BLACK RHYTHMS OF PERU

HEIDI CAROLYN FELDMAN

Black Rhythms of Peru

REVIVING AFRICAN MUSICAL HERITAGE
IN THE BLACK PACIFIC

WESLEYAN UNIVERSITY PRESS

Middletown, Connecticut

Published by Wesleyan University Press, Middletown, CT 06459
www.wesleyan.edu/wespress
Printed in the United States of America
5 4 3 2 1

Library of Congress Cataloging-in-Publication Data

Feldman, Heidi Carolyn, 1965–
  Black rhythms of Peru : reviving African musical heritage in the Black Pacific /
Heidi Carolyn Feldman
    p. cm — (Music/culture)
  Includes bibliographical references and index.
  ISBN–13: 978–0–8195–6814–4 (cloth : alk. paper)
  ISBN–10: 0–8195–6814–7 (cloth : alk. paper)
I. Blacks—Peru—Music—History and criticism. 2. Folk music—Peru—History
and criticism. 3. Dance, Black—Peru—History. 4. Black theater—Peru—History.
I. Title II. Series.
  ML3575.P4F45 2006
  781.62'96085—dc22   2006010984

Contents

Illustrations

Acknowledgments

❖

I wish to thank the following people and institutions, without which this book could not have been written.

For sharing knowledge of Afro-Peruvian music in interviews and conversations: Alex Acuña, Julio "Chocolate" Algendones, Walter Almora, Roberto Arguedas, Susana Baca, Adelina Ballumbrosio, Amador Ballumbrosio, Camilo Ballumbrosio, Carmen Ballumbrosio, Eusebio Ballumbrosio, Luci Ballumbrosio, Maribel Ballumbrosio, Ronaldo Campos, Rony Campos, Félix Casaverde, Ana Corea, Pedro Cornejo, Silvia del Rio, Guillermo Durand, David Fontes, Gino Gamboa, Miki González, Brad Holmes, Orlando "Lalo" Izquierdo, Javier Lazo, Leslie Lee, José Luis Madueño, Mabela Martínez, Juan Medrano Cotito, Teresa Mendoza Hernández, Luis Millones, Juan Morillo, members of the Movimiento Francisco Congo, Daniel Mujica, Manongo Mujica, Victor Padilla, Aldo Panfici, Leonardo "Gigio" Parodi, Ricardo Pereira, Agustín Pérez Andave, David Pinto, Enriqueta Rotalde, Luis "Lucho" Sandoval, Octavio Santa Cruz, Rafael Santa Cruz, Victoria Santa Cruz, Eusebio "Pititi" Sirio, Ezequiel Soto Herrera, Ana María Soto, Carlos "Caitro" Soto de la Colina, Ramon Stagnaro, Efraín Toro, Abelardo Vásquez, Chalena Vásquez, Juan Carlos "Juanchi" Vásquez, and Oscar Villanueva. I am especially grateful to have had the opportunity to hear the memories and thoughts of Abelardo Vásquez, Ronaldo Campos, Pititi, Chocolate, and Caitro Soto, all of whom died before this book was published.

For teaching me how Afro-Peruvian music and dance are performed: Juan Medrano Cotito (cajón), Gino Gamboa (cajón), Oscar Villanueva (dance), Ana María Soto (dance), and Maribel Ballumbrosio (dance).

For facilitating important introductions: Alex Acuña, Susana Baca, Javier León, Juan Morillo, Jonathan Ritter, and Raúl Romero.

For providing lodging and hospitality in Peru: Juan Morillo, Ruthie Espinoza, Lourdes Tuesta, and Iris Tuesta in Lima; Susana Baca and Ricardo Pereira in Lima; the priests and staff of the church in Pueblo Nuevo, Chincha; and the Ballumbrosio family in El Carmen, Chincha.

For hosting me as an affiliate research scholar in Lima: the Center for Andean Ethnomusicology of the Pontificia Universidad Católica del Perú. I especially thank Raúl Romero and Gisela Cánepa Koch for scholarly and friendly companionship, and their assistant, Mariela Cosio, for orienting me to both academic research sources and *peña* nightlife.

For archival research assistance: Ricardo Pereira and Susana Baca (Instituto Negrocontinuo in Lima), Ana María Maldonado (Biblioteca Nacional in Lima), Eva García (Casa de América in Madrid), Luis Lecea (Radio Nacional in Madrid), and José Anadon and Scott Van Jacob (University of Notre Dame's Hepsburgh Library Special Collections in South Bend, Indiana).

For sharing materials from private archives and collections: Susana Baca and Ricardo Pereira, Lalo Izquierdo, Teresa Mendoza Hernández and Caitro Soto, Raúl Romero, Oscar Villanueva, Chalena Vásquez and Monica Rojas, and Juan Morillo and Perú Negro.

For guidance on my dissertation committee: Susan McClary, Steven Loza, Timothy Rice, Jacqueline Cogdell DjeDje, and Tara Browner. I give special additional thanks to Susan McClary for her mentorship and inspirational scholarship and for encouraging me to publish this book.

For patiently awaiting my final manuscript and enabling me to make this a better book: my editor Suzanna Tamminen. For skillful and compassionate guidance during the production process: Ann Brash. For proofreading assistance: Gail Ryan.

For reading drafts and providing helpful critiques: Alex Acuña, David Byrne, Christi-Anne Castro, Andrew Connell, Kevin Delgado, Kathleen Hood, Javier León, Juan Morillo, Rafael Santa Cruz, Victoria Santa Cruz, and Thomas Turino.

For ongoing scholarly dialogues about Peruvian music and culture that have helped shape this book: Javier León, Martha Ojeda, Jonathan Ritter, Raúl Romero, William Tompkins, and Chalena Vásquez. Thank you to William Tompkins and Javier León for allowing me to reproduce their musical transcriptions. I am especially grateful to Javier León for the comparison of notes and ideas that has nourished my work over the years that we have both studied Afro-Peruvian music. Special thanks to Juan Morillo for contributing to the success of this project in so many ways.

Some of the material from this book first appeared in my article, "The Black Pacific: Cuban and Brazilian Echoes in the Afro-Peruvian Music Revival" in *Ethnomusicology* 49, no. 2 (2005). Some of the contents of chapter 3 will appear in "Nicomedes Santa Cruz' *Cumanana*: A Musical Excavation of Black Peru," in *Escribir la Identidad: Creación Cultural y Negritud en el Perú*, edited by M'Bare N'gom (Lima: Editorial de la

Universidad Ricardo Palma, forthcoming). My title is respectfully borrowed from Nicomedes Santa Cruz' poem "Ritmos negros del Perú."

For grants and fellowships that funded research and writing: Social Science Research Council (International Dissertation Field Research Alternate Fellowship), UCLA Latin American Center (Tinker Field Research Grant), UCLA Institute of American Cultures/Center for African American Studies (Research Grant in Ethnic Studies and Predissertation Grant), UCLA Department of Ethnomusicology, and UCLA International Studies and Overseas Program (Ford Foundation Grant and Predissertation Research Grant). For a subvention grant to help defray the costs of restoration and copyright fees for photographs: the Lloyd Hibberd Publication Endowment Fund of the American Musicological Society. For subvention grants to help defray publication costs, the costs of restoration, and copyright fees for photographs: the Lloyd Hibberd Publication Endowment Fund of the American Musicological Society.

For their support and love throughout the years it has taken to produce this book: Ruth Feldman, Gilbert Feldman, Kevin Delgado, and Delilah Delgado. For helping me finish this project in order to begin a new chapter of life: Delilah's little brother or sister, who will be born as this book goes to press.

BLACK RHYTHMS OF PERU

Staging Cultural Memory
in the Black Pacific

The globalization of vernacular forms means that our understanding of antiphony will have to change . . . The original call is becoming harder to locate. If we privilege it over another to make the most appropriate reply, we will have to remember that these communicative gestures are not expressive of an essence that exists outside of the acts which perform them and thereby transmit the structures of racial feeling to wider, as yet uncharted, worlds.—Paul Gilroy, *The Black Atlantic*

The "Disappearance," Revival, and Globalization of Afro-Peruvian Music

I didn't know much about Afro-Peruvian music before I attended a concert in Los Angeles by Susana Baca in 1998. I found the singer and her band captivating—along with the unusual (to me) rhythms and instruments they played, including a jawbone and a small wooden box with a fast-moving lid.

The next day, I attended an International Women's Day symposium at UCLA, where Susana Baca was a panelist. As I listened to her describe her journey along the Peruvian coast in search of African-descended musical expressions that were dying with older generations, I thought about the similarities between art and ethnography. When she made the disclaimer that she is not a scholar, I raised my hand and asked how she thought her work differed from scholarly research about music. She quietly answered that her work is a personal endeavor by an untrained person to find and nurture the Black contribution to popular culture in Peru.

A few days later, it suddenly occurred to me that someone should write a book about the way Afro-Peruvian artists such as Susana Baca (and others who preceded her) have rescued their own traditions from obscurity, performing work that resembles ethnography in order to sustain a living artistic culture. Thus began my unexpected relationship with the topic of this book, which has compelled me to think in new ways about history, memory, and diasporic identity.

The story of Afro-Peruvian music is often told as a metahistory (White 1973), a narrative tale emplotted with tragedy and romance—from disappearance to revival to globalization. Peru, popularly stereotyped as "the land of the Incas," is not known for its Black population. Yet, the first Spaniard to touch Peruvian soil is said to have been a Black man, one of fifty slaves who assisted in the Spanish expedition of 1529 (Dobyns and Doughty 1976, 62). Chroniclers write that his appearance so astonished indigenous Peruvians that they tried to scrub off his color (Mac-Lean y Estenós 1947, 6; Bowser 1974, 4). As the indigenous labor force dwindled, Spaniards in Peru looked toward Africa for replacements. After some enslaved Africans crossed the Atlantic Ocean, they were re-exported (legally or illegally), generally continuing on to Peru from Cartagena by sea (via Panama) or from Rio de la Plata by land (Bowser 1974, 54; Scheuss de Studer 1958, 237). Colonial Peru became an important supplier of African slaves for the Pacific Coast (Bowser 1974, 26–51, 55). As Charles Bowser observes, in the "frantic process of sale and resale, the African's condition was often momentarily even worse than it had been during the Atlantic voyage" (1974, 52).

Enslaved Africans in Peru worked in multiethnic groups on small *haciendas*, in silver mines, or in the urban homes of White owners, facilitating rapid assimilation into White Peruvian coastal society. According to historians, a sizeable minority had already acquired European languages and customs;[1] they were *ladinos* or *criollos* who either had lived as slaves in Spain, Portugal, or the Americas or had been born into slavery in those locales (Bowser 1974, 4, 73; Lockhart [1968] 1994, 196–197; Luciano and Rodríguez Pastor 1995, 273).[2] In fact, the early-sixteenth-century rush of Spanish explorers and their Black slaves from other parts of Spanish America to Peru is said to have left some Caribbean islands nearly depopulated (Bowser 1974, 5).

Black Peruvians inhabited a social space much closer to White criollos than to indigenous Peruvians in colonial times. In general, people of European and African descent lived along the coast, whereas indigenous people primarily occupied inland mountain and jungle regions. Blacks in Peru are said to have fought against indigenous Peruvians in colonial times; for example, the free colored militia helped suppress the largest indigenous revolt against the Spanish, the Túpac Amaru rebellion, in the 1780s (Bowser 1974, 7, 333). Today, many Peruvians still describe their native land as three countries—coast, highlands, and jungle—referring not only to dramatic topographical differences but also to the different inhabitants of those regions.

After 1812, colonial Peru withdrew from the African slave trade, but a law passed in 1847 (after independence in 1821) allowed continued traffic from other parts of the Americas (Blanchard 1992, 4; Cuche 1975, 34). In the post-independence years preceding abolition, Afro-Peruvians developed inventive strategies to earn their freedom and to challenge the institution of slavery (Aguirre 1993; Hünefeldt 1994). Finally, in the midst of a civil war in 1854, Peru's President Echenique freed all Peruvian slaves who enlisted in the national army, and Echenique's successor, Ramon Castilla, issued separate decrees abolishing slavery in 1854 and 1855 (Blanchard 1992, 189–199).

It is often popularly alleged that Peru's Black population "disappeared" by the twentieth century. To be sure, compared with other parts of the Americas, only a small number of enslaved Africans were brought to Peru in the first place.[3] Yet, it is important to remember that the concentration of Blacks in the coastal urban areas of Peru settled by Spanish colonialists was significant. From 1593 on, Blacks made up half the population of Lima (Bowser 1974, 75), and they outnumbered Whites nationwide by 1650. However, in the 1940 Peruvian census (the last to include racial data), Blacks apparently had declined to an estimated 0.47 percent of the country's population (29,000), approximately one third the numerical size of the Black population in 1650 (90,000) (Glave 1995, 15).

The so-called "disappearance" of Peru's African-descended population often is attributed to deaths caused by slavery and military service (Tompkins 1981, 374), but it also resulted from changes in racial self-categorization by people of African descent who identified, as criollos, with a predominantly White coastal culture (Stokes 1987). By the twentieth century, many Black Peruvians demonstrated little sense of belonging to an African diaspora. In fact, Raúl Romero proposes that, with no clearly established collective identity or traditions, Blacks did not constitute an ethnic group (1994, 309–312). Perhaps for this reason, African-descended musical traditions similarly "disappeared" from national collective memory, maintained by only a few families in the privacy of their homes or communities (Tompkins 1981).

Beginning in the 1950s, diasporic consciousness was revived through a social movement to re-create the forgotten music, dance, and poetry of Black Peru. A number of events converged to inspire this musical reclamation of Peru's African past: African independence movements and other international Black rights movements, performances in Lima by African and African American dance troupes, the appropriation of Black culture by White criollos, the Peruvian military revolution (late 1960s to 1970s) and its support of local folklore, and the emergence of important charismatic leaders (both within and outside the Afro-Peruvian community). In 1956, Peruvian scholar José Durand (a White criollo) founded the Pancho Fierro company, which presented the first major staged performance of reconstructed Afro-Peruvian music and dance at Lima's Municipal Theater. Several Black Peruvian artists who participated in Durand's company later formed their own groups. The charismatic Nicomedes Santa Cruz led the subsequent Afro-Peruvian revival, re-creating music and dances, directing plays, writing poems and essays, and hosting television and radio programs. With his sister, Victoria Santa Cruz, he codirected the music-theater company Cumanana in performances at Lima's most prestigious theaters. Victoria Santa Cruz later became choreographer and director of her own dance-theater company and the National Folklore Company of Peru, both of which performed in Peru and abroad. In the 1970s, Perú Negro, founded by former students of Victoria Santa Cruz, became Peru's leading Black folklore company, a role the ensemble still enjoys today with a busy schedule of Peruvian performances and international tours.

The leaders of the Afro-Peruvian revival excavated the forgotten rhythms of Black Peru, conjuring newly imagined links to the past and seeking to separate blackness from the larger criollo culture. Like musical archaeologists, they erected "sites of memory" (Nora 1984–1986) in the form of a canon of stylized songs and dances for the concert stage, forging forgotten histories from scraps of scanty documentation. Out of necessity, the revival leaders used whatever tools were available to excavate their missing heritage, whether or not those tools were condoned by the academy: ancestral memory; "flashes of the spirit" (Thompson 1983); the recollections of community elders; rumors, legends, and myths; and, when all else failed, invention, elaboration, and even the transplanted cultural memories of other communities in diaspora.

Although the music and dances that resulted from this process borrow from the world, they are performed with a uniquely Afro-Peruvian accent. Like the *música criolla* styles that Black Peruvians performed with White criollos before the revival, the core of Afro-Peruvian music is the interplay between *cajón* (box drum) and the criollo guitar. Various percussion instruments (jawbones, a smaller version of the cajón called the *cajita*, *congas*, *bongó*, cowbells, and so forth) and occasional harmony and/or melody instruments are added for specific genres. The music combines traits associated with West African music styles (polyrhythms, layered percussion, call-and-response vocals, metric complexity) with elements of Peruvian música criolla (vocal timbre, guitar melody styles and strumming patterns, the prominence of triple meter, hemiola). Dances range from "novelty" acts to exuberant or sensual choreographies, reminiscent of Peruvian criollo couple dances as well as dances of West Africa and the African diaspora.

By the 1980s, with virtually no local support since the demise of Peru's revolutionary military government, Afro-Peruvian music was reduced to tourist entertainment. Yet, the popularity of the music that had "disappeared" and been revived in Peru rose again in the 1990s, and it reached global markets when Afro-Peruvian singer Susana Baca (under the patronage of producer David Byrne) introduced U.S. audiences to the mysteries of Afro-Peruvian music. Ironically, although Baca represented Black Peru to world music audiences—and to me when I first heard her at UCLA in 1998—I would later learn that her idiosyncratic arrangements of Afro-Peruvian music were at odds with the canon of stylistic authenticity produced by the revival and that she rarely performs in Peru. This was the first of several surprises I encountered on my journey to understand the many faces of Afro-Peruvian music.

Gathering Trees

Ethnographers acknowledge that the idea of "fieldwork" may be outdated. Where, after all, is "the field"? These days, it is often in our own backyards, and the mythologized "Other" is not so easily separated from our own social worlds. In my case, I began my research at Los Angeles' UCLA Wadsworth Theater (about five miles from my apartment) at a concert by Susana Baca, whose audience and touring circuit is located almost entirely in the United States and Europe. This project would later take me to various parts of Peru and to Madrid, Spain; South Bend, Indiana; Reston, Virginia; and finally back to Los Angeles, California.

Anthropologist James Clifford (1997a) argues that culture is translocal. In other words, culture is not rooted in one geographical place; it resides along traveling continuums that defy national borders. Using a similarly decentralized culture concept, anthropologist George Marcus (1995) makes convincing arguments for the practice of multisited ethnography. As anthropologist Renato Rosaldo observes (1993, 30), the cliché of "the Lone Ethnographer riding off into the sunset in search of 'his native'" and returning home with a true account of the romanticized Other—long the backbone of the fieldwork rite of passage—is an archaic image in today's multicultural, globalized world.

This book is a multisited "ethnography of remembering" (Cole 2001) about performed reinventions of Afro-Peruvian music in two locales (Peru and the United States) over a span of approximately five decades (1956–2005). I expand upon the approach of Thomas Turino (1993), whose comparative ethnography of Peruvian *sikuri* (panpipe) musicians examines how that culture is reinvented and shaped in both rural (Conima) and urban (Lima) contexts. Similarly, I analyze various stagings of Afro-Peruvian music in rural (Chincha) and urban (Lima) contexts of Peru, with the added dimension of the international sphere (Peruvian immigrants and world music audiences in the United States). My understanding of these Afro-Peruvian music cultures is based on research I conducted between 1998 and 2005, including forty-seven recorded interviews (nine in the United States and thirty-eight in Peru);[4] archival research in Peru, the United States, and Spain; collection and analysis of rare commercial recordings; observation and documentation of rituals, competitions, performances, and celebrations; and Afro-Peruvian music and dance lessons. Sadly, several members of the older generation of Afro-Peruvian musicians and revival leaders died while I was writing this book. I feel fortunate to be able to include some of their memories and testimonials.

As Peter Wade (1997) observes, Black and Native American participants in "new" social movements (that is, movements focused on identity politics) frequently organize around essentialist views of their own identity and history. As a result, many scholars, whose training encourages them to identify the social constructedness of racial or ethnic identity, find that their analyses conflict with the beliefs of the people they represent. Wade writes, "when academics deconstruct these historical traditions or more generally when they show how 'essentialisms become essential,' they may be weakening those identities and claims" (1997, 116). The best way out of this dilemma, Wade advises, is to juxtapose different versions of identities and the political agendas that created them.

Over the course of my interviews and ethnographic fieldwork, I arrived at a similar conclusion. I discovered that, although the Afro-Peruvian music community in Peru is small, it is not closely knit. Animosity, jealousy, and disagreements over authenticity and performance practice divide practitioners and influence the way history is told and remembered. It was typical for my interviews in Peru to begin with a request for the names of others I had interviewed. Before one such interview, Afro-Peruvian musician and actor Rafael Santa Cruz listened to what by then was a very long list. He paused, then asked, "And have you found any agreement whatsoever amongst these people?" He added that he wanted to read my book because he had no idea what many of the people I had named would say in an interview about Afro-Peruvian music, and he would never be in a position to ask them (R. Santa Cruz 2000b).

Talking to Rafael, I realized that I could make a potentially valuable contribution to the Afro-Peruvian music community. Perhaps only someone like myself, with nothing (apparently) invested in any one version of history or authenticity, could hear all of these stories (of course, my status as an "outsider" may have precluded me from other types of confidences and cultural understanding). By compiling seemingly contradictory remembered histories and their attendant ideologies, I could attempt to describe the full range of ideas about Afro-Peruvian music that circulate and shape contemporary notions of cultural identity. Rafael's question made me realize that I could construct a rarely seen view of the forest if I could gather enough trees.

Charting the Black Pacific in Peru

In my own retelling of how Afro-Peruvian music mobilized (and continues to mobilize) diasporic identity in Peru, I imagine Peru's African diasporic population as inhabitants of what—borrowing from Paul Gilroy—I call the Black Pacific world (Feldman 2005). Although Gilroy's influential book *The Black Atlantic* (1993) challenged the public to imagine a cultural world that connects Africa, Europe, and the Americas through the circulating expressive forms and shared "structures of feeling" (Williams 1977) of the African diaspora, it left uncharted the somewhat different experience of countries in the Black Pacific like Peru. Expanding upon Gilroy's important model, I use the term "Black Pacific" to describe a newly imagined diasporic community on the periphery of the Black Atlantic. According to Gilroy, citizens of the Black Atlantic share a "counterculture of modernity" (because enslaved Africans and their descendants are neither part of nor outside of Western modernism) characterized by critically marginal "double consciousness" (they self-identify as both "Black" and members of Western nations).[5] I suggest that the Black Pacific inhabits a similarly ambivalent space in relationship to Gilroy's Black Atlantic. Whereas Black Atlantic double consciousness results from dual identification with premodern Africa and the modern West, the Black Pacific negotiates ambiguous relationships with local criollo and indigenous culture and with the Black Atlantic itself.

I locate the Black Pacific in Peru and (tentatively) other areas along the Andean Pacific coast (for example, Ecuador, Bolivia, Chile, and Colombia) where the history of slavery, and even the persistence of people and cultural expressions of African descent, is unknown by many outsiders.[6] General studies and maps of African slavery in the Americas often omit these areas, effectively erasing the history of their Black populations (see Whitten and Torres 1998, x). Within the Black Pacific, where ideologies of whitening and *mestizaje* shade the racial imagination (and where larger indigenous populations typically survive), people of African descent are often socially invisible and diasporic identity is sometimes dormant. Because less African cultural heritage has been preserved continuously in the Black Pacific (or at least so it appears), the cultures of the Black Atlantic seem very "African" to some residents of the Black Pacific. Even the ubiquitous metaphors of water and ships linked to Gilroy's Black Atlantic fail to encompass adequately the experience of the Black Pacific, in which enslaved Africans were forced to continue parts of their voyage by land, leaving the Atlantic Ocean behind.

The Afro-Peruvian revival remapped the relational networks of the African diaspora from the perspective of the Black Pacific. A central element of Gilroy's model of the Black Atlantic is its rejection of classic diasporic center (homeland) and periphery (those longing to return) structures in favor of a decentered geography of postnational, multidirectional cultural flow (see also Appadurai 1996a; Cheah and Robbins 1998; Clifford 1994; Hall 1990; Hannerz 1992; Safran 1991; Tölölyan 1996). As I will demonstrate, the Afro-Peruvian revival both embraced and rejected Gilroy's model, illustrating the observation of Ulf Hannerz that "as the world turns, today's periphery may be tomorrow's center" (1992, 266). Confronted with scant documentation or cultural memory of the historical practices of enslaved Africans in Peru, some Afro-Peruvian revival artists found ways to "return" to an imagined ancestral African homeland through music and dance. Others relied in part upon transplanted versions of Afro-Cuban or Afro-Brazilian cultural expressions to re-create the forgotten music and dances of their ancestors and reproduce their imagined past, symbolically relocating the "African" homeland (center) to the Black Atlantic (periphery). Thus, whereas Gilroy and others before him (Mintz and Price [1976] 1992) argue that African diasporic culture was born in the Middle Passage and slavery, what was inspiring to the leaders of the Afro-Peruvian revival about certain Black Atlantic cultures was that they appeared to preserve continuously an African heritage that did not survive in the Peruvian Black Pacific. In fact, leaders of the Afro-Peruvian revival appropriated as "African" heritage some cultural traditions born, creolized, or syncretized in the Black Atlantic.[7] Believing that these practices were continuous retentions of African heritage was an important way out of the anxiety of double consciousness. As Javier León observes, today's Afro-Peruvians continue to seek inspiration from the Black Atlantic, not only for "authentic" musical practices descended from Africa but also for ideas about how to "assert the authority necessary to redefine the very concept of the authentic" (León Quirós 2003, 71).

Throughout this book, I will discuss how Afro-Peruvians positioned the Black Atlantic as a point of reference for the re-Africanization of Peruvian traditions and as a surrogate for "Africa." In my excavation of Cuban and Brazilian influences on Afro-Peruvian music, following Gilroy's emphasis on the way music and other Black Atlantic cultural forms circulate and metamorphose across the diaspora, I seek to avoid a notion of cultural property that would clearly distinguish what is and is not Peruvian. After all, as Gilroy and Néstor García Canclini (1995) remind us, no cultural forms are pure, and the cultural expressions of Latin America and the Black Atlantic are particularly infused with double consciousness, hybridity, and mixed references. However, I concur with Gilroy's critics (Chivallon 2002; Lipsitz 1995; L. Lott 1995; B. Williams 1995) that an overemphasis on a monolithic transnational Black Atlantic culture that ignores the particularities of national struggles, cultural discourses, and differences in national and hemispheric ideologies of "race" results in a skewed understanding of racial politics. Such an approach would obscure the complexity of Afro-Peruvian networks of belonging: Afro-Peruvians identify with the transnational Black Atlantic but also are deeply engaged in an identity project that responds to Peruvian national discourses.

In particular, the national ideology of *criollismo* mobilizes the other half of Afro-Peruvian/Black Pacific double consciousness. Before (and after) the revival, many Blacks in Peru typically identified with criollo (rather than African diasporic) culture, and yet they were denied the social benefits afforded White criollos. Music, dance, cooking, and sports were the only realms in which Black accomplishments were publicly celebrated, and very few Blacks succeeded in business, politics, or other socially prestigious realms accessible to White criollos. Nationalist ideologies condoned subtly racist interpretations of cultural mestizaje while disavowing the concept of "race," creating an environment that Marisol de la Cadena aptly terms "silent racism" (1998). Further, while Peruvian narratives of mestizaje implied that both European- and African-descended elements contributed to the development of Peruvian criollo culture, in practice most criollo traditions were identified with European origins (R. Romero 1994, 314; Tompkins 1981). Thus, Black Peruvians were both inside and outside of criollismo, just as they were both part of and separated from the Black Atlantic diaspora. To resolve the ambivalence resulting from their dual allegiance with Peruvian criollo and African diasporic cultures, Afro-Peruvians (and some White criollos) launched a variety of memory projects to reproduce and stage the Black Peruvian past, variously emphasizing "Africa," the Black Atlantic, or Peruvian criollo culture as points of return.

Memory Projects: Staging the Afro-Peruvian Past

The staging of Afro-Peruvian cultural memory popularized competing visions of an imagined past, shaped by memory projects and technologies. I use the term "cultural memory" to describe how members of a culture group (in this case Afro-Peruvians) remember, with the aid of cultural expressions, elements of a collective past that they did not personally experience (see Bal, Crewe, and Spitzer 1999). By "memory projects," I mean social agendas that reflect present-day goals that direct people—both individually and collectively—to selectively remember certain elements of the past and not others. Such projects may be advanced by technologies (arts) of memory, including techniques that increase the ability to remember (mnemonic devices such as lists and images) and the illusory experiences of reliving the past created by certain films, music, dance, theater, and literature (see Cole 2001, 277–278; Ebron 1998, 96–99; Yates 1966). In my book, the full set of competing memory projects of the Afro-Peruvian revival circulate in what, borrowing from Jennifer Cole, I conceive as a "memoryscape," an imagined space that "encompasses the broad spectrum of commemorative practices through which people rehearse certain memories critical to their personal dreams of who they think they are, what they want the world to be like, and their attempts to make life come out that way" (2001, 290).

This does not mean that I subscribe to a functionalist model of history as a kind of sculpting clay that can endlessly be reshaped to suit contemporary political and social ideologies. Rather, I agree with Arjun Appadurai (1981) that history is a "scarce resource" and that memory projects therefore are constrained in their reproductions of the past by the availability of "raw materials," the culturally determined limits of believability, and the actual persistence of the past in daily life (see also Cole 2001, 26; Schudson 1997). However, when resources are especially scarce or a certain vision of the forgotten past must be legitimized, "memory workers" use creative methods to deliberately invent traditions that "attempt to establish continuity with a suitable historic past" (Hobsbawm 1983, 1).[8]

Although "invented traditions" (Hobsbawm and Ranger 1983) are part of the normal, ongoing processes by which societies write their histories, the Afro-Peruvian revival apparently inspires this question: are some traditions *more* invented than others? I was told many times during my research in Lima that all modern Afro-Peruvian music was invented in the 1960s, based on Cuban and Brazilian models, and therefore has nothing to do with "authentic" Black culture in Peru. The seemingly greater inability of outsiders to forget the inventedness of Afro-Peruvian music—in comparison with reconstructions of an imagined "Africa" in genres such as Jamaican reggae (Hall 1989) or Brazilian samba reggae (Crook 1993)—may be another factor that distinguishes the Black Pacific from the Black Atlantic. Perhaps, indeed, the traditions of the Afro-Peruvian Black Pacific *are* more invented than those of the Black Atlantic, because more was forgotten about the African past on the Pacific coast, and because neo-African origin myths were explicitly attached to reinvented traditions to fill the void of cultural memory. Yet, as anthropologist Paulla Ebron argues, "the task of cultural analysis . . . is not so much to evaluate the purity of cultural claims such as those of African American memory projects as to discover their ability to move and mobilize" (1998, 103).

As Javier León observes (León Quirós 2003, 63–66), ethnomusicologists who write about the reinvention of the Afro-Peruvian past face a special irony. Inadvertently, we invent our own traditions, using creative strategies to fill in gaps and construct comprehensible genealogies, (meta)histories, timelines, and narratives that represent the past. Although I fully admit to my participation in this process, my objective in this book is not to construct the *history* of Afro-Peruvian music but rather to describe how the *histories* of Afro-Peruvian music have been constructed by various memory projects. In this respect, I share with certain scholars of the African diaspora a concern about methods of ethnographic representation. For example, Karen Fields, discussing her efforts to help her grandmother write memoirs, observes that "our scholarly effort to get the 'real' past, not the true past required by a particular present, does not authorize us to disdain as simply mistaken the enormously consequential, creative and everywhere visible operation of memory" (1994, 153–154). Fields' warning inspires questions central to my own ethnographic process. What is the difference between "real" and "true"? Where does "history" end and "memory" begin in the retelling of the past? These questions also motivate David Scott (1991), who argues that anthropological representations of an "authentic" past for African diasporas in the New World raise difficult epistemological issues. How can we ever really know what happened in the past? Is it anthropology's task to corroborate the authenticity of selective discourses about the past?

My approach to each memory project described in this book follows Scott's suggestion that it is more useful to describe how "the past is ideologically produced and used . . . in the construction of authoritative cultural traditions and distinctive identities" (Scott 1991, 268) than to authenticate one version over another. In this spirit, rather than striving to identify the "most authentic" invented tradition in the Afro-Peruvian memoryscape, I analyze the social construction of ideas *about* authenticity and the way several "valid but partial" (Clifford 1986; Turino 2000) versions of Afro-Peruvian history have mobilized diasporic consciousness. Thus, this book is not an authoritative history of Afro-Peruvian music and dance but rather a compendium of vestiges of the remembered histories that endure in today's cultural memory and archival artifacts. I describe not so much what happened but how what happened is remembered and how such memories affect contemporary Afro-Peruvian identity. Ultimately, I suggest that all of the versions of history staged within the Afro-Peruvian memoryscape are "true" for those who experience them as such, whether or not they can be authenticated as "real."

Each of the following chapters explores how prominent individuals or artistic companies deployed particular memory projects to reinvent Afro-Peruvian music and dance: criollo nostalgia, ancestral memory, *negritud*, folklore, tourism and re-created rural origins, immigrant nostalgia, and cosmopolitan world music. I view these memory projects as strategies that helped Afro-Peruvians resolve their Black Pacific double consciousness by variously reconnecting with "Africa" and its diaspora and/or reinscribing their lived relationship with Peruvian criollo culture. Specific memory projects influenced which among many possible music genres, dances, and instruments were to be rescued and which left behind; what meanings should be ascribed to reconstructed genres; and so on.[9]

Chapter 1 describes how White criollo folklorist José Durand (1925–1990) created the Pancho Fierro company for a landmark 1956 performance at Lima's Municipal Theater. This company's debut, with its ethnographic reconstructions of genres such as *el son de los diablos* ("the song of the devils"), is usually cited as the first major staging of Black Peruvian music and dance in the twentieth century. In chapter 1, I describe how criollo nostalgia, the migration of Andean peasants to Lima, and the public stage created a performance of blackness that became the new original upon which future renditions would be based. The Pancho Fierro show was a criollo re-creation of the Black Peruvian past (including the use of blackface), which ultimately reaffirmed the idea that African heritage had "disappeared" into criollo culture. Yet, the Pancho Fierro company opened the door for more Afrocentric and diasporacentric approaches later in the revival.

In chapter 2, drawing from scholarly and artistic work on history, memory, and diaspora, I profile the rise of Black theater and dance as a "site of memory" (Nora 1984–1986) under the charismatic leadership of Victoria Santa Cruz (b. 1922) in the 1960s and 1970s. Victoria Santa Cruz began as co-director of the theater group Cumanana, founded by her brother Nicomedes, and she later became famous in Peru for her re-creation—through what she refers to as "ancestral memory"—of Afro-Peruvian dances such as the *landó* and *zamacueca*. Her theories about rhythm and ancestral memory influenced her young protégés to learn and perform a new conception of Peruvian blackness. Chapter 2 is informed by three intense afternoons that I spent with Victoria Santa Cruz in her Lima home, as well as my interviews with former members of her companies.

Nicomedes Santa Cruz (1925–1992), is the subject of chapter 3. Nicomedes Santa Cruz was internationally famous as a reciting poet and known within Peru for his theories regarding the African origins of coastal Peruvian music. His controversial reconstructions of Black history and music—most notably his theory of the African *lundú*—mobilized powerfully enduring ideas about negritud and Black identity in Peru that challenged the paternalism of the Pancho Fierro show's criollo nostalgia. To reconstruct the history of enslaved Africans and their music in Peru, Nicomedes pieced together remembered song fragments, chroniclers' descriptions of dances, research on the African diaspora in other parts of the New World (especially Cuba and Brazil), and his own imaginative inventions. In chapter 3, I especially focus on how Nicomedes Santa Cruz transplanted Black Atlantic traditions to the Black Pacific.

In chapter 4, I discuss the rise of Perú Negro, Peru's leading Black folklore company since the 1970s. After winning the Grand Prize at the 1969 Hispanoamerican Festival of Song and Dance in Argentina, Perú Negro brought Afro-Peruvian music and dance to international audiences and tourists. In chapter 4, I explore the indebtedness of the company's stylized canon of songs and dances to the nationalist folklore project launched by the 1968 military revolution in Peru. I argue that Perú Negro navigates between two competing connotations of "folklore": nationalist State–driven "local color" versus the "authentic" arts (staged or otherwise) of subaltern cultures within the State. The "Perú Negro sound" that emerged in the 1970s continues to define most Afro-Peruvian genres today (especially the archetypal landó and *festejo*). Musically, it expresses Black Pacific double consciousness through dual allegiance to both the local (música criolla and the military government's folkloric memory project) and the transnational (Black Atlantic models, such as the borrowed Afro-Cuban religious chant "Canto a Elegua"). Perú Negro's choreographic canon, which I address through an analysis of the Dance of the Laundresses, expresses a similarly ambivalent relationship with the past (slavery) and present (Black social invisibility).

In their reproduction of the Afro-Peruvian past, the urban leaders of the Afro-Peruvian revival looked inward to criollo culture and outward toward both an imagined "Africa" and the transnational Black Atlantic. But they also searched for (and re-created) the "African" past in rural Peru, bringing center even closer to periphery. Chapter 5 contrasts the Afro-Peruvian performance practice of rural Chincha with urban Lima, questioning tropes of premodern rural authenticity. Following Dean MacCannell's ([1976] 1989) theories of tourism and staged authenticity (and their postmodern rearticulations), I describe how, in the late 1970s and 1980s, revival artists, scholars, and Chinchanos invented the legend of Chincha as the rural cradle of Afro-Peruvian culture. Two events particularly helped Chincha acquire its reputation for rural authenticity: the *yunza* and the Festival of the Virgin of El Carmen. Ironically, these events are strongly linked to Andean (indigenous and *mestizo*) customs from the highlands. I explore how the legend of Chincha gave rise to a local tourism industry and culture brokers such as the Ballumbrosio family, whose members run a home business in rural Chincha, entertaining tourists with a typical Afro-Peruvian lunch and music and dance show. The Ballumbrosio family also has popularized Afro-Peruvian fusion through collaboration with Spanish-Peruvian rock star Miki González. Following Néstor García Canclini (1995), I argue that Chincha's form of double consciousness promotes the harmonious coexistence of "two Chinchas": the authentic cradle of Black tradition and the modern tourist stage.

Chapter 6 tells the story of how Afro-Peruvian singer Susana Baca was "discovered" in the 1990s by producer David Byrne and promoted internationally as a world music artist. Just as I imagine the Afro-Peruvian Black Pacific as a periphery of the Black Atlantic, I envision Susana Baca as an artist on the cosmopolitan periphery of the Black Pacific. Paradoxically, Susana Baca is considered the least representative Afro-Peruvian artist in Peru, yet she was the only Afro-Peruvian artist most non-Peruvian U.S. residents could name before other Afro-Peruvian artists began to tour mainstream U.S. venues in the early twenty-first century. In chapter 6, I contrast the international career of Susana Baca with Afro-Peruvian folkloric music and dance preservation within the Peruvian immigrant community in Los Angeles, the music of Afro-Peruvian diva Eva Ayllón, and the Los Angeles–based Peruvian band Los Hijos del Sol.

I conclude by describing current trends in the ongoing reinvention of Afro-Peruvian music, including a brief discussion of Teatro del Milenio, the first Black theater group since the days of Victoria Santa Cruz. As a whole, my narrative chronicles the past but is situated very much in the present, informed by the memories of living practitioners.

In the field of Afro-Peruvian music studies, my book is conceptually and chronologically sandwiched between (and greatly indebted to) the historical research of William Tompkins (1981) and the contemporary study of Javier León (León Quirós 2003). Together, the different foci of our works combine in what León describes as an "academic division of labor" (León Quirós 2003, 17), providing readers with both a comprehensive survey of the history of Afro-Peruvian music and analytical tools with which to understand the way different versions of that history shape Black identity in the present. I am also particularly indebted to Raúl Romero's work on the Afro-Peruvian revival (1994), Chalena Vásquez' study of the music of the Christmas festival of Chincha (1982), and Martha Ojeda's analysis of the poetry of Nicomedes Santa Cruz (Ojeda 1997 and 2003).

Unless otherwise noted, all translations are my own. Throughout the book I use words that pertain to the racial and ethnic imagination (such as White, Black, Afro-Peruvian, indigenous, Andean, mestizo, and criollo) to denote the self-described or externally perceived identity of individuals. People identified as "White" in Peru typically would not be considered "White" in the United States. Similarly, many people in Peru who call themselves "mestizo" or "criollo" are called "White" by "Black" Peruvians, and people who fall within the perceived category of "Black" often self-identity as "*mulato*," "*zambo*," "mestizo," or a variety of other terms that imply subtle gradations or degrees of "blackness." Following Peruvian practice, I use the term "Andean" to describe indigenous and mestizo expressive culture (both in the Andean highlands and in Lima). Although sociocultural and racial categorizations are imperfect at best, I have tried to use these descriptive terms in ways that make sense in context.

I am inconsistent in the use of first versus last names. I mean no disrespect to those individuals to whom I sometimes refer by their first names. Because there are only a few "royal families" of Afro-Peruvian music, many of the people who figure most prominently in my narrative have the same last name. For example, in the case of Victoria and Nicomedes Santa Cruz, to simply used the name "Santa Cruz" would result in confusion. Moreover, some of the individuals who figure in my book are usually referred to by their first names, whether or not the speaker knows them personally.

Finally, I have tried to remain faithful to and respectful of all the generous and knowledgeable people who have contributed to my learning process. However, it is likely that persons who are invested in one or another ideological stance will find shortcomings in my work. I sincerely apologize for any perceived misrepresentations, and I encourage my readers to listen to and respect all the voices represented herein, whether or not everything I say or repeat is agreeable. Unwieldy, contradictory, disjunctive, yet somehow predictable, the events that take place within these pages are not always what we wish had happened, but they are true in someone's memory, somewhere.

CHAPTER I

The Criollo *Nostalgia of José Durand*

The ultimate uncertainty of the past makes us all the more anxious to validate that things were as reputed. To gain assurance that yesterday was as substantial as today we saturate ourselves with bygone reliquary details, reaffirming memory and history in tangible format.—David Lowenthal, *The Past is a Foreign Country*

Lima and the Limeños live saturated in the past. It has thus been decided that our city is impregnated with a "misguided nostalgia"[1] . . . Where do our historical eyes turn? They gaze at the illusion of an age that did not have the idyllic character tendentiously attributed to it, an age ordered by rigid social classes of privileges of fortune and well-being for the few, to the detriment of the great majority . . . The colonial myth . . . hides itself in criollismo. —Sebastián Salazar Bondy, *Lima la horrible*

Criollo *Nostalgia*

In the Peruvian coastal capital of Lima, music enacts criollo nostalgia, which, as Javier León writes, "maintains not only a connection to the past but a means through which to keep the past alive" (León Quirós 1997, 25). León describes how performances of songs such as the late composer Chabuca Granda's beloved "La flor de la canela" (The cinnamon flower) actively unite Peruvians in the project of remembering old Lima. The chorus of "La flor de la canela" begins with the words "y recuerda que . . ." (and remember that . . .). Typically, when the song is performed by a soloist, the entire audience joins in to sing those words, fulfilling the composer's mandate to remember a collectively imagined past. A selective type of remembering is enacted by música criolla; as León writes, "we find not only musical material representative of composers from different time periods, but also images of a past that most people have never experienced and that comes to life through the lyrics of the songs, the choreographies and the retelling of well known anecdotes" (León Quirós 1997, 25–26).

As Lowenthal, Salazar Bondy, and León all suggest above, the histories in which society members believe most accurately describe the present-day memory projects that produce them. Societies use collective memory to create shifting "social frames" (Halbwachs [1950] 1992) that reproduce the

FIGURE 1.1. José Durand (seated, left) directing the Pancho Fierro company. *Reprinted with permission from* Caretas.

past from the vantage point of the present. Collective memory is sometimes configured by those who "collect" cultures (whether through folklore, history, or field research), especially cultures designated as endangered or traditional. As James Clifford writes: "Cultures are ethnographic collections . . . Collecting . . . implies a rescue of phenomena from inevitable historical decay or loss" (1988a, 218, 231).

This chapter describes how José Durand and his Pancho Fierro company collected and staged Black performance traditions in the 1950s, reinscribing the history of people of African descent in Peru's national memory through criollo nostalgia. After decades of social invisibility, Black Peruvians suddenly were celebrated as culture bearers, and their music and dances were presented as past treasures in need of rescue. In the midst of a rapidly changing urban demographic landscape resulting from the massive migration of indigenous and mestizo people from the rural highlands,

White Peruvians positioned Black traditions as ingredients that had been assimilated into their coastal criollo culture. The Pancho Fierro company's theatrical reconstructions became the new "original" for subsequent revival artists, infusing re-created Afro-Peruvian music and dance with a strong dose of criollo identity that, when combined with African diasporic "structures of feeling" (Williams 1977), I view as an expression of Black Pacific double consciousness.

The term "criollo" (see the introduction, fn 2) originally described the acculturated children of enslaved Africans, differentiating them from "pure" African *bozales* (Bowser 1974, 78–80; Lockhart [1968] 1994, 198). Later, Europeans employed the term to describe the children of Spanish settlers born in Peru, setting them apart from "real" Europeans. In the nineteenth and twentieth centuries, the idea of being criollo, or criollismo, was reappropriated by coastal Peruvians as a means of defining their own national culture (Salazar Bondy [1949] 1964, 20).

Criollismo is a complex concept with several different social meanings (see León Quirós 1997). In its sociocultural manifestation, criollismo's origins are in Lima's multiracial working class communities. Political criollismo, on the other hand, is a nationalist ideology linked to Lima's White elite oligarchy. The political ideology of criollismo inspired the nation-building process of the nineteenth-century Peruvian Republic, in which a small elite Lima-based oligarchy of White families first established their centralist control over the vastly indigenous nation (Poole 1997, 146). Nineteenth-century Lima—with a population of 53,000 Whites, Blacks, and mestizos—was separated from the surrounding indigenous populace not only by walls constructed in 1685 but also by the ideology of modernism and an elite fascination with European culture (Muñoz Cabrejo 2000). As Raúl Romero writes, "Indians, ethnic minorities, and regional ethnic cultures were accepted only insofar as they could integrate and blend into the larger national culture" (2001, 124). A campaign to modernize the capital city resulted in the destruction of the city walls, the construction of paved streets and sanitation systems, the promotion of European theater, and the strict regulation of leisure and arts to exclude Black Peruvian and other "primitive" cultural expressions—all in the quest to develop a new criollo culture that embraced European notions of progress and development (León Quirós 2003, 21–23; Muñoz Cabrejo 2000). During the political debates surrounding the Bolivian Confederation (1836–1839), Peruvian criollismo also developed as a nationalistic strategy, elevating Whites (symbols of modernity) over indigenous Peruvians (symbols of barbarism), with Blacks aligned with White criollos in the national imagination (see Méndez G. 1996; Muñoz Cabrejo 2000).

In several enduring works of nineteenth-century Peruvian literature, sociocultural criollismo was definitively linked with nostalgia for the lost colonial era. Ricardo Palma's multivolume *Tradiciones peruanas* (Peruvian traditions) ([1872–1910] 1957) is a classic compilation of stories that manufacture a Peruvian criollo essence. After most of the contents of Peru's National Library were destroyed by the occupying Chilean army during the late-nineteenth-century War of the Pacific, Palma, as new Library Head, was charged with restoring the collections. At the same time, Palma continued to publish his "traditions" (historical fictions) as a means of rebuilding and preserving criollo cultural memory of the undocumented past. In Palma's depictions of old Lima, power relationships are glossed and Blacks are historicized as part of the colonial scenery (whimsical street vendors, happy slaves, and servants). Javier León notes Palma's "use of nostalgia as a main tool of identity construction" for "lovable working class folk," and he observes that today's criollo gatherings reenact Palma's strategies through musical performances seasoned with anecdotes from the colonial past (León Quirós 1997, 65–66). Palma's harshest critic, Sebastián Salazar Bondy, affirms, "Ricardo Palma proved to be, entangled in his own witticism, the most fortunate producer of literary stupefaction. His formula, as he himself revealed it, was: to mix the tragic and the comic, history with lies" (Salazar Bondy [1949] 1964, 13). Another example of literary criollismo, Manuel Fuentes' gorgeously illustrated *Lima: Apuntes históricos, descriptivos, estadísticos y de costumbres* (Lima: History, descriptions, statistics, and customs) (Fuentes [1867] 1925)—published in French, Spanish, and English—constructed a proud and picturesque national identity for European readers and Peru's criollo elite.[2] Reading *Lima*, a stranger to Peru would quickly formulate the impression that the Peruvian capital was a European oasis. Blacks are portrayed as if they no longer existed, surviving only through the assimilation of some of their traditions into Peruvian coastal culture.

In Peruvian coastal life, as in the literature that celebrates it, to be criollo means to embrace certain cultural practices, no matter what one's racial background.[3] In fact, as Raúl Romero observes, cultural practice, not biological heritage, generally determines "race" in Peru (2001, 28, 30). The site *par excellence* for the performance of criollismo by the multiracial working class in early-twentieth-century Peru was the social gathering known as the *jarana*. Often, *jaranas* took place in *callejones,* or multi-unit colonial buildings that had been converted into communal dwellings for the poor (including many Black Peruvians), with a common passageway for water, laundry area, restrooms, waste disposal, and cooking. In the early twentieth century, members of the White oligarchy fled the neighborhoods where callejones were situated (Muñoz Cabrejo 2000, 256), and in the Afro-Peruvian revival the callejones were mythologized as the site of authentic Black and criollo music.

At the jarana, the communal performance of music enacted criollo unity through shared cultural celebration. Typical jaranas lasted from four to eight days and nights, during which time the door was locked so that no one could leave before the official *despedida* (farewell) (Bracamonte-Bontemps 1987, 233; Tompkins 1981, 93). All guests participated in some way, whether by playing an instrument, singing, dancing, or performing the special rhythmic handclap patterns unique to each musical genre. William Tompkins notes how the music of the jarana expressed the stereotyped criollo personality: "the criollo is usually an extrovert who loves wit and good humor and seldom fails to take advantage of an opportunity to demonstrate his ability as an orator, philosopher, musicians, or dancer . . . The criollo spirit of wit and teasing, and even insult, is present in [the musical and poetic genres of coastal Peru] . . . and is also often projected in the *guapeo* (emotional words and phrases) that accompanies almost all performances of music and dance in the jarana" (1981, 92).

The music of the jarana, música criolla, includes genres of strophic songs in triple meter with frequent hemiola, especially the *marinera* and the *vals* (waltz). Música criolla has been performed, since the mid-twentieth century, on two core instruments that symbolically express the European and African heritages: the guitar and the cajón (box drum). Typically, the lead guitarist plays elaborate solos and active, strongly plucked figures on the upper strings, while a second guitarist performs ostinato patterns (*bordones*) on the two lowest strings and strums rhythmically. In the early part of the twentieth century, these guitar parts, along with the enthusiastic handclaps and singing of participants, were the only traditional instruments of música criolla. However, by the mid-twentieth century, the cajón had been incorporated into certain genres, providing a rhythmic counterpart that freed the first guitar to perform more syncopated solo passages.

The cajón (figure 1.2) is a rectangular wooden box with a sound hole in the back. The Peruvian cajón player (who is usually, but not always, a man) sits on top of the box and plays the face of the drum with the hands. Peruvian cajón techniques produce an impressive variety of timbres. There are two basic strokes: a deep bass tone, created by hitting the center of the drum face with the palm, and a "slap" tone that results from striking the top corners with the fingertips. The Peruvian cajón's origins are uncertain; the only documented drums used by Blacks during the early centuries of slavery were log and clay types (Tompkins 1981, 36, 38). Some say the cajón

FIGURE 1.2. Left: Oscar Villanueva plays the Peruvian cajón. Right: Rear view of cajón. *Photos by the author.*

is the descendant of box drums found in various parts of Africa and the Antilles, whereas others maintain that it was invented by slaves to trick Spanish authorities who had prohibited music-making in Black quarters (a wooden box or crate's identity as a musical instrument could easily be camouflaged). According to William Tompkins, the first documented reference to the Peruvian cajón is found in a description of the zamacueca dance from around the mid-nineteenth century (Tompkins 1981, 143). Whatever its actual origins, the cajón has been naturalized as a powerful symbol of both Black and criollo culture in Peru.

Because the jarana and its music constituted a culture with which both White and Black Limeños (along with some mestizos and Asian Peruvians) identified as criollos, efforts to separate "White" from "Black" music in early-twentieth-century Lima were virtually impossible (see R. Romero 1994). Black musicians were among the most famous icons of criollismo to emerge from the callejones. Yet, although Blacks became known for their contributions to música criolla, a common perception was that African-descended music had disappeared by the first half of the twentieth century.

A dramatic urban migration of Andean peasants began in the 1930s and grew exponentially in the 1950s and 1960s. Whereas at first rural migrants were absorbed into the city's existing physical spaces and social strata, assimilation was no longer possible by 1945 due to the critical mass pouring into

Lima from the Andes (Millones 1985, 86). Massive numbers of Andean peasants extended the urban boundaries of Lima with land invasions that created new neighborhoods called *pueblos jovenes*. José Luciano and Humberto Rodriguez Pastor write that these changes "modified the entire social fabric of the country," initiating the demise of Peru's oligarchy and a process of democratization (1995, 280). The ensuing conflict between Lima elites and the Andean masses extended the ongoing battle for social control of Peru that pitted elite White criollo Limeños against provincial mestizo intellectuals and indigenous Peruvians (see De la Cadena 1998, 145). With the relocation of the regional populations to the urban center, it became more difficult for centralist elites to construct an imagined Peruvian national identity that excluded the provinces (see R. Romero 2001).

At this critical juncture in the 1950s, the same specifically "Black" traditions that had been rejected as "primitive" during the nineteenth-century quest for modernization were suddenly reclaimed by White criollos. Growing interest was nourished by the wave of Black migrants who came to Lima from rural coastal areas, ostensibly bringing with them "purer" traditions forgotten by the city's assimilated Black criollo population (Luciano and Rodriguez Pastor 1995, 281). The revalorization of Black arts was also catalyzed by the perceived threat of the cultural "Andeanization" of Lima as a result of mass migration (see Lloréns Amico 1983; León Quirós 1997 and 2003). Faced with the rapid disappearance of the orderly and homogeneous city they knew and loved, members of the upper and middle classes in Lima expressed a nostalgic longing for the colonial past imagined by Ricardo Palma, and they asserted the hegemony of criollo identity over Andean expressions in the realm of popular culture by reclaiming Black music and dance as criollo "roots."[4] This criollo nostalgia exemplifies the irony whereby, as Renato Rosaldo writes, "agents of colonialism long for the very forms of life they intentionally altered or destroyed" (1993, 69). In Lima, Black traditions allegedly had been absorbed into mainstream criollo popular culture, but now White criollos mourned the passing of those traditions as separate entities. The reclamation of colonial Black dances became a way for criollos to symbolically revisit the Lima that preceded Andean migration.

Was Black music-making really confined to criollo circles until the 1950s, or was there a separate cultural practice unknown to non-Black outsiders? Did accounts of the vanishing of Black culture conjure a mythical past, based on criollo nostalgia? The counter-histories set in motion by the Afro-Peruvian revival, beginning with José Durand and the Pancho Fierro company in the 1950s, illustrate a clash of beliefs regarding the answers to these questions.

Travel Diaries, South Bend, Indiana, 2000: The José Durand
Collection of Rare Books and Manuscripts

I am in South Bend, Indiana, perhaps the last place I expected my Afro-Peruvian research to take me. When I finally locate the University of Notre Dame library building, imposing and solid, I feel like a real scholar. I find my way to Special Collections, an elegant room that seems to breathe the whispered secrets of the colonial era. I am surrounded by old leather-bound books.

The friendly and helpful staff members at Special Collections are excited; I am the first person to consult the Durand Collection, which—although it is only partially catalogued—was inaugurated with a public symposium in 1996. In fact, I only know of the whereabouts of this collection because of a comment shared in passing by José Durand's nephew, Guillermo Durand, over coffee in Lima. When I first found the description of the José Durand Collection of 8,000 rare books and manuscripts on the Notre Dame Library Web site, I was taken aback. To me, Durand was an obscure Peruvian folklorist, important because of his role as a catalyst for the Afro-Peruvian music revival. How little I knew about José Durand.

Bibliographer Scott Van Jacob takes me down to the basement, where he guides me through an awesome array of shelves containing Durand's books and manuscripts, many signed by their authors. Scott tells me that some of these books are now individually worth $30,000. "How did he afford these books on a professor's salary? Obviously he was a real bibliophile," Scott muses. He opens a box and hands me a remarkably well-preserved book: "These date from the Inquisition." I gingerly open the cover to see faded script surrounded by elaborately colored borders. Under the Inquisition-period manuscripts, in an unsorted box, we find a notebook filled with handwritten poetry. Such cuadernos *were guarded jealously, and I wonder who owned this one.*

Durand's specialty was colonial Latin American literature, and his passions were the works of Sor Juana Inés de la Cruz and Garcilaso de la Vega ("El Inca"). Durand spent forty years collecting and reading all the books in Garcilaso de la Vega's library. Some say, in fact, that Durand knew "El Inca's" work so intimately that he had practically become him (Durand's nickname among academic friends was "El Inca"). The breadth of Durand's collection is formidable: from Peruvian history, literature, and folklore to general works from throughout Europe, the United States, and Latin America. Yet, when I finish scouring both shelved volumes and uncatalogued materials (still in boxes), I am disappointed to find very little material regarding Afro-Peruvian music.[5]

When we emerge from the basement, I meet with José Durand's former student, José Anadón. Professor Anadón, a Chilean historian who teaches at Notre Dame, speaks fondly of his old friend and teacher. He tells me about Durand's career in the United States, where he taught at the University of Michigan from

1968 to 1974 and was known for his inspiring classes and close mentoring rela-
tionships with students. Durand then moved to France, where he married, and
he returned to the United States to teach at the University of California,
Berkeley, in 1975. In 1990, Durand died when a blood vessel burst in his brain.

Professor Anadón reminisces about his visits with Durand to the homes of
older Black musicians in Lima. There, the two scholars participated in all-night
jaranas. Walking the streets of Lima, Anadón tells me, Dr. Durand would stop
to talk to Blacks working menial jobs. "They would have a 15-minute conversa-
tion and it would turn out this was a major musician," Anadón remembers.

I explain my research topic to Professor Anadón. I tell him that I see Durand's
work as an example of the way scholarship can yield real results in cultural prac-
tice—some foreseen and some unintentional. Durand researched historical Black
music genres of coastal Lima and directed a company of musicians and dancers
who brought these songs to life on the stage of Lima's Municipal Theater in 1956.
He went on to write articles and produce television documentaries about little-
known Black music genres.[6] When his company split up after only a couple of
years, Black artists and musicians took up the torch, and a full-fledged revival of
Afro-Peruvian music took place in the 1960s.

Dr. Anadón listens thoughtfully, taking notes. "Your research is so impor-
tant!" he tells me. "It is a story that needs to be told. And José Durand's life is
worthy of a book in itself."

José Durand: A Passion for the Past

José "Pepe" Durand Flórez (1925–1990) was a White Peruvian criollo who
worked as a folklore professor at Lima's San Marcos University before
leaving Peru in 1968 to teach in the United States. Educated in Mexico, he
possessed a vast knowledge of colonial Latin American and European literature and customs. Durand had two obsessions, inspired by his love for
the authentic and the old: books and music. His former colleagues remember him comfortably straddling worlds, devoted to both: "In Berkeley,
arguing points of bibliography and bibliophilia . . . in his Lima, discussing
the exact cajón rhythm of an old piece of music with popular musicians. At
work and at play, José Durand was characterized by zeal for the genuine
and fervor for the perfect" (Monguió and de Colombí-Monguió 1993, 11).

Durand was a man with a passion for the past. According to Peruvian
anthropologist and research collaborator Luis Millones, Durand's preoc-
cupation with colonial Lima shaped his perceptions of contemporary
Black culture. "He was always trying to relive colonial times," Millones
told me (2000). Writing about Durand's memorable classes on colonial

literature, Luis Cortest says, "His love for the present was surpassed only by his love for the past. If anyone lived in two epochs simultaneously, it was Durand" (1993, 9).

An addiction to discovering vestiges of the past made Durand an avid book collector. His academic colleagues recall: "Accompanying him on a visit to a library sale in Peru . . . was always a renewed surprise. This man with defective eyesight had a keen ability to see, distinguish, and infallibly identify, among bundles of undistinguished tomes, the rare book, the inaccessible booklet, the useful file of old documents . . . his was the art of searching for the aged and finding the unique" (Monguió and de Colombí-Monguió 1993, 12).

The same spirit of glory in the survival of past treasures characterized Durand's musical avocation. Durand's family was part of the inner circle that attended jaranas where leading Black and White criollo musicians performed in the first half of the twentieth century. Durand often brought his academic colleagues along on trips to Lima's jaranas, where, as in his rare book-finding missions, he reveled in "the genuine marinera, the legitimate vals criollo, the old *resbalosa*" (Monguió and de Colombí-Monguió 1993, 14).[7] On one such night at an "authentic music house," a colleague remembers, "he took me, not to the well-known Lima of Barranco and Miraflores, but to the Lima of the miserable squatter settlements of Cerro de San Cristóbal.8 On a street there, we came across a policeman who was beating a poor boy. Pepe, great man that he was, suddenly launched into them, separated them, and reprimanded the officer for his brutality. That night, his great indignant voice opened a space for liberty" (Monguió and de Colombí-Monguió 1993, 14).

In a similar spirit, José Durand opened a new public space for Black performance in Peru and encouraged other White criollos to view Black traditions as cultural treasures. Under Durand's leadership, the first publicly staged performance of Black Peruvian traditions was shaped by the memory project of criollo nostalgia.

The Pancho Fierro Company

In the 1950s, José Durand combined his passions for academic study and music when he used his skills as a folklorist to re-create historic Black Peruvian music, poetry, and dance traditions for staged performances by his newly created Pancho Fierro company. Although the project lasted only two short years, the Pancho Fierro company lives on in popular memory as a landmark in the invention of a staged tradition of Black Peruvian music. In fact, many Peruvian musicians refer to the Pancho Fierro company as the beginning of all Black Peruvian music in the twentieth century, and the company's debut performance is generally acknowledged as the catalyst for renewed interest in Black traditions among criollo audiences.

Although Durand's Pancho Fierro company is acknowledged as a milestone, a few smaller theatrical initiatives paved its way. Beginning in 1936, Samuel Márquez' Ricardo Palma company performed a mixture of música criolla and a few "old Black songs" in a theatrical performance (Tompkins 1998, 106, 500). In the 1940s, Rosa Mercedes Ayarza de Morales (a White criolla pianist/composer) transcribed, staged, and published symphonic and chamber music arrangements of Black Peruvian songs performed for her by the elderly Ascuez brothers. Pancho Fierro company member Nicomedes Santa Cruz viewed the company as an extension of the Pampa de Amancaes, the site of an annual Lima festival of folkloric and criollo music and dance that was discontinued shortly before the Pancho Fierro company was founded in the 1950s (qtd. in R. Vásquez Rodríguez 1982, 37).

To form a company, Durand sought out members of the few Black families that had preserved music and dance traditions in the rural provinces of the northern and southern coasts, some of whom had moved to Lima during or prior to the twentieth-century migration waves (Tompkins 1981, 106). The Pancho Fierro company was named after a nineteenth-century Peruvian mulato artist whose vibrant and whimsical watercolor illustrations are among the few sources that document the musical instruments, costumes, and dances of Blacks in nineteenth-century Peru.[9] Durand's company breathed new life into Pancho Fierro's canvases by reenacting the Black musical traditions of the past.

José Durand's primary consultant was Don Carlos Porfirio Vásquez Aparício (1902–1971), patriarch of one of Lima's most important Black musical families and a leading source of information about Black Peruvian music for non-Black Peruvians in the 1940s and 1950s. Don Porfirio Vásquez had moved from rural Aucallama to Lima in 1920. There, he married and had eight children. He earned a living as a porter in the Lima Kennel Park dog track, but he lost that job when the park closed in 1945 (N. Santa Cruz 1975, 43). Don Porifirio possessed a vast knowledge of the Black and criollo music and dance traditions practiced in his native Aucallama. By a stroke of luck, his unemployment coincided with the sudden valorization of folklore by the Peruvian government and Lima's criollo elite.

In 1945, a political struggle between Peru's APRA party and the military government was mediated by a compromise coalition called the Democratic National Front. An open election placed this coalition, headed by José Luis Bustamante y Rivero, in power. The Bustamante y Rivero government immediately implemented a folklore initiative aimed at revalorizing national

culture by preserving and promoting the artistic traditions of Lima's growing population of rural Andean peasants (see Fell 1987). The architect of
the Peruvian government's new cultural plan was Luis Valcárcel, Minister
of Education from 1945 until 1947. Valcárcel—a leading intellectual in the
provincial *indigenismo* movement—created the San Marcos University
Ethnological Institute and the Museum of Folklore (now the Museum of
Peruvian Culture), and these organizations embarked on massive projects
to collect oral literature and folklore. Valcárcel also added a new entity to
the Ministry of Education, the Section of Folklore and Popular Arts (Fell
1987, 60–61). To head the activities of this new folklore office, Valcárcel
appointed José María Arguedas, then a student at the San Marcos
Ethnology Institute, as Folklore Preservationist.[10]

As a result of this initiative, newly created Lima folklore academies
employed qualified culture bearers—primarily Andean peasants but also
some Blacks—to teach "authentic" cultural traditions. The authenticity of
Andean musical expressions was defined in terms of fidelity to contemporary regional arts and rigorously monitored by Arguedas. Andean artists
abandoned their previous self-exoticizing "Inca" costumes and performances in favor of more accurate representations of their contemporary
and diverse regional traditions (R. Romero 2001, 97–102). In contrast, neither regional nor historical accuracy was demanded of Black Peruvian
artists, who combined styles from different rural and urban areas, some
still practiced and others as forgotten as the music of the Incas.

In this context, the recently unemployed Don Porfirio Vásquez was
hired as a professor of Black Peruvian dance by Lima's first folklore academy in the 1940s. His reputation soon earned him many private students,
and Don Porfirio augmented his income by teaching private dance classes
in society homes. In so doing, he continued a long-standing Peruvian tradition. From colonial times until the late nineteenth century, famous Black
dance masters taught Lima's White aristocracy in their homes (Tompkins
1981, 60). Because of the skill and versatility of these dance masters, Blacks
gained a reputation for the ability to teach the choreographic traditions of
both their African ancestors and the European-descended aristocracy.
Years later, Porfirio Vásquez taught a variety of social dances to Lima's
"best families," including stylized versions of Black traditions. Perhaps his
prominent role as a bridge to Black arts for the White criollo populace
brought him to José Durand's attention.

Porfirio Vásquez worked closely with José Durand on the selection of
musical repertoire for the Pancho Fierro company, and he introduced
Durand to Black musicians. After a cast was assembled, Don Porfirio
taught songs and dances to the younger members, many of whom were as

uninformed about the traditions of their parents and grandparents as was the White criollo populace.[11] Thus, for some of the younger Black artists, the company offered a chance to unlock the secrets of their own past. Others took a more active role in the reconstruction process (N. Santa Cruz 1964b; Soto de la Colina 2000; A. Vásquez 2000). Each one brought what he or she remembered, and thus the traditions of various Black families and communities were combined as an aggregate that may never have existed before. Former Pancho Fierro company member Abelardo Vásquez remembered, "It was the first time this was done as a company, and unfortunately everyone had forgotten . . . because our music is very obscure, you know? No one wanted to dance festejo, no one did it. And furthermore, it wasn't ballroom music, it was music of the callejón, music of the people, music of poor people, no? And further still, it was performed by Black people" (A. Vásquez 2000).

The Pancho Fierro company made its public debut in Lima's prestigious downtown Municipal Theater on June 7, 1956, and ran in command performances through August 1956. José Durand secured some support from the Peruvian government and private companies, as well as the cooperation of costume designer Rosa Graña and set designer Alberto Terry. According to William Tompkins, whose research on Black Peruvian music in the mid-1970s included consultation with Durand: "Durand's highest goal was to bring Afro-Peruvian folklore to the theater stage . . . This presentation at the Municipal Theater proved to be of great historical importance, for it marked the beginning of organized commercial companies of Afro-Peruvian musicians and dancers, which were to shape the evolution of black music in the future" (Tompkins 1981, 106–107).

The Pancho Fierro company initially included about thirty-five musicians and dancers, most (but not all) of whom were considered Black. Some of the musicians (for example, singers Caitro Soto and Abelardo Vásquez) had previously worked with groups that played música criolla and the popular Cuban *música tropical*, enabling Afro-Peruvian music to be reborn with a "Cuban accent" that would become more pronounced later in the revival. Many of the vocal solos were performed by Juan Criado, who had launched a successful singing career performing with the Ricardo Palma company. Criado's publicly perceived racial identity has been described to me by Peruvians as either White criollo or *sambo claro* (light-skinned Black). His association with "high society" Lima families and his light skin placed him socially in the milieu of White Peruvians. Although some Peruvians state that his facial features suggested Black ancestry, he regularly used blackface when performing alongside dark-skinned Black

FIGURE 1.3. Members of the Pancho Fierro company, 1956. Juan Criado, third from right, holds a *quijada* (jawbone) and is in blackface. Also pictured: Caitro Soto (second from left), Olga Vásquez (fourth from left), Ronaldo Campos (far right). *Reprinted with permission from* Caretas.

Peruvians in the 1940s or 1950s, and press photos for the Pancho Fierro show featured Criado's smiling, corked face (see figure 1.3).

The audience of about 1,200 people for Pancho Fierro's debut performance was presented with a "retrospective vision, transporting the spectator to the Lima of the last century" (N. Santa Cruz 1964b). The printed program announced Durand's intention to prioritize authenticity over aesthetic appeal in the staged performance of popular tradition, stating, "This presentation of traditional Peruvian art . . . does not seek to stylize the dances, poetry, and songs . . . For this reason, complicated scenic movements that would augment the brilliance but detract from the spontaneity of popular arts have been renounced" (qtd. in N. Santa Cruz 1964d). Song-and-dance numbers depicted Blacks in times of slavery, working and playing in the rural fields and urban streets of Peru: "En tiempos de Pancho Fierro" (In Pancho Fierro's times), "La fiesta en el solar" (Fiesta at the big house grounds), "En los cañaverales" (In the sugarcane

FIGURE 1.4. *Marinera* from the Pancho Fierro show, 1956. Pictured: Olga Vásquez and Mendoza Reyes. *Reprinted with permission from* Caretas.

fields), "La marinera de salon" (The ballroom marinera), and "Toro mata" (Bull kills) (N.a. 1956b; N.a. 1956e; Tompkins 1981, 107).[12] At the last minute, probably to ensure an audience, José Durand also contracted Peruvian criolla singer/composer Chabuca Granda, who debuted her new vals "Fina estampa" (N.a. 1956b) and danced a marinera with Peruvian dancer Eduardo Freundt (N.a. 1956c). Newspaper reports, in general, glowingly portrayed the Pancho Fierro company's preservation of Peru's national folklore. Reviewers praised José Durand but rarely mentioned the performers' names or details of specific performances and genres.

One of the most successful and enduring genres revived by the Pancho Fierro company was el son de los diablos (the song of the devils), a Carnival dance. According to company member Nicomedes Santa Cruz, this dance, which opened the Pancho Fierro company's debut performance, captivated the Municipal Theater audience, "whose applause still echoes" (N. Santa Cruz 1970b). Nicomedes noted that much of the appeal resulted from the fact that, instead of the typical cajón-guitar ensemble associated with música criolla, the "virile and diabolical choreography" of el son de los diablos was accompanied by guitars, caijta, and quijadas.

The cajita (figure 1.5) is a small wooden box with a hinged top, suspended from the player's neck by a rope. The player alternately opens and closes the top of the cajita and hits its side with a stick or mallet. Some say the cajita's invention was inspired by the boxes used to collect alms in church (Fuentes [1867] 1925).

The quijada (figure 1.6) is the jawbone of a donkey, horse, or mule. It is alternately scraped or struck with a mallet (or stick) and hit with the fist, the latter of which causes the molars to rattle in their sockets and produce a raspy buzz. The quijada's presence in Peru has been documented since at least the eighteenth century (see F. Romero 1939b; Tompkins 1981, 137).[13]

In the Pancho Fierro company's debut performance of el son de los diablos, the quijada's distinctive sound was exceeded in theatrical value only by the appearance of a group of Black musicians, dressed as devils, striking bony skeletons. A greatly embellished command performance was presented during the company's next run at the Municipal Theater in January of 1957. Alberto Terry, renowned for his elaborate creation of a magical forest in the production of William Shakespeare's *A Midsummer Night's Dream* at the Municipal Theater, designed the sets. Durand and Terry decided to precede el son de los diablos with an all-quijada number titled "Ritmos de quijada" (Quijada rhythms). Eight Black dancers, dressed in black, carried quijadas covered with phosphorescent paint. When a black light was directed at the stage, eight glowing jawbones seemed to float in the air, apparently playing themselves. "The effect was marvelous but the folkloric authenticity was marginal," observed company member Nicomedes Santa Cruz (1970b).

Despite such apparent deviations from the stated prioritization of authenticity over aesthetics in the original program, the Pancho Fierro show is generally considered the "first serious effort to bring Black Peruvian folklore to the stage" (N. Santa Cruz 1970b), and today many performances of el son de los diablos begin with a "Quijada rhythms" prelude.

The Ethnographic Re-Creation of El Son de los Diablos

As director and curator of the Pancho Fierro company, José Durand used the methods of ethnography to collect and stage Black music and dances. Durand regarded the great older Peruvian musicians of the jaranas as

FIGURE 1.5. The caijta. *Photo by the author.*

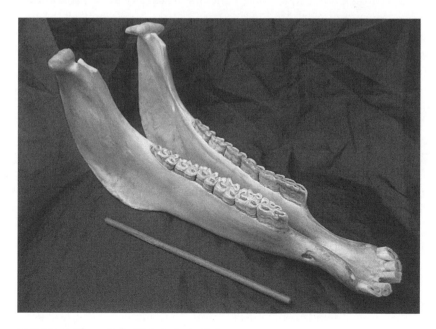

FIGURE 1.6. The *quijada*. *Photo by Javier León.*

sources as valuable as his beloved manuscripts and books, and he described his methods in the quest for the discovery of musical "originals" as identical to those of "modern ethnological science" (J. Durand Flórez 1995, 31). When ethnographic methods failed to produce a complete song or dance, Durand and his company took the liberty of artistic embellishment for the sake of performance.

A good example of José Durand's use of ethnographic methods to create an artistic product was the staging of el son de los diablos. Most scholars concur that el son de los diablos is descended from the Spanish Corpus Christi festivals and morality dramas. It was danced in Peru by members of Black *cofradías* (social/religious organizations) in Corpus Christi processions at least as early as the nineteenth century (Tompkins 1981, 257–258). After the Catholic Church prohibited its performance in conjunction with religious celebrations in 1817 (Fuentes [1867] 1925; Tompkins 1981, 258), el son de los diablos resurfaced in Lima in predominantly Black neighborhoods during secular outdoor Carnival celebrations.

In the twentieth century, performances of el son de los diablos in Carnival gradually diminished. According to William Tompkins (1981, 260) and guitarist Vicente Vásquez (1978), the tradition came to an end after the death of the last *diablo mayor* (chief devil), Don Francisco Andrade (nicknamed "Ño Bisté") in the 1920s. However, former diablo mayor Pedro "Chumbeque" Joya remembers dancing with his *cuadrilla* (dance team) until 1958. After that, according to Chumbeque, all the former diablos moved to different neighborhoods and the cuadrilla disbanded. Chumbeque's testimony is interesting, because it dates the last public street performance of el son de los diablos after the supposedly extinct genre was revived in the Pancho Fierro show. If Chumbeque's memory is accurate, then Durand and his company nostalgically re-created a staged version of a dance that had supposedly "disappeared" but was actually still being performed in neighborhoods not typically visited by White criollos.

To re-create el son de los diablos, Durand and his company began by studying several watercolor paintings of the dance by nineteenth-century artist Pancho Fierro. In one of Fierro's lively scenes (figure 1.7), we see a large, masked diablo mayor dancing athletically. He is dressed in calf-length pants with tiered trim and a large plumed mask, and he is carrying a whip or cane. Following him are musicians carrying a guitar, harp, quijada, and cajita with mallet.[14] Only the diablo mayor is dancing, and behind the band are two onlookers.

When José Durand brought these paintings to life in the Pancho Fierro show, in addition to emulating the costumes documented in Fierro's

FIGURE 1.7. Comparison of *el son de los diablos* scenes: nineteenth-century painting by Pancho Fierro (left) and 1956 dramatic reenactment by José Durand's Pancho Fierro company in Lima's Teatro Municipal (right). *Photos reprinted with permission from* Caretas.

paintings (see figure 1.7), he added two elements about which the images are silent: music and choreography. William Tompkins affirms, "when José Durand undertook the presentation of the almost forgotten son de los diablos in 1955, one of the greatest problems facing the group was the reconstruction of the music" (1981, 267). Durand sought the assistance of three former diablos who had participated in the alleged last cuadrilla to dance in Lima's Carnival: Manuel "Manucho" Mugarra, Cecilio Portugués, and Pedro Torres. Manucho taught the caijta and quijada patterns and what he could remember of the guitar melody to guitarist Vicente Vásquez (who would go on to compose definitive guitar parts for most Afro-Peruvian genres in the revival), and Vásquez embellished the melody fragment to create a complete guitar motif (see figure 1.9) (Tompkins 1981, 267–268). Some variation of these instrumental parts for caijta, quijada, and guitar would be used in all subsequent performances of el son de los diablos, as well as other revived Afro-Peruvian genres.

Although no recordings are publicly available from the Pancho Fierro company's performances, some idea of how this musical reconstruction of el son de los diablos was remembered in later decades may be gained through other recordings and ethnographic documentation. My point is not to reconstruct the exact musical sound and choreography performed in the Pancho Fierro show but rather to explore the musical identity mobilized by that "original" revived performance.

The most striking aspect of el son de los diablos parts for caijta and quijada, as performed in subsequent decades, is the way polyrhythmic patterns combine to create a duple pulse with an internal "swing" that falls somewhere between two- and three-beat subdivisions—a playful sense of musical time that Afro-Peruvian musicians identify as a trademark of their style. The associated guitar melody contains hemiola-like figures that contrast alternating duple and triple phrases (see figure 1.9). Because of this internal metric ambivalence, along with different ways of hearing musical phrase structures, it is possible to notate the music of el son de los diablos in a variety of time signatures ($\frac{2}{4}$, $\frac{4}{4}$, $\frac{6}{8}$, or $\frac{12}{8}$), and the question of how this (and other) Afro-Peruvian genres should best be represented by musical notation results in several choices by Afro-Peruvian musicians and ethnomusicologists. For example, in the three major dissertations about Afro-Peruvian music, William Tompkins (1981, 267) published a $\frac{6}{8}$ transcription of the caijta part (as performed for him by former Pancho Fierro company member Abelardo Vásquez in the 1970s), Javier León (León Quirós 2003, 167) notated the cajita and quijada parts in $\frac{2}{4}$ and I (Feldman 2001, 73) chose $\frac{4}{4}$ with triplet subdivisions (figure 1.8). Of course, these three transcriptions were not based on the same performance, but the point remains that the sense of musical time in most performances of el son de los diablos defies the conventions of simple transcription.

Performances of el son de los diablos were recorded in the 1960s and 1970s by former Pancho Fierro company members (including former diablo Manuel "Manucho" Mugarra, Nicomedes Santa Cruz, and Vicente Vásquez) (N. Santa Cruz y su Conjunto Cumanana [1964] 1994; Various Artists 1998a). In my transcriptions of excerpts from these post-Pancho Fierro recordings (figure 1.9), although I have chosen to notate the cajita parts in $\frac{4}{4}$ using eighth and sixteenth notes, it should be understood that there is a heavy Afro-Peruvian "swing" feeling. The excerpts transcribed in figure 1.9 demonstrate the alternation of duple and triple phrasings in Vicente Vásquez' re-created guitar melody, as well as examples of how the guitar melody, instrumentation, and percussion patterns re-created for the Pancho Fierro show were performed in the next stages of the revival.

Re-creating the choreography of el son de los diablos may have been somewhat easier than restoring its music. Written descriptions of the dance survived, along with Pancho Fierro's paintings and the memories of the former diablo consultants. According to sources, the cuadrillas typically marched through the streets in formation while the diablo mayor kept his little devils in line by cracking his whip. The real dancing was performed for spectators on street corners and in front of taverns in exchange for money and/or bottles of rum (Jiménez Borja 1939; V. Vásquez 1978). Each devil danced a solo within a circle of devils (Tompkins 1981, 259). The *zapateo* (Peruvian-style tap-dancing) may have been the basis for some of the dance steps and configurations (Tompkins 1981, 265), and post-revival

A. Willliam Tompkins' transcription of performance by Abelardo
    Vásquez (1981:267). Adapted and reprinted with permission.

Cajita

B. Javier León's transcription (2003:167). Reproduced and reprinted
    with permission.

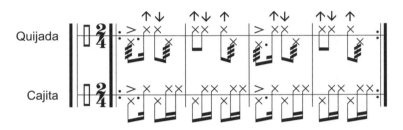

C. Heidi Feldman's transcription (2001:73).

Transcription Notes:

Quijada (B): ↑↓   (upper staff space): Direction of scraping along teeth
         𝆇   (lower staff space): Buzzing sound when jaw is struck
                with fist (León's convention will be borrowed henceforth)
Cajita: Lower staff line/space: Top lid shut
                  Upper staff line/space: Outside surface struck with stick

FIGURE 1.8. Three transcriptions of *el son de los diablos* parts for *caijta* and *quijada*.

staged performances usually include a zapateo contest. The spirit of zapateo—which can feature athletic leaps and daredevil stunts (such as the
salto mortal or "fatal jump" in which the dancer performs a 360 degree flip
in the air and lands dancing [Tompkins 1981, 282])—certainly is compati-
ble with the look of the devilish dance, as depicted in Pancho Fierro's
watercolors. Documentation suggests that twentieth-century Carnival diablos also performed dance steps as part of narrative choreographic figures
including: the *salida del infierno* (departure from Hell), in which the minor

A.. Nicomedes Santa Cruz and Cumanana ([1964] 1994).

B. Cuadrilla de Don Manuel Mugarra 1971 (re-released on Various Artists 1998a).

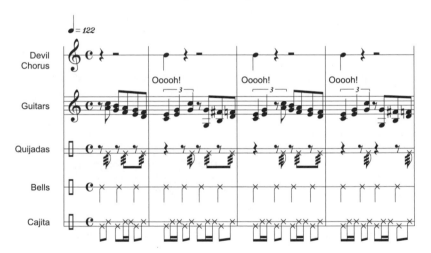

Transcription Notes:
Quijada: Upper staff line: Teeth scraped with stick
            Lower staff line: Jaw struck with fist
            In Example A, the scrape pattern is inferred from an earlier segment of the
            same recording (the other scraper-type instrument renders the *quijada* scrape
            inaudible at the point of transcription). In Example B, no scrape sound is audible.
Bells (B): The bells (probably worn on dancers' ankles) do not sound precisely on the beat.

FIGURE 1.9. Two post–Pancho Fierro show performances of *el son de los diablos*.

devils formed a row, under the command of their captains, and leapt and tap-danced joyfully forward (Jiménez Borja 1939); the *diablo perdido* (lost devil), in which the diablo mayor rounded up his devils only to find that one was lost, necessitating a search and capture (*Son de los Diablos* 1988); and various cross-shaped formations that testify to the dance's Christian origins. Former diablo mayor Chumbeque recalls that his cuadrilla marched in the shape of a cross (qtd. in *Son de los Diablos* 1988), and Arturo Jiménez Borja (1939) describes how the diablo mayor drew a cross in the dirt and forced the minor devils to prostrate themselves before it under penalty of his whip.

Black dance suffered a history of repression in Peru, as in many other American countries. In 1563, Blacks were officially prohibited from dancing in public or within their cofradías. All Black dances were geographically restricted to performance only in the Plaza Nicolás de Ribera "El Mozo" (Tompkins 1981, 28). Particularly objectionable genres of music and dance were banned (Estenssoro 1988, 166). In the nineteenth century, Black dances still were considered indecent by high society. In 1814, an outraged letter-writer to *El Investigador* newspaper protested the *Inga* dance performed by Peruvian Blacks:

> Only the devil could have invented such an instrument for the downfall of man. What an obscene and scandalous dance! Is it possible that in a country of Christians, fathers can forget what they owe God and their children, allowing a scandal of this class in their homes? Founding father, minister of sanctuary, it is your responsibility to eliminate this cancer that is seizing innocent young people! (qtd. in Estenssoro 1988, 166)[15]

Thus, for centuries, Peruvian Blacks who danced in public were described as frightening, disgusting, intimidating, obscene, and worse. Perhaps, then, performing el son de los diablos in Carnival was a way for Lima's marginalized Black population to take back the streets as a stage for the theater of parody, dancing and playing music and performing devilish pranks and acrobatic stunts, with individual identities hidden behind hideous masks. As Juan Carlos Estenssoro suggests, Black processional dances of the Corpus festival historically allowed marginalized and oppressed citizens to express their voices—silenced at other times—and to use the burlesque to parody the extreme, sometimes ridiculous, elements of dominant culture (Estenssoro 1988, 163). If Black dances were characterized by official culture as "invented by the devil," then Carnival set the stage for Black performers to enact a self-reflexive parody in which they became the absurd fantasies of their detractors—devils who scare or shock bystanders but who also make them smile and laugh with their daredevil dancing and burlesque.

As a staged performance in Lima's Municipal Theater, El son de los diablos came to represent something very different—the reclamation of a Black past by the criollo populace. el son de los diablos is one of the few dances in the revived Black Peruvian repertoire that has a fairly well-documented history in Peru. Even if the actual music and dance steps were reinvented based on some guesswork for the Pancho Fierro show, the costuming, instrumentation, role of the diablo mayor, and acrobaticism are consistent with the real Pancho Fierro's nineteenth-century paintings and with archival accounts. This link to the past gave a sense of pride both to Black Pacific "people without history" (Wolf 1982) and to White criollos longing for the past, and thus staged performances were endowed with great historical value by their viewers and performers.

Since the Pancho Fierro show, el son de los diablos has been re-created many times as staged folklore and street theater. Prominent Black Peruvian artists, including Victoria Santa Cruz and Perú Negro, staged it in the 1970s, and, from 1987 to 1990, Lima's Black rights organization Movimiento Francisco Congo worked with former diablo mayor Chumbeque and Grupo Cultural Yuyachkani to reconstruct the street procession for Carnival (R. Romero 1994, 322; *Son de los Diablos* 1988). In 2000, several schools and professional companies in Lima (including Perú Negro, Grupo Teatro del Milenio, Grupo Cultural Yuyachkani, and Chalena Vásquez' CEMDUC program at Lima's Catholic University) performed the dance, both in concert settings and in the streets, and members of the theater companies Grupo Teatro de Milenio and Yuyachkani taught the Black youth of rural El Guayabo to perform it as part of a cultural outreach program.

Because of the status afforded the Pancho Fierro project and the continued performance of its musical re-creations in later years, the reinvented costuming, dance, and instrumental parts of el son de los diablos and other genres were generally deemed "authentic" reproductions of forgotten past practices. Thus, José Durand's staged ethnographic reconstruction of el son de los diablos and other genres became the newly invented "original" upon which all future reinventions were based. In addition, Durand's blending of ethnographic and artistic methods became a model process still used by Afro-Peruvian artists in the 1990s to assert the authority of their own interpretations of the reconstructed past (see León Quirós 2003, 92–101).[16] The ethnographic production of "original" artistic performance thus became a viable substitute for the continuous maintenance of African musical heritage in the Afro-Peruvian Black Pacific.

Like some written ethnographies, the Pancho Fierro company's repertoire privileged a perceived ethnographic present—in this case an amalgamation of the memories of Durand's twentieth-century diablo consultants and the nineteenth-century watercolors of Pancho Fierro—that was reified in later reproductions of the genre, relegating to obscurity the possible existence of alternate performance styles from other time periods and performers. For example, whether or not the costumes of real twentieth-century diablos still resembled the ones in Pancho Fierro's paintings, all known post-Durand reconstructions have featured some variation of this nineteenth-century outfit of short frilled pants and masks. Moreover, the musical accompaniment typically used in post–Pancho Fierro company performances of el son de los diablos privileges the remembered performance style of Manucho and his fellow diablos, regardless of the possible existence, during the dance's long history of street performance, of different instrumentation (as shown in Pancho Fierro's paintings) and other rhythmic patterns and/or melodies performed by different cuadrillas. Variations of the music specifically created for the staged reproductions—including Vicente Vásquez' guitar melody as well as the quijada prelude—have been incorporated into performances in subsequent decades. This is not to say that the Pancho Fierro company's arrangements have been reproduced verbatim; each group has its own variation of the percussion parts and guitar melody (see figure 1.9), and new instruments also have been added. Staged reconstructions often use a cajón in the percussion section, and street parades such as those organized by Movimiento Francisco Congo and Grupo Yuyachkani have incorporated cowbells and West African *djembes*, although no one (to my knowledge) has revived the harp shown in Pancho Fierro's paintings.

Interestingly, the only "original" aspect of the Pancho Fierro company's re-creation of el son de los diablos that Durand contributed from his own personal experience, the song, was discarded in most later performances, suggesting that Durand's ethnographic authority may have been questioned by later revival artists and former members of his company. José Durand's Aunt Catalina had taught him to walk while singing what he remembered as the "son de los diablos song" (J. Durand Flórez 1979b), a nursery rhyme-like tune about a monkey with the chorus "chubaca chumba chas!" According to Durand, this song dated from 1850, thus preceding the memories of his diablo consultants. After he learned Manucho's rhythm patterns, Durand legitimated the authenticity of his aunt's el son de los diablos song by noting that the vocables "chubaca chumba" in the chorus aligned exactly with the traditional el son de los diablos caijta part, and that the syllable "chas!" corresponded with the quijada part (Tompkins 1981, 268). After learning the song from Durand's mother, Juan Criado performed it with the Pancho Fierro company in 1956 (Tompkins 1981,

268). Durand later included the son de los diablos song as part of a video documentary (J. Durand Flórez 1979b) and Arturo "Zambo" Cavero, who played the caijta in that documentary performance, also recorded it with the title "Son de los diablos" (Aviles et al. n.d.). However, later recordings of el son de los diablos by former Pancho Fierro company members and former diablo Manucho eliminated Durand's song, featuring strictly percussion and vocal cries ("oooh!") but no lyrics (N. Santa Cruz y su Conjunto Cumanana [1964] 1994; Various Artists 1998a). Contemporary staged versions of the son de los diablos dance by Perú Negro and CEMDUC use yet another song—a festejo called "El son de los diablos" that describes the Carnival dance and some of its famous performers but was composed after the street performances had come to an end (CEMDUC 1999; Tompkins 1998; V. Vásquez 1978). It is interesting to note that a detailed description of el son de los diablos by Arturo Jiménez Borja (1939) that predates Durand's reconstructions does not mention any lyrics at all, and that ex–diablo mayor Pedro "Chumbeque" Joya remembered yet another song when interviewed for a television documentary (*Son de los Diablos* 1988).

William Tompkins comments: "Despite disagreements . . . considerable data exist for the reconstruction of the son de los diablos. Yet, like many of the other Afro-Peruvian dances, the son has been relegated to the stage, another chapter in its history of changing contexts—from the sacred plays and processions of Corpus Christi to the secular Carnival, and now to the world of the stage as commercialized folklore" (Tompkins 1981, 268–269). Commercialized folklore or not, Durand's ethnographic reconstruction of the son de los diablos and other dances for the theatrical stage became a vital repository for the memories of older consultants, a source that could be consulted by future generations who found these memories missing from national history. Like all acts of remembering, the creation of such a site of memory is highly subjective. Would el son de los diablos exist today if not for José Durand and the Pancho Fierro show in 1956? Maybe. But the music would be different. Vicente Vásquez created the guitar melody that defines the genre today, and the percussion parts were learned from elderly consultants and former Carnival diablos who are now deceased. Thus, the performance of el son de los diablos in the Municipal Theater in 1956, while seeking to represent the traditions of the past, became the basis for presentations of the future.

The Pancho Fierro Company on Tour

After the 1956 performances, the Pancho Fierro company's reputation and popularity quickly grew so strong that other groups vied to emulate them.

In January 1957, the rumor spread that Lima's Pancho Fierro company would perform in Piura, a northern Peruvian province. In an interview with the Lima-based newspaper *La Prensa*, José Durand assured the public that the Pancho Fierro company did not, in fact, have plans to perform in Piura. Apparently, a false Pancho Fierro company had appropriated the name of the Lima-based troupe in order to sell tickets to unknowing audience members (N.a. 1957b).

The real Pancho Fierro company was busy performing in Lima that month. On January 17, 1957, the company participated in a special concert in homage to Chabuca Granda at Lima's Plaza de Acho (Bullring Stadium). Ten thousand cheering spectators watched the company perform el son de los diablos, "Toro mata," "En el cañaveral," and other scenes that by now were part of the recognized staged repertoire of Black Peruvian music. Chabuca Granda, who was not scheduled to perform at her own tribute concert, was moved to tears by the performance in her honor. She responded by presenting the audience with her own renditions of her compositions "Bello durmiente" and "Fina estampa" (N.a. 1957a). In May 1957, the company revisited Lima's Municipal Theater, performed in Arequipa on Peru's southern coast, and finalized plans for tours to Chile, Argentina, and Uruguay.

For the 1957 tour to Chile, José Durand decided to change the name of the company to Ritmos Negros del Perú (Black Rhythms of Peru), commissioning Nicomedes Santa Cruz—who had recently joined the company—to compose and recite a poem by that name. Alberto Terry created a spectacular set for the company's international debut, including a forest with trees more than nine meters tall. Durand selected el son de los diablos as one of the "most representative" numbers for the company, which now consisted of approximately twenty-seven members, to perform in Chile (N.a. 1957c). In addition, the company prepared several new scenes, including "Navidad negra" (Black Christmas). As the first ambassadors to bring the country's Black folklore to audiences outside Peru, Durand and his protégés seemed bound for glory.

Reflections on the Significance of the Pancho Fierro Company

Although Durand's reconstructions of collected Black folklore gave new life to fading genres like el son de los diablos, which continue to be performed today, the promise of the Pancho Fierro project itself was short-lived. According to company member Nicomedes Santa Cruz, while the group began its rehearsals as a solid unit, it later fragmented into separate factions, divided by the geographical origins of members. Santa Cruz also cites the fact that Juan Criado was given a disproportionate percentage of the solos as a source of friction (N. Santa Cruz 1964d). By most accounts, the 1957 tour was a financial disaster, and many company members remained in Chile.

The Pancho Fierro company folded in 1958, but its members went on to found their own groups. Former member Abelardo Vásquez explained, "I don't know if Durand thought it would be so, but it turns out to have been a novelty. To create such a big company . . . attracted a lot of attention . . . When we returned from Chile, the company disbanded. Then other groups followed, and they all did what Pancho Fierro did . . . Cumanana, Gente Morena de Pancho Fierro, these groups, all [are descended] from Pancho Fierro. Including Perú Negro" (A. Vásquez 2000). Discussing the historical importance of the many spinoff companies, William Tompkins adds: "If these early companies seemed a failure because of their short lives, they were from another standpoint a great success for they sparked considerable interest in a disappearing music tradition about which many Peruvians knew little and also initiated the careers of many now famous black artists" (1981, 99–100).

While the Pancho Fierro company should be credited as a catalyst for the revival of Black diasporic consciousness in the 1960s and 1970s, it is also important to remember that Durand's re-creations firmly placed Black cultural identity in the past, as an ingredient of criollo popular culture. In later years, certain Black Peruvian musicians would stress Durand's identity as a privileged outsider, and I noted with interest that several former Pancho Fierro company members whom I interviewed had little to say about Durand, seeming to prefer not to discuss his role. Might such reluctance indicate that Black Peruvians today prefer not to credit the birth of the Afro-Peruvian revival to the efforts of a White folklorist? Could it reveal lingering frustration with Durand for minimizing the agency of his Black cast members and taking too much personal credit for the revival of Black Peruvian music in his role as director?

Without access to the testimony of the late José Durand himself, I can only speculate about the reasons for both the silence of some former company members when his name is mentioned and the public critiques of his leadership and vision that circulate. For example, former Pancho Fierro company member Nicomedes Santa Cruz—who went on to lead the Afro-Peruvian revival in the 1960s—located the company's public perception and Durand's approach within the rubric of paternalistic criollismo. In an interview with musicologist Chalena Vásquez, Santa Cruz insisted that it was the Black company members who gave Durand the idea of reviving Afro-Peruvian music and dance in a staged performance rather than the other way around (qtd. in R. Vásquez Rodríguez 1982, 37). Writing a few years after the group disbanded, Nicomedes strongly questioned José Durand's alterations of Afro-Peruvian folklore for staged performance before a mainstream theater public, charging that "Durand's misguided innovations came about because, wanting to improve the presentation, he believed himself capable of stylizing ancient folklore. He overestimated himself" (N. Santa Cruz 1964c).

A similar critique was articulated to me by Juan Carlos "Juanchi" Vásquez. Juanchi (Abelardo Vásquez' son and Don Porfirio Vásquez' grandson) is a dancer, conga player, and founder of Peru's leading organization for Black rights, Movimiento Francisco Congo. When I met Juanchi in 2000, he was also an (ultimately unsuccessful) candidate for Congress. In an interview in his apartment in Lima, Juanchi reflected upon the social cost he believes was incurred when Durand "cleaned up" Black dances for the tastes of Lima audiences (of course, Juanchi had not yet been born when the Pancho Fierro company performed). Ironically, in Juanchi's retrospective view, it was the staging of Black Peruvian music and dance that caused more "natural" Black cultural expressions to diminish. Thus, he says, although Durand's objective was to revive disappearing Black dances, he accomplished exactly the opposite.

"He brought together all these people," Juanchi explained, "to take [Black music] out of the callejón and bring it to the salons of Lima, no? So the people could appreciate it. But this had its cost, for me, an extremely grave cost for the music. Which was the price of eliminating the *raison d'être* of the dances." This raison d'être, according to Juanchi's reading of Cuban scholar Rogelio Martínez Furé's writings on the Bantu presence in Latin American dances, is an erotic sensibility that unites Black dances of the New World. "So this group, the first one ever, had to leave by the roadside these erotic suggestions that remained in the dances and were the reason for their sustenance. Because this couldn't be performed in a Municipal Theater. So the essence of folklore had to be modified . . ."

Juanchi stressed that Black dances had not "disappeared" in Peru when José Durand set out to reconstruct them. They simply were not seen outside the closed circles of musical families like his own. "People had forgotten that there was also an important Black presence, with its own values, its own culture," he explained. "Now there was the possibility of showing that, and converting it into a theatrical spectacle . . . These Black families that already preserved their traditions who were united for the first time, they were given the condition that if they wanted to bring this music to the theater . . . they had to eliminate the erotic elements. That was the condition. My father [Abelardo Vásquez] has not told me who mandated this, but I suppose it was Mr. Durand, because he was the director of the group, no? Because throughout the epoch of colonial times until the epoch of the Republic, Black music was 'obscene,' 'lewd,' no? . . .

"And this had an effect. Because when people returned from the theater to their houses, they also stopped performing these erotic scenes. That is, 'if the professional artists do this, this is the only correct way,' you understand? So everyone begins to imitate and imitate, and everyone does what they have recently learned, that is they take as their example what they saw in the theater. And this is natural under any circumstance. And they take this as their example, and begin to repeat and repeat and repeat. This makes it part of daily life, and the daily life makes it normal. So now it is a normal affair that these erotic elements are no longer used" (J. Vásquez 2000).

It is significant that the above-cited critiques of Durand's project come from members of two of the most prominent Afro-Peruvian "royal families" that acquired prestige as culture bearers after the Pancho Fierro company disbanded: the Vásquezes and the Santa Cruzes. Nicomedes Santa Cruz' and Juanchi Vásquez' statements implicitly paint José Durand as a cultural outsider, no matter how well-meaning, and they suggest that the criollo nostalgia of his memory project corrupted "real" African-descended traditions. Nicomedes Santa Cruz accuses Durand of overstepping his bounds by stylizing African-descended folkore, and Juanchi Vásquez suggests that the Pancho Fierro shows led to the naturalization of sanitized choreographies of African-descended dances. On the other hand, as Javier León suggests (León Quirós 2003, 219–229), the "cleaned up" versions of staged revival choreographies may also have reflected Afro-Peruvians' own desire to be perceived as "decent," stemming from concerns regarding the dangers of naturalizing stereotypes about Black sexuality.[17] Some Afro-Peruvian dancers maintain that Durand revived "authentic" Black music and dance that was later eroticized for the nightclub audience to conform to stereotyped beliefs about African-descended peoples and their sexuality. In this and other areas, the ways in which "ancient folklore" was changed for the theater remain the subject of speculation, as the "original" fades from accessible memory.

By bringing Black music from the urban callejones and rural homes to the concert stage, José Durand opened the door for the creation in subsequent decades of competing Black performance traditions and styles. Durand's application of academic research methodology to the reconstruction and public celebration of Black music resulted in an unprecedented public acknowledgment of Black culture and music, and Pancho Fierro became the first of many groups to use ethnographic methods to recreate "lost" Black dances of the past. Perhaps Durand's nostalgic obsession with the colonial era lingered in the efforts of subsequent artists, for Black music and dances would continue to be presented almost exclusively as framed visions of history—rather than expressions of a living tradition—in the decades to come. Whereas José Durand's presentation of the past was infused with the colonial nostalgia of criollismo, the Black artists who would perform those same songs and dances for public audiences in the 1960s—especially Nicomedes Santa Cruz and his sister Victoria—had very different social and musical agendas.

CHAPTER 2

Cumanana and the Ancestral Memories of Victoria Santa Cruz

❖

The Diasporic Dance of History and Memory

While José Durand is remembered as the White criollo curator of the first major staged performance of Black music and dance in twentieth-century Lima, Victoria and Nicomedes Santa Cruz are celebrated as the Afro-Peruvian leaders of the subsequent revival of Black arts in the 1960s and 1970s. Under the direction of the Santa Cruz siblings, theatrical productions reconnected Black Peruvians with an African past that preceded the colonial era nostalgically revived by the Pancho Fierro show. Blacks staged their own re-created traditions and began to describe themselves as *afroperuanos* (Afro-Peruvians), signifying a turn toward Africa and its diaspora that was inspired by African independence movements and international Black rights movements (see N. Santa Cruz, qtd. in R. Vásquez Rodríguez 1982, 37). In what I theorize as the struggle to forge a new identity for Afro-Peruvians in the Black Pacific, local criollo nostalgia gave way—in part—to transnational African diasporic "structures of feeling" (Williams 1977).

This chapter describes how Victoria Santa Cruz' reconstructions of Afro-Peruvian music and dance by means of "ancestral memory" in the 1960s and 1970s mobilized a new diasporic consciousness. Chapter 3 focuses on the Peruvian negritud of Nicomedes Santa Cruz. To properly set the contextual stage for my discussion of Victoria and Nicomedes Santa Cruz' leadership in the Afro-Peruvian revival, I will begin with a brief overview of scholarship on diaspora, history, and memory.

The Greek word "diaspora" originally was used to describe the scattering of the Jewish people after their expulsion from Jerusalem by the Babylonians in the sixth century BC. Increasingly, since the 1960s, it also has referred to the coerced geographical dispersal of other peoples (see Boyarin and Boyarin 1993; Butler 2001b; Chaliand and Rageau 1995;

FIGURE 2.1. Victoria Santa Cruz, 1967. *Photo from the collection of Victoria Santa Cruz, reprinted with permission.*

Clifford 1994; Safran 1991; and Tölölyan 1996). As the idea of diaspora has grown to encompass diverse experiences beyond the "classic" Jewish model, scholars have sought to identify commonalties shared by diasporas (Butler 2001b; Safran 1991; and Tölölyan 1996). In its many manifestations, scholars tend to agree that diaspora is not simply a demographic condition but also a state of mind. Diasporic peoples are united by their collective consciousness of loss and forced exodus, sometimes defined by events that happened hundreds of years before their birth. Long after the initial separation of people from a homeland, their shared feeling of belonging to a diaspora connects an imagined past to a lived present.

Normally, in order for diasporic consciousness to remain alive, a group of people must actively maintain collective memory, diasporic longing, and a myth of return to the homeland. Without these elements, descendants of the diaspora tend no longer to identify as diasporic subjects, as was the case in Peru (before the revival) and other parts of the imagined Black Pacific.

Connected to a homeland most have never seen and a past they did not experience, diasporic peoples work with the tools of history and memory to actively define their diasporic heritage by reproducing the past. French historiographer Pierre Nora's (1984–1986) influential notion of "sites of memory" presents memory and history as diametrically opposed rivals in the struggle over how to represent the past. Nora writes that when the acceleration of history (via industrialization) eradicates real environments of memory (*milieux de mémoire*), societies harness memory by linking it to sites (*lieux de mémoire*) such as museums and monuments. Many scholars identify problems with Nora's argument, even as they make use of his model (Fabre and O'Meally 1994; Cole 2001). Critics contend that Nora's strict separation of history from memory ignores the ways history and memory are intertwined and that his reliance on the binary opposition of lieux and milieux reinforces a Eurocentric division of the world into modern and premodern camps.

However, Nora's model offers a useful way to think about how artists in diaspora connect with the past through their creative works. In some cases, dance plays a vital role in the reconstruction and "siting" of dormant or fading diasporic memories—which is particularly relevant to this chapter's overview of the Africanist choreographies of Victoria Santa Cruz. For example, as VéVé Clark (1994) argues, choreographer/anthropologist Katherine Dunham (whose example inspired Victoria and Nicomedes Santa Cruz) inscribed the "memory of difference" in dance through her ethnography to performance method; she studied Afro-Caribbean dances and rituals (real environments of memory) and then transformed them into staged choreographies (sites of memory). Similarly, dancer/choreographer Bill T. Jones describes the historical migration of dance itself from real environments of memory to sites of memory (without actually using those terms). He writes: "In its beginnings, dance was something that we, as a community, enjoyed. It was a way we told our stories. It was a way we expressed what we wanted and what we feared. It is still a ritual, a system of signs and gestures, but we have separated those who dance from those who watch the dance. The dancer and the watcher are held together in a moment. The dancer steps, he pushes the earth away and is in the air. One foot comes down, followed by the other. It's over. We agree, dancer and watcher, to hold on to the illusion that someone flew for a moment. And in this way, all dance exists in memory. This is what makes dance such a supremely human art. It leaves no physical evidence" (1995, 246).

Like dance, history may be viewed as a performance that afterwards exists only in memory. The events that will be recorded as history "dance" before our eyes and we negotiate how to interpret their movements. Taking this approach, "new history" projects depict history as a kind of contract between societies and their pasts, and memory as a history-making technology (see Ebron 1998). Using the technologies of "counter-memory" (Foucault 1977), subaltern people challenge the official memory inscribed by endorsed versions of history. For example, victims and survivors of slavery and genocide have used memory techniques (such as Holocaust survivors' secret diaries and marks on cell walls; Toni Morrison's literary reopening of suppressed memories of African American slavery in *Beloved* [1987]; the late Iris Chang's publication of *The Rape of Nanking* [1997] and her fight against the censorship of the Nanking massacre from Japanese textbooks and world memory; and so forth) to prevent the erasure of their experiences from history. Similarly, Afrocentric projects (for example, Amadiume 1997; Asante 1988; Bernal 1987–; Diop 1986) propose counter-memories that recover the unacknowledged historical contributions of Africa and its peoples.

I suggest, in this chapter, that Victoria Santa Cruz' Afrocentric re-creation of Black Peruvian dances as sites of memory challenged the Peruvian discourse of criollismo. With other leading artists of the Afro-Peruvian revival, she looked toward the Black Atlantic to forge a transnational diasporic identity for Black Peruvians, borrowing musical instruments and cultural expressions. But Victoria Santa Cruz' most celebrated legacy is her idiosyncratic deployment of "ancestral memory" as the cornerstone of a choreographic technique that enabled her to "return" to the African homeland by looking deep within her own body for the residue of organic ancestral rhythms. In particular, through her re-creation of the landó, Santa Cruz believes that she gave life to a danced memory of her ancestral homeland that is more "African" than contemporary Africa. Whether or not this is true, her re-created dances now publicly represent the actual heritage of Afro-Peruvians, and they are performed as such by folklore groups to this day. Moreover, Victoria Santa Cruz trained a young generation of dancers to use her method as a means to reclaim their African heritage, resulting in a lasting role for ancestral memory as choreographic strategy in Afro-Peruvian dance.

"Africa" and "slavery" have long been competing points of reference for scholarly and artistic constructions of a past for Blacks in the New World

(Scott 1991; see also Herskovits 1941; Price 1983 and 1985). Afrocentric projects weigh in heavily on the side of Africa, while other scholars have focused, since the 1970s, on creolization and hybridity. In an influential essay published in the 1970s, Sidney Mintz and Richard Price warned against "the dangers of extrapolating backward to Africa in the realm of social forms" (Mintz and Price [1976] 1992, 54). Mintz and Price argued that the anthropological search for "survivals" of presumed African culture traits (championed by Melville Herskovits in the 1930s and 1940s) should be redirected to focus on the "birth of African American culture," emphasizing the creative African American response to the only cultural experience actually shared by all enslaved Africans in the New World—surviving and surmounting the trauma of slavery. Similarly, Paul Gilroy (1993) locates the beginning of Black Atlantic cultural formation in the Middle Passage and the crisis of modernity that occurred in slavery. While he recognizes the motivational value of Afrocentric projects, Gilroy worries that their ideologies reinscribe essentialist—and ultimately prejudicial—ideas about "race," blindly bypassing the legacy of slavery in order to revalorize imagined constructions of great precolonial African civilizations (see Gilroy 1993, 187–192).

Because Victoria Santa Cruz' rediscovery of African ancestry through bodily rhythms can be interpreted as implying a biological connection to "race" and inherited memory, it represents the kind of Afrocentric position Gilroy argues against (1993 and 2000). However, overly rigid application of Gilroy's and Mintz and Price's models may discount the importance of the emic discourse of members of the African diaspora such as Victoria Santa Cruz (see Scott 1991, 262). If Africa is actively reinvented in the production of diasporic identity, then this retelling of the past is an important aspect of understanding that identity—whether or not it corresponds to the "real" Africa. Moreover, due to the Black Pacific's diasporic isolation, ancestral memory may be perceived as one of the only available routes to recover the remote African past. Yet, it is also important to acknowledge that when Victoria Santa Cruz speaks of Africa as the source of her ancestral memories—like many other artists of the African diaspora who cannot trace their genealogy to a specific place or nation within that vast and diverse continent—she refers to a generalized Africa that no longer exists (and perhaps never existed except in diasporic imagination).

In this chapter, I use the tools of history and memory to reconstruct the ancestral memory project of Victoria Santa Cruz. I begin with a history of Victoria and Nicomedes Santa Cruz' collaboration to direct Peru's first all-Black theater company, Cumanana. The narrative then moves from history to memory, shifting to the recollections of Teresa Mendoza

Hernández, a former member of the Cumanana company. The third section focuses on Victoria Santa Cruz' pedagogical method for the discovery and development of an inner sense of rhythm, her re-creation of Black Peruvian dances (the landó and the zamacueca), and her powerful role in shaping the first generation of Black actors and dancers to perform on Lima's mainstages. To situate this entire reconstructive project where it began, in the present-day collection of memories, I conclude with my personal recollection of my own meetings with Victoria Santa Cruz in Lima.

The Santa Cruz Family and Cumanana

Victoria Santa Cruz Gamarra (b. 1922) and her brother Nicomedes Santa Cruz Gamarra (1925–1992) were born into a family of Black intellectuals, artists, and musicians whose contributions to Peru's cultural life went back six generations (O. Santa Cruz n.d.). Their mother, Victoria Gamarra Ramírez (1886–1959), was the daughter of Peruvian painter José Milagros Gamarra (considered the father of indigenismo in Peruvian painting). Nicomedes and Victoria remember their mother reciting *décimas* and dancing the zamacueca and the marinera.[1] She is said to have had a contralto voice and an ear so fine she could discern whether water poured from a teapot was boiling based on the pitch of the sound it made as it splashed to the ground (R. Santa Cruz 2000a, 179). Their father, Nicomedes Santa Cruz Aparicio (1871–1957), was taken to the United States at the age of nine during the War of the Pacific with Chile, and he lived there until he was a young adult (R. Santa Cruz 2000a, 179–180). He returned to Peru fluent in English and a connoisseur of Shakespeare, opera, and the theater, and his original plays were produced in Lima in the early 1900s (Handy 1979, 97). The elder Nicomedes Santa Cruz and Victoria Gamarra had ten children, of whom Victoria Santa Cruz was number eight and Nicomedes Santa Cruz was number nine.

Victoria Santa Cruz began to dance shortly after learning to walk. By the age of twelve, she was innately drawn to music, dance, and theater, and she began to direct and choreograph dances and one-act plays in high school (V. and N. Santa Cruz 1961). She discovered "Western" arts with the guidance of her father, who exposed his children to the music of Haydn, Handel, Wagner, and Mozart and the plays of William Shakespeare. From her mother, Victoria learned to dance the Peruvian marinera. She observed in her mother what she describes as an "organic connection" to music and dance, which influenced her greatly. As Victoria says, her mother imparted in her children an understanding of the silence where all sound begins (V. Santa Cruz 1991 and 2000). To this day, Victoria perceives a fundamental divide between those who approach knowledge with the intellect and those who understand organically with their bodies. Academic pursuits, to Victoria, are how the mind colonizes the body (V. Santa Cruz 2000).

Victoria and Nicomedes first decided to create a company of Black artists after they were inspired by a performance of dances from the African diaspora by the Katherine Dunham Company at Lima's Municipal Theater in 1951 (V. Santa Cruz 2000). Dunham, an African American choreographer and anthropologist, studied African-derived cultural expressions of the Caribbean and then translated them to staged and stylized choreographies using her ethnography to performance method. Nicomedes later described Dunham's show as the first positive publicly staged demonstration of blackness in Peru (N. Santa Cruz 1973, 24). Nicomedes joined the Pancho Fierro company in 1957, and in 1958 he launched his own Black theater group, Cumanana, which included other former Pancho Fierro members.[2] In 1959, Victoria joined Nicomedes as co-director of Cumanana. With Victoria's choreography, musical compositions, and theatrical direction, Cumanana matured from "revue scenes to what can well be called the beginning of Black theater in Peru" (V. and N. Santa Cruz 1961).

Nicomedes and Victoria worked together as directors of Cumanana from 1959 until 1961, researching and reconstructing what they referred to as Afro-Peruvian folklore. They revived old musical games and re-created forgotten songs and dances. Their approaches were very different. Whereas Victoria developed a method based on rhythm and ancestral memory, Nicomedes engaged in book research, ethnographic collection of folklore, and literary studies. Victoria became famous for her staging and choreography, and Nicomedes was the better-known poet and musician (although Victoria also composed music and poetry). Differences eventually dissolved the partnership, but for a few important years, Cumanana was the focus of their joint collaboration.

The Cumanana company brought Victoria and Nicomedes' re-created Black Peruvian folklore to life in productions mounted at Lima's most prestigious theatrical venues in 1960 and 1961. These plays, generally set in times of slavery, reclaimed forgotten African heritage in Peru. Unlike the Pancho Fierro company's performance of nostalgic criollismo, their plots often included satirical jabs at racism and inequality. The result was an unprecedented public staging of blackness that emphasized racial difference and Black pride.

The first Cumanana production was a three-act play titled *Zanahary*, which opened to excellent reviews at Teatro La Cabaña on March 13, 1960. The first act, "Callejón de un solo caño" (Callejón with only one faucet), dramatized a scene from daily life in the laundry area of a callejón, the typical communal housing facility where many poor Blacks lived in early-twentieth-century Lima. The first act also included the skit "La pelona" (based on Nicomedes' poem about a Black girl trying to rise above her station and race). The second act, "La academía folklórica" (The folklore academy), lightheartedly pointed out the racist implications of musical notation terminology.

The finale and showstopper was "Zanahary," a staged Africanist healing ritual with dancing and drums, conceived and choreographed by Victoria Santa Cruz. As explained in Nicomedes Santa Cruz' related poem "Mi Dios, mi Zanaharí" (My God, my Zanahary), "Zanahary" is the supreme divinity in religious belief systems of Madagascar, an area of Africa not commonly believed to have supplied many slaves to the New World, but whose people are known for rituals of ancestral memory (N. Santa Cruz n.d.[1959?], 29–30, 159; Cole 2001, 9–10).[3] According to a preview of the scene "Zanahary" in the Peruvian newspaper *La Crónica*, "Its primary plot revolves around a maiden suffering under a malignant evil spell. Fanaticism and credulousness bring her before chocolate sorcerers, with the hope that rites, music, chanting, and dances will eradicate the harmful evil spell" (N.a. 1960a). "Zanahary" also included references to an exoticized African heritage in the original song "Karambe" and a ritual dance called *afro*.[4] Because there is little historical documentation of the past religious practices of enslaved Africans in Peru (see Cuche 1975 and 1976), Victoria and Nicomedes Santa Cruz either accessed information unknown to scholars and historians or, more likely, they relied on the pan-African custom of "borrowing" symbols from a wide range of African practices.

The three-act play was a great success, and newspaper reviewers hailed the Santa Cruzes' re-creation of Peru's lost Black Peruvian heritage. However, despite the strategic promotion of an African identity for Black Peruvians, critics reconfigured the Black expressions presented onstage as an important building block of criollo culture. For example, a review in *La Crónica* included the caption "Negroid dance and song contributed a native aspect to the happiness and sharp wit of Lima's criollismo and *mazamorrero*" and praised the dramatic themes and acting as "authentically criollo" (N.a. 1960c).[5] Similarly, the advance feature in the same paper ("Exotic black magic and scenes of the callejón go to the theater with Kumanana") predicted: "'Zanahary' and 'Callejón' . . . will be preferentially incorporated in the archive of national theater, the *costumbrista* theater we have missed so much in this grave era of 'foreignism'" (N.a. 1960a). In the tradition of Ricardo Palma, *costumbrismo* utilizes themes and devices that celebrate local or regional customs, songs, dances, and traditions in order to create what Javier León refers to as "seemingly timeless snapshots of an idealized colonial past that never was" (León Quirós 2003, 56). Thus, the reviewer's reference to costumbrista theater invokes the memory project of criollo nostalgia while turning a blind eye to the competing transnational project of African diasporic memory.

Victoria Santa Cruz followed *Zanahary* with a more complex dramatic production in April 1961. *Malató*, Victoria's first full-length play, was set on a hacienda in 1833. A slave girl (played by Victoria in her acting debut) became the White master's lover and thought herself better than the other slaves. When her lover grew tired of her she was cast off, and the Black slave and sorcerer (Nicomedes) who adored her tried to win her back. The three-act play included Afro-Peruvian and criollo songs and poetry composed by Victoria and Nicomedes, including festejos, *cumananas,* décimas, *lamentos,* and *panalivios* (V. and N. Santa Cruz 1961).

Malató acted as counter-memory by dramatizing the intimate relations between slave and master that were omitted from the country's official history. In the provinces of Ica, Chincha, and Cañete, the popular saying "el mejor plato lo toma el español en la cena" (the Spaniard takes the best dish at supper) referred to the common practice whereby hacienda owners had sexual relations with their female slaves. Chosen partners were often cast aside, after a time, in favor of a new "flavor." Although this practice was not typically acknowledged publicly in criollo society, Lima's national archives are filled with paternity petitions by female slaves whose children were fathered by Spanish hacienda owners, and with documentation of the forced marriage of numerous Spanish and Black parents (Harth-Terré 1971, 12).

Like *Zanahary, Malató* also reconstructed the African-derived religious practices of Black Peru, this time based on information provided by Don Porfirio Vásquez. Nicomedes portrayed a *curao* (enchanted one), who practiced the *brujería* (sorcery) typical of Don Porfirio's rural place of birth, Aucallama. According to the program notes for *Malató* (V. and N. Santa Cruz 1961), Black curaos of Aucallama inserted tiny amulets into their arms, legs, and heads. These amulets, known as *santolino*, were human figures made of marble extracted from the sacred stone of the main altar of the temple. Once the treatment was complete, Black curaos who wore the amulets under their skin were endowed with extraordinary powers enacted through auto-suggestion; they became immune to damage by fire, rocks, or steel.

The process of creating and rehearsing works like *Zanahary* and *Malató* established Victoria Santa Cruz as a charismatic mentor who awakened Black diasporic consciousness, self-awareness, and racial pride in her company members. These young Black Peruvians, bred in a society that hardly recognized their existence, were eager to learn about their African cultural heritage with their bodies and minds. This was the first time an all-Black Peruvian company had performed on Lima's main stages, marking a landmark in the social achievements of Peruvian Blacks and a turn in the Black Peruvian revival from criollo to African diasporic identity-making projects. In the following passage, ex-Cumanana company member Teresa Mendoza turns the pages of her photo album and recalls how it felt to be part of this momentous historical event.

In Her Voice: Teresa Mendoza Remembers Cumanana[6]

My name is Teresa Mendoza Hernández. I danced and sang in Cumanana, Nicomedes and Victoria Santa Cruz' company, in the 1960s. I became a part of it by accident when I was only twenty-four or twenty-five years old. One day I went to visit a friend who worked at the Teatro de la Cabaña. And there, Nico saw me.

"Señorita," he said, "you are perfect for the play we are producing!"

So I said, "Oh, no! I can't dance like that."

"You'll only have to dance the marinera," he replied.

So I said to myself: "This is my opportunity, my ticket!" Because my mother would never let me go anywhere. "Don't even think of turning them down," I told myself. "They're not going to leave me behind!"

And my friend, Juanita who worked at the theater and was a friend of my mother's, told Nico, "Don't you worry, I'll be responsible for Teresa."

She asked my father. "Not a chance!" he said. "Don't even think about it. To the theater, so you come back at who knows what time!"

Juanita, assured him, "Look, don't worry, I'll be her chaperone. I'll take her there and bring her back."

And my mother gave permission.

The rehearsals began, and I danced the marinera. They told me I danced well, and they made me perform the turns again and again, according to the rules of the marinera. They told me I had a very nice figure, a beautiful "look." There were plans to present a play, and a project to travel to France. Finally, my opportunity!

The rehearsals were a thing of beauty. For me it was a party. Oh, how I enjoyed myself! I always arrived early, because my mother taught me to be punctual and this remained with me. And I would talk with Victoria. We were more friends than directors and artists. And in the rehearsals, the more spontaneous you were, the better. Victoria created the scores and the libretti. And everyone contributed his or her part.

We rehearsed for almost a year, a year that made a significant mark in me. It gave me a kind of energy. Because I was not prepared for theater; I was a woman of the house, I had a fashion design workshop. It would never have

FIGURE 2.2. Teresa Mendoza Hernández and her husband, Carlos "Caitro" Soto de la Colina, in their Lima home, 2000. *Photo by the author.*

occurred to me to be part of a theater company. I have so many beautiful memories. But Victoria had her temperament; nobody can tell her what to do!

Almost all of Victoria's plays fired a shot at real life. And at this time that was rarely done. Today, you see the soaps on TV, but a play about authentic Black people? Even now it is just not done. At least that's how it seems to me. And it can be beautiful, because Black people have so many stories, so much history!

So Victoria formed her company, and we started to rehearse a show in three acts. The first act was "Callejón de un solo caño." It took place in a callejón where there was just one water tap for everyone, and they would fight over the use of the tap. The famous water tap. Because, imagine if you had to go to work and everyone left at the same time. There was a quarrel. One lady thinks she'll do her washing, and the other is at the tap, the first begins: "Hurry up! Hurry up!" And the other answers back, and it's a whole quarrel. And it ended in a fight, and the whole callejón came out to see it. And the neighbor was so enraged that she hurled her basin of water! And then they started pulling each other's hair. It was funny!

Victoria mounted this play, and it was as if you were transported to that callejón. Like I tell you, she is a great choreographer.

Also in "Callejón," I played "la pelona."[7] It was a satirical song for a skinny Black girl, and the role fit me perfectly, because I was so thin. Nico told me, "You are ideal for this song!" And I said, "But I can't sing!" I never performed musically. I lacked confidence. Put on whatever music you want and I would dance

FIGURE 2.3. The quarrel from "Las lavanderas" in "Callejón de un solo caño," reenacted in the late 1960s under the direction of Victoria Santa Cruz. Pictured (top photo): Lucila Campos (left) and Teresa Palomino (right). *Reprinted with permission from* Caretas.

FIGURE 2.4. "La pelona," 1960. Pictured (front): Nicomedes Santa Cruz and Teresa Mendoza Hernández. *Photo from the collection of Teresa Mendoza Hernández, reprinted with permission.*

for you. But singing? I said, "How am I going to sing if I can't carry a tune?"
And Victoria said, "Girl, just do it!"

When the performance came, they had to push me out on stage because I was dying of fear! And the people began to applaud. What a stimulus an audience is! I was center stage, and the people were applauding me. Nico started to recite his décimas, and then came the game in which I had to sing: "I won't marry a Black man . . ."

FIGURE 2.5. "La escuela folklórica," 1960. Pictured: Nicomedes Santa Cruz, center. *Photo from the collection of Teresa Mendoza Hernández, reprinted with permission.*

The lyrics say it all. It demonized the Black person. This is a Black woman who thinks she's ahead of her time, the Black girl pretending to be something she wasn't. I was the Black woman who wore heels at a time when Blacks went barefoot. Who imitated the master and the mistress and their lifestyle. The Black girl who wants to be like society people, like a White person of the era. She wants to dress herself elegantly and go out, and now she doesn't even want a Black man anymore. "A Black man? No!" And she dresses up in her hat and her pocketbook, and it's as if today we dressed up elegantly to go to the fields. She had "civilized herself," as they say. She had fixed her hair, painted her lips. I had this dress, a horribly pretentious pocketbook, a terrible hat. Nico's décima goes: "With your witch's head . . ." Because I had no hair, my hair was done up, and I carried a compact and I smoked. Things that weren't seen in the old days. And Nico insulted me ("You with your cigarette, you're a wannabee!"), and I answered back.

So it was very funny. And the song goes: "You'll marry a Black man, marry a shoemaker, marry a carpenter." And I'd say, "That doesn't suit me, because the carpenter who cuts wood will cut me, too!" And next is the breadmaker, and the breadmaker kneads flour, he might knead me, too. The other is the bottle man, and if you marry the man who sells bottles, he might sell you, too. And none of them looked good to me. This was the gist of the song. It was a game. The show was widely accepted, even though I really didn't know how to sing!

The second act was "Escuela folklórica" (The folklore school). Nico was the professor, and he wanted to teach us music. And he said, "Let's learn how in music, a white note [half note] equals this much." And the professor is called out of the room, and then all the students rise up: "How is it possible that a white note [half note] equals two black notes [quarter notes]?" [8] How did the song go? Oh yes [sings]: "Whoever invented musical notes lies and lies, I'm not wrong, lies and more lies. It's not possible that a white note is worth two black notes . . ." And we began to dance. When the professor came back, we all took our seats. It was lovely!

And the last act was "Zanahary," which was about witchcraft. I had never danced the afro. That was for the other girls. One day, Victoria said to me: "Teresa, dance the afro!" I said to Victoria, "I can't—" "Dance!" she said. "Dance. I want to see you." So she made me dance the afro. And from that point on, we began to rehearse and rehearse until we mounted a work that was an enormous hit.

Victoria created this whole ritual that was called "Zanahary." I played a woman who was bewitched, supported by two sorcerers, Ronaldo Campos and Abelardo Vásquez. So we entered, and I sat down. One started to pass a rooster over my body while the other leapt around, and they performed all their rituals until I was freed a bit. And I started to dance a type of ritual with them. The

FIGURE 2.6. "Zanahary," 1960. Pictured: Teresa Mendoza Hernández (center), Ronaldo Campos and Abelardo Vásquez (leaping in air). *Photo from the collection of Teresa Mendoza Hernández, reprinted with permission.*

three of us danced until I was freed. Then there was another dance with my sister and another female dancer. And finally I came forward in a solo: the afro. The ritual, the music, the dance, and everything was African.

Why is it called afro? Because it is authentically African. We couldn't say "African," because we weren't in Africa. The afro is a memory, a memoir, an act of remembering, a style that belongs to Africa. But it is not the African dance of Africa. It is afro. Something that was brought from Africa. And I expressed it.

I felt . . . that is, I came forward, I started to dance, and for me there was no audience. For me everything had been erased. I simply felt the music, I felt the drums, and it is incredible how the drums move you! The batá *drums and the* cajón.[9] *They are so rich, and they're not used in other parts, right? But here in Peru, the Africans came and they hadn't brought anything, so they created the cajón. I danced the afro, and there was no choreography. Now free, free from the sorcery that had cured me, I started to dance. The liberated woman who danced and danced and danced. But all this was in Black rhythm. Drum rhythms. Black African rhythm and African dance.*

When we finished Zanahary, *the next work was* Malató, *and the main characters were Victoria and Nicomedes. And it was also a hit.*

But she left, she went to France. After Victoria left, we went to the Iberoamerican festival in Argentina in 1967. This was "Nicomedes Santa Cruz and his Group." It was just Nico, Abelardo Vásquez, Ronaldo Campos, Pipo Vásquez,

Caitro Soto (my husband), and me. There were seven of us.[10] And the stage was a stadium! When we saw the stage, we wanted to die. Over one hundred dancers came from Mexico. My God. Panama: over one hundred people, and oh! Their beautiful costumes, the beautiful, enchanting women! We began to sweat. What were we doing here? Brazil! I think there were 189 dancers from Brazil. And they carried an old Black woman who was seated on a throne. And there were Brazilians and Brazilians and more Brazilians. And the Brazilians kept coming, and we watched. Actually, I think it was 200 dancers from Mexico. Everyone brought hundreds of dancers, and we had seven.

What could we do, now that we were already there? We were going to perform zapateo and festejo. There were so many people, so many spectators, because you know a group of seven Mexicans will fill a stadium. Over a hundred? Okay, we thought, they've got it all tied up. Nico said, "We have material, we have to do it. We are here, we have to make the best of it."

So we decided to perform Black Christmas, el son de los diablos, festejo, and zapateo. And we also included the alcatraz. When it was our turn: "Peru!" Peru came out. We said, my God, we have to position ourselves as far apart as possible. Imagine how we would have to run like crazy! Seven people in a full stadium, we were just like mosquitoes! But they liked us, because we included el son de los diablos. Caitro was the diablo mayor at that time, and he came out cracking his whip. And the people applauded. We danced festejo and they raved. And after we danced alcatraz, the people couldn't believe it. You know what the alcatraz is? A Black woman with a little tail and a Black man with a little tail carry a candle in their hands. And they try to burn each other's tail. And in this era, we all had good figures!

Black Peruvian dance has a great richness in every sense of the word. Because you move from your feet to your legs, your hips, your waist, shoulders, head, we can't move our hair, but we move our heads. And the eyes are the life of the Black face. The Black dancer lives the dance. No one dances without wanting to. But we have this grace of God and an art that is inside of us. Black people can't dance without being happy. So when we danced the alcatraz . . .

We said, "Thank God they applauded us. We didn't make out too bad, folks!" And what happened? Mexico and Brazil reclaimed the prize, because they said seven people couldn't win a festival when so many members had come to participate. But in reality, we won first prize.

When Victoria came back from France, she remounted the show. But not "Zanahary." Just "Callejón" and the music school. But the truth is, by this time I had my husband, my children. Then they came for me when they started Perú Negro. But I told them, "Look, my time is over. Now I have my husband, I have my children, and I want to dedicate myself to them. I want to enjoy my children."

Our audience was all kinds of people. But mostly rich people. We had a great public. Our work became well-known and the performances were so beautiful and so respectable. Nothing was indecent. At the time, people said that Blacks were saucy, insolent, Blacks are like this, Blacks are like that, marginalized from all sides. Because in this era, you didn't see Black music. You didn't hear it. Look, Ramon Castilla freed the slaves, but for the Blacks, life continued as it had before, marginalized as ever.

When the first Black companies came out, they came from the small towns. So what they presented was small town performance. Their songs, their dances, they even danced in another way. When Zanahary came out, it changed everything completely. Everything. Because they had played their cajón and their guitar as they did in the country. But now Victoria brought in batá drums, which weren't used. The tumbas were used, but not much.[11] Then she used the cajita. And all this enriched the music. She presented us in a beautiful way, even though we never stopped being what we were. We had quality. She dressed us up, she put clothes on us, and although we were still from the small towns, now we were presentable.

Victoria Santa Cruz and the Power of Ancestral Memory

> There are beings who were born to accomplish great tasks, drawing strength from the deepest atavism, recreating lost ancestral voices, giving new life to deceased movements, and above all, surpassing the greatest natural, accidental, and deliberate obstacles. Such is the case of Victoria Santa Cruz: past, present, and future of Peruvian folklore.—(Nicomedes Santa Cruz, qtd. in N.a. 1982)

It has been said that "all song and dance, every ensemble and solo performer that cultivates art with 'afro' roots in Peru is influenced—directly or indirectly—by Victoria Santa Cruz" (R. Santa Cruz 2000a, 181). The mention of Victoria's name provokes that intense combination of love and hate, fear and disdain, dismissal and reverence that is reserved for charismatic individuals who powerfully affect others. Everyone has a "Victoria Santa Cruz story," and not all of them are kind. Yet, those who remember her plays agree that they were a historic and glorious achievement, and more than one person has confided to me, "to see her dance was a thing of beauty."

In popular allegories of time travel, those who go back in time and make even the smallest changes forever alter the future. Victoria Santa Cruz changed history for Blacks in Peru by guiding her young protégés to rekindle their connection to the lost African past and through choreographies that reshaped public notions of blackness in Peru. On Lima's grandest stages, she accomplished what was not acted out in real life: she created a space in which Black Peruvians could celebrate—and be applauded for—the beauty and dignity of their cultural heritage.

Victoria Santa Cruz writes, "I was born a woman, I was born Black, and . . . being Latin American . . . also was an obstacle. Fortunately, the very act of having formed myself in hostility taught me to discover what it means to rise up without looking for someone to blame . . . The act of having suffered, from a very tender age, innumerable difficult situations that obligated me—without my knowing it—to fall back into the depths of myself, with questions such as 'What is life? Who am I?' permitted me, afterward, to discover . . . the incredible advantages of apparent disadvantages."[12] Describing how rhythm connected her to ancestral memories since childhood, Victoria once said, "I remember having awakened one night. I would have been six years old. And in the [adjacent] callejón there was a jarana . . . And I have not slept without thinking about how I would like to be there. That is ancestral! That is ancestral, the source of all vibration." She continued, explaining that among her brothers and sisters, "I am one of the most African. Because I could be listening to rhythmic combinations and they were transporting me to memories. And a time came when one of my brothers told me, 'I go no further!' And I continued traveling in time" (V. Santa Cruz 1991).

Explaining what she means by "ancestral memory," Victoria writes: "What is ancestry? Is it a memory? And if so, what is it trying to make us remember? . . . The popular and cultural manifestations, rooted in Africa, which I inherited and later accepted as ancestral vocation, created a certain disposition toward rhythm, which over the years has turned itself into a new technique, 'the discovery and development of rhythmic sense' . . . I reached my climax . . . when I went deep into that magical world that bears the name of rhythm" (V. Santa Cruz 1978c, 18). Elsewhere, she continues: "Having discovered, first ancestrally and later through study and practice, that every gesture, word, and movement is a consequence of a state of being, and that this state of being is tied to connections and disconnections of fixed centers or plexus . . . allowed me to rediscover profound messages in dance and traditional music that could be recovered and communicated . . . The Black man knows through ancestry, even when he is not conscious of it, that what is outwardly elaborated has its origin or foundation in the interior of those who generate it" (V. Santa Cruz 1988, 85).

Victoria Santa Cruz has spent her adult lifetime developing, teaching, and preparing for publication (2005) the pedagogical method that she calls "Discovery and Development of the Sense of Rhythm." A brief overview of my understanding of the theory behind her method, paraphrased from various writings and discussions, goes something like this:

"Discovery And Development Of The Sense Of Rhythm" (compiled and paraphrased from V. Santa Cruz 1979a; 1988; 1995; 2000): Organic cultures are organizations of human beings who continue to develop an inherited organic knowledge that is interwoven with the fabric of daily life. In organic cultures there is no such thing as "specialization" or "art"; dance and music are part of life, learned from life and enacted for the purpose of living. When organic cultures are destroyed, their knowledge is divided, with vestiges retained within what is called folklore. Rhythm is "the great organizer." It is the key to our connection to the secrets of the organic cultures of the past. We can discover rhythm with the vehicle of the human body, never with the cold, colonizing intellect.

Dance, emanating from the solar plexus, is a medium toward connection with rhythm, but we must remember that dance is not a goal in and of itself. The secret nature of rhythm, inherited from ancestral cultures, cannot be expressed through definitions ("tempo," "beat," "meter," "movement," "order," etc.), for these definitions are only a consequence of rhythm (just as dance is a consequence of rhythm). Education leading to the development of a sense of rhythm is fundamentally necessary for all human beings, not just so-called "artists," bringing about a profound understanding of ourselves and our psychological process. Through rhythmic formulas of African extraction, stressing the binary continuum of sound and silence, this method guides practitioners through the process of starting by finding out and trusting their point of departure—the self—and making a deep connection with ancestral truths through the inner sense of rhythm.

"Ancestral memory" is often understood as part of belief systems in which the spirits of the deceased watch over and intermingle with the living. In the religious rituals of many cultures, ancestors possess the bodies of the living when invoked through music, dance, and offerings. In some cases, ancestors visit the living in their dreams to teach new songs, and the composers "remember" the songs when they awaken. However, Victoria Santa Cruz' performative ancestral memory is unlike these types of ancestral communications received from the dead. Instead, her connection is a geographically unspecific link to a generalized sense of African ancestry (versus a specific ancestor) that she believes she discovered through the vehicle of her body and dance. In this sense, the body itself represents a kind of "Africa" where lost ancestral memories are stored.

Although Victoria Santa Cruz' method is specific to her own experience, it should be noted that certain other artists (choreographers, performance artists, jazz musicians, negritude poets, and so forth) and social theorists do share a similar notion of ancestral memory as a source of creative performativity. For example, dancer/choreographer Martha Graham believed that "blood memory" inspires choreography, providing dancers (whose training makes their bodies open vessels for the imprint of "ancestral footprints") with inexplicable awareness of bodily movements derived from ancient world cultures "in the blood" (Graham 1991). Sociologist

Paul Connerton describes performative bodily practices, in which the body understands and reinscribes "habit memories" linked to social identity and performs them as choreographies (1989, 72–104). And anthropologist Ruth Behar writes, "the body is a homeland—a place where knowledge, memory, and pain is stored by the child . . . The path back leads to an imaginary homeland—the space on the frontier of consciousness where . . . meanings—unspoken, inchoate, raw, and throbbing with life—wait to be found, to be given voice" (Behar 1996, 134).

A basic tenet of Victoria's method is the presumption that a sense of rhythm is innate in all Black people by way of ancestry. "From an ancestral memory of Africa," she explains, "without knowing of the existence of an African continent; I learned the *foundations* of rhythm. Rhythm, without the intellectual connotation of 'time and beat.' Rhythmic combinations inherited, and in the passage of my life, recreated by me, awakened those *inherent qualities* of the human being. *Qualities* which taught me to discover the door that suffering hides, whose secret is not to exit but: To Enter."[13] Victoria believes that the African origin of all Black people is an organic culture with an inherent knowledge of the secret of rhythm. This does not mean that all Black people are in touch with their ancestral memory. It means that, through the method Victoria has discovered, they can reconnect with the knowledge that lies dormant within them, using the tool of rhythm. "Long ago," explains Victoria, "Africa discovered the secret of rhythm, the secret of movement. The Black man vibrates to silence" (V. Santa Cruz 1979a, 7). She adds, "Artisanship, music, song, dance, poetry; these were *means* created since ancient times, to tune the only instrument that cannot be tuned by another: the physical body. The physical body contains secrets that do not belong to the physical-terrestrial plane, being the first step in the process of evolution of the human being."[14]

This placement of ancestral memory in the Black body is both compelling and problematic, seemingly supporting biological determinism and the full range of stereotypical assertions that rhythm, dance, and other essential qualities are "in the blood" of Black people. The lyrics to the song "Pa' goza con el ritmo del tambo," composed by Victoria Santa Cruz and still performed today, proclaim, "to get down to the rhythm of the drum, you have to be Black . . . to enjoy this life you have to know how to feel, let your body go, it will take you by itself . . ." (V. Santa Cruz 1995). While contemporary cultural critics (Appiah 1992; Gilroy 1993 and 2000) take issue with such essentializing notions, arguing that "racial" behavior is learned, not inherent, and that "race" itself is an invention, it is striking that (with the exceptions noted above) most of the prolific scholarly literature on collective memory virtually ignores the concept of ancestral memory. The beauty and the danger of the idea of ancestral memory is that it deftly disables criticism in the same way devout religious belief can never be "wrong."

While Victoria was developing her method in the early 1960s, a French cultural attaché, deeply impressed by Victoria's play *Malató*, arranged for her to receive a foreign study grant from the French government. Victoria quickly taught herself French, and, in 1961, moved to Paris to study theater and choreography, leaving Cumanana in Nicomedes' hands. For five years, she studied with renowned professors at the Université du Theatre des Nationes and École Superieur des Études Chorégraphiques in Paris. During this period, Victoria also visited Africa for the first time as a member of a student theater group that toured Tangiers, Marrakesh, and Casablanca as well as Spain, Italy, Belgium, and Portugal (Revollar 1967, 7). Upon her return to Paris, Victoria directed and mounted her ballet *La muñeca negra* (The black doll), featuring a cast of Black Cuban, African, and Antillean dancers (N.a. 1982). "In Paris, they thought I was African," she remembers. "They didn't know there were Blacks in Peru . . . In contrast, in Africa they spoke English to me. Because of my clothing and manner of walking they thought I was North American" (qtd. in Revollar 1967, 7).

In 1966, Victoria Santa Cruz returned to Peru, proclaiming herself "blacker and more Peruvian" than ever (qtd. in Suárez Radillo 1976, 285). She issued a public call to auditions for her new company, Teatro y Danzas Negras del Perú (Theater and Black Dances of Peru). "I would like all the Blacks in Peru to arrive at my house in Breña and sign up for a test of their abilities," she announced on Peruvian television. "Ah! But don't believe that because you are Black you have an aptitude for dance! After a careful selection of people, everyone—including the *cajonero*—will participate in exercises, because elasticity of movement is fundamental, as are the abilities to improvise and to express oneself. And all this can only succeed with great discipline" (qtd. in Suárez Radillo 1976, 285).

Forty-five hopefuls answered Victoria's call. The presence of eager, multishaded Blacks gave Victoria hope that the Peruvian process of mestizaje had lessened its racist emphasis on "whitening" since her grandparents' time. She stated, "The proof is that when I made this call to all the Blacks in Peru to form a Black theater, Blacks, mulatos, and light-skinned zambos answered, and they are part of my company. This would not have happened earlier, because a zambo did not consider himself Black, and a mulato even less so. Ah! This proves that the Black person is finally comprehending that we are all Blacks, and it is not a question of 'fading' a little . . . because if the discrimination of White against Black . . . is sad, the discrimination of Black against Black is much sadder" (qtd. in Suárez Radillo 1976, 288).

A PEDIDO DE
NUMEROSO PUBLICO

"TEATRO Y DANZAS
NEGRAS DEL PERU"
de
VICTORIA SANTA CRUZ
en el
TEATRO MUNICIPAL
2 Ultimos Días:
SABADO 21   Vermouth 7.30 p.m.
              Noche   10.00 p.m.
DOMINGO 22   Vermouth 7.30 p.m.

FIGURE 2.7. Newspaper ad for Teatro y Danzas Negras del Perú, *El Correo,* 1967. *Reprinted with permission from the collection of the Biblioteca Nacional del Perú.*

For Victoria, Teatro y Danzas Negras del Perú was a triumph. Using her now more fully developed rhythm technique, Victoria guided the members of her new company through the process of self-expression via ancestral memory. She taught them that, to dance, first they must know themselves, because dance is not simply a series of choreographed movements and gestures but rather an expression of inner knowledge. Facing the self within, the members of Teatro y Danzas Negras del Perú learned to confront and accept their own blackness without the shame they had been socially conditioned to feel. This self-awareness and pride was a first step toward confronting Peruvian racism through theater and dance. Once the company members had embraced a positive sense of self, they could project a negritud (or positive sense of Black identity and ancestral values) in performance that would combat negative racial stereotypes.

Because few previous theatrical opportunities existed for Blacks, the members of Teatro y Danzas Negras del Perú had no training as dancers or actors. By trade, the company members were chauffeurs, textile workers, carpenters, and bricklayers (Suárez Radillo 1976, 294). Early rehearsals were lessons in both performance skills and Black cultural heritage. Collaborating theater artists trained the company in the performance of physical exercises and improvisation for actors. At one point, Victoria installed a ballet bar and invited a classical dance teacher (she later abandoned this practice when it did not achieve the desired results). Victoria delivered lectures on culture, theater, racism, and the Black experience of Peruvian mestizaje. Improvisations, dances, and re-creations of Black folklore drew from the company members' internalization of all these elements.

When Victoria felt that her protégés were moving mechanically, disconnected from the process that *results* in dance, she would stop the rehearsal. Turning out the lights, she lit a candle and asked everyone to listen to the cajón and dance what they felt. There, in the darkness, her dancers were encouraged to reconnect with their ancestral heritage and find a corporeal way to express it, enacting Victoria's method (V. Santa Cruz 1991). Photos of Victoria's company taking a break from rehearsal to play a danced game (figure 2.8) present some idea of the costuming (bare chests for men, striped pants, head turbans for women), dramatic body language, close-to-the-ground postures, and choreographic figures (the circle of onlookers around a dancing couple, an image frequently cited by travelers to nineteenth-century Peru who viewed Black dances) that characterized the company in at least one of its dances.[15]

In 1967, Cuban scholar, director, and novelist Carlos Miguel Suárez Radillo videotaped a rehearsal of Teatro y Danzas Negras del Perú, along with testimonials by the company members.[16] Company member Teresa explained that she had "a lot of complexes" about her race before answering Victoria's public call for dancers. She realized, through her involvement with Teatro y Danzas Negras del Perú, that she had not even considered members of her own race before she married a White man, because she wanted her children to have the social benefits associated with being "whiter." Luis credited Victoria's guidance with empowering him to use the word "Black" with pride, rather than hiding behind euphemisms

FIGURE 2.8. Teatro y Danzas Negras del Perú, late 1960s. Pictured female dancer (center): Teresa Palomino. *Reprinted with permission from* Caretas.

like "*moreno*" or "person of color" ("People of color?" chided Victoria. "*What* color? Call things what they are!") (Suárez Radillo 1976, 289–291).

Not all of Victoria's young company members were equally enchanted with her. Opinionated, strong-minded, and forceful, Victoria cultivated more than her share of enemies during her reign as the proprietor of Afro-Peruvian folklore. "The enemy is in your house," Victoria often says, noting that some of her company members called her a "fascist" and said that they would rather take orders from a White man than a Black woman (V. Santa Cruz 1991). Women in many cultures are the bearers of cultural memory, yet, especially in Latin America, women (particularly Black women) do not often take on as prominent a public role as Victoria Santa Cruz. Victoria's extraordinary self-confidence and commanding manner of speech defy cultural stereotypes about submissive women whose work is performed "behind the scenes." Further, some of Victoria Santa Cruz' company members perceived her as part of a "Black aristocracy"; she was born into a family of artists and intellectuals and had traveled and studied in Europe. In the late 1960s, several male members of Teatro y Danzas Negras del Perú left the company and formed performance groups that, in Victoria's opinion, distorted the Black manifestations she had recovered, exoticizing blackness and gratuitously exploiting the erotic aspect of Black Peruvian dance.

From the late 1960s to the early 1970s, Teatro y Danzas Negras del Perú performed in Lima's mainstage theaters and on television, self-described as "a serious group that cultivates coastal theater, music, and dances with African roots . . . recovering and re-creating . . . the original purity of these manifestations and traditions" (N.a. 1982). The company also toured internationally, performing at the 1968 Olympics in Mexico (where Victoria served as director of the cultural delegation for Peru), at the Pan American Games in Colombia, and in Venezuela. In 1972, Teatro y Danzas Negras del Perú revived Victoria's *La muñeca negra* and performed the new comedy *Un marido paciente* (A patient husband) (N.a. 1982).

Victoria Santa Cruz' most enduring accomplishment during the Afro-Peruvian revival was her re-creation of forgotten dances, especially the landó. Victoria writes: "One of my most important choreographic works was the creation of the 'disappeared' landó dance, which had disappeared as a form, but was alive in my ancestral memory" (V. Santa Cruz 1995). Through her choreographic re-creation of the landó, Victoria believes that she recovered a musical memory of her ancestral homeland that is more "African" than contemporary Africa. Victoria has been to Africa, and she perceives Africans who lived under colonialism as more European than African (V. Santa Cruz 2000). Thus, Victoria's Afrocentric re-creation of the landó creates an "island of time" (Assman 1995) by skipping over the Middle Passage entirely to recover a direct link with the Africa that pre-ceded slavery and colonialism.

Victoria first became acquainted with the Peruvian landó when she was a child. She recalls, "The first time I heard this beautiful and simple melody was from the lips of my mother's sister when I was barely six years old; this was one of the clues that moved in me unforgettable memories related to ancient ancestral connections" (V. Santa Cruz 1995). In this melody's rhythm, years later, she found the blueprint for its choreography. Victoria writes, "just as I discovered that all melodic lines implicitly carry their own harmony, I also rediscovered that the rhythmic combinations in a rhythmic phrase or unit also generate their respective movement and gesture, provided that we find a level of psychic connection" (V. Santa Cruz 1995).

Although Victoria Santa Cruz is unanimously credited with having rescued the landó's choreography from obscurity, Afro-Peruvian musicians and scholars disagree about whether or not the choreography performed as landó since the revival (see chapter 4) is the one she re-created. When I asked Victoria, herself, her answer was elusive. She responded that "choreography" is simply a word that describes movements and figures that are the result of a process. That process is what is important and should be remembered (V. Santa Cruz 2000). Thus, writing about Victoria Santa Cruz' re-creation of the landó presents the same challenge as describing José Durand's reproduction of el son de los diablos for the Pancho Fierro company. In both cases, no recorded or visual documentation is readily available, yet the re-created choreographies (and the processes that inspired them) live on as new "originals" in popular memory and contemporary performance.

In 1968, Victoria publicly presented her reconstruction of the zamacueca, a Peruvian couple dance dating to the nineteenth century. Documentation suggests that the zamacueca was historically performed by all races and classes, but it was believed by Peruvian scholar Fernando Romero and Afro-Peruvian revival artists to have originated as a Black social dance (F. Romero 1939a; Tompkins 1981, 62). Like many American dances that made their way from the popular classes to the elite, it was at first considered scandalous and overly suggestive; in 1829, shortly after its arrival in Chile, Bishop Manuel Vicuña prohibited its performance and called it a "thing of sin" (qtd. in Tompkins 1981, 68). In Peru, the zamacueca was stylized in the exclusive salons of the upper classes and danced suggestively at the Pampa de Amancaes. A pair of nineteenth-century watercolors by Pancho Fierro (figure 2.9) suggests the way this dance may have been performed (and racialized) in each context.

As Pancho Fierro's paintings clearly show, the zamacueca was a "handkerchief dance." In the nineteenth century, a couple typically performed the courtship dance to the musical setting of three verses of sung romantic poetry accompanied by cajón, guitar, harp, and/or *vihuela*. Onlookers shouted guapeos (encouraging phrases typical of Peruvian coastal music and dance). During the first verse, the couple circled each other, advancing and receding "like birds in a mating ceremony" (Tompkins 1981, 64),

FIGURE 2.9. Two nineteenth-century paintings of the Peruvian *zamacueca* by Pancho Fierro. Left: "Decent *zamacueca*." Right: "Licentious *zamacueca*." *Reprinted from Angelica Palma's* Pancho Fierro: Acuarelista limeño *(1935, 22–23)*.

waving their handkerchiefs in the air. The courtship became steamier in the second verse; the man redoubled his efforts to win over the feminine object of his desire, but the woman resisted and the man grew impatient. In the third and final verse, the man displayed all his dancing prowess, performing fancy zapateo steps while the dancing couple's circles became smaller and smaller and their handkerchiefs waved madly in the air. Finally, overcome by seduction, the woman either fell into the man's arms or threw her handkerchief on the floor as a flag of surrender (F. Romero 1939a; 1940; Tompkins 1981; Vega 1953).

In contrast to her re-creation of the landó, a dance that had completely disappeared from contemporary performance, Victoria's staging of the zamacueca altered the way an existing dance was performed. Folklore companies in the 1960s, taking their cue from Pancho Fierro's watercolors, used a woman's costume that ballooned at the skirt. Victoria affirmed that this costume was absurd; what Fierro had painted was in reality a fashion of the day, whereby a handkerchief was tied around the hips. Aided, again, by what she calls an "ancestral memory," Victoria restored the zamacueca's "correct" costuming (N.a. 1982). The handkerchief costume, in turn, led Victoria Santa Cruz to discover a more "authentic" choreography (before Victoria Santa Cruz' innovations in the 1960s, most companies danced the zamacueca using steps that were a variation of another Black Peruvian folkloric dance, the festejo).

In the aftermath of the revival, the zamacueca typically is performed in a manner that may have been inspired by Victoria's placement of the handkerchief. The modern choreography emphasizes the woman's prowess—and also the sensuality of her body movements—before she surrenders. Each dancer waves two handkerchiefs (a characteristic of the nineteenth-century *moza mala* dance painted by Pancho Fierro, which was more closely associated with Blacks and eroticism than was the zamacueca [Tompkins 1981, 74]), and the handkerchief literally becomes the net of seduction. During the finale, it is the woman who performs bodily pyrotechnics, while the man frantically attempts to harness her by tying his handkerchief around her hips. Once the man has captured his prey, she belongs to him. He ties the remaining handkerchief around his own hips, and the couple dance off together. According to William Tompkins, Afro-Peruvian musician and *jaranero* Augusto Ascuez criticized this "Africanization" of the zamacueca, claiming that the original choreography was identical to that of the marinera (Tompkins 1981, 110–111).

In 1968, a Peruvian coup launched a military revolution led by General Juan Velasco Alvarado. The government enacted drastic social and economic reforms, nationalizing industries and rejecting foreign capitalist control, especially from the United States. Velasco promoted patriotism by supporting the dissemination of national music in order to combat the previous domination of Peruvian radio stations and listening tastes by U.S. rock music and Caribbean música tropical (Lloréns Amico 1983). In addition to quotas mandating the promotion of Peruvian music on television and radio programs, the Velasco government established a National School of Folklore, under the auspices of the National Institute of Culture. In 1969, Victoria Santa Cruz was appointed director of the National School of Folklore, and in 1973, she was named director of the newly established Conjunto Nacional de Folklore (National Folklore Company).

The Conjunto Nacional de Folklore enacted the Velasco government's cultural policy by promoting, at home and abroad, two different groups of musicians and dancers under Victoria Santa Cruz' choreographic direction: indigenous dances of the Andes and African-influenced dances. In *Folklore*, a magazine she edited for the government in the 1970s, Victoria Santa Cruz described the Conjunto's goal, "to compile, preserve, research, and disseminate national folklore in the form of dance, music, songs, and musical instruments," which furthered the agenda of the military revolution. As she explained: "the current process of changes entails the valorization of essential elements of our popular traditional culture, with the high quality and technical level that the folkloric richness of Peru demands. Considering that the dynamic of the revolutionary process and the changing international situation demand different proposals and actions, the Conjunto Nacional de Folklore uses totally new criteria to focus its work" (1978a, 14).

These "new criteria" entailed the eradication of European pedagogical methods in favor of techniques more suited to Peruvian reality. In auditions, preference was given to dancers who had learned folkloric traditions at home. Yet, Victoria believed that folkloric dance had become distorted. To recover Peru's inherited folklore and disseminate it to local and international audiences, the Conjunto Nacional de Folklore used methods such as Victoria's "Discovery and Development of the Sense of Rhythm." In their rhythm education classes, company members studied "rhythmic combinations with African roots," which helped them develop a "psychosomatic aptitude and attitude" that allowed them to approach dance in a new way. Through her work with the Conjunto dancers, Victoria came to revise some of her previous beliefs, acknowledging, "the thesis that folklore cannot be taught has been surmounted" (V. Santa Cruz 1978a, 15).

Under Victoria Santa Cruz' direction, the Conjunto Nacional de Folklore debuted in Lima's Municipal Theater in December 1973. During the next nine years, the company performed indigenous and coastal dances in engagements throughout Peru, Latin America, the United States, Canada, and Europe. When the company performed in Paris in 1974, audiences were surprised; a French critic wrote in *Le Monde* that the Afro-Peruvian dances seemed more representative of Africa than Peru (qtd. in Tompkins 1981, 110). A glowing review of the company's 1975 Hunter College performance by *New York Times* dance reviewer Anna Kisselgoff called the Conjunto "one of the best and most interesting folk dance companies to be seen here in years," praising the company for avoiding the "unattractive slickness" of companies like the Ballet Folklorico de Mexico. Kisselgoff succumbed to the charms of the "exquisite dancing and . . . humor that traces the history of Indian culture in Peru," calling the Andean dances "supremely fascinating" from an ethnic standpoint. Describing the Black dances of Peru, however, she seemed less fascinated, referring to "numbers whose African origins make them appear familiar and close to similar rites, Carnavales, and work dances from other parts of Latin America and the Caribbean that have Black culture. Much of the good-humored ribaldry and vibrancy of the program comes from this section." Kisselgoff went on to note: "Class consciousness is not absent from this program, although it is always presented as reflecting historical truth rather than propaganda" (1975).

The military revolution and its support for local folklore came to an end in 1980, and, by 1982, problems with the Conjunto drove Victoria not only to vacate her position as director but also to leave the country altogether. She was hired, and later granted tenure, at the Theater Department of Carnegie-Mellon University in Pittsburgh, Pennsylvania, where she disseminated her methods in a rhythm class for actors. While Victoria still believed firmly in the essentialism of organic cultures, she now felt that she had discovered universal truths that transcend the experience of Black Peru. In 1995, she wrote: "I have arrived at this stage of my life by way of an ancient culture that, although very African, I now know to be cosmic. From this knowledge arises my interest in sharing and exchanging" (V. Santa Cruz 1995).

During her seventeen years in Pittsburgh, Victoria applied her method to guide students through the process of rediscovering their connection to their own cultures. "I don't teach, I touch," she would say to her English-speaking students. She also continued to stage theatrical productions, codirecting *Peer Gynt* and *Antigone* and collaborating (along with other international professors and directors) with Peter Brook on the epic *Mahabarata*.

In 1999, Victoria Santa Cruz retired and moved back to Lima. Just as her departure from Peru had been a secret (many Peruvians had no idea that she was in the United States), Victoria returned quietly. At this writing, she lives in her family home near the sea, and she is working with physicians, architects, and other interdisciplinary professionals to found an international organization called Health, Equilibrium, and Rhythm. She has published a book on her beliefs, *Rhythm: The Eternal Organizer* (2005). "I have important things to leave on this Earth before I go," she says fervently (2000).

When word spread that Victoria Santa Cruz was back in Peru in early 2000, she was interviewed by newspaper reporters and on television programs. Many hoped and expected that she would mount new Afro-Peruvian theater or dance productions. Victoria Santa Cruz' name is still synonymous in Peru with the Afro-Peruvian revival of the 1960s and 1970s.

But Victoria told me, during my meetings with her in 2000, that that phase of her life was long over.[17] For her, much of the Afro-Peruvian music performed in Peru distorts the ancestral rhythms and folklore she worked so hard to revive. Victoria does not dwell on this problem; she has moved on. She observes, encapsulating the crisis of Afro-Peruvian music, "We are always running behind something, looking for an answer by projecting ourselves into the past. We evoke a false future by not living in the present. This is the great trap" (V. Santa Cruz 1991). After reading an earlier version of this chapter, Victoria Santa Cruz wrote to me, "We are, still, in time to reorganize our Life in *action*, to stop swimming in an ocean of words. 'The last ones will be the first ones,' it was said. Not the first to have the upper hand, of course, the first to sound the call of alarm, saying: If we do not unite, if we do not struggle elbow to elbow; something can befall the *Human Family*. Of course, before uniting oneself with others, it is necessary to unite with *oneself* . . ."[18]

Travel Diaries, Lima, 2000:
Meeting Victoria Santa Cruz[19]

"Nothing happens by chance," Victoria tells me, welcoming me to her home in Lima. I had planned to travel to Pittsburgh to meet Victoria Santa Cruz, hoping to sit in on her rhythm class and ask her for an interview. But in December 1999, I learned that Victoria had just retired after seventeen years of teaching. I call her in Lima, nervously explaining who I am and why I want to meet her. She is ever so gracious, complimenting me on my Spanish. She tells me she is extremely busy. Can I come over this afternoon?

Victoria stands in the doorway of her family's lovely home, smiling broadly. Dressed in jeans and an oversized shirt, she stands like a dancer. When she tells me later that she is seventy-seven years old, I can't believe it. She sits in a chair with the grace of a cat stretching after a nap, and she imitates people with gestures and postures that perfectly capture the essence of what she conveys.

We sit down together and she repeats, "Nothing happens by chance." I tell her my grandmother used to say that. She smiles. Why am I here, what could possibly have brought me, a North American student, to make a connection with her? It takes me about an hour to answer her question. I am interrupted many times. I am learning a great deal about Victoria Santa Cruz. What we talk about, for almost three hours, is me.

Going to see Victoria is a little like visiting a sage or a spiritual guide. She speaks in proverbs and poems, her sentences are like melodies sung in a deep alto voice with remarkable range, she dances as she moves, and she turns every question back upon its asker, interrupting thoughts before they are fully formulated.[20] *She gracefully, yet brusquely, flips a mirror, and I see myself reflected with all my inadequacies and imperfections. I have had this feeling before during my fieldwork in Peru, but never so intensely. My "informants" frequently turn the tables on me by asking me questions for which I should have much better answers. I am reminded of the moment in the folklore shows of Lima's nocturnal* peñas *(nightclubs) when the tourist is inevitably called to dance onstage, challenged to perform exaggerated and difficult moves that show off his or her foreign-ness and unpreparedness. I have danced this dance before, but Victoria is my slipperiest, most graceful partner. She insists on leading, and I fumble through efforts to follow. She often asks me, after she tells a story or recites a truism, "Are you following me?"*

I will see her three times while I am in Lima, spending three or more intense hours with her each time. She will not let me record our conversations. A recording is a dead thing, lacking the timbre of the voice, the living energy of our human exchange. After we are no longer in each other's presence, this conversation will cease to exist. Why preserve it? I do not interview Victoria Santa Cruz. Instead, we talk. She asks me questions about my culture and my project, and I ask her questions about herself. I suspect that she is using her method on me.

She quickly determines that I am ignorant of my own culture. When she asks me to describe it, she says, I just give her words, telling her things I've been taught, not real answers. If I don't know who I am, how can I possibly hope to understand Afro-Peruvian music? As for ethnomusicology, it is absurd. How can we teach the cultures of the world when we don't know our own? And what is "ethno" anyway? The intellect imprisons us, it is only through the body that we can be free, and only from the school of life that we can truly learn. Yet, she senses what she calls "a strong thread" in me, but it is a thread "surrounded by dust." I must come to know myself, to love myself, to respect myself, and to look for the Truth. I must come back next week with very specific, concise questions.

After our first meeting, I walk by the sea, thinking about the astonishing woman I have just met. She is relentless, because she believes in Truth. I think her greatest talent is her ability to instantly pinpoint the essence of a person or a situation, and I wonder if that was what made her such an effective dancer and choreographer. Yet, that very talent can lead to a reductionism that sometimes troubles me, especially when it is directed at the description of a racial or religious group—or at me.

When I arrive the following week, Victoria immediately asks me to describe the central focus of my research and to articulate my specific questions. I tell her that I want to help people in my country understand the Peruvian context for Afro-Peruvian music.

She laughs and interrupts me. For what? In your country this music would be performed as part of a "folklore extravaganza." And what you will find here in Peru is not Afro-Peruvian music but a cheap copy—performers selling their blackness to become famous, to make money.

But that is what I want to explain, I start to tell her. I want to reveal the larger context. I want to understand what happened in the 1950s and 1960s so I can figure out what is happening today.

But you can't possibly understand what happened then! That would be impossible. In a word, she throws cold water on my entire project.

We talk for a long time. Victoria's answers to my questions about specific songs or choreographies always end in long explanations of the cosmic truths she has discovered about organic cultures. We talk about Cumanana and the plays,

Nicomedes, Afro-Cuban music and religion, José Durand, Pancho Fierro, Pittsburgh, dance, the solar plexus, and the secrets of the cosmos.

She tells me frequently that I must be honest with myself when I write my book. Don't write anything unless you honestly know it is true. And remember at all times that you are writing it for yourself. This is part of your own journey to understand yourself. Sometimes we travel so far to find what is so close to us—inside ourselves.

We will come together one more time, Victoria tells me, and this will be the final meeting.

The last time I saw Victoria, she had just returned from a week in Pittsburgh, and I was getting ready to leave Peru. She had arrived at dawn and barely slept. She told me she had been thinking about me on the way back to Peru. As usual, Victoria got right down to business. What did you expect to find before you began your research, what did you actually find, and what do you intend to do with it?

You were right about something, I tell her. I imitate her speaking style and melodious inflections: "But my love, you can never understand what happened in the 1950s and 1960s. That would be impossible!" She laughs. I tell her I know that I can't go back in time and understand that era as if I had lived it. But that history endures today in contradictory memories and staged performances. I am struck by the way other Peruvian researchers, and even musicians, have assumed, upon meeting me, that I am here to research the centuries-old origins of Black music in Peru, dismissing its contemporary manifestations as unimportant and invalid. I realize that what I must describe in my book is the present, even when I am writing about the past.

But of course! This is self-evident to Victoria. How can we hope to understand anything if we don't understand the present? All understanding starts with yourself. And it's not who you are, it's what you're doing.

I go on. I tell Victoria that I want to write about the way Black Peruvian music has been reconstructed by artists who have conducted a type of research similar to the work of anthropologists or ethnomusicologists. She doesn't connect with this idea. We get stuck in definitions. But you are talking about artists when there is no such thing as art, only artesanía! Research is scientific, cold, disconnected, nothing like the process of connecting with the past. Anthropologists are Western outsiders who go to a foreign country and presume to describe what they see. Impossible!

We go around in circles. We move on, talking about Victoria's meeting with Katherine Dunham in the United States. We discuss what Victoria perceives as distortions of African religions in Haiti and Cuba, and we talk about Bach and the early music authenticity movement. Ridiculous, she says, to try to perform Bach as if we were in his time. Impossible! She seems unaware of the irony of her *statement. She tells me about her book and the organization she is founding to promote health through the development of the sense of rhythm.*

Toward the end of our meeting, the exchange necessitated by my research clearly comes to a close. Victoria brings out a plate of chips and two glasses of Sprite, and the rhythm of our encounter changes. It slows down and becomes less intense. We talk about personal things. We linger.

As she shows me to the door for the last time, Victoria hugs me and tells me how much she has enjoyed our exchange, and that we will keep in touch (we do). She has already told me not to thank her, because we are sharing, this is a two-way street. I hug her warmly and promise to remember to be true to myself when I write my book. Just in time, I remember not to say thank you.

CHAPTER 3

The Peruvian Negritud of Nicomedes Santa Cruz

Nicomedes Santa Cruz is a big man, very black, with a big mustache that totally covers his upper lip and a marvelous, huge voice. Seeing him, one thinks of Nicolás Guillén, Yambombo, Babalú, Drume Negrita, of "Todo' lo' negro' tomamo' café," of mamá Inés, of "Vito Manué, tú no sabe ingle"; seeing him with his white shirt, and his big teeth, strong like a prehistoric animal, one thinks that Nicomedes was conceived long before original sin, when the world wasn't Africa or Asia or Europe or Latin America, but one perfect and elastic unity . . . And Nicomedes sings, he sings of love, of the flight it enables, of the sky in summer, of the fate of working people, shouting "the song should cost dearly, so much that it has no price," he sings and dances in his hotel room until the telephone rings, until his wife, as small and blonde as he is tall and black, tells him they are waiting for him below . . . —Elena Poniatowska, Mexican journalist and author, 1974

Dear old Nicomedes, don't you remember me? We have come to America together, and suffered and endured on the same slave ship. Now we are also together in rebellion and victory!
—Nicolás Guillén, Cuban poet, to Nicomedes Santa Cruz, 1974

You are the poet of Latin America.
—Léopold Senghor, President of Senegal, to Nicomedes Santa Cruz, 1974

Nicomedes Santa Cruz: Archaeologist of Black Peru

Nicomedes Santa Cruz (1925–1992) is remembered as the literary voice of Peruvian negritud and the father of the Afro-Peruvian music revival.[1] Nicomedes employed both research and performance methods to argue that the monuments of Peruvian criollo culture were built not only from European but also from African musical materials. As a record producer, director, composer, music arranger and performing poet, he reconstructed the forgotten performance traditions of Black Peru. As a folklorist and "cultural archaeologist" (see Feldman forthcoming), he excavated the African origins of Peruvian música criolla, and he researched the musical traditions of Blacks in other countries.

FIGURE 3.1. Nicomedes Santa Cruz and his wife, Mercedes Castillo. *Reprinted with permission from* Caretas.

Nicomedes Santa Cruz shared with the international negritud(e) movement a propensity to strategically essentialize peoples of African descent, identifying and celebrating their common traits and experiences. This pan-African perspective made it logical for him to appropriate the known histories and traditions of Blacks in other parts of the world in order to reproduce the forgotten Black Peruvian past (a typical Black Pacific strategy). Under Nicomedes Santa Cruz' leadership, Afro-Peruvians began to forge new diasporic links with the Black Atlantic, especially Brazil and Cuba, as a source of knowledge about their own "African" past and a surrogate for Africa.

In this chapter, I strive to present an honest evaluation of Nicomedes Santa Cruz' leadership in the Afro-Peruvian revival, including both problems and unprecedented achievements. Situating Nicomedes' legacy in a narration of his life events, I examine his strategies to promote Peruvian negritud in the Black Pacific through poetry and song and the way his legacy mobilized new performances of Peruvian blackness.

Negritud(e) *in Comparative Perspective*

Contextualizing Nicomedes Santa Cruz' Peruvian negritud calls for a brief overview of the international negritude movement.[2] Negritude was a literary movement of Black poets and intellectuals from French colonies in Africa and the Americas in the 1940s and 1950s. Its founders (Leopold Senghor, Aimé Césaire, and León Damas) were influenced by the leaders of the U.S. Harlem Renaissance who created new cultural forms based on African and African American folk art in order to "elevate the race" (E. Jones 1971, 13–15; Floyd 1995, 106). Similarly, negritude sought to rehabilitate blackness from European colonialist denigration by affirming the shared positive qualities of all Black cultures and minimizing ethnic differences among Africans and their descendants in the New World. This "strategic essentialism" (Spivak 1988) later was criticized by Black intellectuals for reinscribing the same racist stereotypes imposed by colonialism (see Fanon 1966). However, at the dawning of the postcolonial era, negritude's racializing strategies were an important form of resistance against racism and European domination.

It seemed to many outsiders that Blacks in Spanish Latin America—especially in the Black Pacific—were unaffected by the spirit of negritude that flourished elsewhere. In the 1940s, according to Afro-Hispanic literature scholar Richard Jackson, the image of the Black Latin American that circulated among many U.S. African Americans was that of a man "too seduced by song and dance to concern himself with civil rights, justice and freedom . . . more interested in musical rhythms and in imitating the white man than in establishing bonds of solidarity with his Black brothers around the world" (1976, 91). For example, U.S. African American journalist George Schuyler wrote in 1948, "Peruvians of negroid ancestry were about where the free Negroes were in our northern states in 1776, and as a group they were not going forward" (qtd. in Rout 1976, 226).

However, it is risky to make unstudied comparisons between the experiences of Blacks in different national and cultural contexts. The idea of race in Latin America differs from its counterpart in the United States, and Black consciousness manifested itself differently in Peru than in it did in the Harlem Renaissance as a result. As Richard Jackson notes, "Nowhere is Fanon's assertion, in effect, that 'there is no black culture and the black people are fast disappearing' more true than in Latin America . . . Nowhere is the negritude of synthesis as the opposite of racialism more significantly close to the concept supported by Senghor, the poet and the theorist of synthesis, than in Latin America . . . Despite this core conception of negritude, black consciousness and the clash of cultures originally posited by negritude, though softened by *mestizaje* in Latin America, are vividly evident in much of the literature by Afro–Latin American writers who reject and condemn white racism and its products, while simultaneously reaffirming the black past and asserting the black present" (1976, 92–93).

In fact, an *Afrocriollo* literary movement swept Latin America beginning in the 1920s. This sensibility first manifested itself in the *negrismo* of White writers who depicted Blacks and their "picturesque" traditions. In Peru, the dramas of Felipe Pardo (1806–1868), whose stereotyped Black characters spoke a parodied Black Spanish, were an early predecessor to negrismo. Peruvian negrismo coincided with the indigenismo movement (in which urban mestizos celebrated Peru's indigenous/Inca heritage), and its major texts were *Estampas mulatas* by José Diez Canseco (1938) and *Matalaché* by Enrique López Albújar ([1928] 1991), the first Peruvian literary works with Black protagonists.[3]

Latin American negrismo opened the door for Black negritud authors who sought to destroy racial stereotypes. Haitian poet René Dépestre described the difference between negrismo and negritud as that which exists "between an ordinary wick and the wick of a stick of dynamite" (qtd in Jackson 1984, 7). Nicomedes Santa Cruz was the sole voice of Peruvian negritud from the late 1950s until approximately the 1970s, and he is the only Peruvian representative in several anthologies and critical studies of Afro-Hispanic literature and Latin American negritud (Jackson 1976 and 1979; Lewis 1983; Nuñez n.d.).

As the following discussion of Nicomedes Santa Cruz' musical, folkloric, and poetic endeavors reveals, his negritud shared much with the international negritude movement. However, Peruvian negritud must be understood within the Peruvian/Black Pacific context of mestizaje, criollismo, and Black social invisibility. Most of all, Peruvian negritud (along with its impact on the Afro-Peruvian revival) bears the personal stamp of its founding champion, Nicomedes Santa Cruz.

Politicizing the Peruvian Décima

Rafael Nicomedes Santa Cruz Gamarra was born in Lima in 1925. When Nicomedes was a boy, the Santa Cruz family lived in a neighborhood where Blacks held social gatherings and jaranas with music, dance, food, and storytelling. Although some describe the Santa Cruz family as a kind of "Black aristocracy," they were neither wealthy nor strangers to blue-collar work (Nicomedes' father was a playwright who earned his living as a refrigeration technician). Nicomedes described his childhood as filled with the creativity that poverty demands; he remembered playing in ruins and listening to the ghost stories and tales of slavery that his aunts and grandmother told at Sunday reunions ("Nicomedes Santa Cruz Gamarra" n.d., 2).

With his mother's encouragement, Nicomedes quit school at the age of eleven and apprenticed with a locksmith, ultimately opening his own blacksmith shop in 1953. As a young man, Nicomedes turned his attention to the arts and Black culture after he met Don Porfirio Vásquez, whose Lima home was a mecca for Black poets. There, Nicomedes opened a new chapter in his education, dedicating himself to the art form that would consume him for the rest of his life—the Peruvian décima.

Nicomedes Santa Cruz was above all a poet, and his first calling was his love affair with the décima, the vehicle through which he initially awakened a spirit of Peruvian negritud. The Spanish décima's golden age coincided with the conquest of the New World. Although the décima became obsolete in Spain, it spread throughout Latin America, where popular poets recited décimas at weddings, dances, parties, and religious events. The most popular décima type in Peru is the *décima de pie forzado* (forced foot décima), which contains four octosyllabic ten-line stanzas (décimas), preceded by an octosyllabic quatrain (*glosa*) that dictates the content of each subsequent stanza. The first décima must end with the first line of the glosa, the second décima with the second line of the glosa, and so on.

Until the mid-twentieth century, Peruvian décimas normally were recited in contests held at parties, jaranas, private homes, or taverns. Two competing poets either improvised verses or drew upon their memory of hundreds of existing ones. The criollo qualities of satire, humor, and the Picaresque guaranteed a successful performance. The contest began with exchanged poetic greetings (*saludos*), followed by biographical décimas (*décimas de presentación*) and then by décimas performed by each poet in alternation, accompanied by a guitar melody called *socabón* (Tompkins 1981, 162). Each competitor performed an entire forty-four-line décima, and the guitar player added melodic interludes during pauses between each couplet (while the poet ostensibly was composing his or her next rhyme) (N. Santa Cruz 1975, 24). The first decimista (composer/performer of décimas) set the theme for the contest, and the rival decimista responded with a new forty-four-line décima expressing the same theme.

The themes normally employed by decimistas fell into the overall categories of the sacred and the secular: "*a lo divino*" or "*a lo humano*." Decimistas chronicled Peru's most important historical struggles: the Spanish Conquest, the rebellion of Túpac Amaru, independence, and the War of the Pacific. As José Durand wrote, "the memory of a country, written in humble verses by those who work in peace and give their blood in war, cannot be lost" (1979a, 79). Yet, because décimas were primarily an oral tradition in nineteenth- and twentieth-century Peru, many have, in fact, been lost. Some of Peru's greatest decimistas were illiterate, and those who could write jealously guarded their cuadernos (notebooks of poetry) and sometimes even were buried with them (Handy 1979, 84).

Beginning in the mid-1800s, the Peruvian décima apparently was abandoned in literary, "cultured" circles, and some members of the middle and upper classes assumed that it was extinct (N. Santa Cruz 1982, 69; Tompkins 1981, 160–161). The décima survived, however, in lower- and working-class neighborhoods. As a child in the late nineteenth century, Nicomedes Santa Cruz' mother lived across the street from a tavern that was a meeting place and competition ground for decimistas, and years later her children would hear her performing décimas while washing clothes (N. Santa Cruz 1982, 82). A childhood friend of Nicomedes' named Pílade also recited décimas. However, Pilade died when Nicomedes was only five years old, and Nicomedes' mother stopped singing after she suffered a heart condition ("Nicomedes Santa Cruz Gamarra" n.d., 1–2). Thus Nicomedes' relationship with the décima was interrupted when he was a child, only to be renewed through his later mentorship with Don Porfirio Vásquez.

Don Porfirio Vásquez and his brother Carlos grew up frequenting the famous *casa de jarana* (jarana house) in their native Aucallama (on Peru's northern coast) in the early 1900s, where they became students of the legendary decimista Hijinio Matías Quintana ("The Fountain of Knowledge") (1881–1944) and Don Hijinio's brother Manuel Quintana ("The Black Canary"). Don Hijinio was originally from Pisco (south of Lima) and made his living by moving from hacienda to hacienda, reciting décimas to promote cockfights (Handy 1979, 86). At some point, Don Hijinio traveled to Chile in search of new poetic rivals. Upon his return to Peru, he spread the rumor that he had competed against and vanquished the ultimate rival—the Devil himself. Thereafter, Don Hijinio was popularly cast in the role of Mephistopheles (the trickster devil) due to his alleged satanic qualities: he was tall and thin, a legendary womanizer, and it was rumored that he practiced "Black magic" (N. Santa Cruz 1982, 103).[4]

Hijinio Quintana's greatest rival in Peru was Don Mariano González (18??–1934). González' rural home was the site of famous contests between the two poets. Quintana and González have been called the last decimistas; their deaths coincided with the great rural migrations to Lima and the resulting transformation of popular cultural practices. Yet, two disciples survived the passing of these prolific poets and continued the tradition in Lima: Carlos and Porfirio Vásquez. Tragically, Carlos Vásquez (considered the true inheritor of Don Hijinio's gift) died unexpectedly in 1954, leaving not a single pupil of his own (N. Santa Cruz 1982, 81–83, 98, 107).

Nicomedes Santa Cruz met Porfirio Vásquez in 1945. He became what he described as a "coffeehouse docent" (qtd. in Mariñez 1993, 112) to Don Porfirio, studying the rules of décima composition and learning about the rural Black communities that had preserved the competitive art. During this time, Nicomedes' parents forbade him to marry a girl with whom he was in love, and his feelings spilled out on paper, sometimes even on the backside of the diagrams he used at his metalwork job (Mariñez 1993, 112; "Nicomedes Santa Cruz Gamarra" n.d.). Years later, Nicomedes reminisced: "it was an exercise that would come to be the equivalent of going to a coffee shop and intoxicating oneself with rum so as to forget about love" (qtd. in Mariñez 1993, 112–113). He apprenticed with Don Porfirio until 1955, and thus he considered himself descended from the line of decimistas that began in Aucallama and almost ended with Carlos Vásquez' death.

Yet, after several years of talking only "in décimas or about décimas" with Don Porfirio (N. Santa Cruz 1982, 110), Nicomedes realized that his only potential rivals were a few old men in their eighties who lived in small towns. A growing desire to protest racial discrimination was moving Nicomedes' poetic expression in new directions. While he respected Don Porifirio and the elderly rural Black decimistas, he said, "they were contained in a thematic that was totally rural, in lo humano and lo divino, and I saw a series of different events" (qtd. in Mariñez 1993, 113).

In 1955, Nicomedes began to write "solo" décimas that addressed contemporary national and international issues. The next year, he wrote a letter to his mother announcing his career change, against his parents' wishes, from metal craftsman to poet (Handy 1979, 97, 99).[5] He closed his metal shop and traveled throughout Latin America reciting décimas and searching for his destiny ("Nicomedes Santa Cruz Gamarra" n.d., 1–2). He roamed from town to town in northern Peru and Ecuador, performing décimas for birthday celebrations, weddings, and tavern gatherings. When he returned to Lima that year, Nicomedes began reciting his décimas on the radio, and shortly thereafter (in 1958) on national television. In 1957, he joined José Durand's Pancho Fierro company as a decimista.

The first décima Nicomedes ever performed for a live audience in a theater was "Ritmos negros del Perú" (Black rhythms of Peru), which he composed for the Pancho Fierro company's 1957 Chile tour at José Durand's request. "Ritmos negros del Perú" would become a Peruvian anthem of negritud. In fact, it was after this composition that Nicomedes began to describe himself as a negritud poet: "From this point on," he said in an interview, "everything I compose has a vision that is totally folkloric, but also of negritud" (qtd in. Mariñez 1993, 114).

In the opening lines of "Ritmos negros del Perú," Nicomedes paid tribute to his African ancestors. At a time when the history and legacy of African slavery were rarely acknowledged in Peru, he told the story of the Atlantic voyage and hardships of the narrator's enslaved African grandmother:[6]

De Africa llegó mi agüela	My grandmother came from Africa
vestida con caracoles,	adorned in shells,
la trajeron lo'epañoles	Spaniards brought her
en un barco carabela.	in a caravel ship.
La marcaron con candela,	They marked her with fire,
la carimba fue su cruz.	the branding iron was her cross.
Y en América del Sur	And in South America
al golpe de sus dolores	to the beat of their pain
dieron los negros tambores	black drums sounded
ritmos de la esclavitud.	*rhythms of slavery.*

He then reclaimed forgotten Black music heritage by naming the "rhythms of slavery"—the song and dance genres invented and performed by enslaved Africans in Peru:

En la plantación de caña	On the sugar plantation
nació el triste socabón,	was born the sorrowful socabón,
en el trapiche de ron	at the rum press
el negro cantó la saña . . .	the Black man sang the *zaña* . . .
. . .	. . .
Murieron los negros viejos	The old Blacks died
pero entre la caña seca	but in the cane fields
se escucha su zamacueca	one hears the sound of their zamacueca
y el panalivio, muy lejos.	and the panalivio, far in the distance.
Y se escuchan los festejos	And one hears the festejos
que cantó en su juventud.	my mother sang in her youth.
De Cañete a Tombuctú,	From Cañete to Timbuktu,
de Chancay a Mozambique	from Chancay to Mozambique
llevan sus claros repiques	their clear drumrolls carry
ritmos negros del Perú.	*black rhythms of Peru.*

Whereas recited décimas traditionally were accompanied by socabón melodies on guitar, in 1964 Nicomedes recorded "Ritmos negros del Perú" to the accompaniment of one of the "rhythms of slavery," the Afro-Peruvian panalivio (N. Santa Cruz y su Conjunto Cumanana [1964] 1970). Later, on an LP recorded with Cuban drummer El Niño, Nicomedes placed the décima in a re-Africanized musical context, reciting "Ritmos negros del Perú" and other poems to the accompaniment of Afro-Cuban drum rhythms of *Santería* and *Abakwá* (N. Santa Cruz y su Conjunto Cumanana [1968] 2000).[7] This use of Afro-Cuban rhythms to accompany a poem about Afro-Peruvian rhythms projects the kind of pan-Africanism characteristic of Nicomedes' personal vision of negritud.

Nicomedes took other liberties with the musical accompaniment of the décima to bring it out of retirement and back to popularity, including the adoption of a more "Spanish" guitar accompaniment pattern. When he brought the décima to the stage, radio, and television in the late 1950s and early 1960s, Nicomedes lamented the existence of only one "listless" socabón melody to accompany décimas (figure 3.2) (N. Santa Cruz 1975, 24).[8] Perhaps the ubiquitous C major tonic chord, repetitive parallel third harmonies, tonic-dominant alternation, and predictable bass motion lacked the sense of drama Nicomedes sought to evoke with his recited décimas. Whatever the source of his dissatisfaction, in 1948, working with guitarist Vicente Vásquez, Nicomedes revived a slowed-down version of the guitar melody of an obsolete Afro-Peruvian genre called *agua'e nieve* as an alternate accompaniment for the décima. The agua'e nieve was a guitar pattern historically used to accompany Peruvian zapateo contests and possibly related to the seventeenth-century Spanish dance called "*agua de nieve*" (Tompkins 1981, 277). Of the agua'e nieve melody, Nicomedes wrote: "its incredible registers bring us close to reminiscences of the Andalusian rhythms that Spanish orators used as the basis of their *romances*" (N. Santa Cruz 1975, 24). Indeed, the new melody (figure 3.3) promoted characteristics stereotypically associated with Spanishness: triple meter with hemiola, flirtations with ambiguous open voicing and major-minor modulations, and flamenco-type tetrachord descent.

In 1959, Nicomedes published the first printed book of Peruvian décimas (N. Santa Cruz [1959] n.d.), and he went on to publish several other collections of his work (N. Santa Cruz 1962; 1964a; 1966; 1971a; 1971c). He also wrote and published *La décima en el Perú* (The décima in Peru) (1982), an in-depth history and analysis of the poetic form with more than 300 pages of collected décimas dating from the colonial period to the contemporary era, including many transcribed from oral performances or the unpublished cuadernos of legendary poets.

Thus, Nicomedes "went public" with the jealously guarded secrets of the décima, previously passed down from master to student and hidden away in cuadernos. After perfecting his technique and developing a repertoire, Nicomedes brought the décima out of oblivion and into the public consciousness. Using a highly complex Spanish poetic form, he broke the barrier of Black Peruvian invisibility. By the 1960s, with books published in three countries and records sold internationally, Nicomedes was an internationally acclaimed literary figure. With the world listening,

Guitar

FIGURE 3.2. Traditional *socabón* guitar accompaniment for décimas. *Excerpted and reproduced from a 1959 handwritten score signed by Nicomedes Santa Cruz in* Décimas y poemas: Antología *(N. Santa Cruz 1971a, 97).*

Guitar

FIGURE 3.3. Excerpt from Vicente Vásquez' *agua 'e nieve* guitar accompaniment for décimas. *Excerpted, adapted, and reproduced from "The Musical Traditions of the Blacks of Coastal Peru" (Tompkins 1981, 545).*

Nicomedes' décimas projected a Peruvian negritud that Peru's official history had ignored all too long.

Reviving the Festejo: "No me cumbén"

In 1958, Nicomedes founded the theater company Cumanana, which he used as a vehicle to bring his recited décimas—now infused with a "rebellious and proud negritud" (N. Santa Cruz 1982, 110)—to the mainstream public. In addition to providing a public forum for his décimas, Cumanana was a showcase of Nicomedes' and Victoria's research on Black music and dances. One of the most important and enduring genres staged in Cumanana's productions was the festejo.

Whereas Nicomedes Santa Cruz maintained that the festejo was first performed by Black slaves of Congolese origin in seventeenth-century Lima (1970a, 61) and Afro-Peruvian folklorist Lalo Izquierdo calls it the "oldest dance among the manifestations of negritud" in Peru (1999, 1), U.S. ethnomusicologist William Tompkins' research produced no evidence of musical works called festejo that existed before the nineteenth century and no mention of the genre in the pre-twentieth-century literature. Tompkins acknowledges, however, that the festejo may have existed musically under another name (1981, 240–241).

Unlike the landó, which had nearly disappeared from performance practice, nineteenth-century festejos were still remembered and performed in mid-twentieth-century family reunions and theatrical performances.[9] After the Pancho Fierro company and Juan Criado popularized Black Peruvian songs in the 1950s, many new festejos were introduced and recorded, enabled by the emergence of large recording companies that concentrated a significant portion of their catalogues on "folklore" recordings (see R. Romero 2001, 112). Most of these festejos were new arrangements of old song texts and melody fragments collected from older Black musicians in rural areas. Difficult copyright issues were raised by the "collect, arrange, and publish" approach in the 1960s and 1970s (see Tompkins 1981, 118–119, 246); unfortunately, some musicians of the era allegedly published in their own names songs they actually had collected from older residents of rural areas. Claims of authorship were complicated by the fact that many festejos share standard features and sound alike, enhanced by the common practice of setting new lyrics to melodies borrowed from other festejos, or *contrafacta* (see Tompkins 1981, 241).

True to the festejo's name (derived from the Spanish verb *festejar*, which means "to celebrate"), although most festejo lyrics depict the hardships of slave life, the music and dancing express an exuberant, joyful quality. This mood is supported by what William Tompkins describes as a "surging" rhythmic accompaniment (1981, 239) and a sense of metric ambiguity. In some festejos, the guitar, quijada, and/or cajón emphasize a feeling of duple meter with triple subdivisions (see figure 3.4), while the vocal line may be in either duple or triple meter (see León Quirós 2003, 164–166; Tompkins 1981, 250–251). The most common time signature used to notate the festejo is $\frac{6}{8}$ (Aliaga and Aliaga 1991; Casaverde 2000b; Tompkins 1981, 250–252), which corresponds to the timing of chord progressions and strumming patterns in the guitar parts, but the festejo also has been represented in $\frac{2}{4}$ (R. Vásquez and Rojas n.d.) and $\frac{12}{8}$ (Acuña 1999). In some cases, multiple time signatures have been used to represent different parts within the same festejo transcription (León Quirós 2003, 164; Tompkins 1981, 250–254, 515–524). Certain performers' contemporary dance steps also juxtapose duple and triple meter; while the right foot moves front and back and the hips trace a figure eight to a count of four, both arms circle three times in front of the body. The typical festejo's harmonic structure

Cajón

R R L R   R L L R L   R R L R L   R L L R L

Transcription Notes:
Lower staff line (● noteheads): Bass strokes (palm on drum face)
Upper staff line (× noteheads): Slap-like strokes (fingers on top corners)

FIGURE 3.4. A cajón pattern for the festejo, learned from Juan Medrano Cotito.

consists of I–IV–V chord progressions in the major mode, outlined by standard guitar bassline and strumming patterns.

In the 1960s, only a few elderly Black Peruvians remembered seeing the early-twentieth-century festejo danced (N. Santa Cruz 1970a, 61). Some said there were specific steps, whereas others maintained that the choreography was "freestyle," and there was further disagreement about whether the dance was performed as a male solo or by groups (Tompkins 1981, 247; A. Vásquez 2000). In 1949, Don Porfirio Vásquez was hired to teach the festejo's choreography in one of Lima's new folklore academies (see chapter 1). Because no standard dance steps existed, Don Porfirio invented a choreography by combining aspects of other Black folkloric dances including the resbalosa, zapateo, son de los diablos, agua'e nieve, and alcatraz—"and from this succulent mixture was born the contemporary festejo!" (N. Santa Cruz 1970a, 61; also Casaverde 2000b; Tompkins 1981, 247–248). According to Nicomedes Santa Cruz, the festejo choreography subsequently taught to students and performed in tourist nightclubs was "whitened" until it no longer resembled either the African past or the Black Peruvian present (1970a, 61).

Under Nicomedes Santa Cruz' direction, Cumanana's first theatrical production featured a festejo he had collected and revived. Nicomedes did not publicly reveal how he had learned this song, and later recordings attribute its composition to Nicomedes himself (Various Artists 1995a; Various Artists 1998b). "No me cumbén" (That doesn't suit me) was performed as part of the theatrical skit "La pelona" in 1960 and Cumanana recorded it in 1964 (N. Santa Cruz y su Conjunto Cumanana [1964] 1970).

The Cumanana arrangement of "No me cumbén" (figure 3.5) suggests the indebtedness of the festejos of the early revival to the reconstructions of the Pancho Fierro company. While the I–IV–V bassline and guitar strumming patterns are similar to those found in later festejos, there is no cajón (the percussion parts are limited to quijada and cajita). This is significant because the cajón, as a naturalized symbol of blackness, became an

FIGURE 3.5. Excerpt from "No me cumbén" *(N. Santa Cruz y su Conjunto Cumanana [1964] 1994).*

indispensable part of the festejo's instrumentation later in the revival (see chapter 4). Moreover, the quijada and cajita parts appear to be variations of the son de los diablos rhythms reconstructed by the Pancho Fierro company (see figures 1.8 and 1.9). In fact, Javier León observes that, during the early stages of the revival when the festejo was reinvented and stylized, performers borrowed rhythmic and melodic parts and instrumentation from other related genres including el son de los diablos (see León Quirós 2003, 167). Thus, Cumanana's recording of "No me cumbén" supports the idea (introduced in chapter 1) that the instrumentation, rhythmic patterns, and "swing" of the festejo were derived from the basic ingredients of the "original" Black Peruvian folklore sound established by the Pancho Fierro company (in which Nicomedes Santa Cruz and several of the other Cumanana musicians performed).

The lyrics of "No me cumbén" are provocative, providing a striking commentary on Peruvian ideas about race and marriage:[10]

No me casara con negra	I wouldn't marry a Black woman
ni aunque el diablo me llevara,	even if the devil dragged me
porque tienen los ojos blancos	because they have white eyes
y la bemba colorada	and thick red lips
¡Como aquella que está sentada!	Like that one sitting down!
¡Como aquella que está parada!	Like that one standing up!

Tampoco me casaría	I wouldn't marry a mulata
con mulata o zamba-clara,	or a light-skinned zamba either
porque dejan a los negritos	because they leave Blacks
por los de "cara lavada"	for people who've "whitened" their faces

| ¡Como aquella que está sentada! | Like that one sitting down! |
| ¡Como aquella que está parada! | Like that one standing up! |

According to Nicomedes Santa Cruz (1970a, 61), these lyrics were sung as part of a game played by Black children in Lima until the 1920s. A soloist sang the first section (above). When the soloist came to the lyrics "like that one sitting down," she or he pointed to a child who was sitting down, and that child immediately stood up to escape being "the one" alluded to by the lyrics. In the second section (lyrics not shown), the boys offered potential suitors to the girls (for example, carpenter, bottlemaker, breadman), who turned them all down (singing "así no me cumbén" or "that doesn't suit me") for a variety of comic reasons (carpenters cut wood, they could cut me too; bottle-makers sell bottles, they could sell me too; breadmen knead flour, they could knead me too; and so forth).

Nicomedes' revival of "No me cumbén" resulted in its rebirth and continued performance in Peru. In the late 1970s, William Tompkins collected the following additional verse (1981, 372):

Quiérome casá	I want to get married,
y no sé con quién	and I don't know to whom
Cásate con negro Mandinga	Marry a Mandinga[11] Black man,
que eso a tí sí cumbén	yes, that will suit you

Ese negro café	That coffee-colored Black man
a mí no me cumbén	doesn't suit me
La Mandinga mancha la gente	The Mandinga stain people
puede manchar a mí también	he might stain me, too

Tompkins presents these lyrics as evidence of the prevalent ideology among Black Peruvians that "whitening" by intermarriage (or through the adoption of "White" or European cultural practices) was the only road to social mobility.

"Whitening" describes the belief that blackness will gradually diminish and eventually disappear after generations of intermarriage. Typically, whitening ideologies were employed by White elites leading early-twentieth-century nationalist movements in various Latin American countries, in an effort to unify heterogeneous populations under a constructed homogeneous national identity influenced by the Social Darwinist rhetoric of the era. For example, in his influential book *Lima* ([1867] 1925), Manuel A. Fuentes likened Peruvian mestizaje to the process of mixing paint until the original non-White hue is indiscernible, illustrating the assumption that "superior" White blood always dominates over other types. Reading the following passage, it is easy to see why Richard Jackson (1976) describes whitening ideologies as a form of societal "ethnic lynching" (see Ojeda 2003, 19):

> Of the three colors, representing the three different races, the following combinations result: white and yellow . . . *mestizo; mestizo* and yellow, white; black and yellow, not the green that results in the painter's palette but the color which is called *Chinese Cholo* in Lima; [Chinese *Cholo*] and black, Chinese *prieto*; [Chinese *prieto*] and white, light-skinned Chinese; white and black, *Zambo*; [*Zambo*] and white, *mulato*; [*mulato*] and white, *cuarteron*; [*cuarteron*] and white, *quinteron*; [*quinteron*] and white, white.
>
> The population of Lima offers . . . a range of shades from the finest and most brilliant black to this yellowish color; there can be no monotony. Since the introduction of African blacks stopped in 1793, blacks have diminished considerably, and the African race has made itself so rare that there is hardly one ancient black man to represent it. (Fuentes [1867] 1925, 79–80)

Between 1908 and 1932, when the game "No me cumbén" was popular among Black children, Blacks were the Peruvian racial group second most likely (after Asian men) to intermarry (*Boletín Municipal de Lima* 1900–1932, cited in Stokes 1987, 187). However, the lyrics of "No me cumbén" express a slightly different perspective than that conveyed by Fuentes—anxiety over the "blackening" that might result from marrying a person of African descent. The narrator of the song could either be a White (or other non-Black) person who is afraid to marry a Black person (in which case the feared "blackening" outcome would contradict Fuentes' whitening scenario) or a Black person who wants to "improve" his or her race. In either case, the end result is to discourage members of any race from marrying someone who is "too" Black. Because Nicomedes identified the song as part of a game played by Blacks in Lima, it can easily be imagined that its performance socialized Black children to avoid being identified with stereotyped characteristics of the Black race if they were to be marriageable and to actively seek out partners who did not appear to be of African descent.

Why, then, did Nicomedes Santa Cruz, a proud champion of negritud, revive this seemingly racist children's game? Understood in the context of the revival, Nicomedes' use of this festejo reveals a second possible reading. If taken literally, the racist lyrics demean Blacks and urge others not to marry them. However, if they are understood as satirical, they ridicule the attitudes of those who are afraid of marrying Blacks by comparing their reasons with others that are equally absurd (such as the fear that a breadmaker will knead his spouse).

In his written notes accompanying the Cumanana recording of this song (N. Santa Cruz 1970a, 61), Nicomedes refrained from commenting on the seemingly racist content of the lyrics, focusing instead on its African traits (parallels to other African children's games, solo-chorus antiphony, and vestiges of bozal speech). However, Nicomedes' theatrical use of the song in "La pelona" suggests that he viewed it as an example of the Peruvian art of satire, which he described as the gift of being able to perceive the ridiculous and skillfully reveal it with the perfect joke or nickname (N. Santa Cruz 1982, 61).[12] As Teresa Mendoza Hernández explained in chapter 2, she played "la pelona," a Black girl who imitated White women to catch the eye of a White man. When she returned to the callejón in makeup and fancy clothes, with her short and nappy hair bound closely to her head under a hat designed for White women with straight and long hair, Nicomedes insulted her for being ashamed of her race with the recited décima "La pelona" (see figure 2.4). In this poem, as Martha Ojeda observes (2003, 19–21), Nicomedes recalled the strategies of the negritude poets by embracing stereotypes about both Blacks and Whites in order to fight Black self-hatred and promote racial pride. In the first verse, he painted an unflattering portrait of "la pelona":[13]

Te cambiaste las chancletas	You traded in your sandals
por zapatos taco aguja,	for high heeled shoes,
y tu cabeza de bruja	and you fastened your witch's head
la amarraste con peinetas.	with ornamental combs.
Por no engordar sigues dietas	To keep slender you diet
y estás flaca y hocicona.	and you are skinny and thick-lipped.
Imitando a tu patrona	Imitating your boss
has aprendido a fumar.	you have learned to smoke.
Hasta en el modo de andar	Even in the way you walk
cómo has cambiado, pelona.	*How you have changed, pelona.*

Nicomedes continued to use ironic language to castigate "la pelona." He scoffed that she wore a bracelet watch but didn't know how to tell time, and he smiled at her use of powder, asking whether she covered her black skin with a fashionable commercial brand or "dust of the coal yard." In the last verse, Nicomedes implored her to stop her foolishness and marry within her race:

Deja ese estilo bellaco,	Drop that cunning style
vuelve a ser la misma de antes.	go back to how you were before.
Menos polvos, menos guantes,	Less powder, less gloves,
menos humo de tabaco.	less tobacco smoke.
Vuelve con tu negro flaco	Return to your skinny Black man
que te adora todavía.	who still adores you.

After Nicomedes made this plea, "la pelona" (Teresa Mendoza Hernández) sang "No me cumbén." Thus, when she announced, "I won't marry a Black man because of his white eyes and thick red lips" in the festejo "No me cumbén," it was not her use of stereotypes to describe Black men that offended, but rather her lack of pride in those stereotyped qualities of her race. Having already made "la pelona" look foolish for her "White" ways with his décima, Nicomedes used the festejo "No me cumbén" to seal the argument against whitening.[14] In other words, by recontextualizing a festejo that may have taught Black children to be ashamed of their race, Nicomedes foreclosed its literal meaning, insisting instead upon its power as satire and social critique.

Reviving a festejo whose contextually determined meaning could alternately be read as racist or satirical was risky business. After "No me cumbén" was recorded by Cumanana, others performed and distributed the song in new contexts. For example, on a recording by Cecilia Barraza, the song begins with a staged encounter between the White criolla female singer and (presumably) Black men who comment favorably on her appearance and dancing, calling her a "pretty *gringa*," before she launches into the reasons why she won't marry a Black man (Various Artists 1998b). On the compilation CD *The Soul of Black Peru* (Various Artists 1995a), the Cumanana recording of "No me cumbén" was re-released in the United States with no explanation of the song's origins or uses in the Afro-Peruvian revival. Based on these recordings, listeners (especially non-Peruvians) may draw their own conclusions about racializing stereotypes in Afro-Peruvian music.

Thus, the social history of this festejo reveals the dangers of decontextualizing collected song lyrics and commodifying them as popular songs. As "No me cumbén" continues to circulate to new audiences through recontextualized recordings, it acts as a palimpsest; new readings by listeners in post-revival Lima and U.S. world music audiences replace (but do not completely obscure) both its satirical antiracist uses during the Afro-Peruvian revival and its original function as a Black children's game.

Excavating Peru's African Heritage in Brazil: The Lundú

After he advanced the spirit of Peruvian negritud with his décimas and the theatrical productions of Cumanana, Nicomedes Santa Cruz developed anti-imperialist sentiments that led him to look outside Peru for solutions to local problems. "I am a revolutionary!" he announced in a décima printed in the newspaper *Libertad* in 1962 (N. Santa Cruz 1971a, 28–30).

Enamored with the Cuban Revolution, Nicomedes believed that Peru needed a similar radical uprising.

By this time, Nicomedes was a published poet, prolific journalist, and co-founder of the newspaper *Expreso*. In what Martha Ojeda describes as his "social and political engagement period" (2003, 29–56), Nicomedes' newspaper columns and recited poetry expressed solidarity with the struggles of oppressed peoples laboring under military dictatorships and other types of repression. Yet, Nicomedes' audience in the late 1950s and early 1960s was primarily members of high society and the criollo oligarchy that had controlled Peru since independence (Mariñez 1993, 118). In 1960, Nicomedes began to alienate his audience by protesting capitalist abuses in poems such as "Talara, no digas yes" (N. Santa Cruz n.d. [1959?], 95–96) (which compared the exploitation of Peruvian petroleum by the United States and the Peruvian oligarchy to Black exploitation), and "El café" (N. Santa Cruz 1971a, 319–321) (in which he used coffee as a metaphor for the bitterness of slavery and colonialism). As a political statement, Nicomedes performed "El café" in front of an audience that included the President of the Association of Latin American Coffee Plantation Owners. However, Nicomedes realized that he was in a position of privilege as a Peruvian poet for the upper classes; one décima earned him up to fifty times the monthly wage of a factory worker (Mariñez 1993, 118). Fed up with Peruvian politics, he went to Brazil in 1963.

Nicomedes entered a new phase in his development as a poet and folklorist during his trip to Brazil. He was deeply affected by what he described as a "beautiful and unforgettable" country with its "colossal" population of "20 million Blacks" (N. Santa Cruz 1971a, 16). Nicomedes remembered, "There, the most extraordinary thing that had happened in my life occurred, when the first thing I encounter on Mariscal Floriano Avenue is a monument to the Brazilian nation, which has . . . four sculptures in the base . . . the Portuguese colony, the Tupí-Guaraní Indian, the *caboclo*, and the Black.[15] When I see a Black man in bronze . . . this is when I say: 'This country is extraordinary' . . . The experience in Brazil changed my life" (qtd. in Mariñez 1993, 119). Nicomedes sought out Afro-Brazilian popular culture (particularly *Candomblé*, an Afro-Brazilian religion involving music, dance, and spirit possession) in Salvador da Bahia, and he formed intellectual relationships with Brazilian folklorists and scholars Jorge Amado, Edison Carneiro, and Luís da Câmara Cascudo. Nicomedes would long remember how he was embraced by practitioners of Candomblé, who, at a *terreiro* (Candomblé ceremony house), "tell me I have something, that I can help them a lot, that they will give me secrets nobody knows" (qtd in. Mariñez 1993, 119). At the University of Bahia,

Nicomedes attended an international conference where he saw delegates from Africa for the first time. His artistic muse was sparked. In Bahia, Nicomedes wrote several of his most famous poems reflecting his new engagement with international struggles ("¡Ay mama!" "Muerte en el ring," "Congo libre," "Johanesburgo," and "América Latina"). When the poet returned to Peru, he stopped performing in the high society clubs frequented by the Peruvian oligarchy and began to read his poems and décimas to university student groups instead (Mariñez 1992, 262–263).

Shortly after his return from Brazil, in 1964, Nicomedes produced his most enduring and influential musical legacy: the ethnographic double-LP album and booklet *Cumanana*, featuring his company of the same name. Along with recited versions of Nicomedes' most famous poems, the album contains the first recordings of many revived Afro-Peruvian genres, collected and arranged by Nicomedes Santa Cruz. *Cumanana* was the first recording of Peruvian music presented in the same format as European symphony and opera recordings (a hard box containing multiple LPs and a detailed booklet, printed on high-quality oversized paper in color). The accompanying booklet contains more than one hundred pages of song lyrics, photographs, artwork, and commentary by Nicomedes. Released by Philips (then the parent company of Peru's El Virrey label), *Cumanana*'s first edition (1,000 copies) was distributed to seventy-one countries including Nigeria, Israel, France, Holland, Spain, and the United States (N. Santa Cruz 1970a, 8). In Peru, copies were presented to the president, the cardinal, and diplomatic leaders (Levano 1965, 30, 33). Second (1965) and third (1970) editions were printed, and total distribution reached 10,000 copies (N. Santa Cruz 1975, 64). In 1994, a CD version was released.

Cumanana is probably the ethnographic and artistic document that has exerted the most lasting influence on contemporary ideas about the Black musical past in Peru. The most influential (and controversial) theory Nicomedes presented in the booklet that accompanied *Cumanana* (N. Santa Cruz 1970a, 18–20) demonstrates how his trip to Brazil influenced his excavations of Afro-Peruvian music and dance history. In *Cumanana*, Nicomedes Santa Cruz popularized a genealogy of the origin of the Peruvian marinera, a coastal couple dance considered the ultimate expression of música criolla (figure 3.6). Nicomedes affirmed that an African couple dance called lundú was the progenitor of the forgotten Afro-Peruvian landó, which later developed into the zamacueca, an older name for the marinera (N. Santa Cruz 1970a, 18). This genealogy definitively declared that Peru's música criolla was of African, as well as European, heritage.[16]

Nicomedes further asserted that the African lundú gave birth not only to the Peruvian landó but also to more than fifty couple dances found

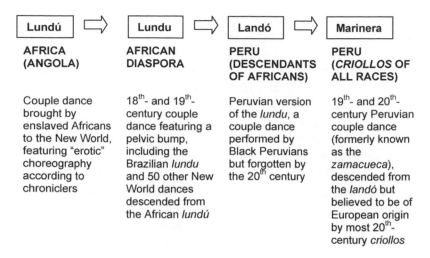

Lundú ⇨	Lundu ⇨	Landó ⇨	Marinera
AFRICA (ANGOLA)	**AFRICAN DIASPORA**	**PERU (DESCENDANTS OF AFRICANS)**	**PERU (CRIOLLOS OF ALL RACES)**
Couple dance brought by enslaved Africans to the New World, featuring "erotic" choreography according to chroniclers	18th- and 19th- century couple dance featuring a pelvic bump, including the Brazilian lundu and 50 other New World dances descended from the African lundú	Peruvian version of the lundu, a couple dance performed by Black Peruvians but forgotten by the 20th century	19th- and 20th- century Peruvian couple dance (formerly known as the zamacueca), descended from the landó but believed to be of European origin by most 20th- century criollos

FIGURE 3.6. Nicomedes Santa Cruz' theory of the African origins of the Peruvian marinera.

throughout Portugal, Spain, and the Americas beginning in the fifteenth and sixteenth centuries.[17] The *leitmotif* (in Nicomedes' terms) shared by these dances and their descendants was a "*golpe de frente*" or pelvic bump. He wrote, "The purpose of these African dances, in rites of initiation or betrothal (*m'lemba:* marriage), was that the male-female couples, displaying a choreographed pantomime of copulation, gave each other the 'frontal hit,' pelvis against pelvis, or thigh against thigh, or navel (*cumbe* in African [sic]) against navel." Explaining that the golpe de frente survived in the Peruvian landó only in symbolic onlookers' calls of encouragement during the couple dance, Nicomedes observed, "Here in Peru, it seems that everything was limited to shouting 'que le da' [give it to him] (the bump) and 'zamba [Black girl], que le da'." Nicomedes also affirmed that the golpe de frente was retained in a more inhibited form in the choreography of the marinera (N. Santa Cruz 1970a, 20, 47).

Nicomedes' emphasis on the lundú and its golpe de frente reignited African diasporic consciousness in Peru by linking Black Peruvian dance to a choreographic expression assumedly shared with other diasporic subjects throughout the Black Atlantic. At the same time it linked the reconstructed African past (the lundú and landó) to the criollo present (the marinera). The emphasis on the lundú served as a self-essentializing version of the same kinds of danced markers that, according to Zoila Mendoza, separate indigenous and mestizo bodily performances in Peru (Mendoza 1998). As Mendoza argues in her analysis of folkloric dances of Cuzco, dancers continuously move between imagined pure and hybridized identities through the use of markers such as close-to-the-earth movements (indigenous) and synthetic fabrics (mestizo). Choreographies reclaimed in the Afro-Peruvian revival—such as the golpe de frente—accomplished similar goals, enabling Blacks to move back and forth between racial difference and their local criollo identity. Thus, if the pelvic bump was a marker that enabled Afro-Peruvian performers to move toward their African diasporic identity, resisting that choreography (or performing it symbolically versus literally) was a way of identifying with the moral culture of criollismo. In sum, Nicomedes Santa Cruz' lundú theory demonstrates what I view as Black Pacific double consciousness; it simultaneously maintains Black ties to Peruvian criollo culture, promotes a strategically essentialist and Afrocentric vision of premodern African origins, and embraces kinship with the Black Atlantic.

How did Nicomedes learn of the lundú and the African origins of the Peruvian marinera? In *Cumanana*, his primary proof that the lundú's golpe de frente choreography was at one time performed in Lima is a cited paragraph from Manuel Fuentes' nineteenth-century book *Lima* that describes the "shocking" way Black Peruvians danced (Fuentes [1867] 1925; N. Santa Cruz 1970a, 20). Yet, Fuentes does not name the dance he describes, and a search of Nicomedes' writings for further direct references to the source of his knowledge comes up empty. Careful reading of *Cumanana* and knowledge of Nicomedes' life events and personal library point to one explanation.[18] He based his theory on his transferal of Brazilian scholars' writings about Afro-Brazilian music and dance to the Afro-Peruvian context.

According to William Tompkins (1981, 288–296), there is no historical evidence that a dance called lundú existed in Peru, although chroniclers in colonial times described dances with similar-sounding names (landó and *ondú*). However, Edison Carneiro (1961) and Luís da Câmara Cascudo (1954) wrote about the Brazilian lundu, a dance that rose from the Black populace to society salons in the eighteenth and nineteenth centuries. Its choreography, said to be derived from a dance of Congo–Angolan African origins, was subjectively characterized by Portuguese chroniclers in Brazil as "lewd" sexual pantomime by a couple who performed pelvic thrusts while surrounded by a circle of spectators. According to Carneiro (1961), the lundu was the source of the *umbigada*, or pelvic bump motion, in the Brazilian *samba* dance. Nicomedes met and formed a close relationship with Edison Carneiro during his 1963 trip to Brazil, and he owned several of Carneiro's books, along with Luís da Camara Cascudo's *Dictionary of Brazilian Folklore* (1954) and the writings of Cuban scholar Fernando Ortiz. Because these are the primary works he cites in *Cumanana* as evidence of his lundú thesis (N. Santa Cruz 1970a, 18), Nicomedes apparently hypothesized that the Peruvian landó must have had the same African origin as the Brazilian lundu, and that it contained the same characteristic pelvic bump. His evidence for this correlation remains mysterious, suggesting that Nicomedes may have relied on nothing more than the similarity of the names of two lost dances—landó and lundu— that originated in Black populations of completely different countries. In other words, the cornerstone of Nicomedes' theory, the lundú, is probably based on a colonial Afro-Brazilian dance that survives in the subjective descriptions of Portuguese chroniclers and that may or may not ever have been performed in Peru.

Nicomedes Santa Cruz' turn to the Black Atlantic was not surprising or unusual, given his isolated position in the Peruvian Black Pacific. Discussing the strategies of Black nationalism, George Lipsitz writes that African Americans have sought to "turn national minorities into global majorities by affirming solidarity with 'people of color' all around the globe . . . Everywhere, diasporic Africans have used international frames to remedy national frustrations" (Lipsitz 1994, 31). In an interview with Pablo Mariñez, Nicomedes Santa Cruz explained why he transferred the findings of Brazilian and Cuban scholars to the Peruvian context, observing that, although tyrants and oligarchies had ruled those countries as well, scholars in Brazil and Cuba acknowledged the Black contribution to national culture.[19] "For this reason," he said, "I have discovered in the works of Camara Cascudo, Nina Rodriguez, Arthur Ramos, and in the works of Fernando Ortiz, Luciano Franco, and in all the ethnomusicological research and literature . . . many points of clarity about African roots and African transculturation which I have adapted to the Black reality [in Peru], which has gone unresearched and unquestioned" (qtd. in Mariñez 2000, 88–89). Nicomedes' friend, Pablo Mariñez, reiterates that Nicomedes' "trip to Brazil and the relationship he established with Edison Carneiro and other intellectuals contributed greatly [to his thinking about blackness in Peru]. In reality, Nicomedes began to solidly formulate himself by way of the Brazilian Africanists, as well as the Cubans. If one reviews the sources used in his works, as well as many of his statements, we find that these Africanists constituted an important—perhaps decisive—part in the intellectual grounding of our author." Mariñez goes on to explain that Nicomedes' reliance on the works of Cuban and Brazilian scholars is understandable because of the greater level of academic research about the Black presence in those countries. "Nicomedes," Mariñez writes, "could not possibly attain an intellectual formation in this realm within the vacuum that existed in Peru" (Mariñez 2000, 18).

Although it is true that there was little scholarship about the African origins of Peruvian music before the work of Nicomedes Santa Cruz, one historian, Fernando Romero, provided a foundation. Romero was a White retired mariner with a PhD. in history whose love for his childhood nanny had launched a lifelong fascination with Black culture.

Romero sought to disprove the claims of Argentinean musicologist Carlos Vega that criollo dances such as the zamacueca were of purely European origin. As evidence for the lack of African influence on the Peruvian zamacueca—a dance that spread throughout South America—Carlos Vega noted its stereotypically European traits (cadential phrases and functional harmony), and the absence of typically "African" rhythms (Vega 1936 and 1953). To disprove Vega's theories, Romero relied in equal measure on stereotypes about "European" versus "Black" music and dance. Using etymological associations and trait testimonials that described "African" characteristics, Romero set out to show that the Peruvian zamba (the dance he identified as the zamacueca's progenitor) was of African origin (F. Romero 1939a; 1939b; 1940; 1946a; 1946b). Based on his readings of eighteenth- and nineteenth-century descriptions of dances performed by Blacks in Peru, Romero suggested a genealogy very similar to the one Nicomedes later proposed in support of his lundú theory. Romero inferred that the Peruvian zamba was descended from the African quizomba (Angola) due to similar choreographic traits, especially the golpe de frente (pelvic bump) or Bantu "m'lemba," which simulated sexual intercourse. According to Romero, the golpe de frente was at one time performed as the epilogue of the Peruvian zamacueca, demonstrating the survival of an African trait (F. Romero 1940, 99).

Therefore, Nicomedes' genealogy of the origins of the marinera expanded upon and popularized earlier research by Fernando Romero, although Romero did not mention a dance called lundú (see F. Romero 1939a; 1939b; 1939c; 1939d; 1940; 1946a; 1946b; 1947). Nicomedes' turn to Cuba and Brazil also mirrors Romero's reliance on the works of the Africanist scholars of those countries.

In addition to the writings of Fernando Romero and Brazilian and Cuban scholars, Nicomedes used a surprising source to support the lundú theory. In the first paragraph of Nicomedes' treatise on the lundú in *Cumanana*, he refutes Carlos Vega's contention that couple dances (such as the zamacueca) are a purely European phenomenon not found in Africa or its diaspora by citing a staged dance performance by the Katherine Dunham Company (N. Santa Cruz 1970a, 18).

As noted in chapter 2, the North American Katherine Dunham Company brought the theatrical results of Dunham's "ethnography to performance" method to Lima's prestigious Teatro Municipal in 1951. The Dunham Company's repertoire that evening spanned the African diaspora, from West Africa to Cuba and the United States. The piece that particularly impressed Nicomedes was the West African "Rites of Passage" dance (including the scenes "Masculine Puberty Ritual" and "Fertility Ritual") that concluded the first act. Seeing the "Fertility Ritual" and its simulation of sexual intercourse (described in the program as a "ceremony that develops in the primitive community on the occasion of marriage" [Dunham y su Compañia 1951]) started Nicomedes on the path toward his theory of the African lundú. Twenty-two years later, he wrote, "The Katherine Dunham Company showed us, in the Municipal Theater, the positive aspect of the Black presence in the world . . . I remember as if it were yesterday how the aristocratic ladies of our hypocritical society abandoned the orchestra level and the boxes of the Municipal [Theater] halfway through the show because they couldn't stand the scandalous scene of a 'rite of passage,' in which a *yao* (Lucille Ellis) received instructions for conjugal living from a *babalao* (Lenwood Morris) in choreography that pantomimed the copular act, as is the custom on the edge of the sacred Oyó River in Nigeria.[20] I could swear that some of these horrified ladies who abandoned the theater . . . showed at the ends of their half-fingered gloves: typical Black nails! And under their mink coats appeared: Black calves! And the snub nose, wrinkled up from a supposed stench or funk that they imagined came from the stage—well that, too, was the nose of a Black person!" (N. Santa Cruz 1973, 24).

In this remembrance, Nicomedes casts Lima's snobbish high society audience in the role of the Spanish and Portuguese chroniclers who condemned Blacks for their disgracefully erotic dances. At the same time, he points out that the very members of Lima's criollo, European-identifying elite who distanced themselves from the Black dance performed onstage were the product of racial mestizaje including African ancestry. Thus, in Nicomedes' eyes, the reaction of Lima's "White" audiences to the Black dance performed onstage reenacted the absurdity of European chroniclers' aversion to the eroticism of African dance, dramatically illustrating the hysteria provoked by fear of the Other within oneself. It was this social denial that spurred Nicomedes' research and gave rise to his theory of the lundú, through which he sought to create a counter-memory that would challenge the official invisibility of the African contribution to Peruvian coastal culture.

Because the negritud of the *Cumanana* recording was specifically manifested as a dignified reconstruction of Black traditions *of the past*, it was easily understood and co-opted by the Peruvian mainstream as part of the criollo nostalgia memory project, leaving intact the myth that Black culture had disappeared from contemporary Peru. For example, Peru's *Caretas* magazine pronounced the album a "stupendous proof of the indomitable power of black song," but echoed the whitening philosophies described earlier in this chapter, postulating, "If some musical genres were lost after the colonial era, they were not lost by decree, but because of their inadequacy for cultural mestizaje . . . The greatest merit of this whole part of the recording seems to be that it confirms the enormous contribution of Blacks to the musical personality of Peru. Destined, perhaps, to physically disappear in Peru, his color blending with Indian and mestizo, the Black man has survived through his dance and his song. These records are his testimonial" (Levano 1965, 32–33). Ironically, this critique renders contemporary Blacks invisible even as it praises a recording by living Black artists.

Moreover, scholars disputed Nicomedes Santa Cruz' theories and questioned his methods and motivations. For example, José Durand charged that "the work of Nicomedes Santa Cruz . . . [is] motivated by his obsessive desire that everything be Black, forgetting that Peru is not: neither Black nor Indian nor White" (J. Durand 1980, qtd. in G. Durand Allison 1999, 37), and William Tompkins criticized Nicomedes for positing speculation as if it were scientific fact (Tompkins 1981, 293). From the standpoint of the university-trained scholar, Nicomedes' thesis appears poorly presented, offering no documentation of the existence or nature of the lundú of Angola and its alleged dissemination in Peru. Further, his idea that a family of more than fifty American dances was derived from the lundú seems to be based on the vague and biased description of "erotic" dances by European chroniclers, because these are the only sources he cites.

However, these apparent shortcomings reveal as much about the different research and documentation parameters of community-based "organic intellectuals" (Gilroy 1993) versus university-based scholars as they do about the possible shortcomings of Nicomedes' research. As Nicomedes himself described his approach, "perhaps following the example of José Carlos Mariátegui [the Peruvian Marxist social critic who described his character as both "extra-university" and "anti-university"], I have never seen things through the lens of academic, sociology, ethnology, or anthropology, but rather from their popular origins" (qtd. in "Nicomedes Santa Cruz Gamarra" n.d., 3).

What seems to bother both scholars and lay critics most about Nicomedes' assertions is that he was so certain that they were true. Critics of the Santa Cruz family often delegitimize their work by pointing out that they lived a comfortable urban life, insinuating that they didn't *know* Black music and culture, they *learned* it. This point of view is rooted in the belief that twentieth-century urban Blacks like the Santa Cruzes had completely assimilated into the criollo way of life, and that "authentic" Black culture came to Lima with Black rural migrants. Thus, while Nicomedes and Victoria refer to songs, dances, and stories learned from their grandparents and passed down by their ancestors, detractors quickly assert that the Santa Cruz family lived in Lima for many generations, and that Nicomedes learned how to compose and write décimas from Porfirio Vásquez, a native of rural Aucallama.

It is also important to note a disturbing antagonism toward Afro-Peruvians on the part of Peruvian scholars. According to historian Frederick Bowser, "the post-abolition attitude of national intellectuals toward Afro-Peruvians has been largely hostile" (Bowser 1974, 223), and anthropologist Marisol de la Cadena (1998) reveals how twentieth-century Peruvian academia's "silent racism" (masked by the replacement of the notion of "race" with progressive classifications based on morality, culture, class, education, and intelligence) has continually forged new ways of affirming the superiority of White intellectuals while denying the existence of Peruvian racism. De la Cadena writes that "silent racism acknowledges the right of every Peruvian to belong to the nation. Yet it also positions individuals on a differentiated scale according to their intellectual capacity and academic knowledge . . . The hegemony of Western hierarchies deriving from formal education makes 'racism' without race not only possible but virtually invulnerable" (1998, 160). Thus, in the 1960s, efforts to reinscribe Black difference into national Peruvian culture were viewed with suspicion, and it was considered normal that White Peruvians dominated research on Black Peruvian culture. With the publication of *Cumanana* in 1965, Nicomedes inserted his voice into ongoing polemics among White scholars about the origins of Peruvian coastal music, insisting on the importance of listening to Black people in the quest to understand the Black experience.

Cumanana became a Peruvian classic. Long out-of-print in its original form, photocopies of the booklet from the third edition circulate in Peru as unofficial Black history texts. Through this opus, Nicomedes Santa Cruz—whose grammar school education prohibited his admittance to the elite category of "*gente decente*" (Whites and honorary Whites) (see De la Cadena 1998)—was able to popularize and disseminate his theory of the African lundú so widely that, decades later, most Peruvians who know anything about Afro-Peruvian music are aware of it. Many Peruvians positively state that the landó came from an African dance called lundú, and that these dances are the basis of the marinera. Javier León observes that this public repetition of Santa Cruz' theory over a period of several decades has "transformed something that could be plausible into an incontrovertible fact" (León Quirós 2003, 106). Whether or not the theory is historically accurate, the fact that so many people *believe* it is true is an important element of the construction of Peruvian blackness by way of the Black Atlantic in the twentieth century. As Janheinz Jahn wrote in *Muntu*, "The Africa presented by the ethnologist is a legend in which we used to believe. The African tradition as it appears in the light of neo-African culture may also be a legend—but it is the legend in which African intelligence believes" (1961, 17). With the resounding achievement of *Cumanana* and his lundú theory, Nicomedes empowered the Black community to speak for itself. More important than the credibility of Nicomedes' argument is how it affected the future racialization of music and dance, especially the rebirth of the Peruvian landó.

Re-creating the Landó: "Samba malató"

Despite the popular appeal of Nicomedes' theory of the African ancestry of the marinera, it did not generate additional research or interest in reconstructing the African lundú. Instead, Black Peruvian performers emphasized the middle child, the Afro-Peruvian genre called *landó* that had been invented and forgotten in Peru. The *landó* became a symbol of the African ancestry of Black music in Peru. Decades after the publication of *Cumanana*, Black musicians and dancers often say that the landó is the mother of all Black music and dance in Peru, and that all Black rhythms come from the landó.

In the previous chapter, I explained how Victoria Santa Cruz re-created the forgotten choreography of the landó through her process of embodied ancestral memory. In this section, I will explore the strategies that Nicomedes Santa Cruz (with guitarist Vicente Vásquez) employed to musically re-create the landó. Through these musical strategies (and those that followed later in the revival), the landó became a double link, connecting Afro-Peruvians both with an African past (shared with the Black Atlantic) and with contemporary criollo practice.

The actual history of the landó in Peru is difficult to ascertain, because there is little documentation of the genre's pre-twentieth-century existence (Tompkins 1981, 288–296). Nicomedes and Victoria Santa Cruz reconstructed the landó from descriptions of elders who had witnessed the dance in the early twentieth century, fragments of song texts and melodies, and their own memories, both childhood and ancestral. In so doing, they challenged the primacy of historical documentation over collective memory, reclaiming Black agency in the history-making process. As Nicomedes proclaimed at a 1974 conference on negritude in Dakar, Senegal, "Colonialist slavery wrenched us from our ancestral land, and over the last four centuries we have reconstructed many of our customs and traditions, thanks to our gift of ancestral memory![21] But our history doesn't begin in America, it begins in Africa. There, the other half of our being remained, which is why we have always felt the imperative call of distant blood, of the homeland, of Mother Africa . . . Our history cannot be written by the descendants of these same White slavers . . . It is we, ourselves, who write our own history" (N. Santa Cruz 1978, 370).

Thus, reviving the landó—by any means necessary—was an integral part of revising official history to restore the African heritage erased from the colonialist narrative. At the same time, the landó's re-creation and subsequent stylization was informed by the vocabulary and sensibility of the music closest to its performers' local identity—Peruvian música criolla. In fact, to support Santa Cruz' thesis that the landó was of African origin and that it later developed into the marinera, the re-created landó had to sound both "African" and similar to the criollo marinera (reflecting a kind of double consciousness). Africanisms in the landós re-created by Nicomedes Santa Cruz and others in the revival included solo–chorus call-and-response form, layered percussion, polyrhythms, and the presence of various non-Peruvian Afro-Latin percussion instruments such as cowbell, *tumbadoras*, and bongó. Other elements of reconstructed landós were reminiscent of música criolla, especially the instrumental core and interplay of two guitars and a cajón, the use of triple meter or triple subdivisions, and the incorporation of a slower version of the guitar strumming pattern associated with the marinera's final section (see León Quirós 2003, 229–248; Tompkins 1981, 110–111, 303).

The first landó ever recorded was "Samba malató," which was re-created for the *Cumanana* album in 1964. Nicomedes and Victoria remembered seeing their grandparents dance landó and hearing their mother and aunt sing this verse fragment: "La samba se pasea por la batea, landó, samba malató, landó" (The Black woman moves past the washbasin, landó, samba malató, landó) (N. Santa Cruz y su Conjunto Cumanana [1964] 1970). The elderly Ascuez brothers, who were considered major culture bearers of Afro-Peruvian music and música criolla in Lima, remembered a variation of the same landó verse.[22] For the *Cumanana* recording, the lyrics of the remembered fragment were arranged and sung in responsorial form by Nicomedes Santa Cruz, a solo female vocalist, and the Cumanana chorus (figure 3.7). The melody is typical of later landós in its apparent avoidance of the downbeat. The landó is often notated in $\frac{6}{4}$ (Tompkins 1981, 297, 546–552; R. Vásquez and Rojas n.d.), but some scholars and Afro-Peruvian

FIGURE 3.7. Excerpt from the vocal arrangement of "Samba malató" *(N. Santa Cruz y su Conjunto Cumanana [1964] 1994).*

musicians use $\frac{12}{8}$ (or combinations of $\frac{6}{4}$ and $\frac{12}{8}$) due to increasing metric ambiguity in the performance of landós since the 1970s (Casaverde 2000a; León Quirós 2003, 230–237; Tompkins 1981, 550–552). Following León, in my notated examples of the landó I combine $\frac{12}{8}$ and $\frac{6}{4}$ time signatures to suggest the possibility of multiple ways of hearing musical time.

Reconstructing the harmonic and rhythmic accompaniment required more creative supplements to existing memory. By 1964, according to Abelardo Vásquez, only a "skeletal rhythmic base" was remembered from the original landó (qtd. in Tompkins 1981, 303). Guitarist Vicente Vásquez composed a now-classic introduction (which returns at interludes throughout the song) by inferring a basic rhythm from the cadence of the sung melody fragment, and a number of percussion parts were added around the guitar (V. Santa Cruz 1995; R. Vásquez Rodríguez 1982, 44; V. Vásquez 1978). This repeating introductory motif (figure 3.8) set up an "Africanist" contrast between different ways of feeling musical time that continues throughout the song (this would become a trademark of the post-revival landó). While the bell and bongó divide the measure into three pulses with duple subdivisions, the handclaps mark four pulses with

Transcription Notes:

Flam stroke

Bongó Round notes on lower staff line: Tone on lower-pitched drumhead

FIGURE 3.8. Instrumental introduction, "Samba malató" *(N. Santa Cruz y su Conjunto Cumanana [1964] 1994).*

triple subdivisions. These contrasting ostinati, in combination with the rhythmic phrasing of other instrumental patterns and dance steps performed during the song, alternately reinforce a shifting $\frac{12}{8}$, versus $\frac{6}{4}$ feel (see chapter 4). For example, in the cajón and guitar parts in figure 3.8, the six steady eighth notes in the first half of the measure either may be heard as reinforcing the feeling of $\frac{6}{4}$ (as I have shown them) or as conforming to $\frac{12}{8}$, (see León Quirós 2003, 231), while the second half of the measure is more clearly felt in $\frac{12}{8}$. The vocal arrangement of the lyrics presents the same pattern of ambiguous alternation between duple and triple subdivisions (see figure 3.7, measures 3–4). Interestingly, the complex rhythms of the recreated landó bear little resemblance to scholarly reconstructions of the Brazilian lundu's straightforward duple feel (see Tompkins 1981, 295).

As the revival progressed, the landó's redefinition via changing cajón and guitar parts revealed the double consciousness of its (re)creators,

FIGURE 3.9. Development of *landó* patterns for *cajón* and comparison with West African/ Black Atlantic timeline and *marinera* patterns.

expressing both a transnational Black Atlantic/African diasporic identity and the continued participation of Black Peruvian musicians in national música criolla. In fact, as Javier León argues, stylistic ambiguity and the encouragement of multiple ways of hearing (including the alternate accent implications of $\frac{6}{4}$ versus $\frac{12}{8}$, time signatures) paradoxically became a defining characteristic of the genre (2003, 229–247). While the original cajón pattern for "Samba malató" doubled Vásquez' guitar motif and the rhythmic phrasing of the lyrics (see figures 3.7 and 3.8), a new landó pattern and variations, displayed in figure 3.9 as "Landó Variations #1 and #2," emerged sometime in the 1970s (Various Artists 1998a; V. Santa Cruz 1995). This pattern, generally attributed to Caitro Soto's innovation [Casaverde 2000a; León Quirós 2003], is rhythmically similar to a timeline pattern frequently used in music of West Africa and the Black Atlantic (see figure 3.9), potentially promoting a more "African" feel among listeners familiar with such music.

Interestingly, while cajón players that I consulted all played patterns similar to Landó Variations #1 and #2 when specifically asked to demonstrate landó, the patterns more commonly used to accompany the landó in performances (sometimes in counterpoint to Landó Variation #1 or #2) are variations of the zamacueca, such as the one shown in figure 3.9 as "Landó/Zamacueca Variation #3" (Perú Negro 2000). Because the zamacueca is rhythmically similar to the marinera (the landó/zamacueca variation in figure 3.9 offsets the standard marinera pattern by half a measure) and serves as the link between the landó and the marinera in Nicomedes Santa Cruz' theory of origins, its reintroduction brings the landó forward from Africa and the Black Atlantic to the domain of música criolla. Whether these similarities are intentional, subliminal, or purely accidental, they provide further evidence that the landó's rhythmic personality continued to be "remembered" in new ways that evoked Afro-Peruvian double consciousness (in other words, both Black Atlantic and criollo ways of hearing and feeling music) throughout the revival.

The most obvious Africanism in the re-creation of "Samba malató" was a stretch of artistic license that Nicomedes Santa Cruz came to regret. When he recorded "Samba malató" on *Cumanana*, Nicomedes expanded upon the remembered fragment with a new verse that included what he later called "arbitrary Afroid wordage" (lyrics that either sounded "African" or were borrowed from other African American musical and religious traditions) (N. Santa Cruz 1970a, 47). The "Afroid" words he added, performed in solo–chorus call-and-response style, are as follows: "Anambucurú, e ioñá, ioñá; a la recolé, uborequeté; babalorishá, e anambucurú; oyo cororó, oyo cororo; anambucurú, e ioñá ioñá; a la recolé, e tiri tiri; babalorichá, e mandé mandé; oyo cororó, oyo cororó; anambucurú . . . landó!" (N. Santa Cruz y su Conjunto Cumanana [1964] 1970).[23] Some of these words are, or resemble, names of people and places in Africa (for example, "Oyo" was a kingdom in Yorubaland and "Mande" is a West African ethnic group descended from the kingdom of Mali), some are Spanish or Portuguese adaptations of Yoruba words (for example, "babalorichá"), whereas others are of unknown origin.

Perhaps Nicomedes' 1963 trip to Brazil and his introduction to Afro-Brazilian Candomblé influenced him to "fill in the gaps" in his reinvention of lost Afro-Peruvian songs and musical traditions, hoping to make them sound even more "African," just as he used bits and pieces of Brazilian and Cuban research to help put together his theory of the African lundú. It is also possible that Nicomedes' added verse reflected his engagement with the inventive strategies of other negritud(e) poets, whose creation of Africanist idiophonic words became what Josaphat Kubayanda calls a type of "drum poetics," with "a distinctive poetic and grammatical logic" that "projects the drum as a principal paragon for poetic expression" (Kubayanda 1982, 37, 47). In particular, Cuba's negritud poet Nicolás Guillén—whom Nicomedes greatly admired and emulated (see Handy 1979, 154)—used onomatopoeic syllables to evoke Afro-Cuban culture and drum rhythms (Moore 1997, 212).

Whatever his motives were, in the third edition of *Cumanana*, Nicomedes publicly repented for his invention of pseudo-African terminology. He transcribed only the lyrics of the original fragment in the newly reprinted liner notes, stating that only that verse was "authentically folkloric" and admonishing other recording artists to banish the contrived verse from the repertoire. "I hope," he wrote, "that the mistake of adding verses is not committed with new recompilations, an indiscretion for which I do not forgive myself" (N. Santa Cruz 1970a, 47).

Nicomedes' change of heart came too late. Ironically, despite his written apology and warning, the LP recordings released with the third edition of *Cumanana* replay the exact sound recording of the original 1964 version, invented lyrics and all (as does the 1994 CD edition). Decades later, unaware of (or unconcerned with) Santa Cruz' plea, other groups continue to perform and record the song—which has become an Afro-Peruvian standard—with its invented pseudo-African lyrics, perhaps believing that the words are a survival of the language of their African ancestors in Peru.

Michel Foucault writes that "history teaches how to laugh at the solemnities of the origin" (1977, 143), questioning societal reification of an imaginary moment of original purity "before the Fall." Yet, whether or not such moments of origin ever existed, their invention in cultural belief systems mobilizes real ideas about identity and ancestry. Although the recent reinvention of the festejo and landó makes them "very modern traditions" (Waterman 1990), they have come to represent a centuries-old essence of Black Peru for performers and audiences. Ironically, for many listeners, the lyrics of the recently composed pseudo-African verse especially mark "Samba malató" as an inherited legacy of African heritage in Peru. Thus, like the Pancho Fierro company's re-creation of el son de los diablos, Cumanana's recording of "Samba malató" became a new "original"—a monument to Nicomedes' Black Atlantic excavations and a site of memory in his reproduction of the Afro-Peruvian past.

Moving Forward and Looking Back

After Nicomedes Santa Cruz' early work with the Cumanana company, both he and the Afro-Peruvian revival moved in new directions. In 1967,

Nicomedes was invited to Cuba to perform for a group of almost 2,000 delegates at an international conference on protest music sponsored by Casa de las Américas. Participants from eighteen countries performed in theaters, open-air venues, factories, schools, and on the radio and television. In the evenings, there were impromptu musical exchanges of British ballads, Italian protest songs, songs expressing solidarity with South Vietnam, and Latin American *nueva canción* (Ossorio 1967, 139–141).

Nicomedes' experience in Cuba made him want to march back to Peru to work toward revolution and racial equality in his own country. Upon his return, Nicomedes performed his poetry before indigenous audiences in the Peruvian highland city of Cuzco for the first time, initiating what Martha Ojeda calls his "integrationist period" (Ojeda 2003, 22–28), during which he produced poems expressing solidarity with indigenous Peruvians and other oppressed peoples of Latin America. Although he embraced the goals of the international Black community, Nicomedes' deepest personal commitment was now to the cause of Peruvian integration and equality. He explained this double consciousness in an interview: "Being Black is, at times, admitting a type of diaspora, a universality of blackness. But at the same time you feel that this land where you were born is your homeland, that you did not come here by your own will, but that all the richness of this people was won with your sweat . . . for others. Well then, fighting for a national integration and fighting against those who do not want it forces me toward the reality of the universal Black, linking me with my brothers from Africa and the United States, but without losing sight of my reality as a Peruvian committed to the cause of his people" (qtd. in Lewis 1983, 79).

A few months after Nicomedes returned from Cuba, he married Mercedes Castillo González in Spain. The newlyweds returned to Peru shortly after General Juan Velasco Alvarado's military revolution took power in 1968. Although Velasco's takeover seemed to Nicomedes to be a military action without the support of the people (qtd. in Mariñez 1993, 123), he worked for Velasco, performing throughout Latin America.[24] The nationalist government's emphasis on promoting Peruvian music over the airwaves helped Nicomedes establish two radio programs: "Así canta mi Perú" (My Peru sings like this) and "América canta así" (America sings like this). Nicomedes supported the Velasco government's campaign to end the dominance of U.S. music and cultural imperialism on the Peruvian radio, hoping that Peru would at last undergo a cultural revolution.

However, by the mid-1970s, both the Afro-Peruvian revival and the military revolution proved bitter disappointments for Nicomedes Santa Cruz. After the publication of *Cumanana*, the folklore that Nicomedes had constructed as a documentary of the forgotten past was transformed into a living theatrical spectacle. Revived genres such as the landó and festejo were performed in folklore shows that horrified Nicomedes with what he perceived as Africanized commercialism. In the third edition of *Cumanana*, he wrote: "In 1965, conscious of the extinction of black folklore, we believed that we left a testimonial to a dignified death in *Cumanana*. But soon, the nocturnal market of Afro-Peruvian 'shows' proliferated . . . with exotic effects . . . What we believed was a dignified death has become indecent agony . . . *Cumanana* did not anticipate such grave problems . . . and couldn't stop the process . . ." (N. Santa Cruz 1970a, 11). Like Dr. Frankenstein, Nicomedes had given life to Black folklore and he could not control its manipulation by Black Peruvian artists, the culture industry, the military government, or the upper class Limeños and tourists who formed its audience. In 1971, he and Victoria helped mount the first Festival of Black Arts in rural Cañete; the next year Nicomedes is said to have written a newspaper article about the festival with the title: "My God, I have Created a Monster!" (R. Santa Cruz 2000b).

In his recording projects during the 1970s, Nicomedes tried to regain control over the presentation of Black folklore and combat its commercialization. His double LP *Socabón* (N. Santa Cruz y su Conjunto Cumanana 1975) is a kind of audio textbook of Afro-Peruvian folklore, with brief examples of the correct way to play the major instruments associated with Afro-Peruvian music, re-elaboration of the theories first voiced in *Cumanana*, and a heavy emphasis on the criollo marinera to contrast the Africanized re-creations of festejos and landós. Similarly, his compilation LP *Los reyes del festejo* (The festejo kings), dedicated to Porfirio Vásquez, who died during the recording process, redefined a canon of "authentic" folklore. The record contains selections by the "authentic" folklore groups that had spun off from the Pancho Fierro company: Gente Morena, Cumanana, and the Vásquez family. Nicomedes wrote on the album's back cover:

> This album has been conceived and structured to be useful to all the educational centers where our folklore is practiced. Peru is living a renaissance of Black music and dance . . . a universal movement with its origins in the recent independence of African countries and the struggle that Africa and Afroamerica preserve against neocolonialism and racial discrimination. But in this Afro-Peruvian renaissance, serious (or at least sincere) innovations and stylizations are performed alongside hoaxes, base plagiarism, and aberrations of groups prostituted by alienating commercialization, led subtly by the dominant class, whose ethnocentrism will never allow them to give up the hegemony of popular Peruvian culture. We also think this work will give pause to those musicians who for two decades have tried to internationalize the festejo, a dance representing Black Peruvian mestizaje. And we think so highly of this record

because its authenticity and purity—we don't use a single foreign element—are the primary materials for any serious musical and choreographic attempt. (N. Santa Cruz 1971b)

By 1973, perhaps sobered by the commercialization of Black folklore, Nicomedes demonstrated new caution about publicly theorizing African "survivals" in Peru. On the occasion of the National Dance Company of Senegal's debut in Lima, the editors of *Caretas* magazine asked Nicomedes to write an article "summarizing his impressions of the show, the possible Senegalese origin of some Blacks during the three centuries of slave traffic, and the ethnic and cultural survivals that might have remained" (N. Santa Cruz 1973, 22). Beginning with the disclaimer that proper research on the specific origins of Africans brought to Peru during times of slavery had yet to be conducted, Nicomedes added that it was impossible to draw conclusions about Black Peruvians' possible Senegalese heritage based on a theatrical performance from contemporary Senegal. This conclusion is striking, first because Nicomedes devoted the 1960s to creating music and dance that he described as an authentic representation of the unwritten history of Black Peru, and second because he supported his theories about the African origins of Peruvian dances with knowledge gained from the staged presentation of the Katherine Dunham Company in Lima in 1951.

He wrote: "We don't believe that the circumstances of . . . a theatrical function allow us to arrive at a series of conclusions about the possible affinities that might exist between our Blacks and those of Senegal. One, because notwithstanding the quality of the company and the authenticity of some dances, it is still a theatrical spectacle where concessions have been made to satisfy the public, including perhaps some drums that aren't strictly from the region or some dances in whose choreography 'the hand of the White man' is seen. Two, because the same thing has happened with our Black-influenced folklore since 1956, when it was brought to the stage for the first time as a theatrical spectacle (*Estampas de Pancho Fierro*). Since then, there has been a movement back to the origins of the loincloth and the drum with the retreat from the authentic folkloric heritage to the 'show' of TV and criollo restaurants" (N. Santa Cruz 1973, 22). Nicomedes admitted to similarities between the Peruvian festejo and certain rhythms performed by the Senegalese company, and he noted that the physicality of some Senegalese artists corresponded to the body types of some Black Peruvians. But he cautioned his readers that contemporary Senegal, like Peru, was a melting pot of races and cultures. To draw conclusions about the past based on theatrical performances in the present would be foolhardy.

In 1974, Nicomedes traveled to Dakar, Senegal, where he was invited to participate as a speaker at an international colloquium on negritude in

Latin America.[25] There, Nicomedes presented his lundú theory of the African origins of the marinera (N. Santa Cruz 1978). In his address, he stressed the importance of evaluating the influence of Africa on the formation of Peruvian culture, striving to answer the vital question "Who are we?" an endeavor far more complicated than filling notebooks with speculations about African survivals.

Pablo Mariñez joined Nicomedes on the trip to Africa, and he later recalled an experience in the streets of Dakar that made both men aware of the ocean of cultural difference separating Africans from African Americans. He wrote: "In a regular neighborhood, we came upon a group of young men and women heating up the drums and making a circle while they sang, laughed, and clapped their hands with a type of little drums, and one of them threw himself into the circle to dance. To us, this was a whole show. We had the satisfaction of knowing that it was not prepared for tourism, but rather a form of the people's popular recreation. After over a half hour of dancing, I was stupefied when Nicomedes threw himself into the ring, performing the steps he had carefully observed. We believed that we could go unnoticed, as just one more in the group. It was later that we realized that there, in the group of dancers, everyone knew perfectly well that we were foreigners, visitors, and they could not confuse us with the native inhabitants of Senegal. We suffered tremendous disillusionment" (Mariñez 2000, 27).

When Nicomedes returned from Africa to Peru, it was apparent to him that "even the revolutionaries no longer believed in their revolution" (qtd. in Mariñez 1993, 123). Recognizing that he was more appreciated abroad than at home, he began increasingly to travel internationally for professional engagements. With Velasco's departure in 1975 and the emergence of a new vanguard of intellectual poets, Nicomedes produced very little poetry or music, taking refuge in his radio and television programs. Once hailed as a great leader and artist, Nicomedes found himself without an audience in his home country. Even worse, as he confided in an interview, he had become the subject of ridicule: "Teenagers, 14 to 17 years old, who had respected me, made fun of me in the streets. It was the opposite of how even the trolleys of this era stopped so I could cross the rails, and if I came into a café to buy cigarettes the people started spontaneously to applaud me . . . And the cry that they direct at all the Blacks: 'Uh, uh, uh,' imitating my voice and everything, but in the streets and plazas, with humiliation and cruel ridicule. It is then that I realize that all is lost" (qtd. in Mariñez 1993, 124).

Alienated from his true native land, Nicomedes left Peru for good in 1980, settling in his wife's Spain. In Madrid, he began to work actively again. He hosted radio programs on Latin American music and worked as a journalist for Spain's Radio Exterior; gave invited public seminars and addresses; published journal articles on slavery and racism in Iberoamerica; traveled to Mexico, Guinea, the Dominican Republic, Peru, Brazil, and Cuba to participate in conferences and give lectures; participated in the compilation of a recording series on Spanish folk songs; and completed and published his book on the Peruvian décima (N. Santa Cruz 1982). In 1986, Nicomedes was awarded the IV International "Spain" Radio Broadcasting Prize, and, in 1990, the Peruvian Embassy in Spain bestowed upon Nicomedes a special award for distinguished services ("Nicomedes Santa Cruz Gamarra" n.d., 1).

Nicomedes' Spanish radio broadcasts and epic book on the Peruvian décima reveal how, in his final years, he moved beyond his Peruvian reputation as a staunch Africanist and promoter of Peruvian folklore.[26] He emerges as a thoughtful, mature, and vastly knowledgeable lay-ethnomusicologist, with a passionate interest in diverse musical and poetic styles of the Americas. His radio programs are peppered with rare recordings, references to scholarly works, historical tidbits, and perceptive insights and opinions. His program on Spanish-American song, in particular, reveals that Nicomedes was as interested in the European origins of his own music as he was in its African roots, and that, for him, African and Spanish cultures were inseparably intertwined long before slavery in the New World.[27] In this respect, he projected a more nuanced understanding of Peruvian music's multicultural origins than did many trained scholars who were strict Europeanists or Africanists.

On February 5, 1992, Nicomedes Santa Cruz died of lung cancer in Madrid. His widow donated his personal collection of books, articles, manuscripts, and sound recordings to the archive of Casa de América. There, a display case in the back room features photos of Nicomedes and several of his LPs, and the archive's music collection is named after him. On March 29, 2000, Radio Nacional de España opened a Radio Study Room at Casa de América in Nicomedes Santa Cruz' name. Yet, in an address to the Peruvian Congress that same year, Nicomedes' nephew Rafael mourned, "Nicomedes Santa Cruz is the most important popular poet and . . . the most important Black person of this century in Peru . . . Nicomedes has a music archive that bears his name in Madrid, he is the favorite son of the city of Bahia in Brazil, he is remembered in Argentina and loved and studied in Cuba, he is a distinguished member of the Academy Our Lady of Africa, at one time an agent of an African State wanted to name him Minister of Education of his country, and here in his land there is not even a plaza in his name" (R. Santa Cruz 2000a, 182–183). Later that year, at long last, the outdoor amphitheater of the newly renovated Gran Parque in downtown Lima was named after Nicomedes Santa Cruz.

Travel Diaries, Lima, 2000: National Library of Peru

I am in the basement of the National Library of Peru, and my hands are covered with black ink. There are little scraps of paper all over the desk where I am reading. My research materials are disintegrating as I touch them. I feel guilty every time I turn a decrepit page.

I have come to Lima secretly, not calling any of my friends or consultants. I am here for a short time, to fill gaps in my research on the 1950s and 1960s. In the National Library, I find a treasure trove of old newspapers from the era, and I turn the pages, looking for clues.

I find out that Nicomedes Santa Cruz was a far more prolific journalist than I had realized. I am reading through his weekly newspaper columns, which treat topics from racism and folklore to the theme of death in Latin American poetry and song. Looking up, I notice that Nicomedes' nephew, Octavio Santa Cruz, is sitting at a table nearby, quietly conducting his own research. Having met Octavio a year ago at a public lecture, I reintroduce myself, and he invites me to a poetry event at his private peña. After he leaves, I smile to myself, thinking how serendipitous it is that, in an enormous city like Lima where Blacks are supposedly "invisible," I should run into a relative of Nicomedes Santa Cruz while I am reading his newspaper columns.

As I turn pages of old newspapers, my attention is drawn by events that scream out of headlines between Nicomedes' columns and mentions of José Durand: the Cuban revolution and subsequent disappearance of Che Guevara, the Yom Kippur War, the assassination of Dr. Martin Luther King. Outside the solid metal door of the National Library, protesters march daily, calling for the resignation of Peru's President Alberto Fujimori. Nicknamed El Chino (the Chinaman), Fujimori (a Japanese Peruvian) initially was welcomed by Peru's mestizo majority as a departure from the long line of White criollos (and mestizos who "passed" as Whites) who had served the interests of either the oligarchy or the military.[28] A political unknown, Fujimori's surprising defeat of White criollo novelist Mario Vargas Llosa proclaimed the power of the popular mestizo vote. Fujimori promoted his allegiance to the Peruvian masses by wearing a traditional indigenous-style poncho for public appearances.

The Peru inherited by Fujimori was ravaged by terrorism and economic chaos. He soon developed a reputation for using strong-armed tactics to save Peru from terrorists, largely through the capture of the leader of the Sendero Luminoso (Shining Path) terrorist group in 1992 and his attack on the MRTA group that held hundreds of diplomats and government officials hostage at the home of the Japanese ambassador to Peru in 1997. In what was called the "auto-coup," Fujimori rewrote the national constitution in 1992, dissolving Congress and lengthening the possible presidential reign to two terms, supposedly to *abolish corruption and reconstruct democracy. When he manipulated Peruvian law to enable himself to campaign for yet a third term in 1998, Peruvians became uneasy about his dictatorial tendencies.*[29]

Race and ethnic origin again come into play in the ill-fated elections of 2000 that form the backdrop of my archival research trip. Alejandro Toledo, a Harvard-educated mestizo, challenges Fujimori's dictatorial policies and foreign interests, and he campaigns strongly to the indigenous and mestizo populace on the basis that he is one of them. A commonly shouted campaign slogan demonstrates the racialization of the Peruvian election of 2000: "El Cholo Sí, El Chino No!"[30]

Tear gas usually disperses the anti-Fujimori crowd outside the library toward the end of each day, filling the streets with throat-stinging smoke. I am overwhelmed by my own immersion in history at a moment so very present in Peru's volatile political life. Did Nicomedes Santa Cruz' life's work make any difference in today's racial politics?

Travel Diaries, Madrid, 2000: Casa de América

When I walk into the research library at Madrid's Latin American cultural center, Casa de América, I want to cry. Nicomedes Santa Cruz' archive of personal research materials is carefully preserved in an elegant, palatial room. The difference between this facility and the archives and libraries I have visited in Lima embodies the stereotyped difference between Latin America and Europe—poverty versus opulence.

Every day for three weeks, I come here to pore through Nicomedes' books and listen to his recordings. I try to reach his widow and son (who still live in Madrid) by e-mail, but I am unsuccessful. On weekends and evenings, I visit the archive of Spain's National Radio. There, I meet Luís Lecea, who worked with Nicomedes and remembers him well. He regales me with stories of Nicomedes and his LP collection. He tells me how much he learned from Nicomedes, not just about Peruvian and Latin American music but also about Spain's cultural heritage.

I reflect upon this irony: in Peru, Nicomedes Santa Cruz is a national celebrity, but his articles are crumbling in the National Library. Here in Madrid, his possessions are preserved in a mansion with exquisitely carved furniture and art-covered ceilings, yet the only people I have met who know his name are librarians and archivists. In Peru, he is remembered as the revivalist who fought for Peruvian negritud through poetry, music, theater, and journalism. In Spain, his radio programs reveal his knowledge of and interest in so many countries and their musical histories. A devoted student of Africa, Spain, and Peru, Nicomedes left many legacies, some intended and others accidental.

The Unintended Legacy of Nicomedes Santa Cruz

Beyond collections of his work or monuments to his name, Nicomedes Santa Cruz' legacy lives on in contemporary performances of Afro-Peruvian music and ideas about blackness. Ironically, it was Black musical genres such as the landó and the festejo, not his beloved décima, which were reborn as a result of Nicomedes' endeavors. Today, although many Peruvians have an elderly relative who still knows and can recite décimas, decimístas are rarely heard in public venues in Lima.[31] The Afro-Peruvian festejo and landó, on the other hand, are part of virtually every public performance of Afro-Peruvian music, exemplifying Peruvian blackness in the national musical and choreographic vocabulary.

As will become apparent in the next two chapters, Nicomedes and Victoria Santa Cruz' revival of Afro-Peruvian music quickly spun out of their control. Despite their objections, in the 1970s groups like Perú Negro recast the Santa Cruzes' revived artifacts as a newly stylized commercial folklore performed for tourist audiences and on international stages. Increasingly, the landó was reconstructed as supremely sensual and the festejo as explosively happy, promoting stereotypical Black archetypes that were complicit in the essentializing depiction of contemporary Afro-Peruvians—by Blacks and non-Blacks alike—as happy, smiling, and "naturally" sexual. That these stereotypes were unintentionally empowered by the re-creation of African musical heritage echoes one of the most fundamental critiques of both the negritude movement and postcolonialism. Using "the master's tools" (often the only tools available), it may never be possible to shake off entirely the effects of colonization and reinscribe precolonial histories.

Yet, Nicomedes' purpose in reconstructing the landó and festejo was to restore dignity and pride to Black Peruvians by recovering their cultural history—even if that meant excavating African heritage in the Black Atlantic and the writings of biased chroniclers. A close look at the early revival of the landó and the festejo has revealed that what Nicomedes and Victoria created, through his research and her ancestral memories, were vibrant, interesting, and uniquely *Peruvian* sounds and gestures. And, as their nephew, Rafael Santa Cruz, reminded me after reading an earlier version of this book, "the legacy of the Santa Cruzes goes beyond a poem or a choreography; their great contribution is to allow an entire group of human beings the possibility of speaking out loud and feeling that they are equal to any other individuals . . . The Santa Cruzes, through these disciplines [dance, theater, and music], sought to help improve the way of life, in every sense, of the people who worked with them."[32] Thus, while competing memory projects have cast the Santa Cruzes and the folklore groups that succeeded them as rivals in the reproduction of the past, Nicomedes and Victoria Santa Cruz unquestionably opened the door to that past, forging the raw materials that would be stylized in the second phase of the revival.

CHAPTER 4

Perú Negro and the Canonization
of Black Folklore

I have been in Peru on an exploratory research trip for a week and I have yet to see Afro-Peruvian music and dance performed live. Tonight I will see Peru's pre-eminent Black folklore group, Perú Negro, at Manos Morenas restaurant and peña (nightclub). I have heard Perú Negro's recordings, but I have never seen the dancing that accompanies the music.

I arrive around 9:45 PM for a 10 o'clock show. Hardly anyone is there. I have not yet learned the concept of "Peruvian time," whereby many performances begin up to two hours late. The man at the door, dressed to the nines, asks how many in my party. When I tell him only one, he smiles disapprovingly. "I don't believe it," he teases. He leads me to a bright room where tables are set for groups of two to twenty. Discreetly, he seats me at the smallest table near the back of the room.

I order a pisco sour (a Peruvian alcoholic beverage made with frothy egg whites) and look around as the room begins to fill. Groups of people are seated at tables, laughing and chatting in various European languages. Alone, I feel self-conscious, so I take out my notebook and busy myself with note-taking. Finally, the lights dim and the show begins.

It is Perú Negro's Thirtieth Anniversary season. A White woman in a long, multi-tiered white dress announces each dance, explaining its historical signifi-cance in times of slavery. As I watch smiling Black dancers, costumed as slaves and servants, entertain a roomful of White tourists, I am reminded at times of a minstrel show. This is not what I was expecting. The dancing bodies, tourist spectators, and poor acoustics alter my previous experience of the music, formed from recordings alone. Obviously I will have to approach understanding this music in a new way that encompasses what I see as well as what I hear. But I want "thicker descriptions" (Geertz 1973) than those offered by the woman in the

FIGURE 4.1. Perú Negro dancers. Pictured (left to right): Fiorella Ayala, Percy Chinchilla, Olga Gallardo, José Durand. *From the private collection of Perú Negro, reprinted with permission.*

white dress. Where did this canon of Black folklore come from, and what does it mean to the dancers of Perú Negro and their local audience?

Folklore and the Peruvian Revolution

Ask most Peruvians about Black Peruvian music, and soon they will name Perú Negro, the only Afro-Peruvian music and dance company with a continuous history of more than thirty years of performance. Perú Negro is an institution in Peru, and membership has long been a goal and success marker for young Blacks. For many years, as former Perú Negro member Juan Carlos "Juanchi" Vásquez explains, "Perú Negro was Perú Negro, period. There was nobody else . . . That is, for Lima's Black families, in order for their children to be successful on a professional level, either they had to play for Alianza Lima, play for the Peruvian Association, or be in Perú Negro . . . Play ball or dance in Perú Negro. That was it" (J. Vásquez 2000).

How did this company earn such prestige? The rise of Perú Negro is linked to the Peruvian government's elevation of folkloric arts as emblems of the nation's identity in the 1970s. Working with the raw materials forged in the first stage of the revival, Perú Negro continued to redefine Black identity in Peru through a process of stylization and canonization enabled by its collaboration with White intellectuals and the new nationalist government.

The birth of Perú Negro coincided with the dramatic political and cultural change that swept the country as a result of General Juan Velasco Alvarado's military revolution, which had overthrown the previous government in 1968. Velasco initiated a dramatic agrarian reform program, seizing large estates and plantations that exploited indigenous labor and converting them into cooperative developments; he officially declared the word *indio* (Indian) racist and replaced it with *campesino* (peasant); and he passed legislation making Quechua (one of the two primary indigenous languages spoken in Peru) an official national language and a mandatory part of university curriculum. In an effort to counter U.S. cultural imperialism, locally produced music and cultural arts were embraced as national folkloric treasures that should be preserved, researched, and performed. Velasco imposed quotas increasing the diffusion of Peruvian music (and decreasing popular U.S. and European music) on radio stations. Live performances of national music also were cultivated through folklore schools, competitions, and government-supported performances for tourists and foreign dignitaries. Although Andean music received most of the government support, Afro-Peruvian music also benefited. In addition to funding and nurturing the *casas de cultura* (cultural centers) and folklore academies (as well as the Conjunto Nacional de Folklore directed by Victoria Santa Cruz), the Velasco government actively financed and guided the early developmental period of Perú Negro. Thus, State patronage was a deciding factor in Perú Negro's early formation and the nationalist character of its folklore.

In the 1970s, the Velasco government provided a steady flow of work for Perú Negro through folklore shows for foreign visitors (Lee 2000), and it provided the company members with salaried positions teaching Afro-Peruvian music and dance classes (Izquierdo 2000).[1] Perú Negro became a professional, staged demonstration of Peruvian culture that Velasco could tap as a showcase for foreign audiences or nationalist causes. Peruvian guitarist Félix Casaverde recalls working with Perú Negro in 1975 in a series of events sponsored by the Velasco regime in which the company performed songs by Peruvian poets about national heroes (Casaverde 2000b). Similarly, Leslie Lee, a visual artist who worked with Perú Negro as lighting designer and general manager in the early 1970s, remembers that, at a performance for the Lima meeting of the Congress of Unaligned Countries in 1972, Perú Negro performed the rousing finale, dancing a zamacueca with red and white handkerchiefs to symbolize the colors of the Peruvian flag (Lee 2000).

During the Velasco years, Perú Negro also benefited from the financial backing and guidance of Luis Banchero Rossi, a philanthropist who made a fast fortune exporting fish meal to Europe. In the early 1970s, Banchero connected Perú Negro with artists, poets, and scholars. He set up meetings with historians so that the company members could learn about their own culture from non-Black scholars who had studied it. Perú Negro founder Orlando "Lalo" Izquierdo recalls, "We would sit and converse and he would tell us, 'Okay, I am giving you a rocket, so that you can take off and be the pilot of your own plane, following your own path. If the rocket crashes, it is because of bad piloting!'" (Izquierdo 2000).

In 1972, Banchero was murdered mysteriously in his home. Banchero's death was a tragic blow for Perú Negro; never again would the company have the luxury and security of that level of financial support and guidance. However, Perú Negro continued to prosper throughout the revolutionary era of the 1970s, aided not only by Velasco's support but also by the managerial guidance and artistic contributions of numerous White criollo intellectuals and artists loosely affiliated with Banchero or the Velasco government.

I have noted in previous chapters that the music and dances revived by José Durand and the Santa Cruzes were described as Black Peruvian "folklore," and that Victoria Santa Cruz was employed by the military government to direct the Conjunto Nacional de Folklore. At this juncture, in order to understand how Perú Negro and the Velasco government canonized Afro-Peruvian folklore as a facet of national identity in the 1970s, some background on the concept of "folklore"—both its European origins and its Latin American/Peruvian usage—is needed.

The European genesis of the concept of folklore is deeply rooted in the "us-and-them" binaries of modernity. Coined by W. J. Thoms in an 1846 letter to the British journal *The Athanaeum*, the term "folklore" initially described popular cultural traditions perceived to be disappearing due to European industrialization. The prefix "folk" implied both "the people" and "the nation." It was related to the German term *volkgeist*—linked with the Romantic response to the Enlightenment—which described organic culture, expressed through the songs, customs, rituals, and stories of the people (Rowe and Schelling 1991, 4).

In many Latin American countries, the English word "folklore" has been adopted into the vernacular, sometimes with spelling modifications (folklor, folclor, foklor). As William Rowe and Vivian Schelling explain (1991, 4), cultures designated "folkloric" by Latin American governments and elites are often autonomous subcultures that present potential challenges to the authority of a politically defined State. Modernizing Latin American nations discovered in the twentieth century that the promotion (and recontextualization) of national folklore was a means to integrate and dominate their ethnically and racially "different" rural populations.

However, the word "folklore" can have more than one connotation—ranging from paternalistic decontextualization to authentic cultural expression—depending on whether it is used by the government, elites, or members of "folk" cultures. Peruvian governments and elites have sought, at various times, to domesticate alternative voices within the nation by reconfiguring their traditions as folklore. For example, in the early-twentieth-century indigenismo movement, urban mestizo artists and intellectuals worked to document, preserve, and disseminate the cultural practices of Peru's indigenous peoples, but the paternalistic nature of their efforts resulted in the presentation of indigenous folklore as a premodern extension of the romanticized Inca past (see Mendoza 2000, 52–53; Poole 1997, 182–185). Similarly, during the 1950s, White criollos celebrated only those Black Peruvian traditions constructed as folkloric performances of the colonial past and times of slavery (see chapter 1). In such movements, as Néstor García Canclini writes, those who seek to recover the premodern past turn a blind eye to the transformative effects of modernity on the cultures they view as "folkloric." As a result, "the people are 'rescued,' but not known" (García Canclini 1995, 149).

However, as Zoila Mendoza observes (2000), Peruvian "folk" also use the word "folklore" to describe their cultural expressions. Mendoza, who studied ritual dance performance in the Cuzco region, writes that she initially was surprised when locals described their performances and *fiestas* as "folklore." Before her experience in Cuzco, Mendoza understood "folklore" only as the process whereby national and regional elites stylized and decontextualized local arts, converting them into emblems of identity that promote negative stereotypes. In fact, her first thought was that local performers used the word "folklore" to simplify their explanations for her benefit. "However," Mendoza writes, "I overlooked that, as part of this process, the performers of Andean expressive forms had gained new spaces and recognition for their creative efforts. In a seeming contradiction, the folklorization had provided them the means to rework and contest social values and stereotypes promoted by such elites" (2000, 237–238).

Similarly, in the Afro-Peruvian revival, the concept of "folklore" slowly shifted from criollo paternalism to popular revalorization and finally to a mixture of the two. José Durand's criollo nostalgia project staged and recontextualized as folklore the Black traditions of the colonial era, which were configured as premodern ingredients of criollo culture. Later, Nicomedes and Victoria Santa Cruz used the word "folklore" to refer to the cultural expressions they had revived. In an editorial for the government magazine *Folklore*, Victoria Santa Cruz discussed the term's double meaning and argued for a national reconceptualization of "folklore" informed by greater appreciation of so-called "folkloric cultures" (1979b). Similarly, in an interview with Elena Poniatowska, Nicomedes Santa Cruz proclaimed, "We no longer accept that the word 'folklore' has this discriminatory, pejorative sense given to it by Western culture. Rather, we are revalorizing the folkloric and the popular as our maximum exposition of culture that is not inferior but different from Western culture, and we are filling it with a message with respect to our revolutionary historical process." When Poniatowska suggested that "all the underdeveloped countries cultivate folklore for the consumption of tourists, and this is in a certain way a form of slavery, of servitude for the powerful," Nicomedes responded "That is nonsense created by imperialism to confuse us!" (qtd. in Poniatowska 1974, 40).

As Jonathan Ritter observes in his study of the Afro-Ecuadorian *marimba* (1998), such seemingly polarized interpretations of folklore (State domination versus local resistance) may coexist in the "contact zones" (Pratt 1992) of tourist shows and folkloric performances. In fact, Perú Negro navigated between both connotations of folklore. On the one hand, the company became what Poniatowska might call a servant of the military revolution's nationalist folklore project and a staged attraction for tourist audiences. On the other hand, the leaders of Perú Negro used the government's resources and the new visibility of Afro-Peruvian performance to continue the Afro-Peruvian revival's re-creation and celebration of what they proudly called "folklore," permanently inscribing a canon of Afro-Peruvian music and dances in the nation's cultural repertoire. Thus, the same performances by Perú Negro may be analyzed as examples of State-driven co-optation or of transnational Afro-Peruvian identity formation. As this chapter will demonstrate, the songs and dances choreographed and stylized by Perú Negro similarly open themselves to multiple readings, a nuance not always apparent at first glance to outsiders such as myself.

In her study of the staging of Cuban religious traditions by the Conjunto Folklorico Nacional de Cuba, ethnomusicologist Katherine Hagedorn uses the term "folkloricization" to describe the process of "making a folk tradition 'folkloric'" (Hagedorn 1995, 10; 2001, 12). She writes, "'folkloric' in this case is not simply an adjectival form of folklore, but implies a highly secularized and often commodified, staged, outward-directed version of a tradition that originates in sacred, noncommercial, nonstaged, inward-directed performance" (Hagedorn 1995, 10). "Folkloricization" is a useful way to conceptualize Perú Negro's staging of folklore in the second phase of the Afro-Peruvian revival. While

Hagedorn's usage of the term highlights the difference between staged (secular) and community-based (religious) performance, I think of Perú Negro as having "folkloricized" (through further stylization and refinement) the "folklore" that was initially re-created and staged by José Durand and the Santa Cruzes, thus marking the second phase of the Afro-Peruvian revival.

Offering yet another level to this analysis of staged folklore in the Afro-Peruvian revival, former Perú Negro guitarist Félix Casaverde uses the term "neo-folklore" to question the authenticity of Afro-Peruvian music's origin myths. He points, for example, to the erroneous belief that certain recently invented songs and dances of the revival (such as "Samba malató") are of "ancient" or African origin due to their re-created African-sounding lyrics or Africanist choreographies (Casaverde 2000a). As this chapter will reveal, Perú Negro's stylization and canonization of genres re-created in the revival contributed greatly to this aura of African-ness and to the naturalization of socially constructed performances of Black identity. By the 1970s, the Afro-Peruvian past that had been re-created based on José Durand's criollo nostalgia, Nicomedes Santa Cruz' Black Atlantic models, and Victoria Santa Cruz' ancestral memory was *neo-folkloricized* (to combine Hagedorn's and Casaverde's terms) as if it had been a continuous heritage from Africa, and it was celebrated (and supported by the government) as Peruvian folklore.

The government-sponsored memory project of folklore provided employment and acclaim for the performers of Perú Negro, but it also framed their performances as premodern "local color" in order to counteract the popularity of foreign (especially U.S.) music and dance styles. This prescribed space for the performance of blackness confined Perú Negro to folkloric reenactments of the past, inhibiting the development of contemporary Black culture. Thus, Perú Negro's containment within the nationalist folkloric vision resulted in an ambiguous relationship between their performance of music and dances from times of slavery and their lived experience of criollo/mestizo modernity. This ambiguity (or double consciousness) expressed itself in the simultaneously re-Africanized and criollo "Perú Negro sound" and in the company's choreographies.

How was Perú Negro selected as the vehicle for the State-sponsored process of folkloricization? What factors molded the group's re-Africanized—yet still criollo—performances of Black Peruvian identity? How did Perú Negro earn the ability to dictate a folkloric canon of Afro-Peruvian repertoire and style? Why, more than thirty years later, is Perú Negro the only group still surviving from the period of the revival? As this chapter chronicles, the company's relatively inauspicious origins could not have predicted such a prestigious future.

The Origins of Perú Negro: "The Land Became Ours"

On February 26, 1969, four young men who were members of Victoria Santa Cruz' Teatro y Danzas Negras del Perú formed their own music and dance group. The project was the brainchild of Ronaldo Campos, who worked as a cajonero with a música criolla group in El Chalán restaurant (one of Lima's many culinary establishments featuring typical coastal Peruvian cuisine prepared for tourists by Black female cooks), and the other three founding members were Orlando "Lalo" Izquierdo, Victor "Raúl" Padilla, and Rodolfo Arteaga.[2] At the urging of El Chalán's owner, Campos spiced up the restaurant's musical offerings with a "typical" Black music and dance show by the new group he called Perú Negro. Victoria Santa Cruz criticized her young protégés for exoticizing their blackness for tourists, but one of the founding members pointed out to me that this was a much-needed opportunity to earn an income (Padilla 1999). In Victoria's group, he explained, performance was a labor of love, with only minor monetary compensation.

Only a few months after Perú Negro was founded, the company won first place at the 1969 Hispanoamerican Festival of Song and Dance at Luna Park in Buenos Aires, Argentina. Overnight, the international acclaim and grand prize of $10,000 (a considerable sum in 1969) transformed Perú Negro and its Afro-Peruvian folklore into a national treasure in Peru. At the Argentina festival, Perú Negro performed a show titled *La tierra se hizo nuestra* (The land became ours), which included many pieces that became part of the canon of folkloric repertoire. Although no video documentation of the original Argentina performance is publicly available, I have partially reconstructed the scope and feel of the performance from a combination of interviews with Perú Negro founder/choreographer Lalo Izquierdo (2000), a review of the Argentina performance in *Caretas* (Enrique Gibson 1969), a printed program from a later performance of the same show (Calvo n.d. [1970s] a), and a video of a command performance of the show performed twenty-four years later (Perú Negro 1993).

La tierra se hizo nuestra demonstrated how Perú Negro navigated between local Peruvian and transnational African diasporic identity in its folklore. As Perú Negro founder Lalo Izquierdo explains, "The show was called *La tierra se hizo nuestra* because when the African arrived [in Peru], he slowly detached himself from Africa. And the children of the Africans were born in this land, so it is their land too. The message of the program is this: 'the land became ours.' That is, the African arrived from afar, but he made the land of his children his own land" (Izquierdo 2000).

FIGURE 4.2. Program cover, 1970s Perú Negro show *La tierra se hizo nuestra. From the collection of Caitro Soto and Teresa Mendoza Hernández, reprinted with permission.*

On October 13, 1969, Perú Negro took the stage at Luna Park in Buenos Aires. Over the P.A. system, the male voice of an unseen narrator (White Peruvian poet César Calvo) introduced the group to 20,000 audience members:

> We come from Peru. Our country, however, has no limits, no borders. Our blood is Africa. Our language, dance. We come to tell you our history: chains, blood, and wind. We will begin with an African dance, which the first fathers danced in the first land, outside, free . . . (qtd. in Enrique Gibson 1969, 36)

This opening dance was called afro, and it was described in *Caretas* as "a frenetic dance." An all-percussion ensemble (cajones, congas, cowbell, and bongó) performed interlocking ostinato patterns. To this accompaniment, six dancers (three male and three female) enacted a choreographed drama, beginning with slow gestures and concluding with vigorous body-shaking encounters. According to *Caretas*, "Rolando Arteaga . . . ended it with erotic and primitive pelvic spasms, entering into a tribal trance" (Enrique Gibson 1969, 36).[3]

Perú Negro founder Lalo Izquierdo, however, clarifies that this dance does not represent trance but rather commemorates degradations endured by Black slaves in Peru. He explains, "The African dance—or descendent of an African dance—that we represent is a dance of procreation. In olden times, in Surco, there was a hacienda owner.[4] This hacienda owner had a Black 'breeder' and made him procreate with the girls to generate his own 'litter.' That is, to conduct business, to raise Blacks to a specified age and sell them, avoiding a series of taxes. Part of the experience of this hacienda has been implanted in this dance. A moment arrives when the male dancer is in the center of the three female dancers, and this is the representation of procreation. That is, the Black 'breeder' who procreates with the maidens, who might be called virgins" (Izquierdo 2000). Such images of Black subordination paradoxically were dignified by the revival work of Perú Negro, because they reinscribed the suppressed history of Black slavery and suffering into Peruvian collective memory.

Next came the Dance of the Machetes. While Eusebio "Pititi" Sirio portrayed a barefoot and shirtless slave cutting a tree down with a machete, César Calvo recited the following poetic text, with the punctuation of the cajón:

> We were ancestors of the baobab and the panther. But suddenly we were others, and another land was ours. We agonized in the plantations, under the painful sun of the land that gave us no shade. We did not even have one name: neither Congo, nor Angola, nor Mandinga, nor Yoruba, nor Carabalí . . . (qtd. in Enrique Gibson 1969, 34)

FIGURE 4.3. *Afro. From the private collection of Perú Negro, reprinted with permission.*

According to Lalo Izquierdo, the ensuing dance illustrated the division among Black slaves that resulted when one was made foreman, ending in a battle with machetes (2000).

Next was a vocal solo by Lucila Campos, the slow lament "Pobre negrito," with its typical *habanera* rhythm. "Poor little Black man," the first verse begins, "how sad he is. He works hard and earns nothin'. Poor little Black man, how sad he is. His owner is gonna beat him."[5] Bold, brassy, and soulful, Lucila Campos' voice epitomizes the Afro-Peruvian sound for many Peruvians. Yet, it was the next lively dance, el alcatraz, that sealed Perú Negro's success. According to *Caretas*, "after 'el alcatraz,' Peru had won the festival. The ovation, number after number, was unanimous and closed. And the attention lent to the history narrated by César Calvo was almost devotional" (Enrique Gibson 1969, 37).

The alcatraz (figure 4.4), revived by Victoria Santa Cruz and popularized by Perú Negro, is a dance said to have been performed by slaves for after-hours recreation. The word alcatraz (pelican) is commonly believed to be a distortion of alcartaz (paper cone). Dancers affix a small paper "tail" to their rear ends. Dancing in male–female couples, each partner tries to burn the other's "tail" with a lit candle, while the other gyrates rapidly so as to avoid being burned. If the man burns the woman's tail, according

FIGURE 4.4. Perú Negro dancers perform the *alcatraz* at the Hispanoamerican Festival in Argentina, 1969. Pictured (left to right): Pilar de La Cruz and Victor Padilla. *Reprinted with permission from* Caretas.

to the game, she belongs to him. The genre is musically characterized by a festejo-like cajón pattern and by lyrics that describe the dance. Typically, in addition to cajón, the musical accompaniment includes two guitars and other percussion such as congas, scrapers, and/or quijada.

After the rousing alcatraz, Lucila Campos returned to belt out a tune that would become a signature classic for Perú Negro: "El payandé."[6] This habanera-style ballad lamenting the bitterness of slavery is generally believed to describe the experience of slaves in Peru. Ironically, "El payandé" was originally composed (with slightly different lyrics) in the nineteenth century, not by Afro-Peruvian slaves or their descendants, but rather by two upper class White criollos (León Quirós 2003, 50–54). "El payandé" was followed by a zapateo (Peruvian-style tap-dance contest). Next came a song genre that recalls the colonial days when the streets of Lima were filled with Black street vendors who sang to advertise their wares—a *pregón* (street cry) called "El tamalero" (The *tamale* vendor).

After the slow pregón, Perú Negro performed a lively festejo, followed by a zamacueca and a related couple dance from the northern coast of Peru, the *tondero*. Finally, *La tierra se hizo nuestra* concluded with another afro, reinforcing the message in Perú Negro's printed program:

> *La tierra se hizo nuestra* tells, through dance, music, and text, the story of Black Peru from slavery to our times. PERÚ NEGRO, the company directed by Ronaldo Campos, interprets "the enchanted dances of Afro-Peruvian folklore" evoking the far off native land and past life among totemic beliefs, founded in centuries of captivity, overwhelming labor, poverty, and hope. Through the voice of the dances, they tell us their message, their outlook as a people, their generous and heroic history, their untiring struggle for liberty.
>
> This is not, then, one more show of dance for dance's sake and music for music's sake. This is a show that comprises the renewing quality of its choreographies, the lilting and surprising rhythm of its dancers, the coherence and rebelliousness of its message. Let us hear it. Because PERÚ NEGRO has come not only to dance and sing, but also to recount for us the moment possibly most stirring and luminous in our history, a moment that continues still, that has never stopped, because liberty—like art—has to shape itself at every moment, has to prevail day after day. (Calvo n.d. [1970s] a)

The Perú Negro Family

The company of young musicians and dancers that won the Grand Prize in Argentina was like a family, and in fact, many of the members were related either by extra-familial ties or by blood. Former manager Leslie Lee described to me some of the ways in which Perú Negro behaved like a family: many of the members lived and rehearsed together in a big housing complex in La Victoria, they jealously guarded songs and cultural traditions only among "family," and they acted as a unit (Lee actually uses the word "tribally") when any member was wronged or hurt. According to Lee, the members of Perú Negro even had their own private language—they spoke Spanish backwards (Lee 2000).

Many artists whose names are household words in Peru today emerged from the first generation of the Perú Negro family, including Ronaldo Campos, Caitro Soto, and Lalo Izquierdo. Brief portraits of these three Afro-Peruvian musicians may help to illustrate the composite personality of the original Perú Negro family.

FIGURE 4.5. Ronaldo Campos de la Colina. *From the private collection of Perú Negro, reprinted with permission.*

Ronaldo Campos de la Colina (1927–2001), director and patriarch of Perú Negro, was born in the southern coastal town of San Luis de Cañete. As a child, he worked the fields, planting rice and picking cotton during school vacations. His father, José Luís Campos, worked as a truck driver at Cañete plantations, and his mother, Lucila de la Colina, was a cook. At the age of fifteen, Ronaldo Campos moved to Lima, where he worked as a textile laborer, a bus driver, and a bricklayer's assistant. He married Bertha Ponce and had four children. In 1956, Campos joined the Pancho Fierro company as a cajonero, and in the 1960s he played cajón and danced in the productions of Nicomedes and Victoria Santa Cruz (Calvo n.d. [1970s] a).

Some say that Ronaldo Campos played cajón and danced zapateo as a child; others say that he learned to dance zapateo in the Pancho Fierro company under the tutelage of Porfirio Vásquez. While some characterize Ronaldo's attitude toward Afro-Peruvian folklore as "conservative," it is generally agreed that he was a gifted cajonero and that his rhythmic innovations are definitive guides for most Afro-Peruvian styles. Campos served as director of Perú Negro from the company's founding until his death in 2001, when the directorship passed to his son, Rony Campos.

Carlos "Caitro" Soto de la Colina (1934–2004) also was born in San Luis de Cañete, and he grew up in a family of seven brothers. Caitro and Ronaldo Campos were technically cousins, but they considered themselves brothers. Caitro's father died when he was seven years old. Because his family was poor and his mother needed his help at home, Caitro was forced to give up school in the sixth grade. His family worked as agricultural laborers at the local haciendas, and Caitro remembered singing and dancing to make work go quicker (Soto de la Colina 1995, 41–42). He also remembered hiding under the furniture to spy on the adults during after-hours jaranas in his home (Soto de la Colina 2000).

Caitro and his elder brothers moved to Lima in search of a better life. "In Cañete," Caitro explained, "there was no future for us. Everything was reduced to the fields" (Soto de la Colina 1995, 47). By the age of fourteen, Caitro was working in the meat transportation business in Lima, earning a salary fifty times that of his mother. Subsequently, he made his living as a construction worker, a longshoreman, a dockworker, and a taxi driver. In Lima, Caitro learned to play cajón at the jaranas of his Aunt Valentina. He began to sing popular Cuban music with a group called Tropical Estrella (Tropical Star), performing on the radio and in private parties at the homes of wealthy patrons (Soto de la Colina 1995, 53). In the 1950s, Caitro joined the Pancho Fierro company. Shortly after Perú Negro was formed, Caitro joined as a vocal soloist, and he performed with them until he left to play cajón for singer/composer Chabuca Granda, to whom he became a surrogate son, in the 1970s.

Caitro lived in Lima, until his death in 2004, with his wife Teresa Mendoza Hernández, their two children, their son-in-law, and their granddaughter. In the last years of his life, the government of Peru

FIGURE 4.6. Carlos "Caitro" Soto de la Colina. *From the private collection of Perú Negro, reprinted with permission.*

declared Caitro a national culture-bearer, and he frequently was invited to speak at universities in Lima and honored at public events.

Orlando "Lalo" Izquierdo (b. 1950) is considered by many Peruvians to be one of the country's finest and most graceful *zapateadores* (tap-dancers). Izquierdo learned to dance as a child, and he worked for a shoemaker at the age of fourteen. His sister, who danced in Victoria Santa Cruz' Teatro y Danzas Negras del Perú, repeatedly invited him to join the group, and one day he gave it a try. To his surprise, there was no audition. Lalo explains that, while he was dancing with Victoria Santa Cruz' company as a teenager, he asked himself, "'Why am I doing this?' I know it is because I belong to this group of people, because it is part of my Black folklore, but why do I do it? What does it mean? And so my investigation began . . . And I listened to people who call themselves teachers, but they were not specific. Because they are people who have heard about this but they haven't seen it . . . so they have written about it in their own manner. Thus, they have distorted many aspects of Black folklore" (Izquierdo 2000). According to Lalo, in Victoria Santa Cruz' company there was no explanation of folklore, just "pure choreography. That is why we [the former members of Victoria Santa Cruz' company who started Perú Negro] dedicated

FIGURE 4.7. Orlando "Lalo" Izquierdo. *From the private collection of Perú Negro, reprinted with permission.*

ourselves to revealing the oral tradition that pertains to us, so we can disseminate the dances and their meaning" (Izquierdo 2000).

Izquierdo worked with Perú Negro as lead dancer and choreographer for its first decade. In 1978, Lalo left Peru for Venezuela, where he continued his studies of the African musical diaspora. Further studies took him to Trinidad and Tobago, Curacao, and Aruba. Izquierdo returned to Peru in 1993 and was employed as a professor at the National School of Folklore.

As a professional folklorist, Izquierdo disseminated theories and brief articles supporting the African origins and Peruvian history of Perú Negro's folkloric re-creations. For example, Izquierdo writes that the Peruvian cajón is a descendant of the *nkakwa*, a wooden drum used in the Fanti-Ashanti zone and Bantu-speaking areas of present-day Angola and Mozambique (Izquierdo n.d.). Further, Izquierdo maintains that the movements expressed in Afro-Peruvian dance are survivals of the corporal system of communication developed by enslaved multiethnic Africans in Peru to overcome the language barrier. When he teaches dance, he explains the exact significance of each movement: movements of labor, movements of salute, movements of the soul, and movements that signify giving and receiving love (Izquierdo 2000).

Lalo Izquierdo is semi-retired from Perú Negro, but he was still called upon in the 1990s when outsiders asked for an interview (he was a major source for this chapter). In 2000, he moved to Los Angeles, where he taught Afro-Peruvian dance classes at a Peruvian restaurant. In 2005, he was performing and teaching Afro-Peruvian music in the San Francisco Bay Area.

Ronaldo Campos, Caitro Soto, and Lalo Izquierdo are but a few of the familiar personalities who composed the "Perú Negro family" in its golden age. With their initial productions, this close-knit group of Black artists radiated a contagious spark of excitement and cultural achievement. The charismatic Perú Negro family attracted a circle of onlookers and friends, some of whom were as important as "the family" itself in the formation of Perú Negro's repertoire and style.

Friends of the Perú Negro Family

During the 1970s, several White and mestizo artists and intellectuals associated with leftist movements became active with Perú Negro. These advisers, administrators, and artistic collaborators contributed greatly to the formation of the company's folklore style. Thus, it is important to remember that, although Perú Negro represents the essence of Peruvian blackness to Peruvians and foreign audiences, Whites and mestizos helped craft many of the company's early staged performances and programmatic directions. As William Tompkins points out (1981, 113–114), by the time Perú Negro emerged, Whites and mestizos had long been involved in Black Peruvian music as its leading scholars, performers, composers, and arrangers, so the company's collaboration with non-Black Peruvians was not considered unusual.

One of Perú Negro's most important non-Black collaborators was singer/composer Chabuca Granda (1920–1983), who arranged for the company to participate in the 1969 festival in Argentina. For this reason, many people say that Chabuca actually created Perú Negro, but this claim fails to acknowledge the brief history of the early company formed by Ronaldo Campos at El Chalán. However, Chabuca Granda enabled Perú Negro's metamorphosis from a small-time tourist entertainment troupe into a nationally and internationally acclaimed staged performance ensemble.

Chabuca Granda first met Ronaldo Campos in 1956, when she performed with the Pancho Fierro company as a guest artist. Five years later, she hired Ronaldo Campos and Caitro Soto to perform slave roles in her musical theater production "Limeñisima," a nostalgic re-creation of "24 hours in a day of the life of the end of colonial Lima" (N.a. 1961a). When Chabuca Granda was invited to serve as a juror in the Hispanoamerican Festival of Song and Dance in 1969, the Argentinean authorities requested that Granda recommend a Peruvian folklore company. Granda first invited Victoria Santa Cruz to bring Peru's Conjunto Nacional de Folklore, but the Conjunto had a previous engagement in Venezuela (Enrique Gibson 1969, 37). Next, Granda turned to Perú Negro, and they eagerly accepted. The Argentinean festival organizers underwrote travel and airfare, a Peruvian company contributed 20,000 *soles* for costumes, and celebrated costume and fashion designer Mocha Graña "worked miracles" (Enrique Gibson 1969, 37).

Chabuca Granda and Perú Negro continued to collaborate in the company's early years, touring and performing together in Mexico and Spain. When Chabuca Granda expanded her artistic repertoire in the 1970s to include "airs" loosely based on Afro-Peruvian rhythms, she hired some of Perú Negro's musicians as accompanists and arrangers. As a highly visible non-Black composer and performer of stylized versions of Afro-Peruvian folklore, Chabuca Granda did much to publicly affirm the place of Black music at the core of Peruvian criollo identity before her death in 1983.

If Chabuca Granda launched Perú Negro to success by inviting them to the Hispanoamerican Festival, Peruvian poet César Calvo (1940–2000) played an equally formative role by creating a poetic and narrative identity that would continue to define the group for decades. A member of

FIGURE 4.8. Chabuca Granda, César Calvo, and members of Perú Negro at the Hispanoamerican Festival in Argentina, 1969. Pictured (left to right): Sara de La Cruz, César Calvo, Chabuca Granda, Ronaldo Campos, Esperanza Campos, Pilar de La Cruz. In background: Victor Padilla and Linder Góngora. *Reprinted with permission from Caretas.*

the left-wing Hora Cero group of poets, Calvo also was friendly with the circle of artists and intellectuals who came to the forefront in Lima during the Velasco years. He became involved with Perú Negro in its early days, serving as artistic director and general coordinator. Calvo became an unofficial member of the Perú Negro family, a privilege conveyed upon few Whites or mestizos (Lee 2000).

Although he was not Black himself, César Calvo endowed Perú Negro's programs with a poetic spirit of transnational blackness. As narrator, in a typical program, Calvo wove together explanations of Afro-Peruvian folklore, religious elements from West African–derived rituals of ancestor worship, and writings of negritude poets. For example, in the 1970s show *Navidad negra* (Black Christmas), Calvo intertwined the texts of Martinican poet and negritude founder Aimé Césaire with the story of Jesus. The plot revolved around a Black Christ child and connected the Black Christmas theme to Cuban Yoruba-derived Abakwá practices, especially the *diablitos* (little devils) tradition of the secret *Ekué* society. To link these Black Atlantic traditions with Afro-Peruvian folklore, Perú Negro members, dressed and acting as "devils" possessed by their ancestors, appeared and spoke to the audience before each dance. Toward the end of the show, the devils performed Calvo's "Canción para Ekué" (Song for Ekué), a *villancico* (Spanish Christmas song) with African-sounding lyrics and references to visitation by the ancestors through the bodies of the devils. The program ended with the traditional Afro-Peruvian el son de los diablos performed by the costumed "devils," thus connecting Afro-Cuban Abakwá diablitos with the Peruvian Carnival tradition revived by the Pancho Fierro company (Calvo n.d. [1970s] b) (see figure 4.9).

After Calvo left the company, Perú Negro continued to employ outsiders (usually White) to fill the narrator role he had created, a programmatic element that emphasizes the staged folkloric nature of the performance and the framing of the company members as their slave ancestors. It is important to note that César Calvo performed his narrator role in blackface, and that blackface performances by non-Black collaborators played a quiet part in the Afro-Peruvian revival. Because this aspect of the Afro-Peruvian revival is not often discussed, I would like to offer some reflections on the use of blackface.

As noted in chapter 1, Juan Criado began performing festejos in blackface in the 1940s or 1950s, and his blackface numbers were featured prominently in the Pancho Fierro show in 1956, lending a certain character of counterfeit to that first public performance of "authentic blackness" on the Peruvian stage. The masquerade continued with Calvo's performances in blackface with Perú Negro in the 1970s.

Because the artists of the Afro-Peruvian revival, from Pancho Fierro to Perú Negro, sought to revalorize Black culture, it may seem incongruous to some readers that blackface was used.[7] However, it is important to remember that there has never been a widespread public outcry against blackface as a form of racism in Peru, and that Peruvian uses of blackface typically have been isolated occurrences rather than part of an organized tradition comparable to minstrelsy in the United States (with the possible exceptions of Black comic theatrical characters in Spanish colonial dramas and *negritos* dances in the indigenous highland communities). When an (apparently) White actor in blackface played the lead in the 1988 Peruvian television miniseries *Matalaché*, based on a famous Peruvian novel set in times of slavery (López Albújar [1928] 1991), few voices rose in protest (see R. Santa Cruz 1988). Similarly, in my interviews with Afro-Peruvian musicians, including former members of Pancho Fierro and Perú Negro, those who discussed Calvo's or Criado's use of blackface did so with a smile and a laugh, as if it were an amusing costume. In fact, no one that I interviewed about Pancho Fierro even bothered to mention that Juan Criado performed in blackface when we discussed his participation. I finally realized that Criado "blacked up" when I came across a 1950s photograph

FIGURE 4.9. Top: *El Ñanigo* (lithograph of *Abakuá diablito* by Cuban artist Victor Patricio de Landaluze). From *Los tipos y costumbres de la isla de Cuba* (1881). Bottom: Perú Negro performing *el son de los diablos*, 1970s. *From the private collection of Perú Negro, reprinted with permission.*

clearly showing his smiling, corked face (see figure 1.3). When I asked several Afro-Peruvian musicians whom I had previously interviewed about my newfound knowledge, they laughed at this amusing but apparently trivial fact and then informed me that César Calvo also "painted himself Black" when he performed with Perú Negro.

While I noted in chapter 3 the risks of drawing cross-cultural parallels—and that caveat still applies here—the use of blackface in the Afro-Peruvian revival invites culturally contextualized comparisons with minstrelsy in the Spanish Americas and the United States (especially Hollywood films such as *The Jazz Singer* that were popular throughout Latin America). As critics of North American minstrelsy point out, the spectacle of blackface may conspire to produce a particular structure of racial feeling long before it is publicly acknowledged as a racist act (Lhamon 1998; E. Lott 1993). Moreover, it is not just the mask that makes the minstrel show, in which a stereotyped and imagined culture is attached to Blacks through staged music, speech style, dance, physicality, and behavior. In addition to the use of blackface, several unsettling elements of some Afro-Peruvian music and dance performances resemble aspects of the minstrel show: the White narrator; emphasis on childlike humor; oversexualized Black bodies; prominent use of the jawbone as a musical instrument; emphasis on the "spectacle of vulgarity" (E. Lott 1993, 138) in musical numbers and dances; and explicit display of blackness and scenes from times of slavery as spectacle for White (criollo) audiences. Thus, although the use of blackface should be analyzed in cultural context, I believe that this aspect of Perú Negro's collaboration with non-Black "friends of the family" must be remembered as a revealing element of the staged construction of blackness in the Afro-Peruvian revival.

The Perú Negro Sound

In the 1970s, Perú Negro created standardized choreographies and a "Perú Negro sound," which would come to define Afro-Peruvian music for the next two decades. As Javier León observes, Perú Negro is one of the most prestigious of several "dynasties" that reign over Afro-Peruvian performance style. For young Afro-Peruvians who want to learn the "right way" of performing Afro-Peruvian music, apprenticing with Perú Negro is considered an avenue to success. Moreover, the fact that Perú Negro members and former members dominate the faculty of Lima's National Folklore School has resulted in the canonization of Perú Negro's musical style and choreographies as "the" way to perform Afro-Peruvian music and dance (see León Quirós 2003, 79–92).

In the revival music of the 1950s and 1960s, while cajón patterns and added percussion instruments established a sonic difference between Afro-Peruvian music and música criolla, most arrangements still were dominated by vocals and guitar styles that borrowed heavily from música criolla's participatory aesthetic. Beginning in the 1970s, Perú Negro molded the musical legacy of the Pancho Fierro company and the Santa Cruzes into an Afro-Peruvian sound that retained the flavor of música criolla while showcasing virtuosic drum-based rhythmic play in a dense and high-velocity soundscape. This new Perú Negro sound satisfied the government folklore project's emphasis on the Peruvian "others" who populated an idealized past—minus the rebelliousness negritud of the Santa Cruzes. Perú Negro's arrangements in the 1970s produced a newly powerful percussive presence by increasing the number of cajones in the ensemble (two or three for most standard works, with special numbers involving six or seven cajones playing in unison), and they established a regular role for the Latin percussion instruments that had already found their way into the Afro-Peruvian repertoire—bongó, congas, and cowbell—playing rhythms derived from West Africa via Afro-Cuban music.

The integration of Afro-Cuban instruments and rhythms was accomplished with the knowledge and enthusiasm of Cuban bongó player Guillermo "El Niño" Nicasio Regueira (who had first worked with Ronaldo Campos in Nicomedes Santa Cruz' Cumanana company) and later El Niño's son Guillermo Macario Nicasio (known as "Macario"). Both El Niño and Macario helped integrate Cuban instruments and rhythms into the Afro-Peruvian percussion arrangements of Perú Negro, adapting and codifying conga and bongó parts for each genre (J. Vásquez 2000). Thus, Perú Negro altered and indigenized Afro-Cuban instruments and rhythms as part of a new and more complex percussion tapestry with which to accompany Afro-Peruvian genres.

The cajón patterns that identified each genre—many of which had been created by Ronaldo Campos in Nicomedes and Victoria Santa Cruz' groups in the 1960s—also were standardized during the early days of Perú Negro. With a basic rhythmic "personality" for each genre more clearly defined, Perú Negro created increasingly complex arrangements of Afro-Peruvian revival classics. At some point, a cajón solo—sometimes with bell and bongó—was also instituted in the middle of some musical numbers, reminiscent of other Afro-Latin musics featuring drum solos. Meanwhile, certain guitar strumming patterns were replaced with more elaborate and soloistic figures that were indebted to criollo guitar styles (see León Quirós 2003, 169–170, 174).

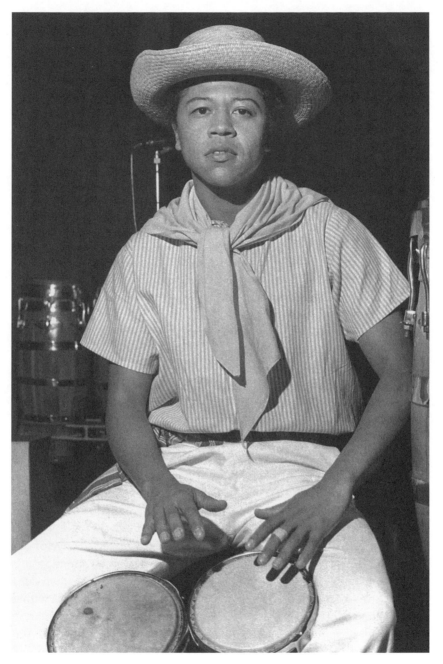

FIGURE 4.10. Guillermo Macario Nicasio. *From the private collection of Perú Negro, reprinted with permission.*

Thus, building upon the musical innovations of the first phase of the revival, Perú Negro established the new sound that would define Afro-Peruvian music, and the group continued to use contemporary aesthetic criteria to expand that sound musically after the 1970s (as evident in the new material and arrangements in Perú Negro's 2000 and 2003 recordings). In contrast, the choreographies first developed in the 1970s are normally performed verbatim decades later, both by Perú Negro and by other folkloric dance companies in Peru.

Creating a Choreographic Canon

Rafael Santa Cruz notes that all Afro-Peruvian dance is indebted to the choreography of Victoria Santa Cruz, who trained Perú Negro's founders (2000a, 181). However, Perú Negro moved Afro-Peruvian dance in a new direction in the 1970s with their enduring canon of staged choreographies. With the lack of public support for national folklore after the fall of the military government, virtually no new choreographies were created (or recreated) in the 1980s and 1990s. As a result, almost all Afro-Peruvian dance companies perform the dances created or stylized by Perú Negro in the 1970s. Therefore, it is important to understand how Perú Negro first developed these performance models.

Continuing the process of artistic ethnography pioneered by José Durand in the 1950s, Perú Negro engaged in community research, using human sources (their relatives and other rural Black Peruvians) to create a living "site of memory" (Nora 1984–1986) in the form of staged repertoire. Unlike José Durand or the Santa Cruzes, the founding members of Perú Negro came from poor families in rural areas where Black music and dance had been preserved, and they viewed their elders as a cultural resource untapped by scholars and previous revival leaders. Lalo Izquierdo explains how the cultural memories of Perú Negro's older relatives inspired his choreographies: "At the choreographic level, it is the direct message of our ancestors. In my case, my great aunts imitated how their grandparents danced, the movements they made . . . in a jarana. Jarana is what we call a family get-together where there is drinking, food, happiness. And within this happiness, through creativity, remembrance results" (Izquierdo 2000).

Two older relatives were particularly important links to cultural memories: Lucila "Chila" de la Colina (Ronaldo Campos' mother, a singer and vihuela player) and Benedicta de la Colina (Caitro Soto's mother). From these women's memories of dances and song fragments, Perú Negro built a tradition, filling in gaps and creatively staging remembered dances in audience-pleasing ways.

Lalo Izquierdo explains how the process worked: "Lets take the 'Toro mata' dance . . .[8] We talked a lot with Chila, Ronaldo Campos' mother; Benedicta, who is Caitro Soto's mother. Ronaldo talked with his mother, too, because it is a very closed family, very thick. Now she has passed away. We talked a great deal with them, because they experienced these things in situ, they participated . . . So based on the orientation they gave us, we pieced together the movements . . . Of course, obviously we gave it a choreographic touch to exhibit the dance, so that it wouldn't end up being monotonous or tiresome . . . The people who participated in the callejones, in Amancaes, where these dances were performed, they have knowledge. Perhaps not complete dances, but some knowledge. This knowledge is what we make known by way of practice and investigation" (Izquierdo 2000).

In addition to consulting family members, Perú Negro conducted rural field research. Beginning in the early 1970s, members of Perú Negro began to visit the rural towns of El Carmen and El Guayabo in the province of Chincha, interviewing the residents and collecting and recording their musical memories. Leslie Lee, who accompanied the group on these research trips, remembers: "We would make a trip, the whole of us, all who wanted to go. They were interested, the girls and the boys. They were discovering themselves. Because the contact with Pepe Durand, Chabuca Granda—and all these people after all were non-Blacks—did give them the idea that they had a background and they had a history . . . We would go there [Chincha] to, what we would call to investigate . . . The contact was mainly done by César Calvo, who was not Black, he was the one who would go and record the words to the songs and all this. And of course Ronaldo and the others would be listening to the music" (Lee 2000).

Based on their research with elderly relatives and in rural communities, Perú Negro created a canon of stylized Afro-Peruvian dances that both expanded upon and opposed the folklore of Nicomedes and Victoria Santa Cruz. Ultimately, because of the departure of the Santa Cruzes in the 1980s and Perú Negro's special role in the Velasco government's folklore project, Perú Negro's vision of Afro-Peruvian folklore became the dominant national memory.[9]

Artistic Repertoire: The Dance of the Laundresses and "Canto a Elegua"

Two examples of the musical and choreographic results of Perú Negro's early investigations are the Dance of the Laundresses (performed to the song "Samba malató") and "Canto a Elegua." These performance numbers illustrate how Perú Negro's folklore "danced" between double readings:

domination versus resistance, premodern past versus redemptive present, and local folklore versus transnational diaspora.

Readers may recall that "Samba malató" first was recorded on Nicomedes Santa Cruz' *Cumanana* album in 1964, and that its forgotten choreography was re-created by Victoria Santa Cruz in the 1960s. As noted in chapter 2, it is unclear to what extent Victoria Santa Cruz' choreography differed from the Dance of the Laundresses that Perú Negro (and virtually every other Afro-Peruvian dance group) performs with "Samba malató." Regardless of who originated its choreography, Perú Negro popularized it.

Perú Negro's Dance of the Laundresses may be viewed in live performances and on noncommercial videos that circulate privately in Peru. The following description is based on a videorecording of the original members of Perú Negro performing in the company's Twenty-fourth Anniversary concert (Perú Negro 1993), as well as my viewing of several live performances from 1998 to 2005. The song begins with the guitar introduction created by Vicente Vásquez for the original *Cumanana* recording in 1964 (see figure 3.8). However, the landó is more "African" in Perú Negro's hands. The three guitars (bass, rhythm, and lead) reiterate variations of the initial motif, while an expanded percussion ensemble (three cajones, three congas, and bongó) executes a combination of unison figures marking the dance moves and soloistic variations on landó patterns (see figure 3.9). Evoking the landó's characteristic playful ambiguity, the dancers' steps and drummers' strokes accentuate triple meter at times and quadruple meter at others. All three cajoneros demonstrate a freedom to improvise that was absent from the *Cumanana* recording. Perú Negro always includes the pseudo-African lyrics penned by Nicomedes Santa Cruz (which, as explained in chapter 3, Nicomedes later asked others to abandon). In fact, Lalo Izquierdo apparently believes them to be in the African Yoruba language. He observed to me, "There is a song that 'la lavandera' sings that has a part in the Yoruba language . . . 'a la mucurú.' This obviously has nothing to do with a Black woman washing clothes, but since it sounds good as melodic content it has been put there despite the results" (Izquierdo 2000).

As the dance begins, six female dancers enter in a line formation. They are wearing the traditional garb of Black domestic servants: kerchiefs covering their heads and tied around their foreheads, white short-sleeved dresses with ankle-length skirts over petticoats, aprons, and bare feet. Each dancer carries a large washbasin, and they slowly sway from side to side with each step. When Nicomedes Santa Cruz' pseudo-African lyrics ("a la mucurú," and so forth) begin, the laundresses are energized, and they take larger steps, jumps, and struts. As the vocals and guitars drop out for a percussion interlude, the laundresses set their basins down in a line at the front of the stage and make a great show of wringing towels while shaking their hips and grinning broadly at the audience (figure 4.11). Every movement and every smile is in unison, doubled by the planned punctuation of the drums. Their work forgotten for the moment, the laundresses dance joyfully with their swinging behinds facing the audience, and then they twirl their hips playfully on outstretched toes as the guitars and vocalists return. The melody fades out once more as the laundresses clap their hands rhythmically. The male vocalist urges the dancers on with calls typical of Afro-Peruvian music ("¡Eso!" "¡Joo ja!" and so forth), as they slowly turn, swivel their hips, and jump. They dance in a circle, arm-in-arm with petticoats swishing, and the vocalists sing: "con la batea la negra se menea" (the Black girl moves with the basin) over and over again. The dancers form couples and mirror each other's gestures, hands on hips and shoulders bobbing, then slowly make their way back to the line of basins at the front of the stage. As the laundresses pick up their basins and resume their work, they exit in single file with a renewed spring in their step (in fact, on every fourth step, each dancer leaps forward).

Interpreting dance is a tricky business, for its meaning is embedded in body movements, costuming, facial expressions, and other elements with culturally and individually varying interpretations. Dance enables multiple readings, even if structures of power privilege some readings over others (see Wade 2000, 9–10). The Dance of the Laundresses invites at least two completely different interpretations: celebration or domination.

For its choreographers and many other viewers, the Dance of the Laundresses dignifies the historical labor and beauty of Black women in Peru. In fact, the image of Black women doing laundry appeared throughout the Afro-Peruvian revival as a symbol of Black women's roles "behind the scenes" in Peruvian history. These laundresses were not only domestic servants or slaves but also Black wives and mothers who spent their days performing household chores for their families.

Lalo Izquierdo explains, "We wanted to represent part of the worklife of the Black woman in the callejón, so we created the Dance of the Laundresses, which represents women's work . . . This Black woman . . . works to support her household. I lived in a callejón, and my mother washed clothing too. She would wake up early to prepare the detergent or the soap. The soap came in a bar and she dissolved it in water and added a fruit called *boliche* that whitened and strengthened cotton clothes, and they came out extraordinary! Next, she put two bricks, firewood, and a can with the water to dissolve the soap, and while she was preparing the soap she selected the clothing . . . And while this process was taking place in the

FIGURE 4.11. Perú Negro performs "Samba malató," 2004. Pictured: Fiorella Ayala (left) and Vanessa Rivadeneyra (right). *Photo by Rosa María Ruvalcaba, reprinted with permission.*

callejón, there was always a birthday or someone's party . . . The party would last two, three, four, five days, and this was normal. And she would see a neighbor with a bottle of cane liquor or rum or *chicha* and she would ask her for a little drink 'to make the morning pass quickly.'[10] So she would dry her hands and take a little drink—and then another little drink 'to give her courage.' And now she would go back to the washing. [Lalo stands up and dance-walks in a swaying fashion.] She would go back to wash—with rhythm! So we wanted to create this sequence in one of the dances, to represent something that was an everyday occurrence" (Izquierdo 2000).

However, for some viewers, the image of the Black laundress represents negative associations with servitude, slavery, and the premodern social space occupied by Black Peruvians in the racial imagination. Seen from this perspective, the joyfulness of the dancers seems to minimize the hardships of Black servitude in order to perpetuate the image of Black women playfully washing clothes (whether for a slave master or their own families) as a symbol of Black culture in national collective memory. The image of a dancing Black woman washing laundry recalls the fact that a large percentage of enslaved Africans were women brought to Lima to perform domestic work and that many Black women continue to earn their living in this way in part because of the lack of more lucrative or socially prestigious opportunities. Because Perú Negro's choreography has not changed in several decades, the laundresses appear to be frozen icons of a premodern past, endlessly repeating their hip-swaying, smiling, and cloth-wringing for the pleasure of modern audiences.

Thus, the dancing laundresses of "Samba malató" are part temptress, part servant, and they are applauded for their joyful complicity in both roles. But they also represent the real women who raised the founders of Perú Negro—Black women whose behind-the-scenes labor and wisdom had long been invisible and uncelebrated. As Javier León writes, "the ambiguous space that is occupied by these choreographic reconstructions of the landó, with their multiple readings, parallels the equally ambiguous place that the dance occupies between past and present, pre-modern and modern, African heritage and Peruvian actuality" (León Quirós 2003, 229).

If "Samba malató" invites the double reading of domination versus resistance, "Canto a Elegua" demonstrates how the transnational was indigenized as local folklore—by now a recurrent theme in the Afro-Peruvian revival's Black Atlantic appropriations. It is also an example of the neo-folkloricization (Casaverde 2000a; Hagedorn 1995 and 2001) of borrowed and invented emblems of "African" heritage.

In 1979, Perú Negro performed "Canto a Elegua" on a Venezuelan television program. In response to my questions about the choreography of "Canto a Elegua," Lalo Izquierdo graciously shared his video recording of this program with me. Captured on aging videotape in black and white, as the song opens, a man and a woman (Caitro Soto and Marina Lavalle) stand on the dance floor in front of a raised platform stage. The woman holds a flaming bowl; the man holds a microphone. Onstage are nine musicians (playing three congas, two cajónes, bongó, cowbell, and three guitars). Twelve Black dancers (six male, six female), all barefooted, form a processional. Women are dressed in short black skirts and white tops, and men wear white calf-length trousers and no shirts. Guitars strum a continuous tremolo while Marina Lavalle sings the opening chant:[11]

> El agua lloré, el vichiló
> El agua lloré, agua y lloré
> El vichiló

The chorus of dancers responds quietly on two descending pitches that echo the soloist's last phrase: "aye." Then Caitro Soto fervently sings a second chant:

> O tiri maché, olonde
> O tiri maché, o tiri maché, olonde

Again, the chorus quietly sings its echo, "aye." The woman places the fire vessel in the center of the stage. The dancers encircle the burning flame. Silence. The drumming begins (the three guitars are silent for the rest of the dance), with congas, bongó, and cowbell performing hocketed rhythmic patterns of interlocking eighth notes, organized around a time-line played by the cowbell (figure 4.12).

The vocal soloists perform three verses, echoed in responsorial fashion by the chorus. The rhythmic accompaniment remains unchanged until after the third verse is completed, when the tempo speeds up and the cajones enter with a different rhythmic pattern.

1. (female soloist echoed by chorus)
Ibarra bo ago mo yuba, ibarra bo ago mo yuba,
Omo ne gon de moyu barra bo, ago mo yuba
Elegua ko lona

2. (male soloist echoed by chorus)
Ishon shon abe, ishon shon abe
Odara kolone y yuba de Elegua

3. (female soloist echoed by chorus)
Eshu o elegua lae, eshu o elegua lae
Elegua la moforibaye, elegua lae

The vocal soloists deliver these lyrics with great emotional conviction. The dancers initially are restrained; women sit cross-legged on the floor and men stand behind them, all performing rhythmically synchronized hand motions that beckon toward the sky. As the chants intensify, the dancers rise and form a fast-moving circle around the fire vessel. The two cajón players finally join in and the music speeds up, then stops; the dancers freeze. After this break, the music begins again, faster this time. The women finally leave their seated position and the dancers leap forward in duple time on the balls of their feet while crossing their bodies with extended arm motions. The cowbell can be heard prominently executing the West African/Black Atlantic timeline pattern that I previously compared to the landó (see figure 3.9). The dancers come together in a tight knot around the fire vessel, shaking their bodies and reaching for the sky. The drumming climaxes, the dancers fall to the ground, and the song comes to an end.

In many parts of the Black Atlantic, music very much like this was pre-served as an African legacy by the descendants of slaves who worshiped *orishas* (a pantheon of ancestral spirits central to the religious belief system of the Yoruba peoples of West Africa). In fact, despite some variations (performance style, melodic intervals, pronunciation, and so forth), Perú Negro's "Canto a Elegua" appears to reproduce the same chants used in Afro-Cuban Santería, Afro-Brazilian Candomblé, Afro-Trinidadian

Transcription Notes:

Bongó   x notes on upper staff line: Slap on high-pitched drumhead
Round notes on lower staff line: Tone on lower-pitched drumhead

Congas 2-3   A single player alternately hits high-pitched (upper space) and medium
pitched (middle and lower staff lines) *congas* with separate hands.
x noteheads: Timekeeping touch strokes
➍ noteheads: Open tone strokes
■ noteheads: Bass tone strokes (palm in center of drum)
Low sound quality and few visuals of the player made this part difficult
to transcribe; I have reproduced it to the best of my ability, aided by
comparison with another recording (L. Campos [1970s] n.d.).

Conga 1   Lowest-pitched *conga* drum playing open tone strokes.

FIGURE 4.12. "Canto a Elegua" excerpt *(Perú Negro 1979)*.

Shango, and other West African–derived religions to invoke the orisha Elegua (also known by the names Eleggua, Elegbá, Legba, Esu, Eshu, and Echu).[12] A number of percussion instruments might be used to accompany these songs to Elegua. In Cuba, sets of three religious drums or gourds typically play the interlocking patterns, whereas in Peru a similar-sounding accompaniment pattern is produced on bongó, congas, and cowbell. Interestingly, elements of Perú Negro's choreography (the fast tempo, fire vessel, vigorous gestures, and so forth) are more reminiscent of Congolese than Yoruba-derived dances.[13]

But in Peru, African-derived religions involving ancestral spirits did not survive to the twentieth century, and it is not known to what extent they ever existed (see Cuche 1976). So how did this song get to Peru, and what does it signify in its Peruvian context? Could this be a retention from Yorubaland, preserved in Perú Negro's repertoire, testifying to the diffusion of the same African traits in both the Black Atlantic and Peru? After all, Peru's Black slaves came by way of Brazil or the Caribbean, and Perú Negro's founders derived early repertoire from ethnographic field trips to predominantly Black rural areas where cultural memory of African-derived traditions allegedly was better preserved.

Although such an explanation is theoretically possible, scholarship on the African diaspora since the 1970s cautions that traditions invented in the New World can easily be mistaken for African retentions (see Mintz and Price [1976] 1992). I learned how this song really came to Peru (or at least one version of its oral history) in interviews with members and former members of Perú Negro.

The man who called himself El Niño (Guillermo Nicasio Regueira) was either African or Cuban, depending on who tells the story. Sometime before 1950, poet and journalist Juan Liscano made a recording in Venezuela of El Niño performing "Canto a Elegua" with his touring Cuban batá drum ensemble Conjunto El Niño (Various Artists 1998d). In 1947, El Niño came to Peru as a bongó player with the Havana Cubans orchestra (N.a. 1967).[14] He married in Peru and never went back to Cuba. El Niño collaborated with both Nicomedes Santa Cruz and Perú Negro, creating rhythmic accompaniment parts for revived Afro-Peruvian genres. He taught the members of Perú Negro a medley of religious chants from Cuba, and he helped them adapt the tonal rhythmic accompaniment patterns to locally available Cuban percussion instruments. He taught them the choreography, too, and he explained the significance of Elegua, but he never disclosed the meaning of the lyrics. Perhaps, like many practitioners of religions that incorporate liturgical chants in a foreign or ancestral language, he did not know their literal translation.[15]

The Peruvian history of "Canto a Elegua" is a particularly interesting expression of Black Pacific double consciousness because, although its ritual context does not exist in Peru, it is part of Perú Negro's canon of folklore developed in the 1970s. In numerous interviews, I asked members and former members of Perú Negro to talk about the song, its history, and its assumed meaning. Perú Negro co-founder and choreographer Lalo Izquierdo (2000) confirmed that El Niño had explained the general significance of Elegua and taught them the choreography. The late Caitro Soto (the male vocal soloist in the 1979 video) also told me that he learned the song from El Niño. When I asked if El Niño taught him the meaning of the lyrics, he responded, "The African dialect, no. But the meaning, I knew what it was. Because all Black music is erotic, they are sexual symbols" (Soto de la Colina 2000). Finally, Silvia del Rio, Perú Negro's second lead vocalist in the 1980s and 1990s, confided that, although Perú Negro's late director, Ronaldo Campos, taught her to pronounce the "difficult" lyrics, she had no idea what they meant. Campos implied to her that the song was an African survival in Peru, but he was mysterious about the details. "And I don't know, even today, what it means!" Silvia told me. "Imagine, what shame if by chance I [perform for a foreign audience] and [they say]: 'Oh, how awful! That's not how the words go!'" (Del Rio 2000).

Is "Canto a Elegua," as performed by Perú Negro, music of the Black Atlantic in disguise? Or does the special history and significance it has acquired in Peru make it Peruvian? Typically, Perú Negro performs "Canto a Elegua" for audiences of tourists and upper class White Peruvians. The song usually is not introduced or explained, leaving the impression (whether strategic or accidental) that it is part of the Peruvian heritage. And in fact, while my reconstructed history reveals that "Canto a Elegua" was not brought directly from Africa to Peru, when viewed from the strategic perspective that designates the Black Pacific as a periphery of the Black Atlantic, "Canto a Elegua" now belongs to Afro-Peruvian folklore. Cuban and Peruvian versions of "Canto a Elegua" are not the same, and the Peruvian performance revises and reinvents even as it appropriates and indigenizes transnational Black Atlantic culture. It is precisely because it has no ritual context in Peru that "Canto a Elegua" is so very meaningful to the founders of Perú Negro, representing the lost African heritage they preserve through staged performance and the past they wish to reclaim.

Musical Archetypes of Blackness: Festejo and Landó

In addition to developing the "Perú Negro sound" and a canon of standard choreographies, Perú Negro reinforced certain archetypes of blackness through the musical "personalities" attached to Afro-Peruvian genres. Of the many folkloric genres stylized by Perú Negro, the two most widely performed and recognized in Peru at the turn of the twenty-first century are the festejo and the landó. Afro-Peruvian music aficionados frequently repeat that the festejo is the most representative Afro-Peruvian dance and the landó is the mother of all Black Peruvian rhythms. Through repeated staged performance, these two genres have become archetypes of publicly imagined Black Peruvian identity: the festejo stands for exuberant joy while the landó symbolizes Black sensuality. Yet, just as the attribution of archetypal qualities to a racial group is a social construction, Perú Negro stylistically rearticulated the landó and festejo in ways that musically emphasized selected characteristics of folkloric "blackness."

Festejos performed by the major groups of the 1950s and 1960s (Gente Morena de Pancho Fierro 1964; N. Santa Cruz and Cumanana [1964] 1994; Various Artists 1998b) had featured harmonized choruses and a balance of attention between guitar, vocals, and cajón and/or quijada. Indeed, some maintain that the pre-1940s festejo survived purely as sung melodies with guitar accompaniment and that the cajón was introduced later (as noted in chapter 3, the 1964 Cumanana recording of the festejo "No me cumbén" did not include a cajón). In Perú Negro's festejos, the cajón—a new symbol of Peruvian blackness—gradually came to dominate the guitar as the focus of musical attention.

In the early festejos of the 1960s, cajón patterns were not yet standardized, often doubling or only slightly varying guitar ostinati or other rhythmic parts. Perú Negro's late director Ronaldo Campos is generally credited with having created the basic cajón patterns for the festejo when he worked for Victoria Santa Cruz in the 1960s. According to Lalo Izquierdo (2000), Campos refined and polished these patterns with Perú Negro in the 1970s, composing the common variations and ornamentation styles used by most Peruvian cajoneros. As percussionist and record producer Manongo Mujica affirms: "Ronaldo feels that he owns several Afro-Peruvian genres. He basically invented them" (1998). Although Ronaldo Campos did not invent the festejo, his way of playing the festejo was richer and more syncopated than the earlier patterns, and it would become definitive.

In addition to enhancing the role of the cajón, as stated previously, Perú Negro also standardized the use of Afro-Latin drums and percussion instruments as part of Black Peruvian folklore (with the help of El Niño and Macario). Former Perú Negro guitarist Félix Casavarde observes, "What is interesting is the process of how the instruments like congas and bongó and the introduction of the cowbell totally enlarges the percussive platform of the festejo and creates a different dynamic. That is, from the moment of Perú Negro, from 1970 on, the dynamic of the festejo changes from the festejo that was played by Pancho Fierro . . . it was another format" (Casaverde 2000a). Casaverde attributes the changes in the festejo to the appropriation of Afro-Cuban music, which began with Nicomedes and Victoria Santa Cruz and continued with Perú Negro. At the same time, as noted in chapter 3, instruments and accompaniment patterns were borrowed from other related Afro-Peruvian and criollo genres, including quijada and cajita parts from el son de los diablos and guitar patterns that may have been transplanted from the zapateo and the alcatraz (see León Quirós 2003, 166–169).

In Perú Negro's festejo ensemble of the 1990s and beyond, two or three cajones often play at the same time, accompanied by congas (playing a variation on the Cuban *rumba guaguancó* pattern), bongó, and cowbell. This wall of percussion expands upon the "swing" that characterized early reconstructions of el son de los diablos for Pancho Fierro by contextualizing that feeling of metric ambivalence in a more complex sonic groove that tends to line up around a timeline (implied by the cowbell and congas). At the same time, the guitar parts have simultaneously become standardized and more complex, with basic strumming patterns replaced by more soloistic ostinati (see León Quirós 2003, 169–170). A typical Perú Negro–style festejo may begin with a song that layers vocalists and three guitars over this percussion section, and then, when the festejo proper (that is, the dancing) begins, the vocals and guitars melt away to make room for serious drumming. Some festejo contexts (such as dance contests) do away entirely with the guitar part and verse (which, ironically, were the original raw materials from which the festejo was reconstructed). Thus, while William Tompkins asserted that the 1970s festejo was popular primarily as a song form, since its choreography had been invented specifically for the stage (1981, 254), by the 1990s the festejo was inseparably linked with virtuosic cajón playing and dancing.

As explained in chapter 3, the festejo choreography had been forgotten and was reinvented by Porfirio Vásquez in 1949. Teresa Mendoza, who remembers the way the festejo was danced in the time of the Pancho Fierro company, says that it was a slow dance, with marked, deliberate body motions (Mendoza Hernández 2000). Félix Casaverde also notes how the tempo changed: "[In the early days before Perú Negro] it was . . . much slower. Why was it slower? Because it was for older people. But from 1970 on, when the peñas flourish, a demand grows for people to be extroverts, to dance, and it gets faster and faster. Faster because they didn't know how to move, and it is easier to move when it is fast, so they requested that it be played faster. The dancers who did shows of these dances performed in three, four, or five peñas each night and they didn't want to tire themselves out. So they asked for everything to be faster so they could move mechanically. This is why we now see the little girls who look like little machines, 'taca taca taca,' dancing in the contests" (Casaverde 2000a).

Perú Negro's festejo choreography involves specific steps and figures that accentuate a duple meter feel and a sense of exuberance—sometimes demanding simultaneous motions of the feet, hips, arms, and pelvis—performed by male and female dancers who execute choreographed figures both as a group and as couples. Despite these dramatic changes in the festejo over a relatively short period of time, resulting from Cuban influences, cross-genre borrowing, and re-Africanization, it is still widely deemed the most representative genre of all the existing Afro-Peruvian songs and dances (Baca, Basili, and Peirera 1992; Izquierdo 1999; Villanueva 2000).

The landó is the festejo's alter ego, and its music and choreography express the other side of the stereotyped Black personality—sensuality. The landó is typically in a minor mode with a pronounced triple feel. Shifting rhythmic accents in a moderately slow tempo leave the listener off-balance, searching for the downbeat.

Very few existing landós are considered part of "authentic" Afro-Peruvian musical heritage. "Samba malató" was the first reconstructed landó in the 1960s (see chapters 2 and 3). A second landó, "Samba landó," was collected and reconstructed by Perú Negro in the 1970s, based on what William Tompkins (1981) describes as a "sexually provocative" couple dance performed by elderly Blacks in El Guayabo, Chincha, during the *yunza* (see chapter 5). In addition to these two historic landós, new songs have been created in the landó rhythm in recent decades. These songs are generally conceived as ballads without choreography, musically expressing understated sensuality. This innovation began in the 1970s with Chabuca Granda, who would say to her guitarist, Félix Casaverde (who had worked previously with Perú Negro): "Let's compose something 'like' a landó!" (Casaverde 2000a). Casaverde explains how he worked with Chabuca Granda and cajón player Caitro Soto to redefine the landó in the 1970s. He notes, "the landó has not been very well worked out musically, notwithstanding the choreographic figures that begin with Victoria Santa Cruz and the Conjunto Nacional de Folklore, which are afterwards reproduced very prodigiously by Perú Negro" (Casaverde 2000a). Casaverde added what he describes as a "sensual guitar treatment" to the landó pattern for cajón developed by Caitro Soto (see figure 3.9) to formalize a "unit" for Granda's experimental landós that eliminated the "extra" Latin percussion used by Perú Negro (see also León Quirós 2003, 238–242).

Casaverde's testimonial highlights the fact that the landó's musical identity had yet to be established in the 1970s, a decade after it was first re-created and recorded. Paradoxically, then, although Afro-Peruvian musicians and dancers consider the landó to be the most ancient and "African" of all the Peruvian rhythms, it is probably the most modern invention.

If the landó acquires its musical sensuality through seductive rhythmic play and stylistic ambiguity, its danced identity locates this sensuousness in the female body. In the two "authentic" landós that preceded Chabuca Granda's experiments, there is a marked choreographic focus on the graceful display of Black women. The Dance of the Laundresses, popularized by Perú Negro for "Samba malató," emphasizes the sensuality of hip-swaying female laundresses. Similarly, Perú Negro's choreography for "Samba landó"—the couple dance collected in El Guayabo—celebrates female sensuality through its choreographic steps and figures. The basic landó waltz-like pivot step (long–short–short) causes the women's skirts to swirl gracefully with every turn of their hips and accentuates the feeling of triple meter. While the dance (like the festejo) is performed by a group of male–female couples, the choreographic spotlight is on the women. The women frequently turn their backs upon their male partners and dance with each other in figures reminiscent of "Samba malató": circles with clapping games, pairs with mirror dancing, and so on.

The archetypal quality of the landó treads a thin line between overt sexuality and understated sensuality, reductive stereotype and celebratory appreciation. Interestingly, as Javier León notes, while the dancing women sway their hips and "move to be seen," the pelvic bump figure so central to Nicomedes Santa Cruz' theory of the origins of the landó is nowhere in either of Perú Negro's revival choreographies. Yet, audience members often interpret staged performances of the landó as sexual in the same way that European colonizers labeled African dance as obscene (León Quirós 2003, 227–228; Villanueva 2000).

The festejo and the landó so epitomize the dual essence of imagined Peruvian blackness that some musicians assert that all other genres associated with Afro-Peruvian folklore are derived either from festejo or landó. Many scholars and musicians feel that several other dances in duple or quadruple meter (the alcatraz, son de los diablos, and ingá) are rhythmically defined by patterns derived from the festejo, only differing in their dance choreographies (see León Quirós 2003, 171–172; Tompkins 1981, 239). In turn, the $\frac{6}{8}$ zamacueca/marinera/tondero complex is considered to be related to the landó (in keeping with Nicomedes Santa Cruz' theory of the origins of the marinera; see figure 3.6). In addition to the relationship of rhythms in these families, the mood of the dances related to the festejo tends to be joyful, whereas those dances closer to the landó are more sen-sual. It could be argued, then, that the music of the revival as a whole lim-its the Black personality to these two choices. Thus, the folkloric stylization of the festejo and the landó—and their associated families of rhythms—has resulted in prominent archetypal symbols of essential traits of the Black cultural personality that feed the racial imagination of the audience culti-vated by Perú Negro and its folkloric spin-off groups.

Developing an Audience for Afro-Peruvian Folklore

Armed with its canon of re-created and stylized folklore, Perú Negro developed new audiences locally and internationally in the 1970s and 1980s, touring Peru, Latin America, and Europe. Rumor has it that, while on tour, members of the company attended local performances and subse-quently integrated elements of what they had seen into their own reper-toire. In the early 1970s, Perú Negro accepted its first invitation to perform in Europe, at the *Festivales de España* competition. There, Leslie Lee recalls: "They started coming onto the stage with a Moorish kind of shoes, you know, the points and the colors . . . And they weren't on time for the show . . . So I just said to Ronaldo, 'You'd better continue with the group, because I don't like what's happening.' I had great expectations. But they lost the chance of winning the festival, which they had started with a very good chance of winning. They gave that up, and I gave up Perú Negro" (Lee 2000).

Perú Negro continued to perform over the next three decades in Europe's major cities and festivals of Latin American music. The company was also featured on many Peruvian and international television programs, which led to the rise of new dance groups in Peru who imitated Perú Negro's TV performances. In an ironic reversal of origins and copies, some of these groups came from the Chincha area, where Perú Negro first researched authentic Black music and dance traditions (León Quirós 1998). In Baudrillard's terms (1994), Perú Negro's style had become a sim-ulacrum that was now deemed more real than the "original" it had copied in Chincha.

Around this time, commercial peñas flourished in Lima, leading to the dissemination of Perú Negro's folkloric styles to a much wider audience. Neighborhood music centers had emerged in Lima in the early twentieth century as places for working class criollos to congregate. In the 1970s, some of these music centers were converted into organized peñas. After commer-cial elements (such as the sale of food and drink or membership dues) were introduced in the early 1970s, the 1980s witnessed the proliferation of nightclub-style commercial peñas. These peñas usually were owned and operated by a proprietor rather than members, but many tried to maintain the traditional characteristics of a social, members-only peña (participation, spontaneity, and nationalism) (Bracamonte-Bontemps 1987, 253). Thus, while a commercial peña generally is open to anyone, audience members typically may be asked to sing or dance at some point during the night, and the music and ambience promotes a strong sense of *peruanidad*, or national identity.

One of the most famous commercial venues that specialized in Afro-Peruvian music was Peña Valentina, opened by Valentina Arteaga. Valentina was the mother of Perú Negro founder Rodolfo Arteaga, and her fame as a dancer, singer, and jaranera is legendary in Lima. Peña Valentina became known as a place where tourists and Peruvians of all races were welcome to seek out Black culture and Afro-Peruvian music and dance. There, a new style of festejo that some Peruvian musicians call "Valentina-type festejo" (Gamboa 1999) developed, leading to a kind of festejo craze and contests in which very young girls dressed in tiny skirts and midriff tops compete to see who can move fastest and shake her body the most.

The rise of commercial peñas created a new space in which Perú Negro's spinoff groups performed for White upper class Limeños and foreign tourists who came to "let loose" and dance the night away. However, the collapse of the military revolution—compounded by the evening blackouts and bombings in the mid-1980s during Sendero Luminoso's crusade of terror—put an end to Peruvian nightlife and the national folklore project.[16] By the 1980s, Perú Negro had stopped performing in theaters and returned to its origins, entertaining tourists in restaurants and peñas that served *comida criolla* (criollo food) accompanied by an Afro-Peruvian folklore show. With no government support for rehearsals, salaries, or performances, the company halted most of its research and creative activities and began to recycle what it already had created for tourist audiences.

Although Perú Negro made monumental achievements in the dissemination of Black Peruvian music in the 1970s, the company developed an audience that was composed largely of White upper class Peruvians and foreigners. Paradoxically, much of Perú Negro's audience outside Peru in the 1990s was transplanted Peruvians, whereas its audience in Peru was primarily foreign tourists. Former Perú Negro vocalist Silvia del Rio remarks upon this irony with a laugh: "Every time we travel, our compatriots show up. They are who comes to our shows. They come out of nostalgia . . . But when we work here in Manos Morenas [a tourist restaurant/peña in Lima], it's all foreigners" (Del Rio 2000).

Thus, like the Peruvians who attended José Durand's first show of "Black folklore," Perú Negro's tourist audiences in Lima learn—often for the first time—that Peru has a Black population with distinct cultural traditions. Because many of Perú Negro's folkloricized dances emphasize depictions of enslaved Africans that have not changed much since the 1970s, they construct a very specific image of blackness for their audiences and for Peruvians in general.

A Peruvian musician remembers, "It was an innovative movement in its time. But it stayed there, it stagnated because of the director's lack of perspective, and because of the internal personnel. They separated, they were very conflictive people, overly complicated. They should have put their art first. This brought the group down. So the people who had applied themselves, who wanted to bring the group forward, they retired, bored.

"It was a precious project. I remember going to their get-togethers, their rehearsals, their events, because I was happy seeing everything. How they worked, preparing the theatrical texts . . . I feel that Perú Negro today [pauses]—they are beautiful people, they dance beautifully, but they have stagnated. It is like seeing a painting or an old film. There is no more, they don't project anything more. And one feels this."

Perú Negro: The Next Generation

Asked about milestones in Perú Negro's history, Lalo Izquierdo (2000) denoted three periods: (1) the first decade (1970s) or "golden age," when the company developed and researched its repertoire, choreographing most of the dances that would become standards;[17] (2) the 1980s, when new members were trained in the repertoire that had been developed in the 1970s; and (3) the 1990s and beyond, when all original members except director Ronaldo Campos (who passed away in 2001) had left the group, membership had turned over numerous times, and the accomplishment of thirty years of national preeminence was tarnished by the financial and creative price of survival.

The middle generation of Perú Negro—the young dancers who joined the company in the late 1970s to 1980s—were, in many cases, children or relatives of members of the first generation. Dancer Oscar Villanueva, for example, is Caitro Soto's nephew. Oscar recalls the "buddy system" by which standard choreographies were taught to new dancers in the 1980s. Senior members of the company coached newcomers, who were later corrected by director Ronaldo Campos (Villanueva 2000). During the revival, the "golden agers" had established a canon of Black Peruvian songs and dances, but the young artists who were lucky enough to pass Perú

FIGURE 4.13. Members of Perú Negro outside YMCA rehearsal space, 1979. Pictured top row (left to right): "Pichin," Lucho Casanova, Marco Campos. Pictured center row (left to right): Adolfo Menacho, Aldo Borja, Oscar Villanueva, Rony Campos. Pictured bottom row: Jorge Talavina. *From the private collection of Perú Negro, reprinted with permission.*

Negro's auditions were simply charged with their proper execution. Thus, when the meaning or history of songs and dances was taught to the new members, it was conveyed as a fixed lesson, not as something lost and newly discovered.

Rony Campos (son of Ronaldo Campos) belongs to both the middle and the late generations of Perú Negro. Rony was five years old when his father founded the company, and he describes himself as having been "brought up with Perú Negro." According to Rony, music is in his blood (Campos 2000). He learned to play music and dance in his home, where his family and friends frequently gathered for musical reunions. In the 1970s, many of the children and relatives of the original Perú Negro family, including Rony Campos and Oscar Villanueva, became part of the first "Perú Negrito" (Little Perú Negro). When Rony entered the adult Perú Negro company in 1979, he was one of a crew of new members who had danced together in Perú Negrito. Thus, the junior company formed a sort of informal training ground for the adult one.[18] In 2001, when his father died, Rony became director of Perú Negro.

Rony describes the difference between the golden age of Perú Negro and the company he joined in the 1980s. In the early years, he explains, "to create a dance, they played music and the dancers began to dance freely . . . From there, steps were created. And my father arranged them. He made them blacker, more traditional. My father is from Cañete, so he has lived the traditions of the South. And in this way, the dances were formed. And the music was the same. At that time, a Cuban, Macario's father, El Niño, was playing with us. He taught, for example, the dance of 'El vichiló' ['Canto a Elegua'] a ritual dance . . . And they formed the choreography, and they rehearsed. The rehearsals were intense! Much more intense than now. It seems to me that the people were more mature . . . They dedicated themselves with more feeling.

"Now everyone is very lazy," he confesses. "They don't want to rehearse . . . they are lacking a bit of desire. Now, the only one who knows the dances is me. The generation dancing now doesn't include even one from my era. Besides my father, I am the oldest now . . . We are in our seventh generation. And we have lost some of the details of the steps. This results from the manner of teaching. In the old days, to teach a step, one had to take the step apart. So they taught [brushes his foot on the floor to show a dance step] piece by piece. Now there is another manner of teaching. The teacher stands in front, he starts to dance, and those who are learning stay in back. Then the teacher says, 'Okay, do what I do' [Rony dances a few steps]. That way, you are never going to learn anything" (Campos 2000).

The loss of dance steps in the 1990s was serious because no new choreography had been created since the 1970s. Lalo Izquierdo laments: "Our goal with Perú Negro is to rescue a type of dances that were becoming lost with the passage of time. And now what is called 'folklore' (in quotations) is in reality tremendously commercialized. There is no interest in research or in the explanation [behind the dances]. They are only interested in copying a dance in order to go to a peña and make money. And they don't even make money, two or three soles normally!" (Izquierdo 2000).[19]

To some extent, the same is true for the music; Rony Campos has written some new songs for Perú Negro, but usually the company performs the same standard repertoire it stylized in the 1970s. In fact, most Afro-Peruvian groups repeat the canon *ad infinitum*, only varying the arrangements. This phenomenon of repetition is exacerbated by Perú Negro's claim that spin-off groups perform exact copies of the choreography and musical arrangements Perú Negro created in the 1970s. Because of the "copying" problem, Perú Negro guards its choreography jealously. Despite its prominence, the group has released very few recordings in Peru, and requests to record or videotape the group are normally refused.

Rony Campos affirms, "Perú Negro is the master. It is the university of Black music here in Peru. So all the groups have copied Perú Negro. Certainly they don't do it the same way, but they all take from Perú Negro. And the National School of Folklore, those who are teaching there are members of Perú Negro. So they are teaching the same thing . . . Perú Negro is the only group that maintains Black tradition. In rhythms, in dances, in steps, in choreography . . . All the best Black music belongs to my father. All of it. This [performances by other groups] is all a copy. We are the originals" (Campos 2000).

Perú Negro Grows Old

In celebration of Perú Negro's twenty-fourth anniversary in 1993, the original members reunited at Lima's Municipal Theater for a command performance of *La tierra se hizo nuestra*, the show that had launched Perú Negro's career and earned the grand prize in Argentina in 1969. As each Perú Negro alumnus was showcased, the warmth and thundering applause with which they were received belied the humble lives most still led. The golden-age members of Perú Negro had become cultural icons for their Peruvian audiences, but their status did not transcend the theatrical stage. Most continued to live on meager resources and some had died in relative poverty. Sadly, the performance of Black folklore on stage did not repair the injustices of Black social invisibility and inequality in the present.

Although Perú Negro's staged re-creations enriched a historical narrative that obliterated the presence of Blacks, it also could be argued that folklore's exclusive emphasis on the past entrapped Black performers in a cruel time warp. Modern Blacks were lauded for their skill as musicians and dancers, but they were limited to playing the part of their premodern slave ancestors onstage. Framed by folklore's window to the past, they historicized themselves and were applauded only as long as they remained on stage, entertaining White and tourist audiences.

Yet, many Afro-Peruvians continue to argue for the importance of Perú Negro's redemptive folklore, which acts as counter-memory by preserving the lost and re-created Afro-Peruvian past. Because Black history was denied for many years in Peru, the re-creation of this suppressed past is an act of vindication for Perú Negro and other young artists, even if it is rooted in part in neo-folklore. In fact, efforts to create new Afro-Peruvian music styles that express the current aesthetics, interests, and experiences of Blacks in Peru are often viewed as less worthy.

At the millennium, Perú Negro showed signs of a creative renaissance. The company began to choreograph new dances and perform newly composed songs that encouraged racial pride and awareness (still very much in the style Perú Negro popularized during the revival), while continuing to present its traditional canon developed in the 1970s. Perú Negro issued two recordings in the first years of the twenty-first century, both featuring several new songs by Rony Campos and a variety of genres. The second release, which coincided with the company's first major tour of the United States in 2004 (after a U.S. debut performance in 2002), was nominated for a Latin Grammy. After more than three decades, Perú Negro continues to occupy an unchallenged place for most Peruvians as the quintessential representation of the music and dance of Black Peru and the authoritative source for the canon of Black Peruvian folklore.

CHAPTER 5

The Legend of Chincha

Travel Diaries, El Carmen (Chincha), 1998 and 2000: Visiting the Ballumbrosios

I have been in Lima for ten days, and everyone I meet tells me that the origins of Afro-Peruvian music and dance are in rural Chincha. So I go to Chincha. When I get there, everyone tells me that if I want to learn about Afro-Peruvian music, I must visit Amador Ballumbrosio and his family. They live in the district of El Carmen, a small town in Chincha with a predominantly Black population, dusty roads, very few basic services, and a reputation as the cradle of Afro-Peruvian folklore. El Carmen is connected to the Pan American Highway by a long and bumpy dirt road that ends at the entrance to the town's plaza de armas. A concrete wall that marks the entry is painted with a mural that beckons: "Welcome to the district of El Carmen, cradle and capital of the black arts of Peru" (figure 5.1).

Everyone knows where the Ballumbrosios live, so it is easy for a stranger to find them by asking directions in the plaza. Amador, the family patriarch, greets us at the front door. I have come with two women who work for a local church; they know him. They explain that I am a student who wants to learn about Black music. He looks tired. He mumbles that nothing is happening now, but if I return in late August I can see the local festival. He disappears, and his daughter, Maribel, reappears in his place. She tells me to come back tomorrow at 4:00 PM if I want to learn about Black Peruvian music.

The next day, I arrive about five minutes late. Maribel chides me, "I thought you weren't coming!" She is busily sweeping the ubiquitous dust of El Carmen off the floor and ordering children to tidy up the large front area of the Ballumbrosio family home that serves as a living room and music/dance space. The house is a long, rectangular-shaped dwelling with a thatched roof and a cement floor. Individual bedrooms, containing two or more beds each, are separated with curtains from a long hallway that leads to the kitchen. A dirt backyard contains a

FIGURE 5.1. Entrance to the district of El Carmen (Chincha). *Photo by the author.*

cooking area and sink, outdoor bathroom, water receptacles, chickens, roosters, and cats.

"Take off your sweater!" Maribel commands me. I am confused; I thought I was going to have a cajón lesson. Apparently, Maribel assumed that I want to learn to dance. First she tells me to sit on the couch. Two boys, aged about ten and twelve, play cajones while two girls, about five and seven, dance toward me. The girls move on bare feet in a way that is dainty and sensual at the same time, performing delicate hand motions, swivel steps executed almost on toe, and circular and horizontal movements of the arms, hips, pelvis, and shoulders. The boys pound away, the rough sound of their festejo echoing all the way down San José Street while neighbors peer in through the wide window and open doorway.

"Now it's your turn; stand up!" says Maribel. I do. The music starts again, and she joins the girls and tells me to imitate everything they do. I learn the basic festejo step first: the right foot moves forward, returns to neutral, moves back, and then to neutral on a count of four. Good. Now, the arms circle in front of the body to a count of three, providing a metric counterpoint to the movement of the feet. At the same time, the girls' hands and fingertips circle gracefully, outlining their bodies. They do not explain these movements or how to count them; they just dance. Now the hips begin to move in fast and tight figure eights while the pelvis and shoulders move front and back in opposite directions. Just as I begin to grasp this step and wonder if my hip region will ever move that way, a new one is introduced. Similar to what some American students of West African dance call "the chicken step," this figure calls for alternating movements of the pelvis and chest, with hands on hips and elbows out in a triangular "chicken wing" shape. I start to get it, and then they do it about six times as fast, and I can't keep up. My body

doesn't cooperate. The little girls try not to laugh, but I collapse in giggles while Maribel smiles at me encouragingly and slows down to show me how it's done.

After the festejo, the girls show me the landó. They appear to perform exactly the same steps that I just learned as festejo. The only thing that has changed is the cajón accompaniment. I am confused; I thought the festejo and landó were different dances. When we finish the dance lesson, I try to interview Maribel, asking questions about the dances we practiced and their associated rhythms. She gives me very short answers that don't tell me much, and I abandon the effort and spend the afternoon socializing with her and the children.

I come back for the festival in August. Maribel has invited me to stay in her house. She tells me that I should come for dinner; her mother often cooks meals for up to one hundred tourists en route from Cuzco to Lima. I call ahead from Lima to confirm that I am coming. "What great news!" Maribel exclaims.

With Maribel and several of her friends and relatives, I attend the festival in the plaza de armas. We pass around a jar and plastic cup of tutuma, a homemade wine local to the Chincha region. Following the local custom, each person pours a small amount into a single cup and passes the jar to the second person, who drinks from the cup and then pours and passes to the next person. A makeshift stage has been erected, framed by giant illuminated plastic bottles of Inca Kola, the national soft drink of Peru.

The show begins with a short skit by local children. The lighter-skinned and non-Black children play hacienda owners and the darker children portray slaves. As the plot develops, the children playing slaves are whipped for their misbehavior, and the crowd laughs uproariously. I am saddened and bewildered by the performance of this skit by descendants of enslaved Africans, but I note that no one else around me seems disturbed by the onstage spectacle. I am reminded of the comment of a Black Peruvian actor in Lima, who told me he began to conduct workshops in Chincha to cultivate pride in Afro-Peruvian folklore because he heard so many children in that area call each other "Black African" as an insult (Sandoval 2000).

The festival continues. The Ballumbrosio children dance their version of festejo. Little girls in midriff-baring tops, matching skirts, and bare feet move and shake while boys play cajones (figure 5.2). The rest of the festival lineup is live salsa music performed by artists imported from Lima.[1] The sound system blares so loud I wonder if my ears will explode before the night is over. It is almost impossible for me to make out words spoken into the microphone, especially with my still-imperfect Spanish.

The festival is sponsored by Inca Kola, and various prizes are awarded throughout the night to promote the soda company's name. About halfway through the show, the announcer calls for volunteers and lights pan the audience. Spotting a blonde head, the announcer and floodlights stop short. I know what is

FIGURE 5.2. The Ballumbrosio family dance company performs at the Festival of the District of El Carmen, August 1998. *Photo by the author.*

about to happen. When I am called to the stage, I reluctantly come forward. I am asked my name and some other questions I can barely make out over the sound system. The announcer can't understand my name when I answer him, so he christens me after a popular television commercial featuring a blonde woman named Yungay. The audience laughs uproariously. I am given my prizes and sent, embarrassed, back to my new friends, who congratulate me.

More than two years and several visits later, I return to El Carmen and the Ballumbrosios' house for Christmas. Some of Amador and Adelina Ballumbrosio's children have come home from Spain, Illinois, and Lima for the holidays, bringing spouses, children, and friends. We sleep four, five, and six to a room. Several of the Ballumbrosios sleep on mats on the hard floor to make room for their guests. We take turns at the meal table. Some of the visitors in the house include a Belgian photographer preparing a photo exhibition of Afro-Peruvian culture, a video team making a documentary on Afro-Peruvian women, a U.S. woman who is working with one of the Ballumbrosio brothers to create a music therapy curriculum, and a group of young travelers from Switzerland who met another Ballumbrosio brother in a bar in Lima and were invited to his house for Christmas. At one point during the week, in order to explain my enduring nickname, "Yungay," María Ballumbrosio tells some of her visiting brothers and sisters the story of my "performance" at the 1998 festival. But the story has changed quite a bit. Reconfigured in memory, I did not just speak onstage, I also danced festejo, which I did with grace and style because "*Maribel taught her well.*" What is remarkable is that the whole family agrees that this was how things happened, whereas I have no memory of dancing on that stage. I don't contradict them, I just think about the socially constructed nature of truth and how time reconfigures memories.

Chincha: Making the Legend

As the legendary rural cradle of Black music's origins in Peru, Chincha is located at the crossroads of two projects: the reawakening of diasporic identity in Peru and the sight-making process of the cultural tourism industry. Although Chincha was not the only place in Peru where Black heritage was conserved, its uses in the revival singled it out as the center of African and Afro-Peruvian retentions. In fact, the legend of Chincha took such strong root in the national imagination that some Peruvians began to believe that all Blacks in Peru come from Chincha (Martínez 1995, 13). This newly identified site of African diasporic cultural memory then was converted into a rural enclave for the modern tourist gaze (Urry 2002) of urban Peruvians and foreigners.

In the 1960s and 1970s, numerous revival artists, tape recorders in hand, visited Chincha in search of the authentic rural origins of Afro-Peruvian music. While several of the performers in the Pancho Fierro company were themselves originally from Chincha, the urban leaders of Cumanana and Perú Negro traveled to Chincha to collect and record songs and dances, popularizing and staging them in theatrical performances. Later, beginning in the 1990s, Chincha's music was staged in the Afro-Spanish rock of Miki González (1993) and the international world music of Afro-Peruvian singer Susana Baca (Baca 2000a; Baca, Basili, and Pereira 1992). The cumulative effect of the inundation of Chincha's small rural towns with urban Blacks (and non-Blacks) seeking to document, record, and stage local traditions was to position Chincha as a newly validated center for the distribution of African diasporic culture in the Black Pacific, remapping center and periphery once again by relocating the source of African cultural heritage to Peru.

Although Chincha first was "discovered" by revival artists, scholars soon learned that Chincha was the source of many of the songs and dances staged as urban folklore. As a result, beginning in the late 1970s, scholars called public attention to Chincha's status as the place of origin of the music of the urban revival. For example, North American ethnomusicologist William Tompkins visited Chincha in the late 1970s and documented its traditions in his dissertation (1981). Tompkins contrasted the reinvented urban landó of the Afro-Peruvian revival with the community-based landó of Chincha's El Guayabo community, noting that the El Guayabo dance was the prototype for Perú Negro's commercially staged version (1981, 298–299). Later, Tompkins included a description of Chincha's Christmas festival traditions (which had been staged by urban revival artists) in an article in *The Garland Encyclopedia of World Music* (1998). Peruvian musicologist Chalena Vásquez' dissertation on the music of Chincha's Christmas festival, based on her observations and recordings of staged rehearsals by the Ballumbrosio family in 1979, became an award-winning book (R. Vásquez Rodríguez 1982).

A brief discussion of how Chalena Vásquez became interested in Chincha illustrates how it was singled out as the authentic "backstage" of the music of the urban revival. Vásquez originally intended to write her dissertation on the Afro-Peruvian festejo. But when she and a colleague interviewed Nicomedes Santa Cruz and Vicente Vásquez in Lima, they were told that the festejo was a modern invention and that the only "authentic" Black music was in Chincha. Vásquez recalls, "Nicomedes said, 'you come to do your research and you are like someone who picks up a cigar butt and wants to know who smoked it! . . . you want to verify something that no longer exists. The only thing that exists is Amador [Ballumbrosio] over there [in Chincha] if you want to research something.' . . . Nicomedes told me that the festejo was a recreation of Don Porfirio's . . . When Don Vicente [Vásquez] tells me that the festejo was not danced, and when Nicomedes tells me that it doesn't exist . . . that's when I go to El Carmen . . . I changed my topic to the *danza de negritos*" (R. Vásquez Rodríguez 2000a).

The introduction of Vásquez' book demonstrates the clear line she draws between the spontaneous (Chincha's *danza de negritos*) and the commercial (Lima's revivalist folklore groups):

> We realized that we had begun from a false hypothesis. The intense activity of many musical groups of so-called Black, Negroid, and Afro folklore . . . made us think that the music presented on stage also had a spontaneous and intense production at the popular level . . . But the musical practice that we had encountered took place primarily within . . . this frame: the commercial . . .
>
> Later . . . we headed for the South: to Chincha and Cañete, places where the Black population is larger . . . We traversed work settlements and haciendas, whose residents emphasized that "these days that music is hardly ever heard," "that was in the old days," or "there is no money for fiestas" . . . Amid this search, we discovered in El Carmen, a town near Chincha . . . an expression that has great current popularity and is realized as part of the Christmas celebration: the danza de negritos. (R. Vásquez Rodríguez 1982, 9–10)

The attention of revival artists and scholars paved the way for the development of Chincha as a tourist sight. This is not unusual; public validation by scholars often creates tourist sights for public consumption (see Castañeda 1996). In fact, Dean MacCannell affirms that mass tourism is the result of "three hundred years of foreplay" by explorers, soldiers, missionaries, and anthropologists ([1976] 1989), and Edward Bruner (1996) concurs that where anthropologists go, tourists are sure to follow.[2] When the Shining Path's war of terror came to an end in the 1990s and Lima residents once again began vacationing in rural areas, Chincha became a showcase of traditional Afro-Peruvian culture for urban tourists, and, as Javier León observes, "one of the last windows into a way of life that most Limeños have only come to learn through the performances of professional Afro-Peruvian folk dance troupes, newspaper articles, educational television programs and publicity campaigns promoting tourism" (León Quirós 1998, 1–2). In the late 1980s, a Lima-based television production company visited Chincha to film and broadcast scenes of traditional life, including Afro-Peruvian music and dance (*Los negros* 1988). In the 1980s and 1990s, photographer Lorry Salcedo also captured Chincha on film, presenting it to the world as the Black face of Peru in an internationally touring photograph exhibition titled "Africa's Legacy." Tourism infrastructure began to develop, marketing new and existing regional festivals of Black arts as tourist attractions.

In contrast with Adorno's portrayal of museums as "mausoleums" where objects go to die ([1967] 1995, 175), this living display of Chincha's inherited traditions accomplished the dual purpose of supporting the endurance of African legacies in Peru and displaying them for tourists *in situ*. Such exhibitions are common tourism tactics in a world in which, as Barbara Kirshenblatt-Gimblett suggests, "whole countries market themselves as 'the world's largest open air museum,'" providing a kind of intimacy lacking in a real museum while framing real life as "a picture of itself" for the tourist gaze (1998, 131, 144). This technique makes sense in Peru, a country rich in historical and archeological treasures but poor in resources with which to preserve and display them. In Chincha, the nation's African cultural heritage is easily displayed with little or no overhead expense by the tourism industry or government.

By the time I (one more academic tourist with recorder in hand) first arrived on the scene in 1998, Chincha was both the legendary center of Black musical heritage and a full-fledged tourist attraction. All of the markers that identified Chincha as the birthplace of Afro-Peruvian music and an important tourist sight were in place. In my interviews with urban Afro-Peruvian musicians, Chincha frequently was described as a mythical place where the African heritage re-created in Lima had always survived. In live concerts of Afro-Peruvian music, I often heard the name "Chincha" invoked in homage, and musicians from Chincha received special introductions, implying that they added authenticity to the performance. Some of the most frequently performed revival songs mentioned Chincha or chronicled events of its rural life. Scholars, musicians, dancers, cab drivers, and friends in Lima insisted that I must go there, although some warned that it was no longer as authentic as it used to be because of tourism and commercialization.

Yet, the reality I encountered in Chincha in the 1990s—the second generation of tourism—often contradicted what I had been led to expect. Ironically, as noted in chapter 4, while Perú Negro went to Chincha to document and stage its folklore, it was rumored that many of the residents of Chincha later adopted stylized versions of their own dances, learned from Perú Negro's televised broadcasts (León Quirós 1998, 10–11; R. Vásquez Rodríguez 1982, 48) (and, in fact, at parties that I attended, Chincha girls performed the exact festejo choreography routines I had learned at dance classes taught by a former member of Perú Negro in Lima). This creates a postmodern chicken-or-the-egg scenario that complicates simplistic modernist trajectories of authentic rural origin and stylized urban copy. When questioned about their music and dance, young Chinchanos talked about their interest in rock and Afro-Latin hip hop. Several members of the Ballumbrosio family actually live some or all of the time in Lima, the United States, or Europe, where they lead modern lives, playing in rock bands or pursuing professional non-music careers. Whereas taxi drivers and other passing acquaintances in Lima assured me that all children from Chincha are born knowing how to dance festejo because it is "in their blood," any visitor who stays long enough would find that the Ballumbrosio family dancers excel because of a professional system of rehearsals, and that many other local children are unable to perform the steps of Afro-Peruvian dances. Similarly, while I was led to expect that I would arrive in El Carmen and immediately see little Black children dancing zapateo in the main square, in all of my visits to Chincha this only happened once (at the peak of tourist season, clearly for my benefit and my cash). In fact, it was only during tourist season that Chincha appeared to resemble its legendary image, and even at those times contradictions were readily apparent. For example, during "Black Christmas," only two of numerous groups of dancers on display in the town square of El Carmen were composed of Blacks; the majority were mestizos. Yet, somehow Chincha maintained its reputation as the rural cradle of authentic premodern

Black music and dance—despite the signs of (post)modernity, mestizaje, and hybridity readily apparent to visitors who choose to see them.

What could explain such a blending of diasporic consciousness with tourist display, juxtaposing the modernist quest for authenticity with seemingly postmodern role reversals? Searching for answers, I turned to the interdisciplinary literature on tourism and the staging of expressive culture.

Staged Authenticity, Post-Tourism, and Hybrid Cultures

The issue of authenticity in tourism received its seminal treatment from Dean MacCannell, whose groundbreaking book *The Tourist: A New Theory of the Leisure Class* is an "ethnography of modernity" ([1976] 1989, 1). MacCannell argues that postindustrial modern society expands itself through mass leisure and international tourism. Because Modern Man craves the authenticity that was displaced by modernity, the premodern world is preserved in peripheral enclaves for him to experience through tourism. To satisfy his craving, Modern Man (a.k.a. the Tourist) leaves the centers of modernity to visit premodern society, and, despite his nostalgia for a "simpler life," his experiences ultimately reconfirm the superiority of modernity.

MacCannell's major contribution in *The Tourist* was the idea of the "staged authenticity" of tourist spaces, based on sociologist Erving Goffman's frame analysis theory (Goffman 1959 and 1974). MacCannell extends Goffman's binary notion of the front (show) and back (real) spaces of social encounters to the tourist experience, defining six hypothetical regions along the continuum from front to back: (1) Goffman's front region, where tourists are given an obvious show (the tourist trap); (2) a touristic front region decorated to look like a back region; (3) a front region totally organized to look like a back region; (4) a back region open to outsiders; (5) a back region that is occasionally cleaned up for tourists' eyes; and (6) Goffman's intimate and "authentic" back region, "the kind of social space that motivates touristic consciousness" (MacCannell [1976] 1989, 102). The stages between "front" and "back" make it impossible for tourists ever to be certain that they are actually in the back region. Thus, the tourist's crisis of modernity is ultimately irresolvable because what appears to be an authentic premodern experience really may be a hoax.

In *The Tourist*, MacCannell also argues that the "sights" considered important by tourists have no inherent worth. Through the process of "sight sacralization," these previously unspectacular tourist sights are marked, elevated, enshrined, reproduced in effigies or postcards, and canonized ([1976] 1989, 44–45). Local ethnic populations can be sacralized as tourist sights—alongside monuments, works of art, and battlegrounds—and obligated to perform a false version of themselves that MacCannell calls "forced traditionalism." MacCannell writes, "Traditional folks dramatize their backwardness as a way of fitting themselves in the total design of modern society as attractions . . . This process is accompanied by the social production of highly fictionalized versions of everyday life of traditional peoples, a museumification of their quaintness" ([1976] 1989, 178). As Dennis Graburn (1976) adds, these types of human spectacles often result from the government or tourist industry's promotion of previously sublimated ethnic populations and their folk arts as local color and borrowed national identity.

The Tourist launched a new body of interdisciplinary scholarship on tourism (see Crick 1989). Although MacCannell's theories continued to inspire and inform numerous studies two decades later (for example, Bruner and Kirshenblatt-Gimblett 1994; Cooper Alarcón 1997; Desmond 1999), tourism theorists reformulated MacCannell's model from postmodern and poststructuralist perspectives that abandon the notion of the back region because they view all culture as staged and migratory, blurring the boundaries between tourists and locals. MacCannell himself now redefines tourist sites as "empty meeting grounds," or social spaces resulting from new postmodern forms of tourism that cause modern center and premodern periphery to collide, as "ex-primitives" migrate to the centers of modernity and co-produce the tourist experience with postmodern tourists (1992). Similar reconceptualizations of fixed notions of place are found in James Clifford's (1997b) concept of "traveling cultures" and Barbara Kirshenblatt-Gimblett's writings on the museumification of the world (1998). In this new postmodern geography of tourism, the role of authenticity has been reexamined. Erik Cohen (1988) and Yvonne Daniel (1996) argue that authenticity is socially constructed and therefore changeable; what once was viewed as inauthentic can later acquire "emergent" or "creative" authenticity. Cohen (1988) and James Urry (2002) add that tourism often is a form of play in which authenticity is not taken seriously; Urry's "post-tourist" (borrowed from Feifer 1986) is aware of the hoax of staged authenticity but willingly plays the game. Similarly, Edward Bruner and Barbara Kirshenblatt-Gimblett (1994) dispense with the modernist quest for authenticity, describing "tourist realism" as a type of theatrical performance in which tourists willingly suspend their disbelief in order to heighten their experience. Notably, these authors retain MacCannell's central metaphor of tourism as a staged performance.

Is Chincha an authentic center of African-derived culture, a staged back region, or a playful display of post-tourism? Nestor García Canclini's work on tourism and popular culture in Latin America (1995 and 1997) offers an alternative to the mutually exclusive application of modern versus postmodern frameworks to the study of Chincha and other locales. García Canclini argues that Latin American nations are home to hybrid cultures that seem to have been postmodern for centuries. However, such apparent postmodernisms indicate the particularly Latin American state of "modernity without modernization," in which premodern traditions linger but true modernity has not completely arrived (1995, 1 and 6). Latin American folk artists occupy a special hybrid position linked to tourist economies, an existence they navigate with "strategies for entering and leaving modernity." Although these artists live and work in the realm of the "traditional," their premodern existence is enabled and consumed by the modern tourist marketplace, and they eagerly mix elements of both worlds in their lives and expressive cultural forms (García Canclini 1995; 1997, 37–47). Thus, García Canclini urges analysts of Latin American societies to account for the simultaneous existence of modern and "traditional" ways of relating to the world rather than applying a universal framework of postmodernism (1995, 6).

Accordingly, I will argue in this chapter that the social construction of the legend of Chincha reflects elements of both modern and postmodern perspectives on tourism. For example, while postmodern theories accurately describe certain elements of the tourist experience in Chincha, I believe that to announce the universal obsolescence of the modernist quest for authenticity would be premature. It was the myth of authenticity that compelled Afro-Peruvian revival artists, scholars, and tourists to make pilgrimages to Chincha, and the legend of Chincha reinscribed this myth in the national imagination. Certainly, authenticity is socially constructed, but it still matters to many tourists and locals in ways that resemble MacCannell's modernist ethnography of *The Tourist*. At the same time, postmodern theories have elaborated upon the ways tourism is staged, expanding upon MacCannell's initially exclusive emphasis on modernity as the central factor in tourism analysis. Chincha's tourism performances often resemble a postmodern collage, poking fun at master narratives by intermingling modern and premodern, local and tourist, Black and mestizo, past and present. Because the citizens of Chincha live simultaneously in "modern" and "traditional" worlds, their expressive culture alternates between these experiences. Ironically, whereas urban revival artists tended to reify folklore and discount contemporary forms of Afro-Peruvian popular culture, in Chincha both types of performance are equally valued as an expression of local identity—often to the dismay of outsiders who would prefer that Chincha preserve the past without moving into the present.

Thus, as this chapter chronicles, although the creation and promotion of Chincha as a tourist sight for seekers of the origins of Afro-Peruvian culture is, in many ways, a classic case of MacCannell's staged authenticity, it is also an example of García Canclini's hybridization of the traditional and the modern. On another level, the legend of Chincha might be perceived as a postmodern theatrical spectacle of post-tourism (Feifer 1986; Urry 2002) co-produced by scholars, revival artists, tourists, and Chincha residents, in which "tourists" and "natives" sometimes exchange roles. As co-producers, like Dean MacCannell's "ex-primitives," Chincha residents are not passive victim-objects of the tourist gaze; they are skillful agents in their own objectification by tourists. To provide a closer glimpse at how Chincha simultaneously operates as a staged tourist sight and a center of Afro-Peruvian heritage, the following sections describe Chincha's main tourist attractions: the Ballumbrosio family home, the Hacienda San José, and the festivals of Black Summer and Black Christmas.

A Cultural Tourist's Guide to Chincha: The Ballumbrosio Family and the Hacienda San José

Chincha is about two hours south of Lima on the Peruvian coast. Within the province of Chincha is a relatively modern district also called Chincha.[3] About twenty minutes further down the Pan American Highway, a dirt road leads inland to several small districts where Blacks settled after abolition, continuing to perform agricultural labor. The districts of El Carmen, San Regis, El Guayabo, and San José are known for their high concentration of Black residents, folklore and music traditions, and rural lifestyle. Roads are unpaved and most residents lack plumbing or telephones. In many areas, water is drawn daily from a communal tank. However, families take care of each other and expenses are less than those of urban life.

Various Peruvian publications orient the visitor to the area and its musical traditions. In a tourism guidebook to the region, published by the Catholic University of Peru in 1995, the section on "Black Music" reads:

> It arrived in Peru with the African slaves. Their musical instruments no longer exist, but their music became songs governed by rhythm and percussion. This music produced Afro-Peruvian dance . . . The grace and charm of Black women during their dances is proverbial. They display agility, mischief, and cunning coquetry. Their attire is almost always ample skirts and a kerchief on the head. They can dance without shoes, which makes them feel lighter, but they almost never forget to wear hoops in their ears . . . In the area of Black music and dance, the members of the Vallumbrosio family . . . are famous, authentic bearers of the Black arts of Chincha.[4] They reside in the town of El Carmen. They are

proud of their lineage, and they constitute an authentic dynasty of ebony artists. (Del Busto Duthurburu et al. 1995, 25–32)

Documental del Perú, a multi-volume guide to regional Peruvian culture published in 1988, offers this description under the heading "The Negroid":

> In the district of El Carmen of the province of Chincha, there still lives one of the most famous colonies of Blacks in Peru. Happy and dark, simple and profoundly human, descendants of the Blacks brought from Africa for the agricultural labors of past eras, they have given, and continue to give the country famous sports figures, musical instruments, dances, sayings, foods, and customs which have been interwoven in the fabric of the national soul. And today, this hot land of San José and San Regis oozes the life of these colossal brown people, yoked to the sod for centuries, but full of that happy sadness of the coastal "morenos,"[5] as they like to be called. Friendly and musical morenos, famous players of the cajón, the mule's quijada and the guitar, they survive off the thirsty soil, stubborn and wrinkled like a thorny shrub, still believing a bit in their ancestral fetishes, in their crafty and solemn sorcerers, in their "calls," in the "evil eye," in the mysteries of the far-off jungle . . . (N.a. 1988, 64)

These tourist narratives represent Black Chinchanos as frozen in an imagined premodern past when African slaves worked the land, danced, and sang ritual songs. Such "noble savage" descriptions entice not only foreign tourists but also urban Peruvians to visit Chincha's exotic and charismatic Black population. Because Blacks are socially invisible in Peruvian urban areas, they can be described in their rural habitat as an oddity, a museum artifact for viewing by the curious. The Black residents of Chincha perform their identity for tourists in ways that conform to this romanticized premodern past, enacting what Dean MacCannell might call "forced traditionalism" ([1976] 1989). Yet, at least in the case of the prominent Ballumbrosio family, "voluntary traditionalism" might better describe their willing participation in the museumification of Chincha (albeit influenced by the lack of other options).

Amador Ballumbrosio, who proudly claims both African and indigenous ancestry, is generally regarded as the leading culture bearer in the preservation of Chincha's Afro-Peruvian heritage. As a small child, Amador swore to keep Black Peruvian music and dance alive. As the story goes, at the age of four, he nearly drowned in a river, but he was saved by passers-by. Upon his safe return, Amador's mother immediately took him to church. There she made her son promise Jesus that he would dance or play music all his life, carrying on the cultural traditions of the Black people of his town in order to give thanks for the miracle that saved his life (C. Ballumbrosio 2000; E. Ballumbrosio 2000, 170).

Today, Amador Ballumbrosio and his wife, Adelina, are the parents of fifteen children, all of whom play music or dance. The Ballumbrosio family actively promotes two types of performance traditions: dances linked with local religious or festival traditions and staged folklore. Most of the boys and men play drums (cajón, congas, bongó, or drum-set) and dance zapateo. Girls and women are more often seen dancing festejo. Female members of the Ballumbrosio family run a dance academy for local children, offering Afro-Peruvian dance classes free of charge in the Ballumbrosio living room. When the Ballumbrosio family is called upon to perform at the nearby Hacienda San José, in a concert by Peruvian rock star Miki González, on television, or in their own home for tourists, a willing and able corpus of dancers can be supplied.

For tourists and newcomers to Chincha, the Ballumbrosio family home is a mandatory stop on the tour of authentic Black culture. In fact, many tour groups, en route from Machu Picchu to Lima, arrange to visit Chincha for a taste of Afro-Peruvian music (and sometimes cuisine). Tour buses pull up in front of the Ballumbrosio home at specified times, contracted in advance with Maribel by travel agencies in Lima. Tourists sit on benches around the perimeter of the room. The boys play cajón while little girls dressed in skirts and halters festooned with glitter and ribbons dance their way into the room. Festejo is always the rhythm that is performed, and the little girls smile and dance energetically. Tourists marvel at the young girls' skill and agility, but they are not permitted to maintain their comfortable distance; at the end of the performance each of the dancers adopts a tourist and insists upon dancing with him or her. After the show, a baseball cap is passed for tips.[6] Having mingled a bit with the natives, the tourists file back onto their bus and continue sightseeing.

The show in the Ballumbrosios' living room is not limited to the gaze of tourists who physically make the trip to Chincha. In the 1980s, a Peruvian media production company called TV Cultura (in collaboration with Lima's Black rights organization Movimiento Francisco Congo) filmed Afro-Peruvian music and dance scenes in Chincha, including a segment featuring María Ballumbrosio teaching young girls to perform festejo amid a circle of onlookers in the Ballumbrosios' living room (*Los negros* 1988). A clip from this film appears in the JVC/Smithsonian Folkways Video Anthology of Music and Dance of the Americas (Various Artists 1995b), a primary source of classroom video images used by professors of ethnomusicology at U.S. (and other) colleges. Thus, for the virtual tourists who study the musical cultures of the world in college classes (and for their professors), the Ballumbrosios' style of performing for tourists represents "the" festejo.[7]

As Erik Cohen (1988) and Valerie Smith ([1989a] 1995) note, the nature of tourist impact on local culture varies depending on the type of tourists involved. Who are the tourists who visit the Ballumbrosios, why are they there, and what types of tourist gazes (Urry 2002) do they cast upon Chincha? Three kinds of tourists tend to visit the Ballumbrosio family: (1) academic or artistic tourists from Peru and abroad who develop relationships with the family (for example, César Calvo, Perú Negro, Chalena Vásquez, and me); (2) partygoers from Lima who leave the cares of the city behind to attend Chincha's infamous weeklong festivals, where they drink heavily, dance all night, and often find romance; and (3) cultural tourists seeking a brief glimpse of the back region of Afro-Peruvian culture, preferably viewed from a comfortable distance and for a limited period of time (for example, tourists who attend shows in the Ballumbrosio living room).

Like all ideal types, these categories may overlap. However, these tourist types usually can be identified by where they stay, and for how long. The longer tourists stay in Chincha, and the more they venture outside of the tourist "set," the more likely it is that they will see the barely concealed signs of the constructedness of Chincha's staged performances of itself. Academic and artistic types stay in the Ballumbrosios' home; revelers from Lima either stay up all night dancing and catch a bus back to Lima or avail themselves of hotels and bed-and-breakfasts in the district of Chincha; and tourist-travelers either don't stay at all (getting off their tour bus at the Ballumbrosios' house and leaving once the show is over) or stay at the comfortable and elegant Hacienda San José, about ten minutes from the entrance to El Carmen.

The Hacienda San José is the second major stop on the tour of Chincha. Formerly a working hacienda in the district of San José, this elegant building and its lush grounds have been converted into a museum and bed-and-breakfast catering to the wealthy. The building dates from the early seventeenth century and has served as both a sugarcane plantation and a tobacco factory (Del Busto Duthurburu et al. 1995, 27–28). As Denys Cuche explains, the towns surrounding the hacienda were built in part by local landowners who were forced to provide housing for former slaves after abolition but wanted to maintain a comfortable distance from them (1975, 136). It is said that the last descendants of the family that owned the hacienda were murdered on the front steps during a Black workers' rebellion amid the War of the Pacific in 1879. Today, the hacienda remains an otherworldly island of comforts amid the poverty of the surrounding towns, where the descendants of slaves live in substandard housing. Many neighboring residents work for the hacienda in a power relationship not

Figure 5.3. Church, Hacienda San José. *Photo by the author.*

far removed from that of slavery (see Cuche 1975; León Quirós 1998; R. Vásquez Rodríguez 1982).

At the Hacienda San José, tourists take an imaginary trip back to the days of slavery, framing the residents of surrounding communities as their slave ancestors and reenacting the plantation economy for the tourist market, enhanced by tourists' own interactive experience with "the set" and "the natives." Upon entering the grounds, enclosed by a locking gate at the end of a dirt road, tourists are immediately impressed by the well-maintained facility, a sharp contrast to the surrounding towns. Next to the main building stands a church with an eighteenth-century baroque façade and elaborately carved wood altar. The hacienda stairway leads up to a large front porch, adorned with archways. At ground level is a door that opens to a cavern-like room with stone walls, where slave torture instruments (such as ankle and wrist shackles) are preserved and displayed.

Inside the hacienda, an air of comfortable elegance pervades open spaces. The front lobby leads to a courtyard area, with glass cases displaying work tools and other artifacts of slavery. A large back porch overlooks the well-groomed lawn, where a swimming pool and bar are nestled among manicured trees. On the back porch, lavish spreads of comida criolla are served each Sunday while Afro-Peruvian music and dance groups execute dances such as the festejo, alcatraz, and zapateo. Dancers silently perform the role of their slave ancestors, framed by the explanations of a narrator who educates the tourists about the history and significance of these dances for the enslaved Africans who worked the lands surrounding Hacienda San José in days gone by. As in virtually every other performance of Afro-Peruvian music, at some point the tourists are persuaded to leave their seats and learn the hip-swiveling movements of the festejo and other dances, brushing shoulders with "the natives."

Back toward the atrium, tourists are invited to lift the trap door and visit the dark catacombs under the hacienda. They light the passageway with hand-held candles. A tour guide leads the way, explaining that slaves were blindfolded and herded through the subterranean passageways, which are said to have extended all the way from the ocean port to the hacienda, so that they would not know their way back if they were to escape. Human bones can still be found strewn on the ground. The tour guide tells tourists to blow out their candles and imagine what it would be like to find one's way through the catacombs in darkness. Just then, the tour guide disappears, and tourists must find their own way back to the trapdoor. Curiosity briefly turns to anxiety, which is alleviated when the trapdoor opens, flooding the passageway with light. All is well.

A tourist guidebook describes the Hacienda San José this way:

> The music, the jasmine perfume, the history of its catacombs, the religious festivals, and the little Black children with their white dresses make San José seem like a dream. Today, the hacienda house has been converted into a touristic inn, offering visitors double and family-style rooms with private baths, sports facilities, a pool, horses, barbeques and typical foods, Negroid music groups, and a special place for conventions. (Del Busto Duthurburu et al. 1995, 29)

Thus, the hacienda is a dream-like museum of slavery, and the live performances by Afro-Peruvian music and dance groups bring a framed historical encounter into the staged authenticity of the tourist space. By extension, the entire town of El Carmen and the area of Chincha have been socially constructed as a museum of Afro-Peruvian folklore that is visited on weekends and at festival times by both Peruvian and foreign tourists looking for exotic back regions. During most of the year, the town's musical entertainment conforms to the tastes of mainstream Peruvian urban dwellers (which is why the local festival that I attended in 1998, which attracts few if any tourists, was dominated by salsa music). At special holidays and festival times such as "Black Summer" and "Black Christmas," however, Chincha transforms itself into a living exhibition of authentic local color for tourism.

Black Summer: The Yunza

The yunza is a communal ritual dance performed in indigenous and mestizo communities throughout the Peruvian Andes to celebrate the end of Carnival. In the Chincha region, the Andean yunza tradition has been appropriated and adapted to include Black music and dance styles. Although Nicomedes Santa Cruz considered the yunza an "Andean survival" in an Afro-Peruvian community (1969a, 12), the inclusion of Afro-Peruvian music and dance has earmarked the event as a rural showcase of African heritage in the eyes of tourists. Ethnomusicologist William Tompkins observed that, in the late 1970s, the yunza was "one of the few remaining folkloric dances of coastal Peru performed as a community rather than by an esoteric group in a private home festivity" (1981, 349).

As in the Andean prototype, each year a host is responsible for decorating a tree with fruits, candies, gifts, balloons, and whatever else she or he can afford. Musicians are hired to play locally popular styles. According to William Tompkins, a typical 1970s yunza band in Chincha and nearby towns included two or more guitars, singers, a cajón, and a quijada. The yunza that I observed in El Carmen in 2000 featured an ensemble with added Latin percussion: a guitar, singers, cajón, cowbell, and bongó. The structure of the dance seems to have remained fairly consistent from the 1970s to 2000; dancers hold hands and move in a slow circle in both clockwise and counter-clockwise directions around the tree. Periodically, the music speeds up and a male–female couple dances in the center of the circle and then uses an axe to chop at the tree. When the last couple causes the tree to fall, children gather up the goodies that fall from its branches. The couple that knocks the tree down is responsible for planting a new one and serving as host for the following year's yunza.

William Tompkins noted that, in the 1970s, the yunza sometimes was called the *huanchigualo*. Huanchigualo is also the name of a song performed in responsorial solo–chorus fashion with panalivio-style accompaniment during the circle dance around the yunza tree.[8] Tompkins asserts, based on his interviews with elderly jaranero Augusto Ascuez of Lima, that the huanchigualo was not always part of the yunza, belonging originally to the "Ño Carnavalón" burial ceremony on Ash Wednesday.[9] This is particularly important because many urban Peruvians believe that the huanchigualo is the only authentic song of the yunza, and they lament its replacement with "nontraditional" songs and rhythms.

When Tompkins visited El Carmen and El Guayabo in the 1970s, he found that the most prevalent music in the yunza was the huanchigualo, which alternated a fixed chorus with either humorous, improvised verses

FIGURE 5.4. Dancing during the *yunza*, 1992. *Photos by Lorry Salcedo, reprinted with permission.*

or Spanish classical poetry. For example, Tompkins collected the following song lyrics (1981, 356–357):

Anoche me acosté	Last night I went to bed
con una niña bonita	with a beautiful girl
Huanchigualito, huanchigualo	Huanchigualito, huanchigualo
para amante, sólo yo	for a lover, only me
Cuando yo me recordé	When I remembered
era tuerta y rocachita	she was one-eyed and bald
Huanchigualito, huanchigualo	Huanchigualito, huanchigualo
para amante, sólo yo	for a lover, only me

After a few such verses are sung, the instrumentalists change the rhythm and increase the tempo while a couple dances in the middle of the circle. Tompkins observed festejos, marineras, and other coastal dances in this section of the yunzas in the 1970s, and musicologist Chalena Vásquez was told by residents of El Carmen in the late 1970s that the couple dances may include the marinera, tondero, *toro mata*, and other "indecent *bailes de cintura* [dances of the waist]" (R. Vásquez Rodríguez 1982, 63). Verses sung during the couple dance were often sexually suggestive (Tompkins 1981, 358).

The yunza I observed in El Carmen in 2000 illustrates the growth of the tourism industry since the initial construction of Chincha as a tourist sight. The yunza had become part of the fifteenth annual weeklong Carnival festival called Verano Negro (Black Summer). Organized by the Municipality of Chincha to promote tourism, Verano Negro included plays, symposia, concerts, a beauty contest and swimsuit competition, yunzas, and even a yunza competition. T-shirts bearing slogans such as "Vamos pa' Chincha, familia!" (Let's go to Chincha, family!) and decorated with caricature-like images of large-lipped, voluptuous, dancing Black women were sold in the street.

In Verano Negro 2000, the yunza of El Carmen took place very late at night in an open-air neighborhood peña with a dirt patio and a cement dance floor, just outside the entrance to El Carmen. In the patio was a tree, covered with balloons, streamers, and a few other items. At midnight, a crowd of approximately sixty people sat on folding chairs around the tree, drinking beer and talking quietly. That evening's activities had begun with a concert in Chincha at about 10:00 PM, in which the Ballumbrosio family band and dancers were the last of a number of other local acts to perform. Because the instrumentalists in the Ballumbrosio family group were also the musicians for the yunza, the yunza started late. When all the musicians had returned from Chincha, the dancing finally began around 1:00 AM.

FIGURE 5.5. Poster advertising Verano Negro in Chincha, 2000.

Huanchigualo verses alternated with other Afro-Peruvian songs I had heard in Lima. Couple dances performed in the center of the circle were consistent with Tompkins' descriptions of the yunzas of the 1970s: festejo, alcatraz, and free-form dancing, usually with a sense of overt sexuality.

After the tree was felled, the yunza was followed by a dance party with amplified music played by a DJ and liquor for sale all night. Salsa, various Peruvian popular music styles (especially *cumbia andina*), and U.S. rap poured through the speakers until the sun came up the next morning, and adults danced and drank while children scrambled through the branches of the tree looking for fallen treasures.

I videotaped the yunza and later showed my video to the members of the Ballumbrosio family, especially for the benefit of Adelina, who had not attended the yunza in many years.[10] From the amused reactions of Adelina and her children, I learned that most of the participants who danced around the tree were Lima residents who had come to El Carmen specifically for the yunza. Ironically, tourists performed the traditional dance that they had come to El Carmen to watch, while the residents of El Carmen sat and observed the tourists.

Which was the back region: the traditional yunza danced primarily by tourists, or the subsequent party in which Chincha residents danced to music styles popular throughout Latin America and the United States? As the entire evening's topsy-turvy events demonstrate, MacCannell's continuum of staged authenticity should also take into account the multifaceted lives of "the natives" in tourist settings, who experience both front and back regions as a normal part of their daily lives. Indeed, for the residents of Chincha, both the yunza (including its ever-present tourist factor) and the dance party are authentic cultural expressions of their lived realities.

Black Christmas: The Festival of the Virgin of El Carmen

A predominantly Catholic country, Peru was the seat of the Spanish viceroy that governed most of Spanish-ruled South America beginning in the sixteenth century. As a result of this legacy, Peru's Andean communities are renowned for their elaborate Catholic festivals in honor of various incarnations of the Virgin Mary. Chincha's Festival of the Virgin of El Carmen, also known as "Navidad Negra" (Black Christmas), shares many elements with these other national festivals. Its events (including masses and *novenas*, music and dance, and the procession of the Virgin) extend from shortly before Christmas until the Day of Kings (January 6).

The festival is of great and solemn importance to the people of El Carmen, celebrating their devotion to Jesus and the Virgin of El Carmen.

FIGURE 5.6. Procession of the Virgin of El Carmen, 1992. *Photo by Lorry Salcedo, reprinted with permission.*

According to community elders, an image of the Virgin of El Carmen was found in a field in 1761. After the town church was constructed, the image miraculously relocated itself and appeared in the church sanctuary (Tompkins 1981, 330). The people of El Carmen believe that the image of the Virgin of El Carmen can grant miracles, and they honor and revere her in their Christmas festival.

The festivities are organized by brotherhoods affiliated with the church. During the festival, groups of young boys and men from Chincha and neighboring areas, called *hatajos de negritos*, dance and sing to violin accompaniment in front of nativity scenes in private homes, in the plaza de armas and streets of El Carmen, and in front of the church before mass. On Christmas Eve and December 27, groups of young girls (*pallas*) also dance in front of the church, accompanied by a violin and/or guitar player. On December 27, a large float containing the image of the Virgin of El Carmen and adorned with flowers and lights is transported by groups of about twenty-five or thirty men through the streets of El Carmen and neighboring towns from 8:00 PM until about 9:00 AM. The procession is accompanied by a brass band, and the floatbearers alternate every few blocks, allowing time for new flowers to adorn the float and for babies to be lifted up to kiss the Virgin's image. Residents know exactly when the

FIGURE 5.7. José Lurita (violin) and *hatajo de negritos*. *Photo reprinted with permission from* Caretas.

Virgin will pass by their home, and they decorate their streets and come out to greet her, no matter how late the hour. In addition to these religious events, the week is filled with evening parties and dances, fireworks, and family dinners on Christmas night.

In the early 1970s, Amador Ballumbrosio was a zapateador (tap dancer) and dance captain for the hatajo de negritos of El Carmen, and the late José Lurita (figure 5.7) was the violin master. Shortly afterwards, because Lurita was aging and had no apprentice, Amador trained as a violinist. Amador would become renowned both for his skill as a zapateador and his role as violinist and director of his hatajo. By 2000, several of Amador's sons had learned to play violin for the festival. Some, like their father, had made a promise to Jesus to play or dance in the festival for either a fixed number of years or their entire lives. Others simply participated out of their desire to carry on the tradition (C. Ballumbrosio 2000; R. Vásquez Rodríguez 1982, 75).

Amador Ballumbrosio trains and rehearses the hatajo de negritos of El Carmen in his home every Friday night from October until Christmas Eve. On the afternoon before Christmas in the Ballumbrosio family home, Amador Ballumbrosio ritually baptizes himself and then the new members of the hatajo with salty water in front of an altar with a baby Jesus figure in a wooden cradle. Most of the new participants are boys, ranging in age

FIGURE 5.8. Amador Ballumbrosio (violin) and son José (dancing) in Ballumbrosio family living room. Also pictured: Adelina Ballumbrosio (seated). *Photo by Lorry Salcedo, reprinted with permission.*

from four to ten. Many older participants return year after year to dance in the festivities.

The hatajos de negritos' repertoire consists of strophic songs in duple meter sung chorally, accompanied by one or more designated violinists whose instruments typically are decorated with streamers in the colors of the Peruvian flag (red and white). While singing, hatajo members mark each beat with handbells. The violin is tuned in fifths but normally pitched one or more tones below European standard tuning (a common tuning pattern is F–C–G–D). The hatajos draw from a repertoire of twenty-four traditional Christmas songs, each with its own lyrics, melody, rhythmic structure, and choreography (E. Ballumbrosio 2000, 171).[11] The melody is played on the violin's upper string, while the two middle strings articulate a repeated perfect fifth on open strings in rhythmic unison with the melody. The lowest string is rarely used. After the melody is played once, the dancers sing the lyrics, usually in choral unison and sometimes in call-and-response form, to the same violin accompaniment. Between verses, the dancers perform unison zapateo steps in two parallel line formations, their footwork providing both percussive rhythmic counterpoint with the violin (often juxtaposing triplets against duple rhythmic figures) and a visual display.

FIGURE 5.9. *Pallas*, 1992. *Photo by Lorry Salcedo, reprinted with permission.*

The negritos' costumes include a sash adorned with mirrors, bits of ribbon, and sometimes money; a crown-like hat decorated with ribbons and glitter; small handbells; and rope whips, which often are decorated with bells that jingle to mark the beat of the songs.[12] Typically, the members of the hatajo dance in two lines, each line managed by a *caporal* (foreman or captain) who keeps the formation in order and the dancing in time. Traditionally, a *viejito* (old man) wearing a wrinkled mask performed with the hatajo, amusing audience members and keeping them from getting too close to the dancers (Tompkins 1981, 331). In the 2000 Christmas festivities, only one hatajo had a viejito.

The pallas (figure 5.9) are the female counterpart to the negritos, and they normally range from very young to adolescent girls. On Christmas Eve, attired in white dresses, gloves, and bridal veils and carrying tall staffs decorated with ribbons, the pallas perform graceful zapateo steps to the accompaniment of a guitar and/or violin. On the day after Christmas, the pallas change their white outfits for similar pink ones. An older woman carrying a doll-like replica of baby Jesus accompanies the pallas (see figure

5.9), while two younger pallas carrying another baby Jesus figure accompany the negritos.

As a community expression of deep Catholic belief in the miracles performed by the Virgin Mary and Jesus, the Black Christmas festival is a legacy of Spanish colonialism and the conversion of Africans and indigenous Peruvians to Catholicism. The custom of singing and dancing villancicos (Christmas songs) in front of nativity scenes in private homes is an ancient Spanish one, and there is evidence of its adoption in Peru as early as the seventeenth century. Tompkins adds that many of the song texts used by the negritos are Spanish religious verses sung throughout Latin America (1981, 338).

Other dramatic elements of the Christmas festival and its music clearly reference the historical experience of Peruvian Blacks. Most obvious is the fact that the groups are called negritos, or "little Blacks" (although, as I will explain shortly, negritos dances also are performed in indigenous communities). As William Tompkins observes, costumes and song lyrics depict opposing aspects of Black heritage: that of kings and that of slaves (1981, 342). The crown-like hats represent kingliness, whereas the whips, caporal (foreman), and the name *amito* (plantation slave-owner) given to the director of the hatajo recall aspects of slavery. Finally, many of the lyrics of the songs performed by the negritos appear to reference slavery, either directly or metaphorically. For example, the song "Zancudito," which describes a mosquito's bite, is commonly interpreted as a metaphor for the pain of the foreman's whip; and the song "Panalivio" refers to the hardships slaves endured while working in the fields. The festival ends with the ritual burning of costumes at "Bethlehem" (a river bed in El Carmen) and a riverside dance on Epiphany, an important holiday for Christians of African heritage around the world because of the belief that one of the three kings who visited and bestowed gifts upon the baby Jesus was a Black man.

Although tourists who come to El Carmen for the Christmas festival tend to identify it as an "Afro-Peruvian" event, it is important to clarify that similar traditions are practiced in indigenous and mestizo communities in various parts of Latin America (including Mexico, Bolivia, and Peru) where indigenous and African populations were converted to Christianity. In many Andean highland festivals of Peru, dances called negritos commemorate the presence of Black laborers in the Andean mines during times of slavery. Like the negritos of El Carmen, indigenous and mestizo Peruvians, wearing Black masks and carrying whips, dance in two parallel lines directed by a whip-cracking "foreman," accompanied by violin and/or other instruments (depending on the region). Andean negritos sometimes imitate Black coastal dances and behavioral stereotypes (see Bigenho 1998; Cánepa Koch 1998a and 1998b, 106–108). Given the prevalence of Andean negritos dances, the hatajos de negritos of El Carmen, like the yunza, could be an Andean survival in an Afro-Peruvian community (although many believe, in reverse, that the negritos dance of El Carmen is the only remnant of the prototype now imitated by non-Blacks). In fact, most of the visiting hatajos de negritos from towns surrounding El Carmen that performed in the plaza de armas during the 2000 Christmas festivities were composed entirely of mestizos who performed the same songs and dances as the Afro-Peruvian hatajo of El Carmen.

Providing some evidence for the theory of Andean origins, Amador Ballumbrosio affirms that a local Andean composer wrote several of the Christmas song melodies. Further, the song repertoire of the hatajo de negritos often resembles the Andean huayno, the most popular mestizo folk genre. As in the huayno, each melodic phrase of the negritos songs is usually repeated twice, melodic phrases tend to rise and then fall, melodies sometimes use five-note scales (although not the traditional Andean pentatonic ones), and almost all songs are in duple meter (see R. Vásquez Rodríguez 1982, 85–172).[13] William Tompkins notes that, in some songs, Black performers appear to mimic Andean vocal style, especially in the use of a "broken, wailing voice at points where the melody suddenly descends" (1981, 338). The use of the violin (a ubiquitous instrument in many Andean genres) may also be an Andean influence; elsewhere in coastal Peru the guitar is the instrument that accompanies zapateo, and the hatajo de negritos repertoire is the only Afro-Peruvian music played with violin. The zapateo dance style employed by the hatajos (an earthy, stomping, full-footed, close-to-the ground technique) is often considered evidence of a more Andean aesthetic than the more stylized and restrained steps performed in Lima-style zapateo (C. Ballumbrosio 2000; Sandoval 2000).

Like the hatajos de negritos, the pallas group has a parallel practice in Andean communities. In the indigenous Quechua language, the word palla describes a woman of nobility in the Inca Court (N. Santa Cruz 1969a, 12; Tompkins 1981, 338). In the nineteenth century, pallas dances were performed by costumed indigenous Peruvians to the accompaniment of harp and cajón at elegant Christmas celebrations (Tompkins 1981, 327). Contemporary pallas groups perform in the Christmas festivals of indigenous and mestizo communities from the north to central Andean region (especially the provinces of Cajamarca, Ancash, Junín, and Lima), typically dramatizing the conquest of the Incas by the Spaniards and possibly symbolizing the endurance of Inca heritage in post-conquest Peru (Cánepa Koch 1998a).

Thus, the negritos and pallas dances of El Carmen have widespread Andean counterparts, suggesting that they may have been brought to Chincha by indigenous and mestizo migrants from the highlands. Yet, public discourse surrounding their origins, especially the word-of-mouth and tourism promotions that fuel the rush of tourists to El Carmen at Christmas time each year, tends to ignore or downplay Andean parallels in the interest of proclaiming African ancestry.

An interesting example of this emphasis on African origin mythology from the realm of academia is Cuban musicologist Rolando Pérez Fernández' analysis (1988) of Chalena Vásquez' transcriptions of the music of the negritos (Vásquez Rodríguez 1982). Vásquez transcribed the Christmas songs in $\frac{2}{4}$ meter, and she noted that all of the metric subdivisions were expressed in simple duple rhythmic motives, with the exception of one typical rhythmic motif found in both the violin part and the dance that alternated duple and triple subdivisions of the duple pulse (see figure 5.10 and Vásquez Rodríguez 1982, 136). However, Vásquez added that, when combined with the percussive effect of the zapateo, these songs demonstrated a tension between duple and triple subdivisions best expressed by $\frac{6}{8}$ meter (1982, 170–172). In previous chapters, I have identified this type of ambiguity as a central characteristic of the reconstructed music of the urban Afro-Peruvian revival, and therefore this feature of the music is consistent with the idea that Chincha was the "African" origin of the re-created music of the revival. Further endorsing the African origin myth, Rolando Pérez Fernández uses one of Vásquez' transcriptions as evidence that Chincha's rhythms are in an intermediate "ternary–binary phase" of the process of binarization typical of ternary African rhythms in Latin America (1988, 86). However, Pérez Fernández' conclusion excludes both the role of the zapateo cross-rhythms and the equally possible theory that these songs might have originated not in "African" triple meter but in "Andean" duple meter. For example, as figure 5.10 shows, the triplet figure in the "ternary–binary" rhythmic motif could just as easily be viewed as a "ternarized" execution of the basic accompaniment pattern of the Andean huayno, which is also danced in a foot-stomping style.

I do not present this comparison of Afro-Peruvian and Andean rhythms to counter Pérez Fernández' trait-based argument about African origins with an equally trait-based theory of Andean origins. Rather, I wish to point out the pitfalls of relying solely on musical (or other) traits to prove origins and genealogies (a problem also evident in Fernando Romero's Africanist versus Carlos Vega's Europeanist claims about the origins of the

Typical rhythmic motif, hatajo de negritos

Typical accompaniment pattern, huayno

FIGURE 5.10. Comparison of rhythmic motif frequently used in *hatajo de negritos* songs (identified by Chalena Vásquez Rodríguez [1982, 136]) with rhythmic accompaniment pattern of *huayno*.

marinera, discussed in chapter 3). In other words, a rhythmic motif that demonstrates tension between duple and triple subdivisions may alternately be heard as a "binarizing" ternary figure of African origin or a "ternarized" version of binary Andean rhythms, depending on the assumptions and predispositions of the listener. To further problematize trait-based analysis, the Andean huayno pattern often has a "swung" feel that does not conform precisely to duple meter, and duple–triple tension is also characteristic of Spanish folk music and its derivative criollo and mestizo forms in the Americas.

In conclusion, although Black Christmas is considered by many outsiders to be an authentic representation of unassimilated Afro-Peruvian traditions, it actually demonstrates the mingling of a variety of cultural and ethnic traditions practiced in Peru, especially Andean ones. Interestingly, Tompkins noted in the late 1970s that the Black performers of the hatajos de negritos in El Carmen and nearby towns did not consider the tradition to be Afro-Peruvian but criollo (that is, representative of coastal culture) (1981, 329).

By 2000, the word in Lima was that the Black Christmas festival had been commercialized, but that it was still an important cultural expression worth seeing. I had already been to Chincha several times, but I had yet to experience this event, simultaneously rumored to be the most authentic and most touristic expression of Chincha's Afro-Peruvian heritage. Thanks to an unanticipated research grant, I made a special return trip to Peru. The Ballumbrosios had a full house of guests and returning family, but they welcomed me with open arms. They were particularly happy that I had brought a video camera, and several members of the family asked me to be sure to send copies of my documentation. The events of the festival that week alternated between the sacred and the profane, the private and the tourist spectacle. The main plaza was crowded with tourists on the morning when all of the hatajos de negritos from El Carmen and neighboring towns danced in front of the church and on the evening when the negritos and pallas performed, but most tourists were absent at family-oriented events such as evening fireworks, and few ventured inside the church for mass. Party-going tourists returned at night for dances at local bars. On Christmas night, the Ballumbrosios held a celebratory dinner for family and houseguests, with dancing, drinking, and conversation until the early morning.

At 4:00 AM on December 27, 2000, I stood on a dark street in front of the Ballumbrosios' home, waiting with the rest of the neighborhood for the arrival of the Virgin and her procession. While I fiddled with my borrowed video camera and wondered whether the battery was properly charged, I noticed an older woman looking at me intently. In her eyes, I saw myself reflected as the only tourist still on the street at four in the morning. As I looked around at the people standing in front of their darkened doorways waiting for the Virgin, I heard the sounds of a brass band. The parade turned the corner, flooding the street with light, and the float bearing the image of the Virgin made its way down the narrow street, borne on the shoulders of proud men. Some onlookers recited prayers by candlelight, while others reached out to touch the float as it passed by. Then I heard the sound of the violin. On a rooftop, several of the Ballumbrosio brothers began to perform the music and dance of the hatajo de negritos, offering their prayers of devotion to the Virgin as she passed by.

Had I found the back region of the festival of Black Christmas, the sacred ritual behind the profane tourist spectacle? Like many tourists who came before me, I was impressed by the deeply tangible meaning this event held for the residents of El Carmen who stood beside me on that dark street. Whether or not the cultural expressions preserved by the festival had any demonstrable African heritage, clearly this was one of the few remaining events in Peru that brought people of African descent together to celebrate a shared cultural practice and belief system. Despite—or perhaps because of—the apparent contradictions between its multicultural origins and its tourist audience seeking rural African survivals, the Festival of the Virgin of El Carmen remains one vital aspect of who the Afro-Peruvian people of Chincha are today.

The festival traditions of Chincha have long fascinated outsiders because they seem so "real," an antidote to the folkloric commercialism of

Lima's peña shows. The yunza and Christmas festival were the most compelling cultural events to the academic and artistic tourists of the 1970s, and, decades later, they are still the major events on Chincha's tourist season calendar. Although it is true that increasing investment from the tourism industry enables their perseverance, these festivals also persist because they continue to have real significance to the lived identities of the people of Chincha. "The performative magic of ritual," writes Néstor García Canclini, is that "you convert yourself into what you are" (1995, 135). And in fact, in the yunza and Black Christmas celebrations, the residents of Chincha really do become what they are to the outside world—the modern guardians of the flame of the Black Peruvian past. At the same time, in contrast with the re-Africanized folklore of the urban revival, these festivals reveal the unheralded influence of Andean culture and Catholicism on the formation of Black identity in rural Peru. Thus, if, as Paul Connerton argues, ritual is in large part defined by its claim to commemorate continuity with the past (1989, 48), the question is *which* past is commemorated in Chincha's ritual events.

Taking the Exhibit on the Road: Miki González and Akundún

The work of revival artists, scholars, and the Ballumbrosio family popularized the legend of Chincha. But the artist who unquestionably placed Chincha on the map for mass Peruvian and international audiences is Spanish rocker Miki González. A guitarist, singer, and composer, Miki González was born in Spain and lived most of his life in Peru. Tall and thin with long curly hair that is just beginning to gray, Miki speaks an idiosyncratic mixture of Spanish and English (whether or not he is conversing with people who speak English). Miki's cosmopolitan lifestyle enables him to traverse many cultural identities, and his chameleon-like assimilation of international popular culture and styles is impressive. After studying at the Berklee School of Music in the United States in the late 1970s, Miki returned to Peru in 1982 and put aside his interest in jazz and blues to record a more lucrative genre—the Spanish rock that had swept Latin America and was fast becoming popular in Peru. By the 1990s, he was a rock star with a following of young, adoring fans.

In 1992, Miki González collaborated with members of the Ballumbrosio family to release an album called *Akundún* that made Chincha and the Ballumbrosios famous (and Miki González more famous than he already was) in Peru and other parts of Latin America. Distributed initially in Peru and later in the United States (by Polygram), *Akundún*

FIGURE 5.11. *Akundún* CD cover. *Reprinted with permission from Universal Music Enterprises.*

recontextualized traditional Afro-Peruvian music, including songs of Black Christmas and the yunza, in a modern sound collage that blends elements of various music styles of the African diaspora.

Miki describes *Akundún* as a personal project that developed out of his fascination with Black "roots" music (González, 2000). His first musical passion was the blues, which he initially learned about through British bands such as the Rolling Stones and Cream, later discovering bluesmen such as Albert King. In the early 1970s, Miki began listening only to Black artists. The blues led Miki into jazz and the Brazilian experimental fusions of Airto Moreira and Hermeto Pascoal. Like Nicomedes Santa Cruz a decade before him, Miki González visited Brazil for artistic inspiration from 1975 to 1976. Upon his return to Peru in 1976, Miki wondered why there was not an equivalent Black "roots" music in his own country.

One day, Miki saw Afro-Peruvian guitarist Félix Casaverde performing on television. Miki asked César Calvo (the television program's emcee and a friend of Miki's family) to introduce him to Casaverde. Miki explains, "Through Félix Casaverde, I discovered the most authentic Black music. Because the versions that are in the media, on the radio, the television, they are very warped down and commercial. They are versions for the mediocre taste of the mass public" (González 2000).

Félix Casaverde introduced Miki to legendary performers in non-commercial peñas, including Abelardo Vásquez, Caitro Soto, and Ronaldo Campos. In 1978, Miki was learning to play Afro-Peruvian bordones and performing with well-known singer/composer Andrés Soto. César Calvo noted Miki's continued interest in Black music and suggested—as he had to Ronaldo Campos and the members of Perú Negro six years earlier—that they go together to meet Amador Ballumbrosio in the "marvelous town" of El Carmen. In the company of César Calvo, Andrés Soto, and other friends of the Ballumbrosios, Miki González took his first trip down the Pan American Highway to El Carmen in 1978.

Thus, yet another artist knocked on the Ballumbrosio family's door in search of authentic Black culture. But Miki's involvement with El Carmen and the Ballumbrosio family would be longer, more consistent, and of an entirely different quality and impact. A large, framed photograph of Miki and his guitar, displayed prominently in the Ballumbrosio family's living room, commemorates the fact that Miki lived in the Ballumbrosio family home for a year from 1978 to 1979, returning to Lima only on weekends to play gigs. With César Calvo and Andrés Soto, he made a short black-and-white film, "Es Amador," celebrating Amador Ballumbrosio's preservation of cultural and musical traditions (González, Calvo, and Soto 1979). During his student years at Berklee School of Music, from 1979 to 1982, Miki worked to create a new musical style, blending jazz with the Afro-Peruvian music he had learned in Chincha. Miki continued to visit and learn from the Ballumbrosio family on an ongoing basis upon his return to Peru in the 1980s.

Miki remembers: "What I discovered in El Carmen was something unique and different from what was played in the peñas [of Lima]. In all the peñas, the only thing that was played was what Nicomedes Santa Cruz recorded and what Perú Negro recorded . . . In El Carmen there was a great wealth . . . I was White and inoffensive and I didn't know how to play [Afro-Peruvian music]. I couldn't do them any harm, I couldn't steal from them. On the other hand, other Blacks had stolen from them . . . and never given them credit. So they felt very offended. But I was not a menace. 'Nephew, bring your tape recorder!' And they sang a ton of things. And that's how a ton of things from those years are in *Akundún* . . . With the songs that belong to traditional folklore, I have said which belongs to whom. When I steal, I say who I am stealing from! [*Akundún*] is an homage to the people of El Carmen" (González 2000).

Miki insists that what he encountered and recorded in 1978 bore very little resemblance to the music performed in El Carmen in the 1990s. In fact, he claims that the cajón, the quintessential symbol of post-1970s urban Afro-Peruvian music, was not to be found in El Carmen until Perú Negro left one as a gift during a field research trip in the early 1970s. According to Miki, he subsequently gave the Ballumbrosio family their first cajón and other musical instruments (González 2000). Miki remembers, "I arrive in El Carmen and the only Black music was Amador, who was not yet a violinist but a dance captain. He maintained the zapateo tradition, and the elders knew about traditions . . . When I arrived in El Carmen, [Amador's children] did not play music. Jesús knew a little guitar and Filomeno knew how to play the cajón. But there was no cajón, there were no instruments. We gave that house their first instruments as gifts. Since *Akundún*, people go to El Carmen and there are a ton of kids with cajones playing in the street corners asking for tips. It has changed a lot. There is a stereotype of what the Black person should be, and they live up to it. Because people give them money" (González 2000).

Although he is critical of the young people of El Carmen, Miki chose to work with them on his *Akundún* project. When asked why he bypassed the elders, whose knowledge of musical traditions he obviously respected, Miki replied: "The old people were sick. And they—[pauses]. There was no way. I didn't play their music . . . It is as if Miles Davis' band were to pick up young jazz players, but they are people with no prejudice. They have talent and they can follow him in his craziness. So my work, my projects, my experimental proposals, there was no one who had done them. I was the first. So I needed young people who could understand" (González 2000).

The album *Akundún* features the participation of five Ballumbrosio brothers (Jesús, Filomeno, Eusebio, José, and Miguel) along with a special guest contribution by Amador Ballumbrosio (who plays violin, sings, and tap dances on one track). Live on tour in Peru and Brazil, Luci and María Ballumbrosio were included in the act as dancers. The music, composed and arranged by Miki González with the collaboration of the Ballumbrosios and other featured musicians, recontextualizes Afro-Peruvian festejo and panalivio patterns for cajón in an expanded Spanish rock band setting (including drum set, synthesizer, guitar, bass, congas, and cowbell) with hybrid musical arrangements inspired by Jamaican reggae and dance hall and other popular styles of African diasporic music. Some tracks are new arrangements of traditional or previously composed songs, including two songs associated with the yunza ("Huanchigualito" and "La esquina del Carmen") and one from the Christmas festival ("Panalivio").

The album's title track was its biggest hit. "Akundún" sets Miki González' deejay-style recited vocals over a repeating dance hall–inspired rhythm track that combines percussive effects and bouncing reggae after-beat-style keyboard chords with the traditional panalivio rhythm for cajón. As a unit that shifts back and forth between various expressions of national and racial identity, "Akundún" brilliantly illustrates the nature of Miki's musical fusions with the Ballumbrosio family.

The song begins with the synthesizer's articulation of the well-known Andean melody "El condor pasa," which instantly evokes a sense of national Peruvian identity normally tied with the romantic evocation of the Inca past—now associated instead with Peruvian Blacks.[14] Because the theme from "El condor pasa" is linked to Peru's indigenous past in the public imagination, its use as an introduction for the song "Akundún" reinscribes the presence of Black Peruvians and their African ancestors into Peru's official history of national origins. Because Simon & Garfunkel's 1970 recording of "El condor pasa" became a worldwide hit, the use of this theme by Miki González also resonates to world music consumers as an international statement of "Peruvianness."[15]

In the midst of these associations created by the "El condor pasa" lead-in, the song moves into a reggae/dance hall groove. The borrowed Jamaican style suggests a pan-African identification, as Miki's own comments about his arrangements reveal: "Nobody [in Peru] knew reggae music . . . I liked reggae, the melodies of reggae were very African, but it was extremely pop-rock in idiom, especially Marley, who was very much in fashion . . . All these Black rhythms, I felt them the same way I feel reggae" (González 2000). In this section, Miki's melodic recitation style emulates that of Jamaican dance hall deejays. His opening lyrics (below) are an obvious adaptation of Nicomedes Santa Cruz' most famous décima and negritud anthem "Ritmos negros del Perú," thus also creating a symbolic link to the urban Afro-Peruvian revival of the 1960s. The album *Akundún* is dedicated to the memory of Nicomedes Santa Cruz, and the song "Akundún" retells Nicomedes' poem almost line for line from a contemporary perspective. However, whereas Nicomedes' poem explains how painful memories of slavery are embedded in Afro-Peruvians' inheritance of the rhythms created by enslaved Africans, Miki González' "Akundún" claims Black cultural heritage for Peruvians of all races. This thematic treatment diverges dramatically both from the message of Nicomedes Santa Cruz' famous poem and from the historical function of the panalivio, a protest genre performed by enslaved Africans and banned by the Catholic Church in 1722 for its subversive lyrics (N. Santa Cruz 1969a; Tompkins 1981, 343).

For example, Nicomedes' poem begins by telling the story of his (the narrator's) grandmother's journey from Africa:[16]

De Africa llegó mi agüela	My grandmother came from Africa
vestida con caracoles,	dressed in shells,
la trajeron lo'epañoles	Spaniards brought her
en un barco carabela . . .	in a caravel ship . . .

Miki González' lyrics (González 1993), on the other hand, describe a universal African grandmother unrelated to the narrator:

En los barcos portugueses	The grandmother was brought over
ahí trajeron a la abuela	in Portuguese ships
la trajeron de Guinea	they brought her from Guinea
con escala en Cartagena	with a stop in Cartagena
mercadores la trajeron más	merchants brought her
pal el sur . . .	further south . . .

Nicomedes goes on to describe the branding and other hardships his enslaved grandmother was forced to endure while Black drums beat the "rhythms of slavery," the only consolation Black slaves found amid their hard labors and terrible working conditions. Miki, however, only briefly acknowledges the whip of Hacienda San José before asserting that:

Hoy los tiempos han cambiado	Today the times have changed
todo eso terminó	all that is over
hoy los negros ya son libres	today Blacks are free
se abolió la esclavitud	slavery was abolished
y es por esa sangre negra	and because of that Black blood
que el Atlántico cruzó	that crossed the Atlantic
es por eso que yo canto	because of that, I sing
ritmos negros del Perú	Black rhythms of Peru

Thus, the lyrics of the first section of "Akundún" imply that the cultural legacy of a universal Black slave grandmother is part of the patrimony of all Peruvians, legitimizing Miki's fusion experiments with the Ballumbrosios. The upbeat, major key and bouncing reggae afterbeat further emphasize the song's carefree alteration of the panalivio rhythm, and Miki's presence as narrator sends the message that even White European-Peruvians have inherited Black rhythms of Peru.

Next comes a stylistic segue to a section that expresses the international solidarity of Peruvian Blacks with their counterparts in the United States. Significantly, this section is in English, and its lyrics, as well as Miki's phrasing and tone, echo the style and poetics developed by African American rappers of the United States:

> Talkin' about the roots and culture here from Peru
> I'd like to welcome all the world and say how do you do
> And let the people know about this country like no other
> This is Miki González and the Ballumbrosio brothers
>
> I do not sell no sex and I do not sell no violence
> It may not be commercial
> I'm at peace with my conscience
> And welcome all my brothers and say hello how do you do
> Talkin' about the roots and culture here from Peru

Akundún (repeat)

The same text is repeated in Spanish, until the fadeout. Thus, "Akundún" begins with an internationally recognized reference to Peruvian identity not normally linked with Black Peru, continues with the pan-African reggae/dance hall sound, borrows from U.S. African American rap, and uses both a historic Afro-Peruvian protest genre (the panalivio) and a famous negritud poem of the Afro-Peruvian revival to express a newly envisioned image of Peruvian blackness and its contribution to national culture. Like many of the standards of the Afro-Peruvian revival, "Akundún" was created by Afro-Peruvians with the guidance of a White collaborator. However, "Akundún" moves beyond the folkloric frame of revival repertoire by connecting the past and present and offering a contemporary vision of blackness in Peru.

Whether or not it is intentional, the song "Akundún" promotes several stereotypes about Black Peruvians. First is the notion that all Black people in Peru are happy and carefree, which is reinforced by the upbeat tempo and the lyrics, cited above, implying that abolition ended the hardships of Blacks in Peru. That said, it is important to note that the stereotyped image of the Blacks of El Carmen as eternally smiling and happy was not created or imposed solely by Miki González; this album was a coproduction with the Ballumbrosio family, and such stereotypes are actively disseminated by many Black performers in Chincha and Lima (especially in tourist peñas). Camilo Ballumbrosio, for example, explains the surging of national and tourist interest in El Carmen by saying: "It's because it is happy! That is, [El Carmen] is one of the happiest cities in Peru" (C. Ballumbrosio 2000).

Second is the linkage of hypersexuality with blackness (also promoted in Lima's peña shows), most apparent in the dancing that accompanies live performances of "Akundún" and other songs, but also expressed by the song's title and refrain. Although "Akundún" was a hit song in Peru, few listeners could explain the meaning of the title, which is repeated as a refrain between each verse. When I asked Miki, he explained its genesis. In rehearsals, he originally sang "adundún" as a sort of onomatopoetic marker of the rhythm of the chorus section. Quietly, Amador Ballumbrosio began to sing "akundún." Miki liked the sound of the word, and he integrated it into the song. Much later, one of Amador's sons asked Miki if he knew the meaning of "akundún." When Miki responded that he did not, Eusebio Ballumbrosio revealed that "akundún" is a euphemism for sexual intercourse in the slang of older Black Peruvians (González 2000).

Heightened sexuality is a stereotype willingly promoted by the Ballumbrosio (and other) girls who dance with Miki González live in concert, showcasing pyrotechnics of the pelvis and scanty outfits. A public debate surrounds the perceived sexual display of young girls and teenagers who dance Chincha-style festejo, and it is worth departing from the discussion of *Akundún* briefly in order to review this issue. This debate is related to previously discussed questions about the erotic content of Afro-Peruvian music and dance in general and to stereotyped notions of Black sexual excess in Peru. With regard to women's bodies, such perceptions are rooted in a long history of public images contrasting chaste White women with oversexualized Black (and mulata) women.[17]

Proponents of one school of thought celebrate what they perceive as the retention of an African-derived sense of bodily expression. For example, as noted in chapter 1, Afro-Peruvian musician Juanchi Vásquez claims that "sexual" movements are a natural aspect of Black dance, and he anchors this claim in the assumed rural authenticity of the provocative dance styles preserved in "pure" form in Chincha. He says, "You go to Chincha and you see a couple that dances festejo and perhaps it appears that they are making love. But that is within the dance. And it disappeared here [in Lima] . . . The Black presence in Chincha is extremely important, because what happened in Lima didn't happen there, because it is so far from commercialization and the capital. You see people dance there, and they haven't lost the erotic movements" (J. Vásquez 2000). Juanchi's notion of eroticism as a "natural" element of Afro-Peruvian dance, validated by the bodily movements of very young girls from "authentic" Chincha, competes with the analysis of other Afro-Peruvian dancers who feel that eroticism has more recently been added to Afro-Peruvian music in order to please onlookers, and that it has been naturalized after the fact. These critics express discomfort at the sexual objectification of Black bodies for the pleasure of White onlookers. They complain that women's skirt lengths have climbed drastically up the leg since the 1970s to please commercial audiences, and they abhor the recently adopted tiny costumes and overtly sexual motions of very young Afro-Peruvian girls. The underlying assumptions about Black sexuality that fuel both sides of this debate demonstrate the ways in which Afro-Peruvian dance—as performed by the Ballumbrosio girls for Miki González and by others—has contributed to the perpetuation of national fantasies about race and the body.

With *Akundún*, Miki González rode the Ballumbrosio family name to stardom (at the same time making the Ballumbrosio name famous). Yet, the relationship between Miki and the Ballumbrosios goes two ways: he taught the Ballumbrosio children to play commercially viable music, gave them instruments, secured recording contracts for their own projects, provided housing for them in Lima, and hired them to play in his band and tour Peru and Latin America. And, while César Calvo introduced Amador Ballumbrosio to many artists and scholars in the 1970s, Miki González' popular appeal and audience as a rock star offered an entirely different type of exposure. Miki González was also the first artist to foreground the Ballumbrosios by name when he re-presented the Black folklore of Chincha. However, he asserts that "I talk a lot about 'Miki González and the Ballumbrosio Brothers,' but they don't do that much. That is, what is more meaningful is the act of having appeared with some Black Peruvians who seem to be international Black artists . . . We wore African clothes, they had dreadlocks . . . It is the first time Black Peruvians have appeared like this, with a look and freshness. So it was very powerful, they arrive and they are stars. I treat them as if they were very famous in my words and my presentations, but they have never played anywhere. Outside of Miki González, they have . . . never left Peru as Los Hermanos Ballumbrosio" (González 2000).

Miki González is one of the few artists who self-consciously acknowledges his own role in the creation of the ever-changing spectacle called "Black music" in Peru. Yet, his very willingness to express his views and thoughts frankly and "let the chips fall where they may" often leads him to make comments that can cast him in a troubling light. For example, when asked what he thinks Chincha would be like today had he not visited the Ballumbrosio family in the 1970s, Miki answered frankly: "Possibly they wouldn't play Black music. There would be some bands that would play for tourists who go to the Hacienda San José. And El Carmen would not be famous. If Miki González, instead of going to Chincha, had gone to Cañete, the same thing would have happened there historically. *Akundún* would have been a success, but without the Ballumbrosio family, instead with the Campos family from San Luis [de Cañete]" (González 2000). Ironically, when Miki says "they wouldn't play Black music" were it not for him, he suggests that what Blacks played in El Carmen before he arrived in the late 1970s (music that he previously differentiated from the canon created by the Afro-Peruvian revival) was not "Black music." Thus, in Miki's new terms, "Black music" is limited to either Afro-Peruvian rock or the cajón-based revival sound introduced to Chincha by outsiders like himself and the urban revival artists. When examined from Miki's perspective, it appears that the only musical "backstage" in Chincha was constructed by the very tourists who set out in its pursuit.

Two Chinchas

In early 2000, I was browsing at a music fair in Lima when I met the author of a book on the Peruvian marinera. We briefly discussed my research on Afro-Peruvian music. He asked me a few questions to make sure I understood the situation properly. He made it clear that he frowned upon the sexualized commercial style of Black Peruvian dancers in Chincha. "People see that," he complained, "and they think that Afro-Peruvian music is really danced like that!"

Many Peruvians, like the gentleman I met that sunny afternoon in Lima, are genuinely uncomfortable with the music and dance of Chincha, and they do not think it is "real." From their perspective, members of the younger generation in Chincha are milking their cultural heritage to sell tourists a contrived style of dancing and musical fusion that represents staged authenticity and has nothing to do with "pure" Peruvian folklore. Yet, Chincha continues to attract tourists, and the Ballumbrosio family holds a position of prominence unrivaled by any other Afro-Peruvian family from the rural provinces. Camilo Ballumbrosio notes proudly: "In El Carmen, the Ballumbrosios are the most representative . . . Who appears when there is a festival of Black music? The Ballumbrosios . . . People want to hear Black music? They say 'Let's go to the Ballumbrosio's house'" (2000). He continues, acknowledging, "Now, more people are interested than before. Because if you arrive in El Carmen in a car and you want to see someone dance zapateo or another dance, the kids will do it . . . You can always find lots of kids who dance zapateo in the plaza de armas . . . You say, 'do you know how to dance?' . . . they'll dance for you and you give them a tip so they'll be happy. They sell you their art" (C. Ballumbrosio 2000).

When I first visited Chincha in 1998, I did not know that the Ballumbrosios would open their home to me, and I inquired about hotels or guest houses where I might stay in El Carmen. People in the district of Chincha looked dubious: "El Carmen is a very humble town," they told me. When I returned to El Carmen in 2000, a huge Folklore and Tourism Center with lodging and performance spaces was under construction just off the plaza de armas, taking advantage of the growing local tourism fueled by the legend of Chincha.

Like many tourist locales, Chincha's development in the 1980s and 1990s had good and bad results. Tourism brings needed income to a community where many residents lack basic resources, and it celebrates their heritage, folklore, and artistic talents. In a country where Blacks are marginalized, it provides a measure of racial pride. However, the musical depiction of blackness for tourists tends to be heavily weighted with cultural stereotypes and references to times of slavery, framing Chinchanos as a quaint, premodern echo of their ancestors.

Describing the Christmas festival he witnessed in Chincha in the 1970s, William Tompkins astutely commented, "A blend of the sacred and secular is evident in the traditions of the Peruvian negritos, where religion and folklore meet, and a strange, almost contradictory synthesis of meaning as the negritos represent both slaves and kings in one dance genre and costume . . . But for the blacks, this apparent dichotomy of representing both slaves and kings caused no confusion. It was as explainable as kings and shepherds worshipping together, or the Son of God being born in a stable" (1981, 342).

What was evident to Tompkins in the 1970s is still true today: the residents of Chincha are supremely comfortable performing multiple roles, both in their private lives and for tourists. The trajectory that portrays Chincha as a premodern cradle of authentic Black culture is complicated by the fact that visitors who penetrate the so-called "back regions" of Chincha find the same music, modern tastes, and cultural concerns that exist in urban Lima. Certainly, the work of artists, scholars, and rock stars has altered the Chincha that existed in the 1970s. What is often forgotten is that the impact of young Chinchanos moving to the city in search of employment and then returning home, television and radio, and the ongoing growth and development of popular tastes and desires would have caused inevitable cultural change in Chincha, with or without the added factors of cultural and academic tourism.

As this chapter has shown, two versions of Peruvian history explain the legend of Chincha. According to the first, Chincha is the authentic, premodern cradle of African-derived music. It is where people from Lima go when they seek the unassimilated roots of Afro-Peruvian folklore. These pilgrimages began in the 1970s with César Calvo and Perú Negro and continue to this day. The traditions performed in Chincha have been maintained and preserved since times of slavery.

The second story casts Chincha in a completely different light. In this version, Chincha was created in response to the urban need for an authentic cradle of Afro-Peruvian music, providing the perfect premodern origin myth for the reconstructions of modern folklorists. The people of Chincha learned to play Black music and dance by watching Perú Negro on TV, and they learned so well that they made the populace believe Perú Negro had learned it from them. The rise of a tourist industry created a demand for performers who could enact the stereotypes tourists imagined they would find in Chincha, and the need for financial subsistence created a willing and able corpus of Blacks to perform those stereotypes.

I have been to Chincha as an academic tourist, and—even if I wanted to pass judgment—I honestly cannot say which of these stories is "true." Somehow, these two contradictory explanations seem to me to coexist in relative harmony. Just when I begin to believe that I've found the real back region of Chincha and that I know when its front spaces are staged, surprising new evidence of the intertwined nature of Chincha's many stages peeks out of dusty corners, confusing simple interpretations and neat analyses. But determining which of these stories is true and providing academic endorsement is not the task at hand. What is more important is that Chincha easily fulfills both fantasies in the eye of the beholder. Chincha is what you want it to be, reflected back at you, so long as you don't stay long enough to explore its many so-called "back regions."

CHAPTER 6

Susana Baca, Immigrant Nostalgia, and the Cosmopolitan Soul of Black Peru

Telling a Secret

This is secret music—a collection of beautiful songs and infectious grooves that's been hidden for years in the coastal towns and barrios of Peru. It's not the guys with flutes and drums in the wooly hats—it's music of the black Peruvian communities. Black Peruvians! Yes, Peru was involved in the slave trade too—and this wonderful, funky music is part of that legacy.

This music survived (barely) within the black communities, and was not accepted outside of those communities until the spark of black pride, ignited in the 1960s, caught fire in the 1970s and 80's. Now, in the 90's, this music is the pride of Peru—cassettes of it are sold on the street alongside techno, Megadeath and Andean folk groups. And while it maintains its funky roots, it has attracted the creative talents of the best contemporary musicians, writers and poets who have furthered the evolution, growth and spread of this music. It's not a secret anymore—and it's yours to dance to.
  —Back cover of the CD *Afro-Peruvian Classics: The Soul of Black Peru*

How we love secrets. Mysterious and tantalizing, secrets beg to be found out. We long for the moment of discovery—precisely when a secret is no longer a secret. From that moment on, we belong to the special group of people who know the secret and possess the power to reveal. How (and that) a secret is learned is sometimes more important than the secret itself, and the decision to reveal alternately may be considered initiation or indiscretion.

In fact, the history of Afro-Peruvian music, as I have described it thus far, is a tale of secrets revealed by curators who made special claims about the authenticity of their discoveries. In the 1950s, José Durand invited Lima audiences to learn about the secret Black music of coastal Peru. In the 1960s, Nicomedes Santa Cruz revealed the secrets of the African origins of música criolla, and Victoria Santa Cruz used her ancestral memory to find secrets within her own body that led her to reconstruct forgotten dances. In the 1970s, older relatives of the members of Perú Negro shared

FIGURE 6.1. *The Soul of Black Peru* CD cover (Various Artists 1995a). *Luaka Bop Inc., reprinted with permission.*

their knowledge of clandestine dances, and, from the 1970s to the 1990s, artists, scholars, and tourists hunted for little-known Black Peruvian roots music in Chincha. Finally, in 1995, David Byrne introduced U.S. listeners to the secret of Afro-Peruvian music by producing *The Soul of Black Peru* (the first recording of Afro-Peruvian music widely available in the United States) and through his subsequent patronage of Afro-Peruvian singer Susana Baca.

As the text from the back cover of *The Soul of Black Peru* (cited above) illustrates, the secret is an effective marketing tool for commercial world music. Secret music sells by playing into the consumer desire to be part of that special group that is "in the know." Timothy Taylor (1997) and others refer to world music as a type of "sonic tourism," and world music consumers certainly share with tourists the desire to penetrate the back regions of foreign cultures—without leaving their living room CD players.

Although the term "world music" tends to refer to music commercially consumed in the United States and Europe and created anywhere else, as Barbara Browning asks, "If your music isn't world music, where in the world are you?" (1998, 37).[1] The opposite question (if your music *is* world music where in the world are you?) is equally thought-provoking; in the Tower Records in Mexico City, Mexican music is reportedly in the "world music" section (Taylor 1997, 5). As Deborah Pacini Hernandez observes (1998), world music's geography is mapped by assumptions about cultural authenticity often linked to African-derived music styles. Pacini Hernandez notes that, although Latin American music styles displaying strong African influences are often received coolly in their home countries, their perceived Africanness is what makes them competitive in the transnational world music market. The preference for African and African diasporic music was particularly pervasive in world music in the 1990s (when *The Soul of Black Peru* was released), linked to the rhythmic grooves of various dance music styles classified as "world beat" and perceived as African cousins.

World music reveals several types of secrets. In the case of Afro-Peruvian music, the very existence of Blacks in Peru is part of the secret shared with global listeners. Upon first hearing, some world music seems to outsiders to contain secret aesthetic messages, encoded in seemingly impenetrable meters, accents, microtones, and harmonic/melodic structures. Barbara Kirshenblatt-Gimblett (1998) describes this enigmatic quality as "confusing pleasure," meaning a desirable encounter with unfamiliar art without the benefit of cultural translation or mediation. "Confusing pleasure" is often the first reaction of world music audiences to Afro-Peruvian music, inspired by the music's rhythmic play and instrumentation, which simultaneously display both stubborn differences and striking similarities when compared with the more familiar Afro-Brazilian and Afro-Cuban music disseminated in the United States as world music, Latin music, or Latin jazz. Although elements associated with these other African diaspora music styles (call-and-response, metric complexity, an emphasis on percussion) are present, many U.S. listeners are tantalized by what sounds like more Spanish influence in the guitar and vocals. The particular way in which Afro-Peruvian music plays with musical time feeds prevalent U.S. notions about the "difficult rhythms" of African diasporic music, while also separating Afro-Peruvian music from other African diasporic styles. Just when new listeners think they are feeling the groove created by the cajón and guitar, the singer comes in and everything seems to change. Thus, Afro-Peruvian music sounds familiar enough to qualify as world music, but at the same time, different enough to produce confusing pleasure. As Thomas Turino observes, this sonic straddling of the familiar and the foreign is a hallmark of world music's appeal (2000, 334–335).

Although postmodern theorists (Appadurai 1991; Clifford 1997a; Lipsitz 1994) argue that globalization and hybridity challenge localized definitions of "place," "culture," "race," and "nation," world music consumers tend to understand the artists whose works they buy very much in terms of their situatedness in a specific culture group and country and its essentialized style. The previously unfamiliar musical sounds that now fill U.S. radio waves, television commercials, grocery stores, and record stores disseminate site-specific ideas about the cultural identity of Others in often-exoticized places. Ironically, although consumers tend to view world music performers as artistic flags of their countries of origin, these same global performers often are marginalized or unpopular at home, belonging instead to the translocal cosmopolitan culture of world music.

In its classic definition, a "cosmopolitan" is a citizen of the world. Unlike diasporic culture, with its center(s) and peripheries, cosmopolitanism is better envisioned as a "metaculture" (Hannerz 1992, 252) that has no single place of origin but instead consists of links between various locales, often organized around power centers. In the case of world music, the power centers are the United States and Europe, where the recording industries are based. In this sense, the "world" defined by world music culture is limited to certain sectors of the populations of participating countries. As Thomas Turino points out, "'native' cosmopolitans . . . emerge as a distinctive cultural group in their own right, relative to other indigenous groups in the same locale . . . It is . . . at this point that binary conceptions of African/European, insider/outsider, and local/global identities need to be refined" (2000, 9).

In fact, world music artists are part of what some scholars perceive as a postcolonial personnel change in the category of cosmopolitans, originally envisioned as those able to choose their status as "citizens of the world" (free-floating and privileged Western intellectuals) but now broadened to include the globally connected citizens of formerly colonized nations. Rethinking cosmopolitanism, some scholars question the previously assumed mutual exclusivity of national engagement versus world citizenship (Appadurai 1996a; Cheah 1998, 20; Clifford 1997b; Robbins 1998). Emerging hybrid concepts—such as "rooted" (Appiah 1998) and "discrepant" (Clifford 1997b, 36) cosmopolitanisms—acknowledge lingering feelings of national belonging among certain cosmopolitans (see Cheah and Robbins 1998). Scholars also note that separate local and global "cosmopolitan loops" (Turino 2000) and "–scapes" (Appadurai 1996a) may coexist in hybrid cosmopolitan spaces, creating a kind of "late nationalism" (Waxer

2002, 16) in which cosmopolitan groups function very much like nations or culture groups. Embodying these notions of nationally rooted cosmopolitanism, world music artists must belong to two worlds at once. Although their professional activities make them cosmopolitan citizens of the world, they maintain personal, artistic, and/or political connections to their home nations, thereby fulfilling the expectations of "rootedness" among world music audiences for whom they serve as ambassadors (and often tokens) of their local cultures.

This chapter contrasts two manifestations of Afro-Peruvian music in the United States: (1) the emergence of Afro-Peruvian singer Susana Baca as a cosmopolitan world music artist, and (2) cultural preservation efforts in U.S. Peruvian immigrant communities. I will suggest that, if the Black Pacific is imagined as a diasporic periphery of the Black Atlantic, Susana Baca is as an artist on the cosmopolitan periphery of the Black Pacific. Although much of her performance repertoire is indebted to the Afro-Peruvian revival, Susana Baca's primary performance circuit is in the United States and Europe. With the style of her arrangements, the content of her repertoire, and the geography of her performances, she partially turns her back on the Afro-Peruvian Black Pacific imagined by the revival, re-creating diasporic identity and center–periphery structures once again. Yet, Susana Baca can never completely separate herself from her identity as an Afro-Peruvian singer, which enables her international popularity. Thus, her rooted cosmopolitanism extends, rather than opposes, Afro-Peruvian diasporic identity in the Black Pacific.

Meanwhile, in Peruvian immigrant communities of the United States, Afro-Peruvian revival-style music is performed. Unlike the trans-state cultural formations of cosmopolitanisms and diasporas, as Thomas Turino writes, immigrant communities typically are characterized by uncomplicated bilateral relations between a new home community and the old country, and they tend to maintain music and dance from the homeland as a means of preserving group solidarity (Turino 2003, 58–59). Many Peruvian immigrants, especially those who fled to the United States during the Shining Path guerilla organization's reign of terror in the 1980s, live in one world but identify with another. Thus, U.S. Peruvians of all races and cultural backgrounds reproduce the experience of living in Peru through Afro-Peruvian dance contests and through concerts by Afro-Peruvian and criollo artists (who are flown to the United States each weekend to perform for all-Peruvian audiences at Peruvian-style peñas in Los Angeles and other cities).

This immigrant music scene is invisible to the U.S. world music consumers who discovered Afro-Peruvian music in the 1990s. In general,

American global pop producers' and consumers' preferences for the cosmopolitan sound of world music tend to relegate such local versions of ethnic music to obscurity, even if they are more representative of what "ethnic" music sounds like in their home countries. As James Clifford observes, capitalism allows and produces differences—so long as they are the "right" kind of differences (1998, 366). In the case of Afro-Peruvian music, the qualities that make Susana Baca a cosmopolitan Peruvian world music artist, while Peruvians living in the United States are "Peruvian artists" are prescribed by the stylistic economy of the world music market.

The release of David Byrne's 1995 compilation CD *The Soul of Black Peru* generated a number of controversies regarding who has the right to perform Afro-Peruvian music and which performances are authentic—the same questions that have provoked heated disagreement in Peru since the 1950s. As I explain in this chapter, the international circulation of *The Soul of Black Peru* complicates these debates, because of the issues of power and appropriation central to world music. Yet, in many ways, the entrance of Afro-Peruvian music as "world music" on U.S. and European concert stages in the 1990s is a transnational echo of the Peruvian history reviewed thus far. When he introduced the "secret" of Black Peruvian music in the United States, David Byrne reenacted, on a global scale, José Durand's role as White curator of Black Peruvian music in Lima. The lack of public awareness that an entirely different kind of Afro-Peruvian music was simultaneously being performed in Peruvian communities in the United States is cause for reflection about the extent to which any of this music was ever really a secret.

David Byrne: From the Talking Heads to Luaka Bop

Born in Scotland in 1952, David Byrne grew up in Baltimore and later attended the Rhode Island School of Design. There, he formed and fronted the 1970s–1980s rock band Talking Heads. Byrne developed a reputation for his bizarre on-stage antics (including dances such as "spastic," "duck," "knock knee," "Indian-Snake," "guitar," "possession," and "vibration") and dress (large oversized suits and kilts) as well as the biting satire of his lyrics and delivery for songs such as "Psycho Killer," "Once in a Lifetime," "We're on the Road to Nowhere," and "Nothing But Flowers." He experimented with incorporating West African polyrhythms into rock on albums like *Remain in Light* (1980) and *Naked* (1988), and he wove Near Eastern and other types of samples into *My Life in the Bush of Ghosts* (in collaboration with Brian Eno), a 1981 recording that anticipated the 1990s wave of world music and "ethno-techno" releases.

In 1988, after several film-directing and multimedia projects and a formative trip to Bahia, Brazil, Byrne started his own recording label, Luaka Bop (then a division of Warner). Initially, Byrne's company issued anthologies of previously released Latin American and African music. Luaka Bop's first release was the Afro-Brazilian *Beleza Tropical* collection (1989). In 1991, Luaka Bop issued the first Cuban music recording released in the United States since the trade embargo, *The Best of Silvio Rodríguez*, followed that same year by the Cuban compilation *Dancing with the Enemy—Incredible Dance Hits of the '60s and '70s.* Over the next decade, the company released several dozen newly recorded CDs by "offbeat" artists from various parts of the United States, Latin America, Asia, Europe, and Africa.

Although many would categorize Luaka Bop as a world music label, in a *New York Times* article provocatively titled "I Hate World Music" (1999), Byrne writes: "In my experience, the use of the term world music is a way of dismissing artists or their music as irrelevant to one's own life. It's a way of relegating this 'thing' into the realm of something exotic and therefore cute, weird but safe, because exotica is beautiful but irrelevant; they are, by definition, not like us. That's why I hate the term. It groups everything and anything that isn't 'us' into 'them.' This grouping is a convenient way of not seeing a band or artist as a creative individual" (1999, 35–36). Luaka Bop's roster reflects Byrne's idiosyncratic taste and the notion that artists should be valued for their aesthetic contributions rather than their "authenticity." Often, Byrne selects artists who are not popular in their own countries. "Sometimes it takes a naïve foreigner to appreciate what people who live in a country don't realize they have," he says (N.a. 1998e).

Regarding world music consumers' preference for "authentic" sounds, Byrne insists: "The issue of 'authenticity' is such a weird can of worms. Westerners get obsessed with it. They agonize over which is the 'true' music, the real deal . . . White folks needed to see Leadbelly in prison garb to feel they were getting the real thing. They need to be assured that rappers are 'keeping it real,' they need their Cuban musicians old and sweet, their Eastern and Asian artists 'spiritual.' The myths and clichés of national and cultural traits flourish in the marketing of music . . . We don't want them looking too much like us, because then we assume that their music is calculated, marketed, impure" (1999, 34).

To dispel such expectations, Byrne insists upon marketing concepts that highlight each artist's individuality rather than his or her status as a cultural "token": "Overall we think of the music we work with as contemporary pop music and we try to present it as such. While something like Zap Mama's first record could be, and sometimes was, perceived as an ethnic record, we did our damnedest to alter that perception. The CD covers go a long way, in my opinion, to creating this attitude. We didn't do covers that look like folkloric records or like academic records or obscure material of interest only to musicologists and a few weird fringe types. We work with designers to come up with a graphic statement that says 'this music is relevant to your life' . . . So gradually, although Zap Mama might have initially been thought of as an 'ethnic-folkloric' ensemble, they are now thought of just as a cool group" (qtd. in N.a. 1998e).

The story of how David Byrne changed Susana Baca's life and introduced North American audiences to Afro-Peruvian music is a tale of luck and chance encounters. David Byrne enrolled in Spanish classes at a Latin American music workshop led by Argentinean musician Bernardo Palombo in New York. One day, Palombo gave Byrne an assignment—to translate the lyrics of a song called "María Landó" from a video Palombo had made of Afro-Peruvian singer Susana Baca. Byrne was hooked. He recalls, "I had to see it again . . . I asked, Are there more records like this? Where does this music come from? What kind of music is this?" (qtd. in N.a. 1998e). Describing what initially impressed him about Afro-Peruvian music, he said, "It was the rare combination of elements that excited me. That combination of the sadness of the lyrics and the happiness of the music. Musically I found certain things reminiscent of Afro-Cuban rhythms, but I also perceived that there was a difference. Also, I found melodies I wanted to sing almost instantly" (qtd. in Cornejo Guinassi 1998, 51). Byrne took home an audio track of Palombo's video. He learned the song "María Landó," and he performed it on the South American leg of his tour for the Latin *Rei Momo* album.

Years later, after he had launched Luaka Bop, Byrne decided to put together a recorded compilation of Afro-Peruvian music. He wanted to feature Susana Baca. But how would he find a Peruvian singer who had never recorded with a major label? By chance, David Byrne visited a photo gallery while he was on tour in Austin, Texas. He picked up an old catalogue from a show of photographs of Black Peruvians by Lorry Salcedo. Byrne contacted the photographer to ask whether any photos might be provided for his compilation, and he asked whether Salcedo knew of a singer named Susana Baca. Salcedo replied that of course he knew Susana, they were old neighbors (Baca 2000b; Cornejo Guinassi 2000; N.a. 1998e).

When Susana Baca received an international phone call from David Byrne, she did not know who he was. Byrne had a small following in Peru, based on his work as the leader of the Talking Heads, but he was not very well known. However, Baca was delighted by his interest in her music. Later, when she told friends she had received a phone call from someone called David Byrne, she began to realize that he was not just an average fan.

FIGURE 6.2. Susana Baca and Juan Medrano Cotito. *Photo by Lorry Salcedo, reprinted with permission.*

She invited Byrne to visit her in Lima, and she told him that she would help him with his project in any way she could.

In 1995, David Byrne made his first of three important trips to Peru, where he met Susana Baca and worked with local labels to collect the master tapes and rights to all the recordings he would reissue on *The Soul of Black Peru*. Byrne came to Peru with a list of Afro-Peruvian recordings made in the 1970s and 1980s (by Susana Baca, Manuel Donayre, Cecilia Barraza, Lucila Campos, Roberto Rivas with Gente Morena, Eva Ayllón, Abelardo Vásquez and Nicomedes Santa Cruz with Cumanana, Chaubca Granda, and Perú Negro), which he had faxed to Warner's Lima-based representative label, El Virrey, in advance of his visit (Cornejo Guinassi 2000). In Lima, Byrne visited Peruvian peñas, met with artists, and collected the masters of the recordings he needed.

To represent Susana Baca on *The Soul of Black Peru*, David Byrne insisted on using the 1980s version of "María Landó" that had originally captured his attention, rejecting several of Baca's more recent and higher quality recordings of the same song. Susana Baca's 1980s version of "María Landó," which so enchanted Byrne and prompted his journey of discovery, opens the album, and Byrne's version of the same tune closes it. The liner notes state (after a short biography of each artist featured on the recording):

We think it's only fitting to end our story with Susana Baca, who truly was the inspiration for this album. Her soulful rendition of *Maria Lando* captivated us and convinced us to explore more of this music. We found, surprisingly, that though her voice is stunning and she is a very respected singer, she has never had a record released on a commercial label in Peru. A dedicated student of traditional Afro-Peruvian forms—much like the first generation of Afro-Peruvian musicians and ethnomusicologists— Susana nevertheless represents the new generation of singers and com- posers of the more "sophisticated" Afro-Peruvian music. (Martínez and Jarque 1995)

Unappreciated in her home country, Susana Baca perfectly fit the Luaka Bop mold of the type of artists Byrne loves to discover. Byrne's patronage transformed Susana Baca's life and career, after years of frustrating work on her part. Susana Baca released three subsequent solo albums on the Luaka Bop label between 1997 and 2002, and she began to tour the United States and Europe constantly. By 1996, Susana Baca was *the* Afro-Peruvian artist for world music audiences; in fact, she was the only Afro-Peruvian musi- cian most non-Peruvians in the United States could name. Ironically, most Peruvians still didn't know who she was, and many of those who did con- sidered her Afro-Peruvian style "inauthentic."

Susana Baca: From Local Unknown to Global Diva

There are traditional people who sing Afro-Peruvian music in the traditional form. I believe that I am the least traditional. My roots are there. I can't extract myself from them. They are there. But I don't want to . . . become a museum display! —Susana Baca, interview with the author

As a cosmopolitan artist, Susana Baca does not conform to Peruvian expectations of how a Black woman should sing. A Peruvian television and radio show host explains, "She has a very subtle way of singing. She's not the typical Black voice. And sometimes that's why here she's not popular. Because people think that she doesn't know how to sing" (Martínez 2000). A cajón player adds that Susana Baca's style differs from that of most Afro-Peruvian performers because her concerts are "for watching." He notes her "mystical" style, performing barefoot and dressed in white with complex musical arrangements and evocative ambience (Parodi 2000). A recording industry representative and music critic adds that Susana Baca's style is the "new Afro-Peruvian music," affirming "I am sure that the people who like Nicomedes Santa Cruz and Lucila Campos don't listen to Susana Baca. Because Susana Baca's music is super-sophisticated for them" (Cornejo Guinassi 2000). Much of Susana Baca's repertoire con- sists of poetry set to music, and, when she does perform Afro-Peruvian stan- dards, her arrangements discard the revival's canonized stylistic trademarks (established bordones, accent patterns, and a percussion-heavy sound). She has struggled to find an audience in Peru, where she is sometimes accused of "whitening" Afro-Peruvian folklore. "I believe that those who want to maintain folklore are going to kill Peruvian music," she responds (qtd. in Bolaños 1995, 206).

Born in 1944 in Chorrillos, a former fishing village that became part of Lima, Susana Baca learned Afro-Peruvian music and música criolla at home. Her father was a guitarist and her mother a dancer, and she is related to two of Lima's most prominent Afro-Peruvian musical families, the de la Colinas and the Camposes. Her childhood included jaranas and music-making with her aunts, who were the major sources for Perú Negro's reconstruction of Afro-Peruvian music and dance. But it was her academic immersion in Peruvian poetry that drew her to music. As a student at the National University in the 1960s, Susana explored her love of poetry and literature. In a downtown Lima bar called El Palermo, she socialized with poets and intellectuals. As a young girl, she won Lima's Agua Dulce music competition and began to consider seriously a career in music.

Although she views Afro-Peruvian and criollo genres as part of her musical heritage, Susana Baca finds something lacking in the lyrics of that repertoire. She explains, "The majority of the older festejos, their words don't make any sense now . . . I remember, for example . . . one day, I asked myself what is [the song] 'Enciendete candela' saying? What is it? And we have sung this since we were children! . . . It is more about the sound of the words, you have fun with them. But suddenly, when I take notice of the lyrics of these songs, I don't like the words. And I feel that they are not the words that I want to express . . . Above all, valses . . . they treat the woman terribly! . . . I would like to sing something that has nicer lyrics [laughs]. I would like to sing something that, I don't know, that a Russian person can understand in translation" (Baca 2000b).

In the 1960s, Susana Baca began to explore ways to combine poetry and Afro-Peruvian music, retaining the rhythms she loved but adding lyrics that nurtured her poetic tastes. She joined her first musical group, an experimental band called Tiahuanaco 2000.[2] Its members were musically untrained young people who wanted to make sounds without musical or cultural borders. Poet Omar Agamayo wrote song lyrics, and the band members made music by imitating earthquake sounds with sheet metal, using children's toys as percussion instruments, and inventing whatever else occurred to them.

In the early 1970s, singer/composer Chabuca Granda hired Susana Baca as a personal assistant, and Susana moved into Chabuca's house. Together, they attended meetings and recitals by the vanguard poets of the Hora

Cero (Zero Hour) group. As a result of Chabuca Granda's interest in her work, Susana Baca nearly secured a recording contract with Peru's IEMPSA music label in the early 1980s. IEMPSA executives owed Chabuca a favor, and she demanded that the company release a record of Susana Baca's songs. Susana met with IEMPSA representatives, who began to discuss how she might improve her image through plastic surgery ("like a product, they were packaging me like a product!" the artist recalls [Baca 2000b]). In 1983, Chabuca Granda died, and IEMPSA executives informed Susana Baca that they no longer were obligated to record her music. Susana Baca never secured a recording deal on any Peruvian label. Although this made her work very difficult, it also meant that she was able to design and package her own music and style.

Before Susana Baca was "discovered" by David Byrne, she did record several albums using her own resources. Her first recording, a cassette titled *Color de rosa* (1982), fused Afro-Peruvian and Andean rhythms with poetry. Compiled by her husband/manager Ricardo Pereira from preexisting individual tapes, *Color de rosa* was remastered in Brazil in an effort to convince a major Peruvian label to sign Susana Baca. Armed with her cassettes, Susana recalls how she went "knocking on doors with Ricardo, looking for a label that would produce my work. And they said, 'Yes, but you sing poetry! What's more, with piano, cello, guitar, things like that.' Most groups in that time didn't play with those instruments . . . They weren't interested. And it was always the same. 'You sing poetry, poetry doesn't sell, it doesn't do anything for us, we want a product we can sell to the masses' . . . Until, one fine day, Ricardo got tired and he said: 'I am going to create my own label.' And he created his own label" (Baca 2000b).

In the 1980s, Susana Baca's trio (including guitarist Roberto Arguedas and cajón player Juan Medrano Cotito) picked up some work in local pubs, and they began to tour in Peru and abroad, performing in Europe in 1985 and the Soviet Union in 1986. Just before the Europe trip, they recorded a new cassette, this time in Miki González' Lima-based studio. On tour in Russia in 1986, they met Cuban *nueva trova* singer/composer Silvio Rodríguez (whom Susana had known since 1973), who invited them to come to Cuba's Egrem Studios to re-record the album. Back in Peru in 1986, Susana and her trio took part in a festival of Latin American music organized by then-President Alan García. Bernardo Palombo, the Argentinean musician who would later become David Byrne's Spanish teacher, came to Peru for the festival, where he met Susana Baca and arranged to make the music video of her performing "María Landó" that would find its way into David Byrne's hands several years later.

From 1990 to 1992, Susana Baca embarked upon a major project to research the Afro-Peruvian music of Lima and the rural coast, resulting in the CD and accompanying booklet *Del fuego y del agua* (Of fire and water) (Baca, Basili, and Peirera 1992). Susana Baca explains that this project coincided with the period in her adult life "when I discover that I am Black, and what it means to be Black. We are different. In some way, we are different . . . there is a culture, there is a presence, there is a manner of feeling, of seeing things, of cooking, of taking pleasure, of singing, of perceiving life . . . Things like this, knowledge of herbs. Which herb can go in which food to lighten the weight . . . So there are cultural things that are very strong, that are present. This is how my interest began. To learn what is there. To know if the other houses where Blacks live also did these things. So I went researching, asking, moving along, until a moment arrived when we could no longer conduct an investigation in this manner. We had to organize, to conduct a good investigation, organize. And this is how we plunge into the investigation of coastal Peru" (Baca 2000b).

Thus, nearly forty years after the Pancho Fierro company brought forgotten Black music of rural areas to the urban concert stage, Susana Baca retraced the steps and methods of the revival artists. To lend her project academic rigor, she worked with ethnomusicologist Chalena Vásquez, scholar Francisco Basili, and a team of friends and musicians. In addition, scholars and culture bearers in each coastal region assisted the group. Susana remembers: "In Zaña, where Luis Rocca, the historian of Zaña received us, he brought us to a gathering where there was a Black Chinese man, and this man sang *moros y cristianos* like my father did! . . . Another man came who sang décimas and verses. I sang them things, they sang me others. We said farewell in the doorway of his house, with tears in our eyes, weeping with sorrow because when would we see each other again? So we kept singing those marvelous verses" (Baca 2000b).

Susana and her research team recorded music in every town they visited. But, Ricardo Pereira explains, "our idea was not to produce a work of ethnomusicology . . . We don't claim to do this. We wanted to make a record that would have modernity, good sound, all these things, and at the same time that would enable Blacks of different populations, by listening to it, to become interested in the subject of negritud in Peru" (Pereira 2000). With these priorities in mind, when it was time to choose songs for the final recording, Susana Baca strove neither for folkloric authenticity nor democratic inclusion. She chose the songs that pleased her most, reinterpreting them in arrangements that evoked the mood she wanted to create. Susana explains that what she loved best about this project was when she had learned a new rhythm so well she could play with it. "These are intuitions," she says. "I can't tell you a preconceived idea about this. What happens is I take a song, I start to sing it, and I feel things. And . . . if it strikes me as beautiful, it stays" (Baca 2000b). The end product features new arrangements by the project's musical director, Félix Vilchez, of familiar songs from the Afro-Peruvian revival ("Samba malató," "Toro mata," and the Christmas songs of Chincha) as well as lesser-known genres. The musical arrangements incorporate synthesizers, piano, electric bass, and other instruments that purposely modernize the sound and style of the collected musical raw materials, and the musical personnel combines studio musicians with revival artists and popular culture bearers. The booklet that accompanies the CD includes articles on the history of Afro-Peruvian music, memories, music genres, dance, and instruments; excerpts from an unpublished manuscript on coastal Peruvian music genres by musicologist Chalena Vásquez; photographic illustrations from Peru, Nigeria, Cameroon, the United States, and Germany; and a list of references.

Although the artistic content and style of *Del fuego y del agua* departed from the folkloric canon of the Afro-Peruvian revival, in many ways the project echoed and extended the goals of the revival leaders. For example, Susana and her team resurrected Afro-Peruvian drums whose use predated that of the cajón. They found an older man in the northern coast, Don Tana Urbina, who taught them how the *checo* (gourd drum) was played by older Afro-Peruvians, and they revived both the checo and the *botija* (jug drum).[3] Sometimes, Susana Baca explicitly combined the work of revival artists and scholars by piecing together lyrics and melodies from a variety of sources. For example, Susana Baca's version of "Samba malató" (titled "Landó") on *Del fuego y del agua* joins the original verse fragment passed on to Nicomedes Santa Cruz by his mother (see chapter 3) with other verses collected by William Tompkins, Guillermo Durand, and Victoria Espinoza, and then adds a new verse by Francisco Basili (Baca, Basili, and Peirera 1992, 78–79). Interestingly, Nicomedes Santa Cruz' pseudo-African lyrics are not included on the *Del fuego y del agua* track, although in later recordings and concert tours Susana Baca would sing them.

To house and organize the material they collected during the *Del fuego y del agua* project, Susana Baca and Ricardo Pereira created a research and performance institute called Instituto Negrocontinuo. They chose the name "negrocontinuo" as an allusion to the *basso continuo* (figured bass) part of Baroque music, which serves as a kind of pedal point over which all other instrumental harmonies are arranged. Thus, the use of the word *"negro"* (Black) in the name "negrocontinuo" posits Black music as the metaphorical "pedal point" of popular music in Peru (Pereira 2000). To foster more research and awareness of Black music and popular Peruvian culture, they opened a research library, and they created a performance and rehearsal space for young musicians. At first, members of Susana's band (as well as some Cuban expatriate musicians) taught classes on Afro-Peruvian music and dance, music theory, and transcription. Their young students, in return, brought to Instituto Negrocontinuo their own fresh compositions and approaches, ranging from Andean music and *chicha* (a blend of cumbia and huaynos popular in Peru in the 1970s and 1980s) to rock and jazz fusion styles. In the late 1990s, due to financial and organizational development concerns, Instituto Negrocontinuo reduced its curriculum to vocal classes only, but Susana and Ricardo continued to work individually with young musicians and composers, and the library remained open for research.

In 1997, publisher Jacques Hubert, with the help of a Los Angeles–based Peruvian music producer named Juan Morillo, facilitated the U.S. re-release of *Del fuego y del agua*. In the introduction to the English translation of the booklet, Morillo wrote:

> Music aficionados in the northern hemisphere first came into contact with the music of Black Peruvians thanks to the magnificent collection of music recorded in the 1960s and 70s put together by David Byrne. The work of Susana Baca was part of that collection. Susana is not only one of the greatest and most expressive performers of Afro Peruvian and Creole music, but also one of the most dedicated researchers of the traditions.
>
> The work you are about to unveil represents the dedicated effort from Susana, Francisco Basili and Ricardo Pereira to document this music and present it to the rest of the world. The original edition, in Spanish, is now out of print, in fact it sold out within weeks of its release. When we met Susana and Ricardo Pereira and "discovered" this outstanding production, we didn't hesitate to affirm the need to spread the word beyond the ancient land of the Incas. (Baca, Basili, and Peirera 1997, foreword)

From a business perspective, the U.S. reissue of *Del fuego y del agua* was a failure, in part because the release coincided with Susana's lower-priced French-produced recording *Vestida de vida*, a collection of songs of the Americas. However, whether or not U.S. audiences bought the CD–booklet combination, the fact that it was in the record stores gave Susana Baca a reputation as a proud researcher of her own cultural tradition. In fact, the only Afro-Peruvian musician (then a Los Angeles resident) who declined to be interviewed for this book referred me to the *Del fuego y del agua* booklet. "I think it is all in there," he said, before hanging up the phone.

When David Byrne met Susana Baca in the 1990s, years of forging her own path had made her a mature, self-guided artist with a cosmopolitan vision of Afro-Peruvian music that could only "sell" outside of Peru. David Byrne gave new life to Susana Baca's brand of Afro-Peruvian music when he distributed it and sponsored her tours in the United States. Susana Baca became (as she was billed in one concert tour with other female world music artists) a "global diva"—the only Afro-Peruvian singer to break into the world music market and the sole representative of Black Peru for world music audiences in the United States in the 1990s. Gradually, her legitimization by the outside world led to greater acknowledgment within Peru. Her local reputation especially was boosted when she received the 2002 Latin Grammy for Best Folk Music Album—ironically for the unauthorized re-release of an album recorded in Cuba in 1986.[4] As a result of this international achievement, the singer was given a special award by the Peruvian government and honored for her services as a cultural ambassador of Peru in a ceremony at the Peruvian government palace. These and other public recognitions of Susana Baca's work outside Peru have resulted in the radical transformation of her previous status as an unknown in Peru. By the early twenty-first century, Susana Baca would begin to acquire a reputation in Peru as an international star.

Travel Diaries, Los Angeles, California, 1999–2000, and Lima, Peru, 2000: Comparing Susana Baca Concerts

We arrive at the Conga Room in Hollywood, right on time for an 8:00 PM show, only to stand in line for almost a half hour. The performance starts on time, so we miss the beginning. A group of three women in line in front of us speak in mixed English and Spanish. The one with long, straight brown hair describes the "strong quality of the Negroid dances" of Peru. "But what Susana Baca does is subtler, it is different," she explains to the others.

    Inside, I notice that there is a much larger Latino contingent at this concert than at previous concerts by Susana Baca that I've attended in Los Angeles over the past two years. Is this because of the Latino-run venue or because of Susana's growing reputation in the United States? When the emcee asks if Peruvians are in the house at the end of the show, his response is a big cheer. People in the audience know the lyrics, and they sing along. Most are clapping at the right times (with help from the musicians onstage), but one man insists on playing the Cuban clave beat (which does not conform to the rhythmic cycle of the Afro-Peruvian music performed onstage) loudly on a beer bottle. Everyone in the room is dancing to their own personal interpretations of how the music grooves, and the room becomes a polyrhythmic sea of smiling heads and bodies bobbing at different times. My companion whispers to me that Susana's band is definitely a "world music" act because everyone in the audience is moving to a different beat.

❊

I drive to the Neighborhood Church, a small building in a park-like setting in Pasadena, California. Susana Baca's husband and manager, Ricardo Pereira, is standing outside. The sound check is running late, and the staff is having trouble dealing with the logistics of the venue's third sold-out show in recent history. Ricardo motions to me and brings me in through a side door, then shows me the seat he saved for me. I thank him and take my place beside another unaccompanied woman. She is a member of the church who has never heard Susana sing. We chat a bit, and I tell her about my work. She asks me about Susana's research—this must have been part of a press release or ad. I tell her about Del fuego y del agua *and the revival of instruments like the checo gourd drum. In the middle of the concert, she nudges me: "Is that the gourd?"*

During intermission, I eavesdrop on the man seated in front of me, who speaks Spanish until some English-speaking friends come by, when he switches to perfect English. He tells his friend that, if you understand the poetry she is singing, it is amazing. He is overwhelmed. I wonder where he is from, and I notice that all around me are people of color, White people, people speaking Spanish, Black people speaking both Spanish and English, and that midway through the concert someone yells out "Viva Perú!" Susana's audience is no longer the Anglo "world beat" crowd it was when I first saw her perform at UCLA in 1997. Yet it is not the audience that attends events in the local Peruvian community, either.

The last number is "Enciendete candela," leading into "El alcatraz." Cotito plays quijada, Hugo plays cajita, and Susana dances between them. Throughout the show the audience is captivated by her unique manner of dancing, shaking her whole body while appearing to glide at the same time. A standing ovation brings the ensemble back for an encore: "Se me van los pies" (My feet are running away from me). Susana dances from side to side, and I see her delight when the African women on the side of the stage begin to dance to the music. Susana makes her way over and dances with them. The show ends.

❖

I am in downtown Lima for the opening of the newly renovated Gran Parque with its outdoor amphitheater. There is a free concert and inaugural celebration to coincide with the 465th anniversary of the founding of the city of Lima. This will be one of Susana Baca's rare public performances in Peru (she is one of several national artists who will perform a few songs each), and I am curious about how it will differ from her U.S. concerts. I arrive in a taxi and see a line of thousands of people forming around the park. I walk along the perimeter and find my way to the front entrance just as the line divides in four to correspond with the opening gates. It is a madhouse. People are running, pushing, shoving, and laughing. Police are everywhere. Inside the park, the enormous new amphitheater is already full. A huge video screen has been set up outside to accommodate the overflow.

I approach the amphitheater, where a line of police is holding the crowd back. Suddenly, the crowd pushes against the police and breaks the barrier. Inside, gates have been shut to prevent people from entering the theater. People are jumping over fences, boosting each other, and throwing small children up to the staircase in order to enter the theater. I give up on sitting inside and make my way to the video screen.

Susana Baca is scheduled to perform after Cecilia Barraza, a White singer of both Afro-Peruvian music and música criolla. In Barraza's Afro-Peruvian numbers, she switches to intonation and body movements associated with Black folklore. She introduces the song "Chinchiví" by explaining that the title refers to a strong liquor drunk by Blacks. Her Black dancers perform choreographed routines as if they are intoxicated, swirling and teetering. The performance is exuberant and skillful but it also reinforces negative stereotypes about Blacks.

Next, emcee Mabela Martínez introduces Susana as "the most internationally recognized Peruvian singer," referring to David Byrne several times. Susana's concert is similar to those she gives in the United States. Her arrangements are subtler than Cecilia Barraza's, with more emphasis on guitar and no choreographed backup dancers. When she performs "María Landó," she dedicates the song to the working women of Lima.

"The Black Soul of David Byrne"

Although it paved the way for Susana Baca's U.S. success (and later Peruvian acclaim) as a world music performer, the CD *The Soul of Black Peru* was barely noticed in Peru. In order to purchase the CD in Peru in the 1990s, customers had to ask record store employees to look through drawers of CDs behind the counter. In contrast, the recording sold well in the non-Latino U.S. market and was earmarked by *Billboard* as one of Luaka Bop's releases with the greatest potential for popularity (Verna 1995). [5]

Despite *The Soul of Black Peru*'s relatively low profile in Peru and among U.S. Latinos, it became the center of several controversies about cultural and economic rights. First, Peruvian artists charged that Byrne exploited them by reissuing recordings without providing royalties. Second, Peruvian critics found fault with Byrne's selection of non-Black and marginal artists as well as his outdated repertoire choices. Third, Byrne's inclusion of his own rendition of the song "María Landó" launched new debates regarding who has the right to perform Afro-Peruvian music.

A couple of vignettes from my field research in Peru illustrate the first issue, artistic exploitation. In fall 2000, I was in a theater in Lima's

Miraflores neighborhood, waiting for a Latin jazz concert to begin. As I took a seat in the front row, next to the pianist's wife (a friend of mine whose father was a famous composer of Afro-Peruvian music), I overheard one of the members of the band talking to her. "You had better be careful about where you register your father's songs," he warned my friend, "because someone like David Byrne can just come down here from the United States and take everything and you'll never find out about it or see a penny!"

Similarly, as the story goes, Lucila Campos was in a record store one day when her daughter said, "Look, Mom, there's a picture of you on the cover of that CD!" Lucila Campos is said to have been oblivious to the release of *The Soul of Black Peru*, despite the fact that the album cover prominently features a closeup of her face (see figure 6.1) and the CD contains two re-released tracks of her previously recorded performances.[6]

According to Pedro Cornejo, the former employee of Peru's now-defunct El Virrey label who facilitated Byrne's project in Lima, the blame should not fall on David Byrne's shoulders but rather on the recording labels with which Lucila Campos and the other Peruvian artists originally signed their contracts. The recordings Byrne selected for his compilation were originally issued in the 1960s to 1980s. In many cases, the agreements made between artists and Peruvian record companies during that era left artists with little or no rights over their own recordings. As Pedro Cornejo explains, "Let's take the example of an artist who makes a record with El Virrey or IEMPSA in the year 1970. At that time, the recording companies found themselves in a much better economic situation than today . . . So the recording companies, when they signed a contract with an artist, it was normally an artist contract. Which meant what? That the record company recorded the record . . . and became the owner of the material forever, as they say, *per secula seculorem*. This implied that the company could commercialize that record or that song forever . . . So a song recorded by Abelardo Vásquez in 1973 continues to sell today. But what happens? The contract Abelardo Vásquez signed in the year 1973 was a contract that probably said that as a royalty the artist was going to receive . . . one sol! You see? In that era, I don't know if that was a lot or a little. But obviously, that sol in the 1990s means nothing! Absolutely nothing" (Cornejo Guinassi 2000).

Cornejo continues, "the curious thing is that . . . these types of contracts sometimes are not well known by the artists, above all traditional ones. For example, curiously, after the CD was released, I remember that a newspaper article came out that said Lucila Campos protests against David

Byrne's CD because she says 'They haven't paid me! David Byrne has paid me nothing for this song!' So, of course, It appears that David Byrne swindled her . . . And what happened was simply that Lucila Campos didn't have the vaguest idea how these things work. Who should have paid her was not David Byrne but El Virrey, the Peruvian recording label that had the legal representation of her songs . . . But Lucila Campos apparently did not get this. So she thinks that the person who should pay her was David Byrne, [he should] take out his money and give it to her . . . But basically the contract was made between Luaka Bop and local labels" (Cornejo Guinassi 2000).

It should be noted that, because of the types of contracts signed in the 1970s, many of the artists featured on Byrne's compilation similarly received little or nothing when their recordings were re-released on compilations made by Peruvian labels. Even if they had negotiated better contracts, their earning potential in Peru was limited by the fact that the market for Afro-Peruvian music and música criolla in Peru was (and remains) very small. After Peru's military revolution ended in the 1980s, so did the quotas that had increased the broadcasting of national music, and foreign styles once again flooded the market. In a 1998 opinion poll, English-language rock and Spanish-language ballads were the favorite music of the upper classes, and lower and middle class listeners favored Spanish ballads and salsa. National musical styles were preferred by only 13 percent of the surveyed listening audience, and Afro-Peruvian music did not even appear on the list (although it may have been contained within the categories criollo and/or *folklórico*) (Nájar 1999, 378).

From one perspective, *The Soul of Black Peru* did no good whatsoever for its featured Peruvian artists, with the exception of Susana Baca. Few received royalties, and without an infrastructure of follow-up recordings or tours available in the United States, none stood a chance of becoming successful as a result of the album. On the other hand, the recording created a new international audience for Peruvian coastal music—which is under-supported in Peru and rarely leaves the country through export sales or radio broadcasts (Soto Herrera 2000)—opening the door for these artists to create their own U.S. markets. About five years after *The Soul of Black Peru* was released, artists such as Lucila Campos, Eva Ayllón, and Perú Negro (all of whom were featured on *The Soul of Black Peru*) began to appear on other international compilations released outside of Peru. In 2002, Perú Negro made its U.S. debut in Los Angeles, and in subsequent tours they filled concert halls across the country.

After the release of *The Soul of Black Peru*, David Byrne made two more trips to Peru, in 1997 and 1998. The first was to promote Susana Baca's self-titled solo album. Like *The Soul of Black Peru*, the album *Susana Baca* generated little interest in Peru. However, the presence of an international rock star attracted popular attention and press, and Byrne's patronage began to lend credibility to Susana Baca's artistry in the eyes of certain Peruvians. While Byrne was in Lima, he met recording studio owner and musician Manongo Mujica, who proposed that they organize a concert as a tribute to Byrne's role in the international dissemination of Afro-Peruvian music. Byrne agreed to perform (he would be touring his solo album *Feelings*), and the date was set for March 1998.

The concert at Lima's Muelle Uno featured performances by Perú Negro; a percussion group composed of Julio "Chocolate" Algendones, Eusebio "Pititi" Sirio, Rony Campos, Manongo Mujica, and Daniel Mujica; and a final rock concert by David Byrne. Ironically, Susana Baca, who was on tour in the United States, did not perform. Lucila Campos opened the show with her renditions of such classics as "Toro mata" and "Guaranguito." Reportedly, Campos also gave one of the only public performances of the song "María Landó" by a Peruvian artist other than Susana Baca, "to show us that Susana Baca is not the only Peruvian who deserves to be released on a recording by Luaka Bop" (Cachay 1998, 16). A glowing article in one of Lima's newspapers, titled "The Black Soul of David Byrne," praised Byrne for his dissemination of the underestimated cultural treasure of Afro-Peruvian music:

> Since Victoria Santa Cruz set a course for the First World in search of a more intense engagement with the African culture seated in America, Black music of Peru has suffered from an abandonment that has led to the devaluation of some of its most contagious expressions. What is curious . . . is that . . . the mortal who dares to rescue and revalorize [Afro-Peruvian music] . . . is not an heir to the Black Peruvian legacy, but a musician . . . whose greatest connection to rhythm and passion has developed with the incorrigible tunes of rock and roll. (N.a. 1998a)

Not everyone in Peru looked favorably upon Byrne's efforts. At the advance press conference for the Lima concert, Byrne apparently was peppered with questions about his selection of artists for *The Soul of Black Peru* (Cornejo Guinassi 2000). Some Peruvian critics felt that White criolla singers such as Chabuca Granda and Cecilia Barraza should not have been included in a compilation titled *The Soul of Black Peru* (although White criollo artists previously had been included on compilations of Afro-Peruvian music made in Peru). Others criticized Byrne for selecting only music from the 1970s and 1980s, ignoring more contemporary trends such as the Afro-Peruvian rock of Miki González.

To the charge that Chabuca Granda's music was inappropriate on an Afro-Peruvian compilation, Byrne is quoted as having responded, "Chabuca is an exception. She is not an eloquent example of Black Peruvian music, but for me she is a great musician. Chabuca Granda's music is influenced by Afro-Peruvian music, and further, it showed me from the beginning the different branches into which Peruvian music could be divided." Addressing comments about the CD's alleged failure to include the country's most representative Afro-Peruvian artists and repertoire, Byrne replied, "I realize that some artists are missing from this compilation, but in the end it is a question of personal taste. It is not an academic selection" (N.a. 1998c; N.a. 1998f).

The controversy over Byrne's selection of artists highlights ambiguities that have characterized the distinction between Afro-Peruvian music and música criolla throughout the twentieth and twenty-first centuries (see León Quirós 2003, 34–35). Although the Afro-Peruvian revival affirmed the blackness of re-created genres such as the festejo and landó, it resulted in ambiguity regarding whether genres such as the marinera should be considered part of música criolla or Afro-Peruvian repertoires. Many artists, such as Eva Ayllón (a Black performer) and Cecilia Barraza (a White performer), perform both styles in a single concert or recording. Thus, although *The Soul of Black Peru* unapologetically jumbles together the old and the new, Black artists and White artists, *música negra* and música criolla, all of its tracks are within Afro-Peruvian music's sphere of influence, and they outline an honest history of the interracial and musically diverse influences that have shaped its tradition.

Of all the tracks on *The Soul of Black Peru*, the song "María Landó" played a special role in the globalization of Afro-Peruvian music. Although most Peruvians had never heard of the song, it became the only Afro-Peruvian song many U.S. listeners could name in the 1990s. It was a signature tune for Susana Baca's U.S. audiences, always earning applause after the first few bars.

Unlike the songs of the revival, the lyrics of "María Landó," composed by poet César Calvo, make no reference to Africa, slavery, or blackness in Peru. The melody is based on an unfinished fragment by singer/composer Chabuca Granda. It should be noted that neither of the song's composers were Afro-Peruvian. The song begins with a verse that employs a string of metaphors to evoke the passage of time from morning to night:[7]

La madrugada estalla como una estátua	The dawn breaks like a statue
como una estátua de alas	like a statue with wings
que se dispersan por la ciudad	that spread across the city
Y el mediodía canta campana de agua	And the noon sings like a bell of water
campana de agua de oro	golden bell of water

que nos prohibe la soledad	that prohibits our solitude
Y la noche levanta su copa larga	And the night lifts its large cup
su larga copa, larga luna	its large cup, large early
temprana	moon
sobre el mar	over the sea

After setting the scene, the poem describe the sacrifices of María Landó, a woman who cannot stop to enjoy the dawn or look at the moon because she labors from day to night on behalf of others.

Who is María Landó? Susana Baca says the song's heroine is a metaphor for working women who sacrifice themselves for others amid Peru's economic crisis. She explains, "There are so many María Landós. María Landó is the woman who goes to the market to sell things. She is the woman who sells food in a little cart with her child bundled inside. She is the working woman, who works and works and earns four coins. She survives. This is the story of María Landó" (Baca 2000b).

"María Landó" was a poem with an unfinished melody before Susana Baca and her trio recorded it. It is a product of Susana Baca's early experimental efforts to combine Peruvian poetry with Afro-Peruvian rhythms. In the 1980s, César Calvo sang the poem to Susana Baca. Later, her guitarist, Roberto Arguedas, created the musical arrangement. Arguedas had never set a poem to music before—a project that intimidated him at the time. He was unhappy with the final product, and so was Calvo (Arguedas 2000). Yet, Susana Baca claims the interpreter's right to differ from the author: "I feel it in another way," she says. "For me, this is my story. My mother has worked all her life to have a place to live. So I have lived the flesh and blood of this story. I am not going to sing it how he [Calvo] wants!" (Baca 2000b).

Musically, Arguedas' trio arrangement of "María Landó" (as heard on *The Soul of Black Peru*) situates Susana Baca outside the authenticity loop of folklore even as it re-creates the core instrumentation (guitar, cajón, and voice) and rhythmic feel of the landó. None of the Cuban percussion instruments (such as cowbell, congas, and bongó) that found their way into the landós of the 1960s and 1970s are present. Still, Baca's trio evokes the landó's characteristic feeling of metric ambiguity and shifting accents. For example, in the guitar and cajón introduction (shown in figure 6.3), Arguedas' syncopated guitar phrasing (beginning on the second eighth note of the first measure) diverts the attention of the downbeat-seeking listener. When the cajón player, Cotito, enters during this second half of the guitar's first melodic phrase, his alternating rhythmic variations with shifting accents further camouflage the downbeat. He does not play the landó pattern developed during the revival, but he implies it with a cajón part similar to the related zamacueca rhythm (see figure 3.9).[8] Cotito plays bass

Transcription Notes:
Smaller noteheads (guitar part): Ornamental notes and chords, played faintly

FIGURE 6.3. María Landó introduction, as performed by Roberto Arguedas (guitar) and Juan Medrano Cotito *(cajón)* with Susana Baca, from *The Soul of Black Peru* (Various Artists 1995a).

tones lightly, causing the brighter alternating sequences of three and four eighth-note "slap" tones to overshadow the downbeats. In the bars immediately following the passage shown in figure 6.3, guitarist Roberto Arguedas switches to anticipated bass movements and finally plays chords on the downbeats just before Susana's vocal entrance. This rhythmic guitar-and-cajón play teases the downbeat-seeking listener so that, like María, before the sun comes up (that is, before the lyrics describe the dawn) we are already late.

The song continues with a cyclical stylistic alternation between three different Peruvian genres (vals, festejo, and landó), with new sections framed by the repeating guitar motif established in the introduction and shown in figure 6.3. Departing from the typical repeating verse–chorus form of the landós re-created in the revival, the form of the song resembles the verse–montuno structure that characterizes Afro-Cuban music and *salsa* (a montuno section is typically characterized by an increase in tempo and/or energy, improvisation, and call-and-response). The song concludes with a last reiteration of the guitar motif, this time delaying the final cadence to the downbeat. The cyclical repetition of the guitar motif, combined with Susana Baca's calmly flowing vocal delivery, might be interpreted as evoking the metaphorical passage of times of day, alternately suggesting the determinism of María's plight and a sense of hope for tomorrow.

Susana Baca told me that what she likes about David Byrne's performance of "María Landó" is its interpretive passion, and Roberto Arguedas, who is in many ways the song's composer, confided that he only began to like "María Landó" when he heard Byrne's recording (Arguedas 2000). Byrne's lyrical delivery reminded Arguedas of Calvo's original recitation of the melody fragment that he had set to music (Arguedas 2000).

Byrne's performance does not reproduce the feeling of the landó in instrumentation, arrangement, rhythmic structure, or accent. Instead, his rendition expresses his own reading of the poem: linear and dramatic, with lush, stringed orchestration more reminiscent of a *mariachi* orchestra or a Hollywood film score than an Afro-Peruvian ensemble. Strings dominate the arrangement, sometimes doubling the voice, sometimes tracing the scale, sometimes emphasizing the tonic or dominant. There is no percussion until the interlude between the first and second sung verses. The orchestration lends a sense of grandeur to the song that evokes a completely different ambience from Baca's rendition.

Byrne's introduction (figure 6.4) immediately establishes a more straightforward temporal world than that of Baca's arrangement. Because of the centrality of time as a metaphor in the poem, and because of the role of musical time in defining the Afro-Peruvian landó, this difference is significant. Like Baca's, Byrne's introduction is guitar-based, but there is no dialogue with percussion or play of shifting landó accents. The feeling of triple meter is solid: easily countable, steady, and considerably slower than Baca's tempo. The second guitar's steady harmonic motion neatly marks each downbeat, backed by the strings and later the cello, while the first guitar elaborates on the resulting chordal framework. Rather than percussion, the guitars are joined by other strings, which articulate a repeating tonic-dominant progression.

When Byrne enters with vocals (immediately after the second ending in figure 6.4), the illusion of time displacement created by Baca's introduction is absent. Byrne, however, plays more with the vocal line, using a fair amount of rubato, which heightens the dramatic tension. Byrne's narrative style is linear (contrasting Baca's calm, circular style), with a sense of beginning, build-up, prolonged climax, and completion that emphasizes the montuno-like aspects of the end of the song. This element of Byrne's performance may result from the fact that he was learning to play salsa and other similar Latin music for the *Rei Momo* album when he added "María Landó" to his repertoire for the South American tour. He begins his dramatic climax much earlier than Baca, marked by guitar strumming, percussion, and dynamic contrast. At the "montuno" section, Byrne builds even more intensity by punctuating the galloping percussion and guitar

FIGURE 6.4. "María Landó" introduction, as performed by David Byrne on *The Soul of Black Peru* (Various Artists 1995a).

strumming with vaguely Latin-style cries (reminiscent of his Talking Heads song "And She Was"). The ending affirms the linearity of the narrative accomplished by this sense of constantly building climax. The percussion beats out the final count, and the song ends definitively on a tonic chord. In Byrne's performance, the story of María Landó has a beginning, middle and end. In Baca's, it is continuous.

Despite the dramatic differences between these two renditions of "María Landó," it should be noted that recordings can "museumize" performers, freezing one interpretation into an essential original. By the late 1990s, Susana Baca was touring with an expanded quintet including a bass player and percussionist, and her performance of "María Landó" was different than the one included on *The Soul of Black Peru*. The calm, cyclical delivery gave way to a clear drum break and climax leading into the "montuno," fusing Byrne's sense of drama with Afro-Peruvian instrumentation and arrangement.

For many listeners, the pleasant experience of discovering Afro-Peruvian music through *The Soul of Black Peru* was jarringly interrupted by David Byrne's blatantly un-Peruvian interpretation of "María Landó." Some people find fault with Byrne for appropriating what they think is a work of traditional Peruvian folklore, and others are annoyed by Byrne's heavily accented Spanish. The "confusing pleasure" of Afro-Peruvian music's rhythmic play is absent from Byrne's arrangement, and his obvious identity as a foreigner further disappoints consumers seeking authenticity in world music. As a friend of mine proclaimed, "What hubris!"

Scholars who write about world music usually place David Byrne in the category of White First World pop artists who use their power and cultural resources to engage in colonialist cultural mining. For example, critiquing Byrne's Latin album *Rei Momo*, George Lipsitz argues that "these explorations have to be carried out with a self-conscious understanding of unequal power relations, of the privileges available to Anglo-American recording stars because of the economic power of the countries from which they come . . . David Byrne's . . . escapes into postmodern multiculturalism, however well-motivated, hide the construction of 'whiteness' in America—its privileges, evasions, and contradictions" (Lipsitz 1994, 61, 63). On the other hand, Lipsitz contends that non-Anglo artists (such as Ronnie Spector and Baldemar Huerta) who play music from outside their culture become "'more themselves' by appearing to be something other than themselves. Like many members of aggrieved populations around the world, these strategic anti-essentialists have become experts in disguise because their survival has often depended on it. Consequently, their escapes differ markedly from what might seem like similar shifts in identity and allegiance on the part of musicians like Paul Simon and David Byrne" (Lipsitz 1994, 63). Along the same lines, Timothy Taylor (1997) argues that Western artists who integrate African music into their performances are colonialists, whereas African artists who incorporate elements of jazz, R&B, and funk engage in "strategic inauthenticity," purposely borrowing modern Western styles in order to counter Western assumptions about premodern "authentic" African music.

Countering those who maintain that "secret" world music can (and should) only be performed by native practitioners, Paul Gilroy contends that "the most important lesson music still has to teach us is that its inner secrets and ethnic rules can be taught and learned . . . The calls and responses no longer converge in the tidy patterns of secret, ethnically encoded dialogue" (Gilroy 1993, 109–110). In this vein, Susana Baca believes that there is no major difference between herself (an Afro-Peruvian singer) and David Byrne (a Scottish-American singer) when it comes to performing the music of other cultures. She bypasses the "West versus the Rest" dichotomy by reformulating the central question to emphasize artistic integrity. When I discussed Byrne's performance of "María Landó" with her, Susana Baca observed, "I feel that for him it is not just one more song. He has put himself into the song. Some people say

'Oh no! How horrible! And besides, his pronunciation is so terrible!' But it seems unfair to me, because there is a feeling, an artistic engagement. With me, for example, I love 'Summertime.' I love it! It has fascinated me all my life . . . One fine day I said . . . 'I want to sing it.' And I sang it in public. It came out terribly [she laughs]. But I sang it, and it came from my heart. I remember that a North American woman approached me. 'Oh,' I said to her, 'excuse what I said, I lost the pronunciation!' But she said to me, 'You have performed it with feeling, Susana. It doesn't matter.' So it is the way you involve yourself with what you are doing . . . I don't believe that Dave would have said 'I just sing this because I want to.' No! He has put himself into the music, he has put himself into the words. And he has loved it! It is as if something pleases you and they deprive you of the right to express yourself with it. That's not right" (Baca 2000b).

David Byrne responds with a view very close to Susana Baca's, asserting his right to be cosmopolitan without automatically being labeled a cultural imperialist. "I'm not going to restrict myself musically," he says. "We shouldn't feel that music or rhythms are limited to, and can only be played by, one people . . . You can't control musicians that way" (qtd. in Howell 1992, 113). In an e-mail message he sent me after reading part of my book manuscript, Byrne added, "From my point of view cultural imperialism would be me remaking Maria Lando with a view to turning it into a slick pop record. Or 'borrowing' the melody or changes, without acknowledgement . . . To me, these define cultural imperialism, and my skewed, subjective, biased and warped . . . interpretations are something else."[9]

Thus, both Susana Baca and David Byrne want audiences to appreciate performing artists not just for where they were born but also for their creative contributions as citizens of the world. Their arguments suggest that a song like "María Landó" should not be reduced to a vehicle exclusively for the cultural expression of Afro-Peruvianness, an identity that is hybrid and complicated to start. The notion of a frozen cultural or geographical "origin" attached to a piece of music is highly problematic in any music's history (see Gilroy 1993; Radano 2003; Taruskin 1995), and more so in one whose experience of loss and reinvention obscures any direct link to a knowable past.

The case of "María Landó," in particular, illustrates how facile assumptions about the cultural origins of world music may lead to judgment errors regarding questions of authenticity and appropriation. Contrary to what many non-Peruvian listeners may think, "María Landó" is not a traditional Afro-Peruvian standard but a very atypical landó, composed by White criollos and performed almost exclusively by Susana Baca, a cosmopolitan world music artist on the margins of popular Afro-Peruvian performance practice. In fact, it is rarely performed in Peru or by any artist other than Susana Baca. Thus, those critics who condemn Byrne's performance of the song on the grounds of cultural mining may not realize that this particular song did not come from the mine where they think it did. David Byrne's fascination with "María Landó" is responsible for Afro-Peruvian music's dissemination to U.S. and European audiences. As a result, Byrne's inclusion of his recorded cover version on *The Soul of Black Peru* is simultaneously risky, clumsy, and honest with regard to his role in the process of the album's fruition.

Of course, the very fact that Byrne performs on an album devoted to Afro-Peruvian classics can and should raise questions. How does Byrne's performance on the album differ from his inclusion of White Peruvian artists performing Black Peruvian music or Black Peruvian artists performing música criolla? What makes a song Afro-Peruvian: the artist who performs it, the circumstances in which it was composed, its arrangement and performance style, or a combination of all these factors?

One of the troubling aspects of arguments that Afro-Peruvian music should only be performed by Afro-Peruvians is that the "West versus the Rest" dichotomy can become a prison for Afro-Peruvian artists, who become identified solely as culture bearers and not as creative individuals. Susana Baca addresses this problem when she insists, "I wouldn't want to be linked only to Afro-Peruvian music. Because Afro-Peruvian music is only part of my expression. Now, the curious thing is that I am the first, I open a passageway. But I hope it is because of my artistry and not because I am an Afro-Peruvian singer" (Baca 2000b). This struggle between Susana Baca's individual artistic vision and the tendency of her music to circulate as world music "flavor of the month" is at the heart of her rooted cosmopolitanism.

Rooted Cosmopolitanism: Beyond Afro-Peruvian World Music Artist

When I conducted my research in Peru from 1998 to 2000, Susana Baca's band consisted of bassist David Pinto, guitarist Rafael "Fallo" Muñoz, percussionist Hugo Bravo, and cajonero Juan Medrano Cotito. I asked David Pinto, who is also Susana's arranger and musical director, to describe how her musical arrangements are created, and how he (who is not Afro-Peruvian) approaches playing Afro-Peruvian music on an instrument not traditionally used in Afro-Peruvian ensembles. He explained that a spirit of experimentation based on Black Peruvian rhythms guides the band, noting, "Perhaps I speak of that sense jazz has. That it moves, that it changes. And this is what I have done to support Susana. Susana is a person who reminds me of Miles Davis. Because when she sings, she leaves many spaces. She isn't like other singers here, who take a song, start the intro, four bars, the A part, the B part—they don't leave much. Four bars, like a machine! And that's it. Susana . . . listens to a lot of music. She listens to jazz . . . She takes something and she sings and she leaves it there and gives you space so you can create. Like a jazz group. And when she feels it, she comes in to sing. This is a magic that I have not felt with other singers here. They make it more square. They don't leave spaces" (Pinto 2000).

One of the musical sounds that sets Susana's band apart from other Afro-Peruvian groups is David's upright Ampeg electric Baby Bass, an instrument favored by salsa bands for its percussive timbre and ability to play at high volumes. In Susana's band, the Baby Bass performs a harmonic and rhythmic role normally accomplished by the second guitar in both Afro-Peruvian music and música criolla. To arrive at an "authentic" yet fresh Afro-Peruvian sound, David studied old recordings of leading Black Peruvian guitarists such as Vicente Vásquez, and he adapted some of their guitar bordones to his bass. Still, some Peruvians are bothered by the foregrounding of the electric bass in an Afro-Peruvian music group.

Like other non-Black artists who play Afro-Peruvian music, David Pinto speaks of the process of learning how to achieve "Black feeling" in the music by mixing binary and ternary rhythms in such a way that the music is constantly moving (Pinto 2000). David played jazz for many years before joining Susana's band, and he explains that jazz and Brazilian harmonies are an integral element of his arrangements for Susana, as is the inferred sense of what he refers to as clave:[10] "We play with so much syncopation, but the clave is there. So sometimes we play this game and I think people say 'where are they?' Even musicians. They say, 'where are they, where is one?' [David repeats the phrase in English] Where is the one, no? Because . . . we leave the one in space and we don't play it. All four of us are playing and nobody marks the one . . .

"For what harmonies to use, generally the harmonies that have resulted from the mestizaje of Black music in other countries, for example, Brazilian folklore, are rhythmically rich. It's another African rhythm . . . Like Cuban music. But their harmonies are richer than ours. Harmony in Afro-Peruvian music is not very varied. Have you noticed? Almost all the songs use I–IV–V . . . So almost everything is the same. With a few exceptions, it is not harmonically very rich. So I have tried to change the harmonies, to open them up" (Pinto 2000).

Cajonero Juan Medrano Cotito is the only member of Susana's band, other than herself, who is visibly Afro-Peruvian. After their concerts outside Peru, audience members of all races and nationalities inevitably approach

Cotito and tell him they didn't know there were Blacks in Peru. For Cotito, this is one of the most rewarding elements of working for Susana Baca; he feels that he is spreading international awareness of his culture and the music he loves (Medrano Cotito 2000).

Similarly, Susana Baca seeks to remedy the invisibility of Black Peruvians, both inside and outside of Peru. She is inspired to perform, in part, in order to provide a model for Afro-Peruvian children who have been socialized to be ashamed of their race. "I have a mission," she says. "I believe that the world should know what Afro-Peruvian culture is. First they have to get to know Peru. But Peru has denied this culture. It has camouflaged it within the word criollo, and now they argue with me and they say: 'But Black [culture] never existed, it has never been here,' and I don't know what. Everything was criollo . . .

"This negation has caused me to work hard in my way . . . All this time has been to vindicate [Black Peruvian culture] . . . I am the person, the singer, the musician, the Peruvian artist who leaves the country and who disseminates this knowledge of the presence of Afro-Peruvians. So this honor is mine. I feel that it is an honor. But . . . the ignorance about this culture pains me a great deal" (Baca 2000b).

Although she seeks to promote knowledge and understanding of Afro-Peruvian culture through music, Susana Baca does not want to be pigeon-holed as world music's Black Peruvian pin on the map of the African diaspora. At a 1998 press conference in Peru, David Byrne announced: "Susana Baca will survive this cliché called world music" (qtd. in N.a. 1998b). At the turn of the twenty-first century, Susana Baca is riding her success, but she is also fighting to maintain her individuality. This struggle, in part, is a battle against labels such as "world music" and "Afro-Peruvian." In this sense, she exemplifies Paul Gilroy's description of cosmopolitan, post-national "figures who begin as African Americans or Caribbean people and are then changed into something else which evades those specific labels and with them all fixed notions of nationality and national identity. Whether their experience of exile is enforced or chosen, temporary or permanent, these intellectuals and artists, writers, speakers, poets, and artists repeatedly articulate a desire to escape the restrictive bonds of ethnicity, national identification, and sometimes even 'race' itself" (Gilroy 1993, 19). So adamant is Susana Baca that her repertoire be understood for what it is that she hastens to correct those who call her an "Afro-Peruvian" artist ("I am Susana Baca, an artist born in Peru" she says [Baca 2000b]).

The production of Susana Baca's album *Eco de sombras* ("Echo of shadows") (Baca 2000a) illustrates the impact of international stardom and cosmopolitanism on an artist who has always defined her cultural and artistic identity on her own. Artistically, it strikes what Scott Malcomson would call a "strategic bargain" with both essentialism and universality (1998, 234), positioning Susana Baca somewhere between national Afro-Peruvian singer and cosmopolitan world music artist.

As noted earlier in this chapter, Luaka Bop's staff aims to create album covers that market their international artists as popular musicians rather than objects of ethnographic display. In the summer of 1999, I accompanied Susana Baca and her manager/husband, Ricardo Pereira, to a Hollywood photo shoot for the cover of *Eco de sombras*. At the shoot, the young photographer laid out sketches and preliminary photos to demonstrate his design concept. When Ricardo saw the sketches, which depicted Susana among leafy plants and trees, he was very unhappy. I assisted with translation at his request. "Susana is not a little Black girl in the South American jungle," he asked me to tell the photographer. "She is a mature woman, 50-some years of age, who is a mestiza, a mix of cultures. Do not exoticize her." Ricardo later told me: "I would like for Susana not necessarily to be linked with the cliché of the Afro-Peruvian singer. I don't think it should be like that. And I believe in this sense, the new CD will change this. I believe that Susana is a singer who has a talent that is her own. That is, she has her own talent, she doesn't need a cliché. Susana is not going to be more Susana because she is Afro-Peruvian" (Pereira 2000).

Eco de sombras was produced for Luaka Bop by Craig Street, whose work is also featured on albums by Cassandra Wilson, Paula Cole, and Meshell Ndegeocello. Street searched Lima for the best place to record the album, ultimately settling upon Susana's house. He worked with local contacts to bring high-end analog equipment into Susana's home, where he stayed much longer than originally intended to record an album for which many things went wrong and everything happened late. Recordings began at 3:00 AM, after the street noises subsided, and Susana cooked wonderful meals for the musicians and recording crew.

The CD contains ten tracks: half poetry set to music, half new arrangements of Afro-Peruvian standards. David Pinto labored over arrangements of repertoire, old and new. A striking example of Pinto's work is the track "Panalivio/Zancudito." This version of the Christmas songs of El Carmen begins with Pinto's bowed Baby Bass performing short monophonic melodic motifs inspired by the music of the hatajo de negritos (minus the trademark repeated open fifth chord typically played on the middle strings of the violin) to the beat of the cajón, harmonized by arpeggios on an acoustic guitar and chords and slide effects on a second guitar. Bells

FIGURE 6.5. *Eco de sombras* CD cover. *Reprinted with permission from Luaka Bop Inc.*

emulate the handbells played by the young boys of the hatajo de negritos, and Susana sings the traditional Christmas songs. The result is an artistic reinterpretation of the music of El Carmen, clearly different from its source. Although traditionalists might balk at the liberties taken with the Christmas repertoire, the song medley creates its own aesthetic tapestry.

After the album was produced in Lima, extra musical parts performed by U.S.–based musicians were added in New York, with Susana's approval. Mark Ribot and David Byrne play electric guitar solos, Greg Leisz adds a pedal steel guitar (a sound that fascinated Susana in the studio), John Medeski plays piano and organ, Rob Burger adds accordion and organ, Greg Cohen plays bass, and Cyro Baptista contributes *berimbao*, bells, and percussion.

On the song "Xanaharí" (an adaptation of Victoria Santa Cruz' song "Karambe," composed for the play *Zanahary*, described in chapter 2),

David Byrne plays the most Andean of Peruvian instruments, a *charango*.[11] Susana remembers how delighted and amused she was by Byrne's choice: "He came and he was very happy. But I thought he would show up with his guitar. And he arrived with a charango! So he played. When all the [extra] musicians played, Craig Street asked me, 'Do you like it, Susana? Do you like it? It's your record.' So when David played, he also asked me 'Do you like it?' I loved it! I loved it because it was a surprise. The sound of the charango is in my ear as accompaniment for the modern music of Violeta Parra or the Bolivian music and Peruvian huaynos. But I had never heard one accompanying a festejo. It would never have occurred to me [she laughs]. So it seemed fabulous to me. Fabulous!" (Baca 2000b).

While such eclectic instrumentation is a trademark of Craig Street's productions, many of the same people who objected to David Byrne's performance of "María Landó" on *The Soul of Black Peru* also are bothered by the addition of "foreign elements" to the core musical arrangements of Susana Baca's band on *Eco de sombras*. A contributor to Luaka Bop's electronic "Susana Baca Bulletin Board" complained:

> The self-titled album is great, the more recent one is so-so. The difference is that on the first album, Susana is backed by musicians who can create that traditional afro-peruvian percussion sound which blends with Susana's voice, while the second album features more famous artists, thus the sound is more commercial. If you are planning to release any more albums, please use Susana's original backup musicians, at least for music's sake! (Balazs n.d.)

Thus, in the name of individual artistry, *Eco de sombras* tested the limits of world music audiences. Susana's next release, *Espíritu vivo* (2002), moved further in the same direction with covers of songs by Bjork, Mongo Santamaría, Caetano Veloso, and Jacques Prevert. Will world music audiences accept Susana Baca as an individual, not just a pin in their discovery map of world music sounds? Knowing that she is not "traditional," will her audience remain loyal?

As she distances herself from the label "Afro-Peruvian singer," Susana Baca discloses the secret most U.S. audiences don't realize: that she is not a typical Peruvian singer and she rarely performs for Peruvian audiences in Peru. Her music is not the Peruvian equivalent of Cuban *rumba* or Brazilian samba, the next stop on world music's diasporic journey. One can't easily go to Peru and find a community of Afro-Peruvians performing this music in private for ceremonial or social events, and Susana Baca is not surrounded by a community of Afro-Peruvian artists but rather by a crop of young Peruvian mestizo musicians. The real secret is out.

Travel Diaries, Pico Rivera, California, 1999:
Concurso de Festejo

A concurso de festejo *(festejo contest) is held for Peruvian children in Los Angeles each fall. Gino Gamboa, my cajón teacher, suggests that I attend. Prior to the concurso, he tells me that the festejo danced in Los Angeles is a commercial version characterized by shoulder and hip shaking and very short skirts. Gino associates this commercial festejo style with Lima's Peña Valentina, one of the first peñas where non-Blacks could go to learn Afro-Peruvian dance. He equates the "real" festejo style with Perú Negro's longer skirts and choreographed moves, but, he tells me, no one in Los Angeles can teach that style. Peruvian parents want their children to learn their country's dances and must settle for what is available.*

The event, sponsored by the Peruvian Ladies' Committee, takes place in the back room of a nightclub in East Los Angeles. I am struck by the celebratory feeling of the room and the size of the crowd. About two hundred elegantly dressed Peruvians—from babies to elders—are in the room, and not an empty seat is to be found. Balloons and decorations are everywhere and mountains of discarded Inca Kola cans fill the trash. Groups of tables are set up as "barras," or small rooting sections that cheer for their favorite contestant or family member.

I stand on a side staircase with a birds-eye view of the room. Tables are set up around the dance floor, with the judges' table in front and a stage in the back. Onstage are two cajón players (including Gino, my teacher), a bongó player, and a conga player. For this type of danced festejo, no guitars are used. There are very few people of visible African descent in the room (only one musician and one judge are Black and most contestants and audience members appear to be White criollos).

The concurso lasts about seven hours, although I do not stay for the end. Contestants are divided into five categories: chiquitita *(ages three to six),* infantil *(ages seven to eleven),* juvenil *(ages twelve to sixteen),* adultos *(ages seventeen to twenty-nine), and* senior *(ages thirty and up). Each dancer is announced by name, place of birth, and both parents' nationalities, and a queen of the festejo is crowned in each category. The band onstage provides identical accompaniment for each solo dancer. The conga player uses a variation of a Cuban rumba pattern to accompany the two cajón players' festejo patterns. The children's dancing appears to be the "commercial" style Gino described, with vigorous improvisational hip shaking and midriff-baring costumes, while the adults tend to favor choreographed dance steps. The three contestants in the senior category (who appear to be in their thirties and forties) wear graceful long skirts with petticoats and dance with less flamboyancy, evoking a sensuality perceived as appropriate for "older" women.*

After the solo dances are over, the choreography competition takes place. Two local groups of teenagers and children compete: Matices del Perú (Shades of Peru) and Estampas del Perú (Scenes of Peru). The first group's choreography begins with a smoky display of dry ice. The boys run out carrying cajones, which they play in pantomime to a recorded festejo performed by singer Eva Ayllón. Boys wear white pants with sashes and no shirts, and girls wear dresses. The whiteness of the young boys dancing to Afro-Peruvian music is exaggerated by their bare chests. The second group is all female except for a little boy who plays a toy quijada in the corner. A little girl kneels in the opposite corner with a basket of fruit on her head. The children begin by reciting a lyric from a popular song: "Somos la raza mas pura" (We are the purest race) as they prepare to dance to the rhythms of Black Peru. This group performs to live music by the band onstage. Their choreography is imaginative, but the judges give the prize to the first group.

On the way out, I pick up a Peruvian-American newspaper and notice that Lucila Campos—Perú Negro's female vocalist in the company's "golden age"—will be performing soon in Los Angeles. The show is sponsored by Peruvisión, one of two Peruvian-American organizations that routinely bring Peruvian artists to Los Angeles.

Travel Diaries, Los Angeles, California, 1999: Peña *and Show with Lucila Campos*

I drive with two friends to a Peruvian restaurant in the San Fernando Valley to attend the Lucila Campos concert. About one hundred folding chairs (all of which will be occupied by the end of the night) are set up around long tables. In the back corner of the restaurant is a small platform stage. People stream in gradually during the first set, which begins right on time, slightly before 10:00 PM. Everyone in the room appears to be Peruvian except my group and two Anglo men who are seated with Peruvian women.

A local band, led by guitarist Victor Vento, plays the first set. The band features two guitars, congas, two cajones, castanets, and a synthesizer. They play dinner music (Peruvian valses and polcas *and Cuban* sones*) as the audience orders plates of comida criolla. In the second set, Lima-based José Luis Jarro, a young singer of música criolla who also performs festejos, joins the band. The audience begins to get involved in the show now that dinner plates are empty. At one point, Jarro calls upon a woman in the audience to dance festejo (the crowd shouts "¡Arriba, atrás! ¡Arriba, atrás!" to coax the dancer's hip movements faster and faster), and the set ends with a tondero (a northern Peruvian dance similar to the marinera) danced by a couple waving napkins instead of handkerchiefs.*

At midnight, Lucila Campos finally makes her grand entrance to begin the third set. She takes the crowd by storm, performing for four hours with only one five-minute break. Her presence is amazing, and the room comes to life. She starts out by calling up to the stage the two little girls who won the recent Los Angeles festejo competition. The festejo queens are wearing their costumes (ruffled short skirts with midriff-baring tops), and they dance while Lucila Campos sings a festejo with her band. Lucila Campos is one of several artists who perform both Afro-Peruvian and criollo music, and tonight her show consists primarily of festejos and valses with one salsa number. She clearly announces which tunes are "música negra" before she performs them. She jokes with and about her audience (she makes a great show of being offended when she notices a man drinking coffee at 3:00 AM and, amid a gale of audience laughter, she tells him that only alcohol is served in the peñas in Lima).

As the night goes on, people are energized, and Campos begins to perform primarily festejos. She demands that audience members get up and dance. She spots the two Anglo men—both with blonde hair, one with a long ponytail—and because they do not appear to understand Spanish they become the subject of the equivalent of the tourist jokes performed in Lima peñas for the remainder of the show—an odd juxtaposition because they are treated like tourists in their own city.

The feeling of criollo patriotism is heavy in the air. This is a concert for people who share a memory of their homeland and who re-create and imagine it in Los Angeles through music. At 4:00 AM the show is over, and I am not the slightest bit tired. I am moved by the spirit of peruanidad I felt in that room and by Lucila Campos' tireless ability to musically create and maintain it. I have never before been to a Peruvian community peña in the United States, nor did I know they existed. How strange it is that these events take place nearly every weekend, yet they are invisible to most non-Peruvians, who believe the only Afro-Peruvian performer who tours the United States is Susana Baca.

Immigrant Nostalgia in the Peruvian Colonies

Although Afro-Peruvian music was a newly discovered secret for world music audiences in the 1990s, the thousands of Peruvian immigrants living in the United States know all about Afro-Peruvian music, and, what's more, it is alive and well in Peruvian "colonies" in Los Angeles and other cities. On weekends and special holidays, Afro-Peruvian and criollo artists like Lucila Campos, Arturo "Zambo" Cavero, Lucila de la Cruz, Fetiche, Cecilia Barraza, Pepe Vásquez, and Eva Ayllón perform in peñas at Peruvian restaurants and hotels. The audience is 99 percent Peruvian, and advertising takes place by word of mouth and in Peruvian-American newspapers. Further, the same marinera and festejo dance competitions (concursos) held in Peru take place in the Peruvian colonies of the United States. In 2000, the winners of the Los Angeles *concurso de la marinera* were sent to Trujillo, Peru, to compete against their Peruvian counterparts in the annual national competition, where the grand prize was a pair of round-trip tickets from Lima to Miami, Florida. As the Los Angelenos paraded down the street in the pre-concurso festivities in January 2000, a man shouted to the crowd: "They are Americans, but they are our children!"

In the so-called Peruvian colonies, the performance of Afro-Peruvian music nourishes the nostalgia of immigrants far from home and helps them impart a sense of cultural identity to their children. The term "colonies," used by Peruvians to describe immigrant communities outside of Peru, reveals the ideological dominance of the homeland over the identity of Peruvian immigrants abroad. The sound of the cajón evokes, for many Peruvians in the United States, an instant sense of cultural identification and longing for home. Just as Afro-Peruvian music was embraced by Peruvian criollos as part of their own heritage during the Andean "invasion" of Lima in the 1950s, so do Peruvian mestizo and criollo immigrants in the United States reach for Afro-Peruvian music, música criolla, and Andean music as identity markers. Many U.S. Peruvian immigrants left their homeland during Sendero Luminoso's terrorist activities in the 1980s. Thus, Peruvian communities in the United States, made up primarily of Peruvians who left Lima shortly after the rise of Perú Negro and Peña Valentina, celebrate and nourish the specific brand of festejo that developed in that peña in the 1970s, re-creating festejo contests and peña performances as a way of nurturing Peruvian identity in their children.

Susana Baca was generally not well-known or liked by Peruvian immigrants in the United States in the 1990s. In fact, because they lived outside of the cosmopolitan loops (Turino 2000) of world music, many Peruvians in the United States were unaware of her success.[12] Some Peruvian immigrants who did know about Baca's music worried that she brought cultural misinformation to the unknowing American public by performing a very idiosyncratic style more influenced by jazz harmonies and elitist poetry than by Black Peruvian folklore. Interestingly, because jazz is patronized by elite White Peruvians in Lima, jazz harmonies are considered to be a "whitening" element for Afro-Peruvian music, despite their African American associations in the United States and elsewhere. Many Peruvians immigrants, rather than buying tickets for Susana Baca's "highbrow" Afro-Peruvian concerts, prefer to attend transplanted peñas with artists imported weekly from Peru. Susana Baca speaks to a global cosmopolitan audience, but she does not nourish the same immigrant nostalgia.

Re-creating Afro-Peruvian music in the U.S. Peruvian colonies is not always easy. Peruvians who did not seek out their folklore at home suddenly find themselves missing the sounds of home, along with family, friends, and country. Individuals who learned Afro-Peruvian folklore in classes at Peruvian universities or from videos are elevated to the role of specialists, formulating taste and practice abroad based on scanty information and a forgiving public. In other cases, musicians who never played national music in Peru find that they are expected to be fluent in those musical languages in the United States.

For example, Peruvian guitarist Ramon Stagnaro, a successful studio musician in Los Angeles, only wanted to play straight-ahead jazz when he worked as a musician on television and at private events in Lima. In Los Angeles, one of the first bands that hired Ramon was a folklore ensemble called Inca that performs the music and dance of Andean countries. Ramon remembers how he had to learn Peruvian music in order to work in the United States: "What's ironic, in Peru I never had to play Peruvian music. I was doing all kinds of music, you know? Always listening to Peruvian music . . . never got involved. When I got here, I came to play more jazz, right? And they start hiring me: 'Oh, where are you from? Peru? Oh, you know how to play valses!' Well. It's amazing, it's ironic. And then, you know, when I started playing with the Inca group, I had all of my records and I started having a blast! . . . So I just have to learn the mechanics, you know, the sound. But the feeling, the feeling was there" (Stagnaro 1999).

Walter Almora studied Peruvian folk dances as a student at the Catholic University in Lima. He moved to Los Angeles in 1999, where he works as a budget analyst for the Department of Social Services. In 2000, Almora taught Peruvian dance classes at Fina Estampa restaurant in Los Angeles' San Fernando Valley. Relying on the steps he learned as a student in Lima, Almora taught the festejo and the marinera to classes including the children of Peruvians born in the United States and a small number of what he calls "foreign" students (that is, non-Peruvians). He explains: "Here in Los Angeles, we're a reflection of what we see in Peru. We try to keep our roots, our culture, we try to keep in touch with that . . . I mean, we try to go to the source. We get videos, we get whatever it takes. Many of the costumes that we use for the dances or any presentations, we brought them from Peru. Because here, you just don't have it" (Almora 2000).

Perhaps the most essential item needed to perform Afro-Peruvian music and dance is the Peruvian cajón. Gino Gamboa, a former psychologist from Peru, started a cajón workshop out of his Los Angeles apartment in order to promote Afro-Peruvian and criollo music-making in the United States. Tired of seeing cajones used as lamp stands by frustrated beginning students, Gamboa designs cajones whose top corners easily produce the desired high-pitched sound (this sound, similar to the "slap" on the conga drum, requires practice on typical Peruvian cajones). Gamboa's cajones have a space between the face of the drum and its sides near the top, enabling the slightest touch of the fingertips to produce a satisfying slap-like result. Gamboa teaches Peruvians and non-Peruvians alike to play his cajones, he works in several music groups, and he designs cajones for Alex Acuña.

Alex Acuña is Peru's most internationally successful musician living in the United States, and he is widely considered Peru's most talented and versatile percussionist and drummer.[13] A brief history of Alex's work with Eva Ayllón and Los Hijos del Sol parallels the story of David Byrne and Susana Baca, illuminating the different results of Peruvian versus U.S. projects to internationalize the Afro-Peruvian sound.

Alex Acuña left Peru as a teenager in 1964, when he was hired by Mexico-based Cuban *mambo* king Pérez Prado to tour with his orchestra. At the time, a Peruvian newspaper published Alex' proclamation: "One day our Peruvian music will be known just as the Cuban and the Brazilian music is known" (Acuña 1999). Yet, in his early career, Alex developed his reputation as a versatile musician capable of performing all kinds of music, and many people—including some of his closest friends and collabora-tors—did not even know that he was Peruvian. Alex went on to play with an eclectic list of renowned musicians and bands including Weather Report, Joni Mitchell, Elvis Presley, Diana Ross, U2, Paul McCartney, Michael Jackson, Julio Iglesias, Tracy Chapman, and Al Jarreau.

Like Ramon Stagnaro, Alex Acuña never played Afro-Peruvian music when he lived in Peru. For one thing, he left the country only shortly after the revival had begun. For another, Alex affirms, "It was almost prohibited for me to play festejo when I was growing up because I am an Indian" (Acuña 1999). In the late 1980s, however, as he was experiencing several other profound personal changes, Alex Acuña publicly began to incorpo-rate Peruvian music and his own Peruvian identity into his professional career. Having established himself as a drummer and percussionist of inter-national stature, Alex sought to fulfill his 1964 promise to bring Peruvian music to the level of exposure already enjoyed by its Brazilian and Cuban counterparts. Alex Acuña's first foray into Peruvian rhythms was in the mid-1980s with a group called Wayruro that reinterpreted Peruvian huaynos and coastal music with a New Age fusion sound. He also began to bring his cajón to performances and recording sessions, doing what he could to infuse U.S. and other Latin American music styles with Peruvian rhythms.

In 1989, Alex worked with Peruvian producer Ricardo Ghibelini to cre-ate a project of which he speaks with great pride—the international

Peruvian band called Los Hijos del Sol. The project was Alex's gift back to the country, his effort to popularize Peruvian music in the international arena (Acuña 1999). Los Hijos del Sol placed traditional Peruvian rhythms in a Latin smooth jazz context for a 1989 album recorded in a Los Angeles studio. In addition to Alex Acuña (on drums and percussion), Peruvian musicians involved in the project included Ramon Stagnaro and Lucho González (guitars), Oscar Stagnaro (bass), Cocho Arbe (piano), Chino Figueroa (keyboards), and Eva Ayllón (vocals). Some of the non-Peruvian guest artists who lent their talent to selected tracks on the recording included Wayne Shorter (soprano saxophone), Paquito D'Rivera (clarinet and alto saxophone), Ernie Watts (tenor saxophone), and Justo Almario (soprano saxophone). The recording featured a range of Peruvian styles of music (Andean, criollo, Afro) and popular tunes, arranged by a Puerto Rican musician and close friend of Alex's, percussionist Efrain Toro. The band played on tour in Peru a few times, and it regrouped with different personnel to make a second recording in the late 1990s.

In Lima, Los Hijos del Sol's expanded live concerts presented its new international Peruvian sound with jazz arrangements, improvisation breaks, and virtuosic soloing. Special guest artists included Perú Negro legends Caitro Soto and Ronaldo Campos, who performed Afro-Peruvian standards such as the zapateo contest and "Samba malató" with big band arrangements. Ramon Stagnaro describes the band's reception during the Peruvian tours as "like when the Beatles came to America."

Unfortunately, despite Alex's hopes of introducing Peruvian music to U.S. audiences through Los Hijos del Sol, the band did not tour or perform publicly in the United States until 2002, when a special concert was held in Los Angeles to promote the much-delayed U.S. release of the original Los Hijos del Sol recording. Until the 2002 album was released in the United States (receiving a Latin Grammy nomination), lack of U.S. distribution and promotion meant that it was only in Peru that Los Hijos del Sol received attention (mirroring the U.S.-only impact of David Byrne's sponsorship of Susana Baca and his release of *The Soul of Black Peru*).

The most enduring legacy of Los Hijos del Sol in Peru was the rise to celebrity status of the band's lead singer, Eva Ayllón. A Black Peruvian singer with a powerful voice and stage presence, Eva Ayllón was quietly performing música criolla in Peruvian peñas before Los Hijos del Sol made her a national star. She became Peru's most popular living singer of both música criolla and Afro-Peruvian styles (her band in the 1990s included two sets of musicians who alternated to accompany those two racially defined musical styles), with several gold records and an adoring mass of Peruvian fans around the world.

FIGURE 6.6. Eva Ayllón in concert, Los Angeles, 2004. *Photo by Ernesto Hernandez, reprinted with permission.*

Inevitably, when the topic of Susana Baca's success in the U.S. mainstream market comes up among Peruvians, the question "why not Eva Ayllón?" is raised. Eva, many Peruvians feel, has a better voice, is a more natural and authoritative musician, and gives a more exciting show. Peruvians abroad yearn to hear her voice, and tickets for her concerts are priced accordingly ($100 a seat for a concert in San Francisco in the 1990s). Yet, David Byrne selected Susana Baca over Eva Ayllón to promote to U.S. audiences as a Luaka Bop artist.[14]

Peruvian radio and television personality Mabela Martínez sums up the difference between Eva Ayllón and Susana Baca in terms of cosmopolitan networks versus national and immigrant communities when she says, "Eva Ayllón is a local phenomenon . . . she belongs to the Peruvian people. But Susana belongs to the world" (Martínez 2000). And, in fact, when Eva Ayllón toured the United States in the 1990s, she (like other Peruvian performers) normally played for the Peruvian "colony" abroad, in special shows advertised only within that community. In August 2000, she broadened her audience when she participated in the AT&T Latino Cultural Festival in New York City's Queens Theater in the Park. A New York Times critic lauded her performance and began his review by comparing Ayllón to Susana Baca, whose "small but deep American art-music following" was launched by *The Soul of Black Peru*:

But the career of Eva Ayllón, another singer featured on that record, has not thrived here, and from her performance . . . it was easy to see why. It's not for lack of talent: Ms. Ayllón, who is in her mid-40s and whose career began in the late '70s, is a strong and outrageously good singer. It's that her music has the temper of out-and-out romantic pop, which can be hard for those outside its cultural references to grasp. Still, Ms. Baca makes an ingenious cross between folklore and highbrow art music, two concepts that the American "world music" audience well understands . . .

There is cultural consciousness in [Eva Ayllón's] music even at the most showbiz-like level. Ms. Ayllón is a highly-strung, sharp-tongued, funny performer. She lampooned popular singers; made jokes about her ex-boyfriend, the pianist; and executed the trick (for an entirely Spanish-speaking but multinational audience) of singing bits of songs that were popular among Chileans, Puerto Ricans and Mexicans. This was all agreeable, if not that profound. Then she yelled "Ritmo negro!" (Black rhythm!) and a physical, rocking round of percussion flooded in, causing the synthetic guitars and drums to fall away into the background. (Ratliff 2000)

Thus, Eva Ayllón is considered by many to be a great artist. But she is received as a *Peruvian* artist, whereas Susana Baca is a Peruvian *world music* artist.

In 2003, Eva Ayllón disappointed her Peruvian audiences by moving to the United States, where she began to tour more widely and released her first U.S.–produced recording. Her live concerts in 2004 and 2005 began to feature a stripped-down acoustic instrumental combo and a marked emphasis on Afro-Peruvian, versus criollo, song repertoire. Will Eva Ayllón attract some of Susana Baca's audience among non-Peruvians in the United States, or will she remain in the exclusive concert circuit of the Peruvian immigrant community? Both performers speak and sing only in Spanish and perform Peruvian music, and both benefited from "discovery" by internationally known sponsors. But Eva Ayllón's performances are apparently much harder to translate for non-Peruvian audiences in the United States, just as Susana Baca's idiosyncratic arrangements and singing style are displeasing to many Peruvians. Despite the beauty and power of her singing voice, Ayllón's "out and out romantic pop" disappoints those among the English-speaking world music audience who seek "confusing pleasure" (or who don't care for that style for other aesthetic reasons), even though Eva Ayllón's performances are more typical of Peruvian aesthetics than are Susana Baca's cosmopolitan arrangements.

An equally important reason why Eva Ayllón's shows might not play well to non-Peruvian U.S. audiences is their racializing discourse, inherited from the revival, which reveals how notions of blackness differ in the United States and Peru, and how these disparate ideas of race operate in cosmopolitan loops and immigrant communities. The legacy of the Afro-Peruvian revival's celebration of negritud was music and dance that essentializes stereotyped qualities associated with blackness. Thus, the festejo queens link the ability to move one's hips in a rapid and seductive manner with blackness, Eva Ayllón yells "Black music!" to the beat of drums when she is about to depart from her criollo repertoire and perform an Afro-Peruvian number, and folklore groups of the revival perform dances in costumes that depict their ancestors from times of slavery. For U.S. world music audiences, such attitudes might evoke feelings of discomfort based on the U.S. history of blackface and minstrelsy. Conversely, for members of the Peruvian immigrant community who are accustomed to this type of performance of Peruvian blackness, the absence of such overt signifiers "whitens" the music of Susana Baca.

The events retold in this chapter (Susana Baca's success in the cosmopolitan world music sphere, the peñas and concursos de festejo of the U.S. Peruvian colonies, and the Peruvian success of Los Hijos del Sol and Eva Ayllón) demonstrate that traditions—expressed through style in Afro-Peruvian music—are invented not only by performers but also by their audiences. Thus, Susana Baca fulfills certain U.S. world music consumers' desires for confusing pleasure and new (yet familiar) sounds, while peña performances and festejo contests nourish immigrant nostalgia in Los Angeles, and Los Hijos del Sol make Peruvian audiences proud to see their music interpreted by artists of international stature. In an ironic twist of geography and culture, the logic of cosmopolitanism converts Susana Baca's music into U.S. music even though she is a resident of Peru, whereas the music performed in the Peruvian colony of Los Angeles is and remains Peruvian music. Continuing the process of competing diasporic reinventions that began in the Afro-Peruvian revival, cosmopolitan world music and immigrant nostalgia produce very different musical styles, all of which are deeply meaningful—and authentically Afro-Peruvian—for those who believe them to be so.

CONCLUSION

Beginnings

Following the lead established long ago by Leroi Jones, I believe that it is possible to approach the music as a changing rather than an unchanging same. Today, this involves the difficult task of striving to comprehend the reproduction of cultural traditions not in the unproblematic transmission of a fixed essence through time but in the breaks and interruptions which suggest that the invocation of tradition itself may be a distinct, though covert, response to the destablising flux of the post-contemporary world. New traditions have been invented in the jaws of modern experience and new conceptions of modernity produced in the long shadow of our enduring traditions—the African ones and the ones forged from the slave experience which the black vernacular so powerfully and actively remembers.
—Paul Gilroy, *The Black Atlantic*

And so I am finished, just when I have arrived at my starting point—the present. The history and memories I have recounted are only a preface to the myriad reinventions that compose the "changing same" of Afro-Peruvian music today.

There is so much I wanted to say about contemporary issues in Afro-Peruvian performance! But, because the Afro-Peruvian revival's history has never before been substantially documented, I knew if I started my story at the end of the twentieth century I would not be on the same page as most of my readers. Equipped with a better understanding of the twentieth-century staging of Afro-Peruvian music and dance, we finally can look at how young Peruvians in the present are beginning to forge a new Black Pacific consciousness.

Afro-Peruvian music is finally in vogue in Lima in the early twenty-first century. Black (and non-Black) musicians are forging new hybrids from Afro-Peruvian and other ingredients. Their creations have yet to be categorized, and many of these artists perform both "folklore" and what they call "fusion."

For example, Afro-Peruvian guitarist and arranger Coco Linares produced a CD released in the 1990s, *Salsa, son, ritmo y cajón,* that fuses Afro-Peruvian and Afro-Cuban music. In 2000, the hottest Black artist in Peru, with a following of adoring young fans, was Guajaja (José de la Cruz). Pioneering a kind of techno–Afro-Peruvian music with audience participation dance steps, Guajaja brings Afro-Peruvian music to mainstream young audiences. Los Hermanos Santa Cruz—a band fronted by Nicomedes and Victoria Santa Cruz' nephews Rafael and Octavio—presents creative arrangements of Afro-Peruvian folklore using electric guitar, jazz-influenced electric bass, and stylistic elements of rock and Afropop. Their 1999 album is called *Ya no soy negro, ya no soy blanco* (Now I am not Black, now I am not White). Jazz artists José Luis Madueño and Richie Zellon are experimenting with what they call Afrojazz, meaning Latin jazz arrangements based on Afro-Peruvian rhythms (the use of the prefix "Afro" revealing that jazz is not already a predominantly Afro-identified music in Peru).

Although these new waves of fusion, appropriation, and invention finally create an active presence for Afro-Peruvian culture in mainstream Peru, critics worry that they water down, whiten, or Cubanize the Afro-Peruvian tradition, resulting in the loss of its perceived unique identity. The "afróbicos" (Afro-Peruvian aerobics) craze in Lima's health clubs in the 1990s seemed to confirm this fear of the commodification of Afro-Peruvian culture. Critics of Afrojazz often say that non–Afro-Peruvian artists may have learned the rhythms of Black music, but they haven't lived the culture. Afro-Peruvian composer Roberto Arguedas observes: "I am afraid that [Afro-Peruvian music] will lose its own sense . . . I can create jazz, fuse jazz with what is in my head, but if I taste from jazz's plate, I will end up with American jazz, not fusion" (Arguedas 2000). Afro-Peruvian performing artist Lucho Sandoval adds, "People think there are no Blacks in Peru. And Afro-Peruvian music sounds strange to people who listen to African or Cuban music. They listen to Afro-Peruvian music and they say, 'What is this? Where is this from? It is strange, it is really strange!' So this is something we should not lose. Because I believe that difference is beautiful" (Sandoval 2000).

In the social center-style peñas of Lima, proprietors and their clientele strive to maintain both Afro-Peruvian music and música criolla in what is deemed their traditional forms. Classic compositions are performed on unamplified musical instruments, the audience is required to participate, and the shared past is routinely evoked. Nostalgia and emotion mingle with cigarette smoke to fill the air. One night, in one of the most famous of such locales, Peña Don Porfirio (dedicated to Don Porfirio Vásquez and owned and operated by his family), a friend and fellow scholar of Peruvian music leaned over and whispered in my ear: "This feels so real."

The question of what is real has long plagued Afro-Peruvian music. Upon reading this book in an earlier form, Victoria Santa Cruz wrote to me, "Thank you, Heidi, for sending me this work, which undoubtedly constitutes an arduous effort and, because of the partiality of certain testimonials, becomes a sword of contradictions . . . Wouldn't this be a great opportunity for organizing debates, conferences, with specific elements that allow us to understand what commitment means?"[1] In the battle between competing versions of Afro-Peruvian music and dance, everyone's great aunt or grandmother remembers a slightly different story, an alternate choreography, an idiosyncratic lyric, a more authentic jarana. Some elders remember nothing at all, leading their offspring to claim that Black music and dance did not exist in its present form until the Santa Cruzes, and later Perú Negro, came along and "invented it."

For example, Afro-Peruvian guitarist Félix Casaverde maintains that there is no such thing as "Black" Peruvian music, just as there is no such thing as "White" Peruvian music. Instead, he describes genres practiced by both Afro-Peruvians and White criollos as "Peruvian coastal music." Casaverde grew up in the rural town of San Regis (near the Hacienda San José), which at that time housed a predominantly Black population of agricultural workers. Casaverde remembers: "when I was ten years old . . . I would walk around the whole settlement and talk to the old people. And so I am lucky, since I love to ask questions, to have received definitive testimonials, although, unfortunately, they are unrecorded. Look, the people in San Regis danced for the last forty years or more to the Sonora Matancera. The 78 records of these older people were the Sonora Matancera, Panchito Riset, and *tangos*" (Casaverde 2000a).[2] Casaverde adds that he never heard of the festejo, landó, or alcatraz until these revival dances were promoted by Victoria Santa Cruz in the 1960s.

In contrast, Juan Carlos "Juanchi" Vásquez affirms that Black song and dance traditions were preserved by only a small group of Black families (such as his own). His point of view does not contradict Casaverde's, but rather highlights the fact that the extent to which Peruvians believe in the pre-revival existence of certain Afro-Peruvian genres may depend on their own personal experience. Juanchi explains: "It was not just the general population that had forgotten about these rhythms, but rather the entire population, including many Black Peruvians . . . Some things were reinterpreted [during the revival] through the collective memory of the people . . . But not everything had to be reinterpreted. The festejo, for example, is something that never stopped being practiced . . . The alcatraz always existed. It's just that it wasn't practiced very publicly . . . José Durand didn't invent anything. What he did was bring together certain families so they could remember. Now, of the 100 percent of folklore that was supposedly practiced here, Black folklore, today 10 percent exists. The majority of the dances have disappeared. And folklore groups, Perú Negro's type, have invented things. They have invented choreography, they have invented basic rhythmic patterns, they have created dances . . . But not everything. It cannot be said that all of Afro-Peruvian folklore has been reconstructed" (J. Vásquez 2000).

In the 1990s, the process of reconstructing the debated past continued with the emergence of Peru's first Black theater company since the Afro-Peruvian revival—Teatro del Milenio (Theater of the Millennium). In many ways, Milenio's productions reiterate the themes, strategies, and methods employed by Nicomedes and Victoria Santa Cruz (although few members were old enough to have seen their productions), revealing that the public status of Blacks in Peru has not improved much, despite fifty years of the elevation of Afro-Peruvian culture to the concert stage. In 1996, according to the *New York Times*, no Black politician had ever been elected to Peruvian Congress; there were no Blacks in the high ranks of Peruvian companies, clergy, or military; none in the diplomatic corps or judiciary; and the estimated number of Blacks employed in any white-collar occupation in Peru was less than 400 (Sims 1996, 2). In 2005, although there were three Black Peruvians in Congress, critics observed that these politicians had passed no legislation to specifically improve the position of Blacks in Peru (see R. Mendoza 2005). Because many Blacks still feel they do not officially exist in the eyes of the nation, the critiques launched by the politically conscious Black theater of Milenio emit echoes of the past.

Teatro del Milenio's first production, *Karibú*, a noble effort to combat racism and promote Black racial pride, was uncannily similar in approach to the work of the Santa Cruzes thirty years earlier. Like Victoria Santa Cruz' 1961 play *Zanahary*, *Karibú* presented scenes that re-created an imagined African ancestry, in this case using models ranging from Afro-Cuban folklore to images from National Geographic videos. Milenio's artistic director, Lucho Sandoval, explains: "The initial exposition [of *Karibú*] was to speak about our presence in Peru, but above all, the African cultural heritage. Why? Because we began to analyze the fact that Blacks in Peru don't like to be called Africans. We believe that being African is something to feel proud of, and not to feel denigrated. But we feel denigrated because 'African' is associated with 'slave.' And it's not true . . . In not valuing ourselves as Blacks, we have lost our African essence . . .

"[In *Karibú*] we were not concerned with respecting a linear history of a specific African nation. For two reasons. One, because this was not a historical work. And the other, because we didn't know very much. So we couldn't be very faithful . . . We took materials from some videos we have seen or from workshops we have had. Like Oscar [Milenio's choreographer] has had workshops with Senegalese people or workshops with Cubans, and the Cuban music and tradition is closer to the African tradition . . . Oscar

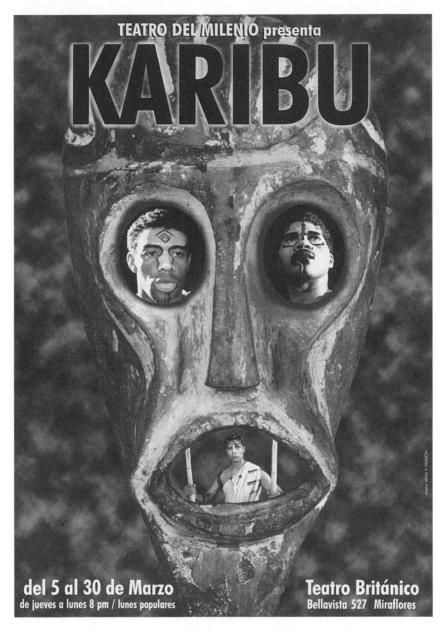

FIGURE C.1. Publicity poster for *Karibú*. Pictured: Oscar Villanueva (*top left*), Jaime Zevallos (*top right*), and Lucho Sandoval (*bottom*).

says to me, 'Everything African is ours' . . . So we took some steps from there. Or from Afro-Peruvian folklore, but we Africanized it more. We took it to the extreme—what we believed, the image we have of what is 'the African'" (Sandoval 2000).

Roberto Arguedas, music director for Milenio, explains how the group retrieved the marimba, an instrument used by enslaved Africans but abandoned by the twentieth century, for *Karibú*. Like Victoria Santa Cruz, Roberto Arguedas says he used his "ancestral memory" to guide him in the composition of Afro-Peruvian melodies for that instrument (Arguedas 2000).[3] When I asked him why the theme of the African and slave past is still so ubiquitous in the contemporary work of Afro-Peruvian artists, Arguedas stated: "The question is, if we don't know our past, how will we move forward to the present? This is also our search for ourselves . . . We must always go back to the past, because first we must visit the past in order to make a new present. Or we will never construct anything . . . For thirty years, everything has been at a standstill, we don't come together. There are not many dance groups, Perú Negro continues to exist but now it is commercial . . . We don't delve deeper there. That was the work of Victoria . . . How will we move to the present? . . . This is our struggle" (Arguedas 2000).

One of the most powerful scenes in *Karibú* offers a rare critique of the contemporary Afro-Peruvian peña. As the scene begins, Lucho Sandoval appears in the role of the smiling *maitre d'* in a nightclub called Peña Negronegro (Peña Blackblack). The musicians have not shown up for work because they found better-paying employment elsewhere. The maitre d' hands the two male waiters the traditional costumes of Afro-Peruvian dancers, including a short skirt and midriff top for the "female" partner. A satirical parody of the overdone stereotypes found in peña performances follows, with the dancers wearing frozen grins. The dance concludes in a puff of smoke, and the men are transported to a dream-like sequence in the African jungle (with musical accompaniment by congas, cajón, and marimba along with jungle sounds) where they dance with large canes and encounter an African healer. Their journey from Africa to slavery in Peru is traced with imaginative choreography before the scene returns to the present—the end of their set in Peña Negronegro. As the applause fades, so do the smiles on their faces. The men look at each other with empathy and sadness; they touch each other's faces (still painted with imagined tribal designs), then each other's shoulders, and they embrace. The female vocalist sings a chant to the Yoruba ancestral deity Yemaya.

Lucho Sandoval explains how the scene evolved: "It came from the necessity to speak about the peña . . . We had to do it, but do it well. For a long time, I took part in a workshop . . . with masks. So it occurred to me that we could work with a facial mask for this moment . . . Why? Because it went with what we wanted to say. The Black man had to wear a mask to satisfy the taste of the public. So we worked with the idea of masks that should be inanimate during the whole scene. That is to say, no matter what we do, we had to act as if we were wearing a facial mask . . .

"We want to revalorize the Black person as a human being," Sandoval continues. "As a human being with contradictions like everyone. We want to revalorize the Black person as an artist who puts his creative-artistic work in a show and people enjoy it . . . We don't want people to go to see the legs of the Black female dancers and say 'Oh, how wonderful these Blacks are, and that's why I go see them.' If it is true that we are happy, we are extroverted, we speak with our entire bodies, etcetera, it is part of our way of being, which nobody is going to take from us . . . We want to be that way naturally without it signifying that we should do it to satisfy the need of others. So we want to be accepted in our reality, our contradictions, we want to be able to speak of profound topics . . . We are not interested in satisfying the market, even though we live, by contradiction, from that market. But we are interested in this market accepting us as artists and not as slaves of the market" (Sandoval 2000).

The peña skit was daring in Peru; it was one of the only public protests against the inherent racism in the cultural economy that only rewards Blacks who portray their slave ancestors or market their sexuality in night-clubs for tourists. However, Sandoval reports that, although *Karibú* was well attended, their satire sparked little public discourse: "I wanted to awaken more polemics. But it didn't generate much public debate. Theater is not going to definitively change society. It is not going to change the manner of thinking. What it can do is give you some ideas to reflect upon. But I believe that it performs its work, it fulfills its function" (Sandoval 2000). Taking an optimistic perspective, ethnomusicologist Javier León observes that, although it might appear that the Afro-Peruvian revival failed to remedy the "real world" problems of Afro-Peruvians, such a view would ignore "the constitutive agency that Afroperuvian musicians and more recently anthropologists ascribe to performance . . . Over the last fifty years, the performance of Afroperuvian music and dance has been the main avenue available to members of the Afroperuvian community to reclaim and promote a past previously denied to them, to appropriate and transform old stereotypes, and to challenge pre-existing social hierarchies" (León Quirós 2003, 74).

In addition, as I have argued, the Afro-Peruvian revival mapped the Peruvian Black Pacific as a periphery of the Black Atlantic. Distinct memory projects enabled Afro-Peruvians to negotiate Black Pacific double consciousness by connecting performances of blackness with criollo, Black Atlantic, or African origins and traditions. As Paul Gilroy observes in this chapter's epigraph, music of the Black Atlantic endlessly blends and transforms inherited African traditions with the modern and newly invented "African" and Creole ones that result from the lived experience of double consciousness. In the Afro-Peruvian music of the Black Pacific, a high premium is attached to competing versions of what is imagined to be the "sameness" of the "changing same." The reinvented past has increased in value because so much was invested in reviving and re-creating its forgotten legacy, and because belief in that past shapes the identity of Afro-Peruvians today.

Like the members of Teatro del Milenio and their predecessors in the revival, I have returned to Afro-Peruvian music's past (albeit a more recent one) in order to understand the present. As I write these words, I hear Victoria Santa Cruz' imaginary response: "You can never know the past you did not experience! Impossible!" Yet, I realize that I initially went to Peru to document performance practice in the present, and what I found there was an enormous dose of the past. Although people say Black Peruvians have no documented history, their past is everywhere today: in Perú Negro's costumes, in the proud way the residents of El Carmen maintain their Christmas traditions, in Susana Baca's journey up and down the coast, in the dance contests of the Peruvian colony in the United States, and in the rebellious theater of Teatro del Milenio. Yet, it is a past that is created in the present to fulfill the needs and desires of both a commercial public and the artists who serve that public. The staging of Afro-Peruvian music and dance since the 1950s has resulted in the creation of a cultural memory of the history of Black Peru, reiterated over and over again through the dramatic performance of a small and circumscribed body of dances, folkloric narration, body image, smiles, gestures, and rhythmic innuendo. It is that cultural memory of Black Peru—a product of the present—that I have documented. The rest, as they say, is history.

Glossary

alcatraz: An Afro-Peruvian dance, said to date from times of slavery, in which male–female partners try to light on fire a small paper "tail" affixed to each other's rear end.

bordón: Typical basslines played on guitar.

cajita: A wooden box with a hinged lid that opens and closes, used as a percussion instrument and played with a stick.

cajón: A box drum played with the hands.

concurso: A contest.

criollo/a: A term originally used to denote the children of Africans born into slavery in Peru that was later employed by Europeans to describe the children of Spanish settlers born in Peru. After independence, the word *criollo* came to describe Peruvians who lived in Lima and coastal areas and identified with a shared set of Europeanist cultural practices.

cuadrilla: A dance team or company.

cumanana: (1) A form of octosyllabic poetry from the northern coast of Peru. (2) Nicomedes and Victoria Santa Cruz' theater company (1960–1961). (3) An ethnographic recording and booklet by Nicomedes Santa Cruz (1964).

décima: A Spanish poetic form, found throughout Latin America, which employs ten-line strophes.

festejo: One of the most frequently performed Afro-Peruvian song and dance genres, with music and choreography expressing exuberant joy.

hatajos de negritos: Groups of male dancers in Chincha and neighboring provinces who perform songs and dances during the Festival of the Virgin of El Carmen.

jarana: A Peruvian criollo party involving música criolla, dance, and typical foods and drinks.

landó: An Afro-Peruvian song and dance genre re-created by Nicomedes and Victoria Santa Cruz in the 1960s. Typically, the landó expresses sensuality through its minor mode, stylistic ambiguity, and shifting metric accents.

lundú: According to Nicomedes Santa Cruz, an African couple dance characterized by the golpe de frente (pelvic bump), which gave birth to more than fifty couples dances practiced by Blacks in the Americas, including the Peruvian landó.

marinera: A couple dance, considered by some to be the national dance of Peru, performed with handkerchiefs in coastal areas of Peru.

música criolla: Music that emerged from lower- and middle-class coastal communities in the early twentieth century, especially the marinera and the vals.

pallas: Groups of girls who dance in front of the church during the Festival of the Virgin of Carmen in El Carmen, Chincha.

Pampa de Amancaes: The site of an annual festival of música criolla until the 1950s.

panalivio: An Afro-Peruvian lament song genre banned by the church in the eighteenth century and revived in the mid-twentieth century.

peña: A Peruvian nightclub or private social center where music and dance are performed and food and drink are consumed.

quijada: The jaw of a horse, mule, or ass, used as a percussion instrument in Afro-Peruvian music.

resbalosa: The "fast section" of the marinera limeña.

son de los diablos: A dance originating in the Spanish Corpus Christi Festivals and later secularized in Peruvian Carnival, in which dancers portray devils and parade through the streets.

vals: A criollo song and dance form descended from the European waltz.

villancico: A Spanish Christmas song sung in front of altars in private homes.

yunza: A group dance around a decorated tree that takes place during Carnival throughout the Andes.

zamacueca: A couple dance performed by Peruvians of all races but thought to be of Afro-Peruvian origin, renamed the marinera after the War of the Pacific with Chile. Related dances are performed throughout South America.

zambo(a): A Black person of mixed racial origin, often including indigenous ancestry.

zapateo: Peruvian-style tap dancing.

Notes

Introduction (pp. 1–16)

1. In James Lockhart's small sampling of 256 slave sales in Lima and Arequipa (1548–1560), 19 percent of slave origins were given as Spain, Portugal, Indies, or "creole" ([1968] 1994, 196). In Frederick P. Bowser's sample of 6,890 slaves sold in Lima (1560–1650), 6.5 percent came from Spain or the Spanish Americas (1974, 73).

2. The English equivalent of criollo is creole. In Peru, the term "criollo" has a multiethnic meaning flavored by local coastal culture. "Ladino" and "criollo" initially described acculturated African slaves, as opposed to *bozales,* or slaves who came directly from Africa (see Bowser 1974, 78–80; Lockhart [1968] 1994, 198). Ladinos were Africans who had lived under European authority and were versed in European languages and customs. Criollos were African offspring born in Europe or the New World. The term "criollo" later encompassed the children of Spanish settlers born in Peru. Since the twentieth century, "criollo" has described people of various racial/ethnic backgrounds who identify with cultural practices particular to coastal Peru and normally ascribed to European origin. I will discuss the cultural politics of *criollismo* in chapter 1.

3. A high point for the documented population of Blacks in Peru, both during and after times of slavery, is 90,000 in the year 1650 (Glave 1995, 15), and it is estimated that imports during the entire slave trade totaled 95,000 (1 percent or less of the estimated entire geographic distribution of enslaved Africans) and that 17,000 slaves were freed at the time of emancipation (Curtin 1969, 45, 46, 89). However, a reliable calculation of the total volume of the Peruvian slave trade has not been produced (see Bowser 1974, 72). A few authors have begun to reconstruct the history and geography of Peru's African slave trade (Blanchard 1992; Bowser 1974; Harth-Terré 1971; Lockhart [1968] 1994; Mac-Lean y Estenós 1948; F. Romero 1994), but most of their findings cover small time periods, and much research remains to be done.

4. I interviewed musicians, composers, dancers, actors, producers, a recording studio owner, a recording label executive, a company manager, a radio show host, scholars, Black political activists, the director of a research center, a music journalist, and the director of Peru's National School of Folklore.

5. Gilroy reworks W. E. B. Du Bois' theory of double consciousness from *The Souls of Black Folk* ([1903] 1994).

6. My model of the Black Pacific is based primarily on my research in Peru, but I am interested in exploring its applicability in areas with similar histories. Relevant ethnomusicological studies of populations demonstrating similar characteristics might include John Schechter's analysis of the indigenous borrowings of the Afro-Ecuadorian *bomba* (1994); Jonathan Ritter's study of the local criollo and African diasporic faces of the Afro-Ecuadorian *marimba* traditions of Esmereldas (1998); Peter Wade's writings on the cultural politics separating the Black populations of

Colombia's Atlantic and Pacific coasts (1993 and 1998); and Robert Templeman's research on the Afro-Bolivian *saya* (1998).

7. Several scholars have deconstructed the belief, central in scholarship on the African diaspora from the 1930s and 1940s, that certain contemporary Black Atlantic cultural practices represent the continuous preservation of precolonial African ones brought by their slave ancestors. As J. Lorand Matory (1999) and Kim Butler (2001a) show, the prevalent portrayal of the Yoruba-derived Afro-Brazilian Candomblé religion as a paragon of African survivals fails to acknowledge the influence of colonial Yoruba culture brought *after* the slave trade by repatriated Afro-Latins, as well as nineteenth-century changes in the practice of Candomblé that involved symbolic uses of Africa. Further, the Yoruba-derived culture that survived in Cuba, Brazil, and other parts of the Americas (and served as a model of African heritage for the Afro-Peruvian revival) did not come from a single unified ethnic group in precolonial Africa; it combined several heterogeneous neighboring groups who shared a spoken language but who did not even call themselves "Yoruba" until much later (Brandon [1993] 1997, 55).

8. I consciously employ the notion of "memory work"—borrowed from Freudian psychoanalytic techniques that recover repressed traumatic memories sometimes alleged to be false—to describe this process.

9. See Raúl Romero's similar analysis of how one genre was elevated above another as worthy of "rescue" in the Peruvian Mantaro Valley (2001, 35–65).

Chapter 1 (pp. 17–48)

1. Salazar Bondy attributes this quote to Raúl Porras Barrenechea.

2. Fuentes was a journalist, cartoonist, head of Peru's Department of Statistics, overseer of the first national census, and—in historian Paul Gootenberg's words— "the social constructor of Limeño reality" (qtd. in Poole 1997, 149–150). For an in-depth analysis of Fuentes' *Lima*, see Poole (1997, 149–167).

3. Criollismo is subtly different from *blanqueamiento* (whitening), another ideological phenomenon prevalent in Latin America in the late-nineteenth to mid-twentieth centuries (see chapter 3). Whereas the philosophy of blanqueamiento espouses that a nation can gradually be "whitened" through intermarriage and subsequent reclassification of children, the ideology of criollismo is not explicitly based on race or skin tone but rather on the identification of people of diverse racial origins with a shared set of cultural practices.

4. Thomas Turino (1996) notes that scholars who study rural to urban migration in Peru often employ an essentialist Andean-criollo dichotomy. Seeking to avoid such essentialism without negating the "essentialness" people feel about their own cultures, he outlines the process by which Andean migrants have redefined their identity in urban Peru. My focus in this chapter is similarly on how criollo culture was redefined in response to the Andean and Black migrations.

5. Whereas one of Durand's former students stated that most of Durand's information about Afro-Peruvian music was "in his head," others feel that Durand's collection of Afro-Peruvian research materials resides elsewhere.

6. See Durand Flórez (1961; 1971; 1973; 1979a; 1979b; 1980; 1988; and 1995).

7. The resbalosa is a section of the marinera.

8. Barranco and Miraflores are two affluent Lima neighborhoods.

9. Although some former company members say the company's full name was La Cuadrilla Morena de Pancho Fierro (The Brown Company of Pancho Fierro), newspaper accounts of the era indicate that La Cuadrilla was actually one of several preexisting subgroups within the Pancho Fierro cast, led by Juan Criado. To further

complicate matters, in 1957 the company changed its name to Ritmos Negros del Perú (Black Rhythms of Peru). However, because most people, and newspaper ads and reviews from the era, refer to the group as Pancho Fierro, I will continue to use that name throughout this book.

10. Among his many activities, Arguedas edited and published the first recordings of Peruvian folkloric music in 1947–1950, arranging for their distribution by Odeon. Arguedas also oversaw the process of "authenticating" folkloric artists, which involved administering questionnaires and strict regulations in order to qualify only "authentic" Andean folklore bearers to perform at huge spectacles in Lima's coliseums and on national radio. These questionnaires, administered to illiterate and semi-literate musicians, solicited detailed information about each candidate's region of origin, folkloric expression, family traditions, project, and living conditions in Lima. A final question was "According to you, should music, song, and costumes be stylized, or should their purity and integrity be respected?" (Fell 1987, 62–63, 65–66). While Eve Marie Fell (1987) notes the irony of the situation in which urban professionals assessed rural authenticity, Raúl Romero stresses that Arguedas was a mentor and father figure to Andean performers and a champion of contemporary regional Andean traditions (2001, 97–102).

11. According to Pancho Fierro company member Caitro Soto (Soto de la Colina 2000), family parties that involved music and dance were conducted behind closed doors after the children had gone to sleep because some Black dances were sexually explicit.

12. This information—an approximation of the original program—was obtained by scanning issues of the Peruvian newspapers *El Comercio*, *La Crónica*, and *La Prensa* from the years 1956 to 1957. See Feldman (2001) for a more complete list of genres, scenes, and artists from the early Pancho Fierro performances.

13. The quijada (jawbone) also has been used as a musical instrument in Cuba, Haiti, Mexico, the southern United States, and other parts of the Americas (N. Santa Cruz 1970b).

14. As Javier León observed in a personal communication, the use of the harp and whip in el son de los diablos dance may reveal Andean influence. The harp (introduced by the Spanish in colonial times) is a prominent instrument in Andean music, and Andean devil dances often feature whipping battles. León further notes that Fierro's paintings depict participants who appear to be mestizos, suggesting that el son de los diablos was not performed exclusively by Blacks (León Quirós 2003, 54n29).

15. For other negative descriptions of Blacks dancing in public from the sixteenth to twentieth centuries, see Tompkins (1981, 27, 36, 72, and 259–260).

16. Javier León suggests that academic research is used, by contemporary Afro-Peruvian performers with no family ties to the constructed rural sites of authenticity, as an alternative to inherited knowledge in the struggle to promote the authority of competing interpretations of Afro-Peruvian traditions (León Quirós 2003).

17. See León Quirós (2003, 224–225) and De la Cadena (1998) for discussions of the twentieth-century social rhetoric of "decency" that masked racist marginalizing practices by White criollo elites in Lima.

Chapter 2 (pp. 49–82)

1. The décima is a Spanish-American poetic form. The zamacueca and marinera are Peruvian couple dances.

2. The word "*cumanana*" refers to a Peruvian genre of sung, octosyllabic poetic quatrains performed in competitive duels. Nicomedes thought the term might be of African origin, and he baptized his group "Kumanana" (changing the first letter to "c" by the mid-1960s) because he was "captivated by its Black sonority" (N. Santa Cruz 1970a, 57).

3. In the glossary of *Décimas*, Nicomedes Santa Cruz defines the term "zanaharí" and clarifies that its Malagasy spelling is Zanahary (N. Santa Cruz n.d. [1959?], 159). Although there is no definitive evidence that Africans from Madagascar were brought to Peru as slaves, several authors cite imports from southern or southeastern Africa (Bowser 1974, 40–43; Curtin 1969, 97; Harth-Terré 1971, 10; Lockhart [1968] 1994, 196).

4. The song "Karambe" (N. Santa Cruz y su Conjunto Kumanana 1959) was revived with different lyrics in the 1980s and 1990s by Félix Casaverde, Miki González, Julie Freundt, and Susana Baca.

5. *Mazamorra* is a typical dessert in Lima (a purple fruit stew) and a *mazamorrero* is someone who either enjoys or makes *mazamorra*. The dish is often invoked as a metaphor for Lima's cultural mestizaje, similar to the "melting pot" metaphor used in the United States.

6. The following narrative is constructed from excerpts of my interviews with Teresa Mendoza Hernández in Lima (2000). Teresa's memories provide an intimate glimpse of the impact of Cumanana on the lives of its young company members in the 1960s. Although I have translated the text of her interviews into English and rearranged and edited it to facilitate chronological flow, the words are her own. I was inspired to "translate" Teresa in this manner after reading Ruth Behar's *Translated Woman* (1993). I decided to highlight Teresa's story because, although she starred in Cumanana's early productions, she retired from the stage shortly thereafter in order to devote herself to her husband and children. Thus, among the many voices clamoring to proclaim the "authentic history" of Afro-Peruvian music, Teresa's is normally absent.

7. Pelona is a nickname for a girl with very little hair.

8. In Spanish, a half note is called a *blanca* (white). A half note's duration value is twice that of a quarter note, or *negra* (black) in Spanish.

9. The double-headed batá drums originate in Nigeria and are used in sets of three in the performance of religious music of Afro-Cuban *Santería*. Batá drums typically were not found in Peru in the 1960s, and the photo in figure 2.6 depicts what appears to be a homemade double-headed drum that may have emulated a Cuban batá drum.

10. Teresa does not name the seventh performer.

11. Tumbas (*tumbadoras* or conga drums) were not used in Black Peruvian music before the 1960s but had been popularized in Peru by Cuban bands in the 1930s and 1940s.

12. Victoria Santa Cruz, e-mail to the author, July 25, 2003.

13. Victoria Santa Cruz, e-mail to the author, July 25, 2003.

14. Victoria Santa Cruz, e-mail to the author, July 25, 2003.

15. According to Victoria Santa Cruz, these photos depict a dance contest in which a glass of liquor is placed on the floor and each dancer must attempt to pick up the glass without using his or her hands or spilling a drop, while the observers sing, "Levántemelo María, Levántemelo José, ¡Que si tú no me lo levantas yo te lo levantaré!" (Pick it up for me, María, pick it up for me, José, If you don't pick it up for me, I will pick it up for you!).

16. I have not viewed Suárez Radillo's videorecording, but an article based on his research (Suárez Radillo 1976) contains written accounts of some of the recorded testimonials.

17. Despite Victoria Santa Cruz' apparent disinterest in returning to the Peruvian theater, in 2004 she directed a new stage production in Lima.

18. Victoria Santa Cruz, e-mail to the author, July 25, 2003.

19. This section documents my three meetings with Victoria Santa Cruz in Lima (2000). Victoria did not allow me to record our discussions, but I wrote extensive journal notes after each one. Thus, Victoria Santa Cruz' statements in this narrative are not direct quotes, but rather my memory of what was said. After reading an earlier draft of this chapter, Victoria Santa Cruz made some corrections and changes, which I have included in the final book version.

20. Although Victoria Santa Cruz speaks fluent English, all of my conversations with Victoria were in Spanish, at her insistence. When we specifically discussed our mutual vocal inflections and accents, Victoria told me that her melodious speech patterns are consistent with the way all "old Limeños" spoke in the early part of the last century.

Chapter 3 (pp. 83–124)

1. I use the spelling negritude to refer to the movement in Paris and French-speaking colonies of Africa and the Caribbean and negritud to refer to the Spanish-language Latin American manifestation.

2. For further background and critical perspectives on the French-African negritude movement, see Beier (1967); Clifford (1988b); Dash (1974); Fanon (1966); Jones (1971); and Williams and Chrisman (1994). For an overview of negritud in Latin America, see Bush (1985); R. Durand (1978); Jackson (1979 and 1984); and Lewis (1983).

3. López Albújar's broader body of work focused on other marginalized populations, especially indigenous and mestizo culture, and thus is part of indigenismo as well.

4. Nicomedes Santa Cruz surmises that Hijinio Quintana's claim to have competed against the devil may have been inspired by his introduction to Chilean Christian décimas that refer to the devil (N. Santa Cruz 1982, 104–105). An interesting cross-cultural parallel could be made with African American blues musicians who made Faustian claims regarding encounters with the devil at a crossroads. Samuel Floyd connects these legends with what he describes as the devilish reincarnation in the United States of Esu, a West African divine trickster (Floyd 1995, 73–74).

5. In addition to Nicomedes' love of poetry, his career change was influenced by the declining demand for metal craftspeople after World War II. To supplement his income, he also launched a career as a journalist in 1958 ("Nicomedes Santa Cruz Gamarra" n.d., 2).

6. The Spanish text of "Ritmos negros del Perú" is reprinted from Décimas (N. Santa Cruz n.d. [1959?], 19–20), and the English translation is adapted from The Peru Reader (Starn, Degregori and Kirk 1995, 290–291).

7. Santería is an African-derived religion practiced widely in Cuba. Abakwá is an African-derived secret male society in Cuba.

8. There is disagreement regarding the number of traditional socabón melodies; William Tompkins (based on information from Augusto Ascuez and José Durand) maintains that, at one time, many socabón variations for guitar accompaniment existed (1981, 164), whereas Nicomedes Santa Cruz believed there was only one authentic socabón melody.

9. Possibly the oldest known festejo, "Molino molero," thought to date from the early nineteenth century or before, was collected by José Durand from Bartola

Sancho Dávila (who had learned it from her aunt, Juana Irujo, a former slave). In 1936, composer Samuel Márquez publicly presented arrangements of remembered fragments of song melodies and texts, including festejos, in a performance by the Ricardo Palma company. Juan Criado subsequently performed and popularized staged versions of festejos learned from older Afro-Peruvians (Tompkins 1981, 240–247).

10. Spanish text of "No me cumbén" is cited from the booklet that accompanies *Cumanana* (N. Santa Cruz 1970a, 61). The English translation is adapted from the liner notes to the CD *The Soul of Black Peru* (Various Artists 1995a).

11. "Mandinga" is used in Peru to mean "African" in general. The most often-quoted use of the term "Mandinga" is Ricardo Palma's saying, "El que no tiene de Inga tiene de Mandinga" (He who does not have indigenous heritage has Mandinga/African heritage), a slogan for the process of Peruvian mestizaje.

12. There is a long tradition of Peruvian parody and satire that is expressed in colonial literature and music (see Estenssoro 1988; Ojeda 1997, 151–168; N. Santa Cruz 1982, 90–94).

13. Spanish text is cited from the booklet accompanying the recording *Cumanana* (N. Santa Cruz 1970a, 27).

14. It should be noted that Nicomedes Santa Cruz was by no means against racial intermarriage, as his own marriage demonstrates.

15. Caboclo is a Brazilian term for the mixture of indigenous and European ancestry.

16. After Peru lost the War of the Pacific (1879–1883) to Chile, Peruvians changed the name of the zamacueca dance to marinera in order to distance it from its Chilean counterpart, the *cueca*.

17. Nicomedes traces the following dances to the *lundú* of Angola and the *kalenda* of Congo: "(Portugal) *lundum, lundu, chorado, chula portuguesa, lado,* etc.; (Spain) *zarabanda, calenda, ondú,* etc.; (New Orleans) *bambula*; (Louisiana) *calenda*; (Mexico) *bamba, maracumbi, paracumbé*; (Cuba) *caringa (calenda), yuka* (which became the *rumba* with its classic *vacunao* pelvic thrust); (Haiti) *kalenda, bambula*; (Puerto Rico) *bomba*; (Panama) *cumbia, tamborito*; (Colombia) *bullarengue, currulao, palacoré, cumbia, bambuco,* etc.; (Venezuela) *chimbanelero, malembe, sangueo*; (Ecuador) *bomba*; (Brazil) *lundu, céco, samba, batuque, tambor de crioula, jongo,* etc.; (Peru) *samba, samba-landó, lundú, samba-cueca, zamacueca, zaña, tondero, zanguaraña, mozamala, polka de cajón, malcito, golpe'e tierra, toromata, ecuador, chilena, marinera*; (Bolivia) *zamba, zamacueca*; (Chile) *cueca*; (Argentina) *zamba*" (N. Santa Cruz 1970a, 24).

18. I examined Nicomedes Santa Cruz' personal library (including books, articles, and handwriting in the margins) in Madrid in 2000.

19. Of course, Cuba and Brazil imported greater numbers of enslaved Africans than Peru over a longer period of time, resulting in the enduring national visibility of Black and African-derived cultural expressions in those countries.

20. *Iyawo* (spelled yao by Nicomedes) is a word of Yoruba origin that refers to an individual undergoing the rites of initiation in Afro-Cuban Lucumí religious societies. The initiate is considered to be the bride of a particular *orisha*, or ancestral deity (regardless of the initiate's gender). *Babalawo* (babalao in the Cuban Lucumí language) is a word of Yoruba origin that describes a priest trained in divination.

21. Nicomedes Santa Cruz occasionally referred to ancestral memory in his writings and public speeches. However, he did not claim—as Victoria did—to have revived Afro-Peruvian music or dance exclusively by means of ancestral memory.

22. "Samba" is a term that refers to a Black woman, often of mixed parentage. "Malató" may be a contraction of *mala* (bad) and *todo* (all), as explained in the theatrical program for the Cumanana play *Malató* (V. and N. Santa Cruz 1961). According to Victoria Santa Cruz (1995), "Samba malató" is actually a *zamba-landó,*

a folkloricized version of the ancestral landó dance. The Ascuez version of the landó is discussed and transcribed by William Tompkins (1981, 298, 546). Another landó was remembered and danced, to guitar and cajón accompaniment, in the rural community El Guayabo during the *yunza* celebration at Carnival time. This version, also discussed and transcribed by Tompkins (1981, 297–298, 547–549), was staged in the 1970s by Perú Negro. See Javier León's discussion of both prototype landós (León Quirós 2003, 230–248).

23. Spelling and pronunciation of these lyrics varies.

24. While Nicomedes Santa Cruz criticized the Velasco revolution in a 1993 interview with Pablo Mariñez, he praised Velasco in a 1974 interview with Elena Poniatowska, even defending Velasco's decision to invite Chilean dictator Augosto Pinochet to the Peruvian events commemorating the anniversary of the Battle of Ayacucho. Of course, there were no longer political consequences to publicly speaking out against Velasco at the time of the later Mariñez interview.

25. Victoria Santa Cruz also attended the conference but did not give a public address.

26. Recordings of Nicomedes' radio programs for Radio Exterior are held in the archive of Radio Nacional de España in Madrid.

27. Even in his early work, Nicomedes Santa Cruz frequently pointed out that Spain's poetic traditions had absorbed African influences before they were brought to the New World. In *Cumanana* and elsewhere, he noted that sixteenth-century Spain had been influenced by the oral poetry traditions of North Africa through its domination by the Islamic Empire, and that the Spanish décima's form of recitation recalls poetic traditions of the Arab world (N. Santa Cruz 1970a, 13–14), as well as the oral poetic traditions of West African *griots* (1982, 69).

28. Peruvians of Asian descent are often called chino or china, whether or not they have Chinese heritage.

29. Fujimori claimed to the courts that he had not yet served two terms under the new constitution, because he was elected under the old one in 1990.

30. Toledo was nicknamed *cholo*, a word (with both derogatory and fond connotations) that describes people of indigenous origin in the process of becoming mestizo.

31. Small poetry groups continue to cultivate the art of décimas. For example, in the 1990s, Octavio Santa Cruz operated a peña where decimistas gathered for poetry readings and competitions.

32. Rafael Santa Cruz, e-mail to the author, August 20, 2003.

Chapter 4 (pp. 125–170)

1. Velasco initiated three arts workshops through the Central Information Office: Coastal Music, Andean Manifestations, and Youth Workshop. Perú Negro was entrusted with teaching Black music of the southern coast in the first workshop, and the company earned a government salary of 7,500 *soles* per person (Izquierdo 2000).

2. Interestingly, whereas most people refer to four male founders of Perú Negro, when I mentioned Perú Negro's founders to Ronaldo Campos' daughter-in-law, Perú Negro lead vocalist Monica Dueñas, in 2005, she added that three female dancers—Esperanza Campos, Pilar de la Cruz, and Sara de la Cruz—were also founding members. The complete list of members of the original Perú Negro company includes: Ronaldo Campos (cajón and dancer), Linder Góngora (first guitar), Isidoro Izquierdo (second guitar), Orlando Soto (quijada and *cencerro*), Caitro Soto and Lucila Campos (voice), and dancers Esperanza Campos, Pilar de

la Cruz, Sara de la Cruz, Lalo Izquierdo, Rodolfo Arteaga, and Victor "Raúl" Padilla. The first generation of the company soon also included Eusebio "Pititi" Sirio (cajón and dancer), Guillermo "El Niño" Nicasio (congas), Julio "Chocolate" Algendones (bongó), and chorus members Sonia de la Cruz, María Laguna, Elizabeth Carillo, Gilberto Bramón, Felipe Carrillo, and Manuel Donayre.

3. This dance was not the same as the afro performed by Teresa Mendoza Hernández in Victoria Santa Cruz' play *Zanahary*. My description of the musical accompaniment and choreography is based in part on later performances by Perú Negro of the afro dance described by Lalo Izquierdo.

4. Surco is a neighborhood in Lima.

5. The Spanish lyrics are "Pobre negrito que triste está/trabaja mucho y no gana na'. Pobre negrito que triste está/su mismo amo le va a pegá" (Perú Negro 1974).

6. The *payandé* is a tree that grows in Colombia (where one of the song's composers was born).

7. Only in recent decades has blackface performance publicly acquired racist connotations in the United States. In the 1920s, it was publicly accepted for performers like Al Jolson to use blackface in Hollywood films (which were also popular in Peru).

8. In Perú Negro's choreography for the song "Toro mata" (The bull kills), Blacks dress in the castoff finery of their White colonial masters and satirize European aristocratic dances.

9. As discussed in chapter 2, the Velasco government also supported Victoria Santa Cruz when she was director of the Conjunto Nacional de Folklore. However, Victoria left Peru in the early 1980s to work in the United States, and Nicomedes left in 1980 to live in Spain.

10. Chicha is a Peruvian alcoholic beverage.

11. All lyrics from "Canto a Elegua" are phonetically transcribed from video (Perú Negro 1979).

12. The three numbered verses, set to similar melodies and accompaniment (arranged for various types of drum ensembles), may be heard on many Cuban and Brazilian recordings (for example, Grupo Afrocuba de Matanzas 1993; Spiro and Lamson 1996; Various Artists 1998d). The first verse (transcribed in figure 4.12) is also similar to a 1939 field recording of the music of the Shango religion in Trinidad, made by Melville and Frances Herskovits and re-released on CD (Various Artists 1998c). The lyrics of these three verses may be compared with transcriptions of Santería liturgical texts (Fatunmbi n.d.; Mason 1992, 72). So far, none of the practitioners or scholars of orisha music whom I have contacted have recognized the opening chant.

13. This observation was made by Kevin Delgado, an ethnomusicologist and specialist in Afro-Cuban religious music, after he viewed "Canto a Elegua" on videotape.

14. The Havana Cubans Orchestra was led by Benetín "Benny" Bustillo, who had previously worked in Arsenio Rodríguez' *conjunto* in Cuba. Bustillo was an Afro-Cuban trumpeter from Guines, Cuba. It is possible that El Niño was also originally from Guines (some Peruvians say he was born in Guinea, Africa). David García helped me piece together this information based on his interview with Arsenio Rodríguez' brother Raúl.

15. I do not know whether El Niño actually was a practitioner of Santería.

16. In 1980, civilian elections marked the end of the military revolution, ironically, exactly at the beginning of the terrorist anti-government campaign of the Maoist guerilla group Sendero Luminoso (Shining Path).

17. "Golden age" is my term, not Lalo's.

18. In 2000, Perú Negro revived Perú Negrito, and the new junior company included the children of Rony Campos and other adult Perú Negro members.

19. Two or three soles was the equivalent of about seventy-five cents in 2000.

Chapter 5 (pp. 171–214)

1. I had a similar experience the previous week, when I attended the annual Festival of Black Arts in the nearby town of Cañete, another famous rural "cradle of Black music." I arrived in town on the first day of the festival, only to learn that the music was scheduled for the following weekend. On the day of the concert, I made the mistake of arriving at the amphitheater right on time (8:00 PM). I waited in the half-empty outdoor amphitheater for three hours. Finally, around 11:00 PM, technicians began to set up the stage and test the sound system. An old man played cajón in the back of the amphitheater. I watched as a drum-set, congas, and several amps were brought on stage, and I began to wonder, heart sinking, what type of music would be performed. The sound system was a typical Peruvian one, and it took two hours for acceptable functionality to be reached. Finally, around 1:00 AM, a teenage band took the stage. The guitarist hit a chord, and the band launched into "The Year of the Cat" by Al Stewart (1976). Feeling foolish, tired, and frustrated, I walked out of the theater, casting a wistful glance at the old man still playing cajón in the stands. I later learned that the only Afro-Peruvian music in the Cañete Festival of Black Arts was scheduled for the final weekend, when, ironically, a number of Afro-Peruvian artists would be brought from Lima to perform in this typically famous rural town.

2. Although anthropologists typically consider themselves to be at work where tourists are at play, some acknowledge that their actual behavior is often similar to that of tourists (see Bruner 1995; Bruner and Kirshenblatt-Gimblett 1994; Clifford 1997a; Crick 1985; Errington and Gewertz 1989; Kirshenblatt-Gimblett 1998; Lévi-Strauss [1955] 1977; Pi-Sunyer 1981; Smith [1989b] 1995).

3. Peru is geographically divided into departments, which in turn are separated into provinces. Within each province are districts, which function as independent towns.

4. According to Amador Ballumbrosio, his family name was originally spelled Vallehumbroso.

5. Brown people.

6. At a tourist performance I witnessed in 2000, the Ballumbrosio family earned $7 in tips from approximately thirty-five tourists. To put this in perspective, a three-course meal in a neighborhood restaurant cost approximately 75 cents in 2000.

7. Singling out certain culture brokers as representatives of their entire culture is a common phenomenon in tourism. Edward Bruner and Barbara Kirshenblatt-Gimblett (1994) describe the similar process by which the Maasai who perform for tourists at Mayers Ranch in Kenya have been constructed by the outside world as "the" Maasai because they have agreed to photographs and are thus the subject of most of the postcards and other public images of the Maasai people.

8. According to Adelina Ballumbrosio, the word huanchigualo refers to a doll that was at one time used in the dance.

9. According to Tompkins, Ño Carnavalón was an anthropomorphic image of the patron of Carnival. The figure was paraded around town and followed by "mourners" and a sobbing "widow," who collected money to help with the "burial" expenses (this money supported the Carnival festivities), and a "notary public," who read a fake will and testament at the "burial." The Ño Carnavalón figure was

thrown into the sea or burned immediately before the yunza (Tompkins 1981, 351–352).

10. My videos of the yunza are held at the UCLA Ethnomusicology Archive and at the Center for Andean Ethnomusicology, the Catholic University of Peru.

11. Chalena Vásquez recorded demonstrations of this music in 1979, and she published transcriptions in her book (R. Vásquez Rodríguez 1982). Vásquez' field recordings were deposited at INIDEF in Caracas, Venezuela, and some are also housed in the Center for Andean Ethnomusicology at the Catholic University of Peru. William Tompkins conducted his research around the same time and also published transcriptions (Tompkins 1981, 560–565). Tompkins' recordings are housed at the British Library Sound Archive, and one song is included on the compact disc that accompanies the *Garland Encyclopedia of World Music* (Tompkins 1998). My videos of the 2000 Christmas festival are held at the UCLA Ethnomusicology Archive and the Center for Andean Ethnomusicology at the Catholic University of Peru.

12. By 2000, according to Amador Ballumbrosio, the hatajo de negritos from El Carmen had abandoned the use of hats because they made them sweat too much (although members of hatajos from neighboring areas that danced in the El Carmen plaza wore them).

13. Chalena Vásquez Rodríguez notes that the prevalence of pentatonicism in the melodies of the repertoire of the hatajos de negritos has been interpreted as indigenous influence. However, Vásquez proposes that the particular five-note scales used in El Carmen more closely resemble church modes than Andean pentatonic scales, and she suggests further comparisons with African pentatonic scales (Vásquez Rodríguez 1982, 164–170).

14. Although many listeners believe that "El condor pasa" is a survival from the music of the Incas, actually Daniel Alomía Robles composed it in 1913 for a *zarzuela* production. Alomía Robles was an urban *indigenista* composer who collected Andean melodies and pieced them together to create new compositions.

15. It is tempting to draw an analogy between Miki González' project with the Ballumbrosios and Paul Simon's career-boosting fusions with artists such as Ladysmith Black Mambazo and Olodum. However, Miki González also formed very close and lasting personal ties with the Ballumbrosio family over an extended period of time.

16. All Spanish sections of "Ritmos negros del Perú" are reprinted from *Décimas* (N. Santa Cruz n.d. [1959?], 19–20) and English translations are adapted from *The Peru Reader* (Starn, Degregori and Kirk, 1995, 290–291).

17. See Deborah Poole's interesting discussion of the eighteenth-century consolidation of race and the body, as expressed by popular images of the criolla tapadas ("White" women who wore a veil that covered their entire bodies except one eye) versus Black, bare-breasted market women (1997, 85–97).

Chapter 6 (pp. 215–258)

1. See Deborah Pacini Hernández' article (1993) about defining world music from the vantage point of Latin America and the Caribbean.

2. Tiahuanaco was a pre-Inca city on what is now the Bolivian side of Lake Titicaca that flourished between the second and sixth centuries AD.

3. The checo was practically unknown in Lima in the 1990s, but a 1970s documentary film by José Durand (1979b) included a brief demonstration of the instrument.

4. The album recorded at Egrem in Cuba was re-released in 2001 by the British label Tumi under the name *Lamento negro*. According to Ricardo Pereira, the British re-release was not authorized by Susana Baca or her management. The new CD features a contemporary photo of Susana Baca and does not reveal the original 1980s recording date.

5. The lack of Peruvian interest in *The Soul of Black Peru* could have resulted in part from lack of marketing. Warner's Peruvian subsidiary El Virrey had entered a financial crisis just before *The Soul of Black Peru* was released. Small Latin American labels like El Virrey had, for many years, functioned as local arms of multinational record labels. In 1994, BMG—one of three international labels represented in Peru by El Virrey—dropped the company and established its own offices in Lima (Sony, Polygram, and other international labels would soon follow suit, effectively destroying several of Lima's major labels). The loss of BMG's accounts considerably diminished El Virrey's marketing capital (Cornejo Guinassi 2000). Although I have seen no actual sales figures, my assessment of U.S. sales is based on a personal communication from record producer Juan Morillo, who has access to industry sales and marketing charts.

6. Because several sources say that Campos met Byrne on his first trip to Peru, it is unlikely that she was totally ignorant of *The Soul of Black Peru* before its release. However, she may not have been aware of the inclusion of her recordings or that her picture would be on the CD cover.

7. Spanish lyrics and English translation are adapted from the liner notes of David Byrne's *The Soul of Black Peru* (Various Artists 1995a).

8. By the late 1990s, Cotito had switched to the typical landó pattern in his accompaniment of "María Landó" during Susana Baca's concert performances.

9. David Byrne, e-mail to the author, November 1, 2003.

10. Clave, a concept normally associated with Cuban music, is a rhythmic time-line pattern that governs the accents of melodies and drum rhythms.

11. The charango is a small guitar-type instrument used to accompany indigenous and mestizo music in Peru and other Andean countries.

12. For example, Susana Baca was interviewed for a Los Angeles Peruvian-American newspaper before one of her local performances. The reporter told her that no one in Los Angeles had ever heard of her and asked how she would develop an audience. Susana Baca had recently performed before a crowd of thousands at the prestigious Hollywood Bowl, a fact of which this reporter—who only frequented events in the Peruvian community—was unaware.

13. Alex Acuña's full name is Alejandro Neciosup Acuña. Like many Latino musicians, Alex anglicized his name when he began his career in the 1960s because producers felt it would be too hard for the American public to pronounce.

14. David Byrne included one song by Eva Ayllón, "Azucar de caña," on *The Soul of Black Peru*.

Conclusion (pp. 259–266)

1. Victoria Santa Cruz, e-mail to the author, July 25, 2003.

2. The Sonora Matancera was a Cuban son orchestra, Panchito Riset was a Cuban-born singer of *boleros* and other genres, and tango is a musical genre from Argentina.

3. See Javier León's dissertation (León Quirós 2003, 306–310) for a discussion of the range of meanings for the term "ancestral memory" as employed by the members of Teatro del Milenio and Victoria Santa Cruz.

References

Acuña, Alex. 1999. Interview with the author. Los Angeles: October 9.

Adorno, Theodor W. [1967] 1995. *Prisms*. 8th printing. Cambridge, MA: The MIT Press.

Aguirre, Carlos. 1993. *Agentes de su propia libertad: Los esclavos de Lima y la desintegración de la esclavitud, 1821–1854*. Lima: Pontificia Universidad Católica del Perú Fondo Editorial.

Aliaga, Francisco, and Elisabeth Aliaga. 1991. *Rhythmes noirs du Pérou: Historique et présentation de musiques et chants enregistrés à Lima–Pérou*. Musical arrangements by Carlos Hayre and Francisco Aliaga. Paris: Lierre & Coudrier Editeur/Wamani.

Almora, Walter. 2000. Interview with the author. Los Angeles: August 4.

Amadiume, Ifi. 1997. *Reinventing Africa: Matriarchy, Religion & Culture*. London and New York: Zed Books Ltd.

Appadurai, Arjun. 1981. "The Past as a Scarce Resource." *Man* 16, no. 2: 201–219.

——. 1991. "Global Ethnoscapes: Notes and Queries for a Transnational Anthropology." In *Recapturing Anthropology: Working in the Present*, ed. Richard G. Fox, 191–210. Santa Fe, NM: School of American Research Press.

——. 1996a. "Disjuncture and Difference in the Global Economy." In *Modernity at Large: Cultural Dimensions of Globalization*, 27–47. Minneapolis: University of Minnesota Press.

——. 1996b. "The Production of Locality." In *Modernity at Large: Cultural Dimensions of Globalization*, 178–200. Minneapolis: University of Minnesota Press.

Appiah, Kwame Anthony. 1992. *In My Father's House: Africa in the Philosophy of Culture*. New York: Oxford University Press.

——. 1998. "Cosmopolitan Patriots." In *Cosmopolitics: Thinking and Feeling Beyond the Nation*, ed. Pheng Cheah and Bruce Robbins, 91–114. Minneapolis: University of Minnesota Press.

Arguedas, Roberto. 2000. Interview with the author. Lima: March 25.

Asante, Molefi Kete. 1988. *Afrocentricity*. New rev. ed. Trenton, NJ: Africa World Press.

Assman, Jan. 1995. "Collective Memory and Cultural Identity." *New German Critique* 65:125–133.

Aviles, Óscar, Lucila Campos, and Arturo "Zambo" Cavero. n.d. *Y . . . siguen festejando juntos*. IEMPSA. Compact disc. IEM 0003.

Baca, Susana. 1997a. *Susana Baca*. Luaka Bop/Warner Bros. Compact disc. 9-46627-2.

——. 2000a. *Eco de sombras*. Luaka Bop. Compact disc. 72438-48912-2-0.

——. 2000b. Interview with the author. Lima: March 28.

Baca, Susana, Francisco Basili, and Ricardo Peirera. 1992. *Del fuego y del agua: El aporte del negro a la formación de la música popular peruana*. Editora Pregón S.R.L. (booklet) and Tonga Productions (compact disc). TNGCD 9301.

———. 1997. *Del Fuego y del Agua*: *Black Contribution to the Formation of Peruvian Popular Music*. English translation edition. Tonga Productions. Compact disc and booklet. TNGCD 9301.

Bal, Mieke, Jonathan Crewe, and Leo Spitzer, eds. 1999. *Acts of Memory: Cultural Recall in the Present*. Hanover, NH: University Press of New England.

Balazs. n.d. *Susana Baca Bulletin Board Entry*. Luaka Bop Web site [accessed 2001]: http://www.luakabop.com/susana_baca/bin/bb.cgi.

Ballumbrosio, Camilo. 2000. Interview with the author. Lima: March 16.

Ballumbrosio, Eusebio. 2000. "Mira el negro cómo está en el campo: los Ballumbrosios." In *Lo africano en la cultura criolla*, 169–176. Lima: Fondo Editorial del Congreso del Perú.

Baudrillard, Jean. 1994. *Simulacra and Simulation*. Trans. Sheila Faria Glaser. Ann Arbor: University of Michigan Press.

Beckford, Ruth. 1979. *Katherine Dunham: A Biography*. New York and Basel: Marcel Dekker, Inc.

Behar, Ruth. 1993. *Translated Woman: Crossing the Border with Esperanza's Story*. Boston: Beacon Press.

———. 1996. *The Vulnerable Observer: Anthropology that Breaks Your Heart*. Boston: Beacon Press.

Beier, Ulli, ed. 1967. *Introduction to African Literature: An Anthology of Critical Writing from "Black Orpheus."* Evanston, IL: Northwestern University Press.

Bernal, Martin. 1987– . *Black Athena: The Afroasiatic Roots of Classical Civilization*, vols. 1–4. London: Free Association Press.

Bigenho, Michelle. 1998. "El baile de los *negritos* y la danza de las tijeras: Un manejo de contradicciones." In *Música, danzas y máscaras en los Andes*, ed. Raúl R. Romero, 219–252. 2nd ed. Lima: Pontificia Universidad Católica del Perú and Instituto Riva-Agüero.

Blanchard, Peter. 1992. *Slavery & Abolition in Early Republican Peru*. Wilmington, DE: SR Books.

Bolaños, César. 1995. *La música nacional en los medios de comunicación electrónicos de Lima metropolitana*. Lima: Facultad de Ciencias de la Comunicación, Universidad de Lima, Cicosul.

Bowser, Frederick P. 1974. *The African Slave in Colonial Peru, 1524–1650*. Stanford, CA: Stanford University Press.

Boyarin, Daniel, and Jonathan Boyarin. 1993. "Diaspora: Generation and the Ground of Jewish Identity." *Critical Inquiry* 19, no. 4: 693–725.

Bracamonte-Bontemps, Laura. 1987. Dance in Social Context: The Peruvian Vals. MA thesis, University of California, Los Angeles.

Brandis, Paul. n.d. [199?]. *Susana Baca Bulletin Board Entry*. Luaka Bop Web site [accessed 2001]: http://www.luakabop.com/susana_baca/bin/bb.cgi.

Brandon, George. [1993] 1997. *Santería from Africa to the New World: The Dead Sell Memories*. 1st paperback ed. Bloomington and Indianapolis: Indiana University Press.

Browning, Barbara. 1998. *Infectious Rhythm: Metaphors of Contagion and the Spread of African Culture*. New York and London: Routledge.

Bruner, Edward M. 1995. "The Ethnographer/Tourist in Indonesia." In *International Tourism: Identity and Change*, ed. Marie-Françoise Lanfant, John B. Allcock, and Edward M. Bruner, 224–241. London and Thousand Oaks, CA: Sage Publications.

———. 1996. "Tourism in the Balinese Borderzone." In *Displacement, Diaspora, and Geographies of Identity*, ed. Smadar Lavie and Ted Swedenburg, 157–179. Durham and London: Duke University Press.

Bruner, Edward M., and Barbara Kirshenblatt-Gimblett. 1994. "Maasai on the Lawn: Tourist Realism in East Africa." *Cultural Anthropology* 9, no. 2: 435–470.

Bush, Roland E. 1985. "Cuba's Nicolás Guillén as Poet of Negritude." *Afro-Hispanic Review* 4:5–10.

Butler, Kim D. 2001a. "Africa in the Reinvention of Nineteenth-Century Afro-Bahian Identity." In *Rethinking the African Diaspora: The Making of a Black Atlantic World in the Bight of Benin and Brazil*, ed. Kristin Mann and Edna G. Bay, 135–154. London and Portland, OR: Frank Cass.

———. 2001b. "Defining Diaspora, Refining a Discourse." *Diaspora* 10, no. 2: 189–219.

Byrne, David. 1999. "I Hate World Music." *New York Times*, Arts & Leisure, October 3, 1 and 36.

Cachay, Raúl. 1998. "Una leyenda en concierto." *La República*, March 29, 16–17.

Calvo, César. n.d. [1970s] a. "La tierra se hizo nuestra." Program from a theatrical performance. Lima.

———. n.d. [1970s] b. "Navidad negra." Program from a theatrical performance. Lima.

———. 1981. *Las tres mitades de Ino Moxo y otros brujos de la Amazonía*. 5th ed. Iquitos, Peru: Proceso Editores.

Campos, Lucila, con el conjunto de Chocolate y su Elegguá. n.d. [1970s?]. *Ritmo negro*. El Virrey Industrias Musicales S.A. LP. VIR 951.

Campos, Rony. 2000. Interview with the author. Lima: March 16.

Cánepa Koch, Gisela. 1998a. "Los *ch'unchu* y los *palla* de Cajamarca en el ciclo de la representación de la muerte del Inca." In *Música, danzas y máscaras en los Andes*, ed. Raúl R. Romero, 139–178. 2nd ed. Lima: Pontificia Universidad Católica del Perú and Instituto Riva-Agüero.

———. 1998b. *Máscara: Transformación e identidad en los Andes*. Lima: Pontificia Universidad Católica del Perú Fondo Editorial.

Carneiro, Edison. 1961. *Samba de umbigada*. Rio de Janeiro: Ministerio da Educaçao e Cultura Campanha de Defesa do Folclore Brasileiro.

Carvalho, Martha de Ulhôa. 1995. "Tupi or Not Tupi MPB: Popular Music and Identity in Brazil." In *The Brazilian Puzzle: Culture on the Borderlands of the Western World*, ed. David J. Hess and Roberto A. DaMatta, 159–175. New York: Columbia University Press.

Casaverde, Félix. 2000a. Interview with the author. Lima: February 23.

———. 2000b. Interview and musical demonstration with the author. Lima. March 24.

Cascudo, Luís da Câmara. 1954. *Dicionário do folclore brasileiro*. Rio de Janeiro: Instituto Nacional do Livro.

Castañeda, Quetzil E. 1996. *In the Museum of Maya Culture: Touring Chichén Itzá*. Minneapolis: University of Minnesota Press.

CEMDUC (Centro de Música y Danza de la Pontificia Universidad Católica del Perú). 1999. *Y dice así* (Lyric booklet). Lima: CEMDUC. Photocopy.

———. 2000. *Achirana*. Pontificia Universidad Católica del Perú. Compact disc.

Chaliand, Gérard, and Jean-Pierre Rageau. 1995. *The Penguin Atlas of Diasporas*. Trans. A. M. Berrett. New York: Viking.

Chang, Iris. 1997. *The Rape of Nanking: The Forgotten Holocaust of World War II*. New York: Penguin Books.

Cheah, Pheng. 1998. "Introduction Part II: The Cosmopolitical—Today." In *Cosmopolitics: Thinking And Feeling Beyond the Nation*, ed. Pheng Cheah and Bruce Robbins, 20–41. Minneapolis: University of Minnesota Press.

Cheah, Pheng, and Bruce Robbins, eds. 1998. *Cosmopolitics: Thinking And Feeling Beyond the Nation*. Minneapolis: University of Minnesota Press.

Chivallon, Christine. 2002. "Beyond Gilroy's Black Atlantic: The Experience of the African Diaspora." Trans. Karen E. Fields. *Diaspora* 11, no. 3: 359–382.

Clark, Vévé. 1994. "Performing the Memory of Difference in Afro-Caribbean Dance: Katherine Dunham's Choreography, 1938–1987." In *History and Memory in African American Culture*, ed. Geneviève Fabre and Robert O'Meally, 188–204. New York: Oxford University Press.

Clifford, James. 1986. "Introduction: Partial Truths." In *Writing Culture: The Poetics and Politics of Ethnography*, ed. James Clifford and George E. Marcus, 1–26. Berkeley: University of California Press.

———. 1988a. "On Collecting Art and Culture." In *The Predicament of Culture: Twentieth-Century Ethnography, Literature, and Art*, 215–252. Cambridge and London: Harvard University Press.

———.1988b. "A Politics of Neologism: Aimé Césaire." In *The Predicament of Culture: Twentieth-Century Ethnography, Literature, and Art*, 175–181. Cambridge and London: Harvard University Press.

———. 1988c. *The Predicament of Culture: Twentieth-Century Ethnography, Literature, and Art*. Cambridge and London: Harvard University Press.

———. 1994. "Diasporas." *Cultural Anthropology* 9, no. 3: 302–338.

———. 1997a. *Routes: Travel and Translation in the Late Twentieth Century*. Cambridge and London: Harvard University Press.

———. 1997b. "Traveling Cultures." In *Routes: Travel and Translation in the Late Twentieth Century*, 17–46. Cambridge and London: Harvard University Press.

———. 1998. "Mixed Feelings." In *Cosmopolitics: Thinking And Feeling Beyond the Nation*, ed. Pheng Cheah and Bruce Robbins, 362–370. Minneapolis: University of Minnesota Press.

Cohen, Erik. 1988. "Authenticity and Commoditization in Tourism." *Annals of Tourism Research* 15:371–386.

Cole, Jennifer. 2001. *Forget Colonialism? Sacrifice and the Art of Memory in Madagascar*. Berkeley: University of California Press.

Connerton, Paul. 1989. *How Societies Remember*. New York and Cambridge: Cambridge University Press.

Cooper Alarcón, Daniel. 1997. "If a Tree Falls: Tourism and Mexicanness." In *The Aztec Palimpsest: Mexico in the Modern Imagination*, 151–187. Tucson: University of Arizona Press.

Cornejo Guinassi, Pedro. 1998. "Sonidos para mayores." *Somos*, n.d., 50–52.

———. 2000. Interview with the author. Lima: February 8.

Cortest, Luis, ed. 1993. *Homenaje a José Durand*. Madrid: Editorial Verbum.

Crick, Malcolm. 1985. "'Tracing' the Anthropological Self: Quizzical Reflections on Fieldwork, Tourism, and the Ludic." *Social Analysis* 17:71–92.

———. 1989. "Representations of International Tourism in the Social Sciences: Sun, Sex, Sights, Savings, and Servility." *Annual Review of Anthropology* 18:307–344.

Crook, Larry N. 1993. "Black Consciousness, Samba Reggae, and the Re-Africanization of Bahian Carnival Music in Brazil." *The World of Music* 35, no. 2: 90–108.

Cuche, Denys. 1975. *Poder blanco y resistencia negra en el Perú*. Lima: Instituto Nacional de Cultura.

———. 1976. "La mort des dieux africains et les religions noires au Pérou." *Archive de Sciences Sociales des Religions* 43, no. 1: 77–91.

Curtin, Philip D. 1969. *The Atlantic Slave Trade: A Census*. Madison: University of Wisconsin Press.

Daniel, Yvonne Payne. 1996. "Tourism Dance Performances: Authenticity and Creativity." *Annals of Tourism Research* 23, no. 4: 780–797.

Dash, Michael. 1974. "Marvellous Realism: The Way Out of Négritude." *Caribbean Studies* 13, no. 4: 57–70.

De la Cadena, Marisol. 1998. "Silent Racism and Intellectual Superiority in Peru." *Bulletin of Latin American Research* 17, no. 2: 143–164.

Del Busto Duthurburu, José Antiono, Juan Luis Orrego Penagos, Sandro Patrucco Núñez-Carvallo, et al. 1995. *Guía turística del departamento de Ica.* Lima: Pontificia Universidad Católica del Perú.

Del Rio, Silvia. 2000. Interview with the author. Lima: March 15.

Desmond, Jane C. 1999. *Staging Tourism: Bodies on Display from Waikiki to Sea World.* Chicago: The University of Chicago Press.

Diez Canseco, José. 1938. *Estampas mulatas.* Santiago, Chile: Empresa Editora Zig-zag.

Diop, Cheikh Anta. 1986. *Precolonial Black Africa: A Comparative Study of the Political and Social Systems of Europe and Black Africa, From Antiquity to the Formation of Modern States.* Trans. Harold J. Salemson. Westport, CT: Lawrence Hill & Co.

Dobyns, Henry F., and Paul L. Doughty. 1976. *Peru: A Cultural History.* New York: Oxford University Press.

Du Bois, W. E. B. [1903] 1994. *The Souls of Black Folk.* Chicago: A. C. McClurg & Co. Repr. New York: Dover Publications, Inc.

Dunham, Katherine. 1969. *Island Possessed.* Garden City, NY: Doubleday.

Dunham, Katherine, y su Compañia de Bailarines, Cantores y Músicos. 1951. Program from dance performance. Lima: Produced by La Organización Artística Renato Salvati, Teatro Municipal.

Dunn, Christopher. 1992. "Afro-Bahian Carnival: A Stage for Protest." *Afro-Hispanic Review* XI, nos. 1–3: 11–20.

Durand Allison, Guillermo. 1999. "Cuatro expresiones negras: Agua'e nieve, cumanana, samba landó e ingá." *Cuadernos Arguedianos* 2, no. 2: 25–38.

Durand (Flórez), José. 1961. "Del fandango a la marinera." *Fanal* 16, no. 59: 10–15.

———. 1971. "De la zamacueca a la marinera." *Mensajes* 15:23–27.

———. 1973. "La resbalosa limeña." *Mensajes* 19:8–14.

———. 1979a. "Décimas peruanas de la Guerra del Pacífico." *Revista de la Universidad Católica* 6 (December 30): 79–106.

———. 1979b. *El señor de la jarana.* Lima: Channel 5. Videocassette recording of television documentary.

———. 1980. *El festejo de Belén.* Lima: Channel 5. Videocassette recording of television documentary.

———. 1988. "El desafio de la marinera." In *Signo e imagen: La marinera*, ed. Willy F. Pinto Gamboa, 52–54. Lima: Banco de Crédito del Perú.

———. 1995. "Ventana al secreto de nuestras canciones." In *De cajón Caitro Soto: El duende en la música afroperuana*, ed. Bernardo Roca Rey Miró Quesada, 31–36. Lima: Servicios Especiales de Edición S.A. del Grupo Empresa Editora El Comercio.

Durand, René L. F., ed. 1978. *Négritude et Amérique Latine, Colloque de Dakar: 7–12 janvier 1974.* Dakar-Abidjan, Senegal: Les Nouvelles Éditions Africaines.

Ebron, Paulla A. 1998. "Enchanted Memories of Regional Difference in African American Culture." *American Anthropologist* 100, no. 1: 94–105.

Eco, Umberto. 1986. *Travels in Hyperreality: Essays.* Trans. William Weaver. English trans. ed. San Diego, New York, and London: Harcourt Brace & Company.

Enrique Gibson, Percy. 1969. "Cuando la tribu entró en trance." *Caretas* (November): 34–37.

Errington, F., and D. Gewertz. 1989. "Tourism and Anthropology in a Post-Modern World." *Oceania* 60, no. 1: 37–54.

Estenssoro Fuchs, Juan Carlos. 1988. "Música y comportamiento festivo de la población negra en Lima colonial." *Cuadernos Hispanoamericanos* 451–452:161–168.

Fabre, Geneviève, and Robert O'Meally, eds. 1994. *History & Memory in African-American Culture*. New York: Oxford University Press.

Fanon, Frantz. 1966. *The Wretched of the Earth*. Trans. Constance Farrington. New York: Grove Press.

Fatunmbi, Awo Fa'lokun. n.d. *Elegba: Ifa and the Divine Messenger*. Plainview, NY: Original Publications.

Feifer, Maxine. 1986. *Tourism in History: From Imperial Rome to the Present*. New York: Stein and Day.

Feldman, Heidi Carolyn. 2001. Black Rhythms of Peru: Staging Cultural Memory Through Music and Dance, 1956–2000. PhD diss., University of California, Los Angeles.

———. 2005. "The Black Pacific: Cuban and Brazilian Echoes in the Afro-Peruvian Revival." *Ethnomusicology* 49, no. 2: 206–231.

———. Forthcoming. "Nicomedes Santa Cruz' *Cumanana*: A Musical Excavation of Black Peru." In *Escribir la Identidad: Creación Cultural y Negritud en el Perú*, ed. M'Bare N'gom. Lima: Editorial de la Universidad Ricardo Palma.

Fell, Eve Marie. 1987. "Du folklore rural au folklore commercial: Une expérience dirigiste au Pérou." *Caravelle* 48:59–68.

Fields, Karen. 1994. "What One Cannot Remember Mistakenly." In *History & Memory in African-American Culture*, ed. Geneviève Fabre and Robert O'Meally, 150–163. New York and Oxford: Oxford University Press.

Floyd, Samuel A., Jr. 1995. *The Power of Black Music: Interpreting Its History From Africa to the United States*. New York and Oxford: Oxford University Press.

Foucault, Michel. 1977. *Language, Counter-Memory, Practice: Selected Essays and Interviews*. Trans. Donald F. Bouchard and Sherry Simon. Ithaca, NY: Cornell University Press.

Fuentes, Manuel Atanasio. [1867] 1925. *Lima: Apuntes históricos, descriptivos, estadísticos y de costumbres*. Paris: F. Didot, Frères, Fils & Cie. Repr. Lima: E. Moreno.

Fuenzalida Vollmar, Fernando, and Enrique Mayer. 1974. *El Perú de las tres razas*. New York: Instituto de las Naciones Unidas para Formación Profesional e Investigaciones.

Gamboa, Gino. 1999. Interview and *cajón* lesson with the author. Culver City, CA: November 2.

García Canclini, Néstor. 1995. *Hybrid Cultures: Strategies for Entering and Leaving Modernity*. Trans. Christopher L. Chiappari and Silvia L. López. Minneapolis: University of Minnesota Press.

———. 1997. *Transforming Modernity: Popular Culture in Mexico*. Trans. Lidia Lozano. 2nd paperback printing. Austin: University of Texas Press.

Geertz, Clifford. 1973. "Thick Description: Toward an Interpretive Theory of Culture." In *The Interpretation of Cultures*, 3–30. New York: Basic Books.

Gente Morena de Pancho Fierro. 1964. Concert at Casa de Cultura, Lima. Centro de Etnomusicología Andina, Pontificia Universidad Católica del Perú, cassette recording, Josafat Roel Pineda Collection, C86/23/151.

Gilroy, Paul. 1993. *The Black Atlantic: Modernity and Double Consciousness*. Cambridge, MA: Harvard University Press.

———. 2000. *Against Race: Imagining Political Culture beyond the Color Line*. Cambridge, MA: The Belknap Press of Harvard University Press.

Glave, Luis Miguel. 1995. "Orígen de la cultura afroperuana." In *De cajón Caitro Soto: El duende en la música afroperuana*, ed. Bernardo Roca Rey Miró Quesada et al., 13–29. Lima: Servicios Especiales de Edición S.A. del Grupo Empresa Editora El Comercio.

Goffman, Erving. 1959. *The Presentation of Self in Everyday Life*. Garden City, NY: Doubleday.

———. 1974. *Frame Analysis: An Essay on the Organization of Experience*. New York: Harper & Row.

González, Miki. 1993. *Akundún*. Polygram Discos S.A./Polydor. Compact disc. 314 519 539-2.

———. 2000. Interview with the author. Lima: February 23.

González, Miki, César Calvo, and Andres Soto. 1979. *Es Amador*. Lima. Video-recording of unpublished short film.

Graburn, Nelson H. H., ed. 1976. *Ethnic and Tourist Arts: Cultural Expressions from the Fourth World*. Berkeley: University of California Press.

Graham, Martha. 1991. *Blood Memory: An Autobiography*. New York: Doubleday.

Grupo Afrocuba de Matanzas. 1993. *Rituales afrocubanos*. EGREM. Compact disc. CD 0058.

Hagedorn, Katherine Johanna. 1995. Anatomia del Proceso Folklorico: The "Folkloricization" of Afro-Cuban Religious Performance in Cuba. PhD diss., Brown University.

———. 2001. *Divine Utterances: The Performance of Afro-Cuban Santería*. Washington and London: Smithsonian Institution Press.

Halbwachs, Maurice. [1950] 1992. *On Collective Memory*. Trans. Lewis A. Coser, ed. D. N. Levine. Paris: Presses universitaires de France. Repr. Chicago: The University of Chicago Press.

Hall, Stuart. 1989. "Cultural Identity and Cinematic Representation." *Framework* 36:68–82.

———. 1990. "Cultural Identity and Diaspora." In *Identity: Community, Culture, Difference*, ed. Jonathan Rutherford, 222–237. London: Lawrence & Wishart.

Handy, Otis. 1979. The Spanish American *Décima* and Nicomedes Santa Cruz. PhD diss., University of California, Berkeley.

Hannerz, Ulf. 1992. *Cultural Complexity: Studies in the Social Organization of Meaning*. New York: Columbia University Press.

———. 1996. "Cosmopolitans and Locals in World Culture." In *Transnational Connections: Culture, People, Places*, 102–111. London and New York: Routledge.

Harth-Terré, Emilio. 1971. *Presencia del negro en el virreinato del Perú*. Lima: Editorial Universitaria.

Herskovits, Melville J. 1941. *The Myth of the Negro Past*. New York: Beacon.

Hobsbawm, Eric. 1983. "Introduction: Inventing Traditions." In *The Invention of Tradition*, ed. Eric Hobsbawm and Terence Ranger, 1–14. Cambridge: Cambridge University Press.

Hobsbawm, Eric, and Terence Ranger, eds. 1983. *The Invention of Tradition*. Cambridge: Cambridge University Press.

Hollinger, David A. 1995. *Postethnic America: Beyond Multiculturalism*. New York: Basic Books.

Howell, John. 1992. *David Byrne*. New York: Thunder's Mouth Press.

Hünefeldt, Christine. 1994. *Paying the Price of Freedom: Family and Labor Among Lima's Slaves, 1800–1854*. Berkeley: University of California Press.

Izquierdo, Lalo. 1999. *El festejo* (Instructional handout). Lima: Escuela Nacional Superior de Folklore "José María Arguedas." Photocopy.

———. 2000. Interview with the author. Los Angeles: August 18.

———. n.d. *El cajón* (Instructional handout). Lima: Escuela Nacional Superior de Folklore "José María Arguedas." Photocopy.

Jackson, Richard L. 1976. *The Black Image in Latin American Literature*. Albuquerque: University of New Mexico Press.

——. 1979. *Black Writers in Latin America*. Albuquerque: University of New Mexico Press.

——. 1984. "The *Afrocriollo* Movement Revisited." *Afro-Hispanic Review* III, no. 1: 5–9.

Jahn, Janheinz. 1961. *Muntu: An Outline of the Neo-African Culture*. Trans. Marjorie Grene. London: Faber and Faber Limited.

Jiménez Borja, Arturo. 1939. "Danzas de Lima." *Turismo* 135:n.p.

Jones, Bill T., with Peggy Gillespie. 1995. *Last Night on Earth*. New York: Pantheon Books.

Jones, Edward A., ed. 1971. *Voices of Negritude: The Expression of Black Experience in the Poetry of Senghor, Césaire and Damas*. Valley Forge, PA: Judson Press.

Jones, LeRoi. 1963. *Blues People: The Negro Experience in White America and the Music that Developed From It*. New York: William Morrow and Company.

Kattar, Jeannette. 1977. "Nicomedes Santa Cruz, poète noir du Pérou." *Annales de la Faculté des Lettres et Sciences Humaines, Université de Dakar* 7:185–205.

Kirshenblatt-Gimblett, Barbara. 1998. *Destination Culture: Tourism, Museums, and Heritage*. Berkeley: University of California Press.

Kisselgoff, Anna. 1975. "Peruvians Bow Here in Dances." *New York Times*, April 11.

Kubayanda, Josaphat Bekunuru. 1982. "The Drum Poetics of Nicolás Guillén and Aimé Césaire." *Prismal/Cabral* 7–8:37–55.

Landaluze, Victor Patricio. 1881. *Tipos y costumbres de la isla de Cuba*. Havana: Miguel de Villa.

Lazo, Javier. 2000. Interview with the author. Lima: March 10.

Lee, Leslie. 2000. Interview with the author. Lima: March 27.

León Quirós, Javier Francisco. 1997. El que no tiene de inga, tiene de mandinga: Negotiating Tradition and Ethnicity in Peruvian Criollo Popular Music. MA thesis, The University of Texas at Austin.

——. 1998. "Que Viva Chincha: The Reconstruction of an Afro-Peruvian Past." Paper presented at the annual meeting of the Society for Ethnomusicology, Bloomington, Indiana.

——. 2003. The Aestheticization of Tradition: Professional Afroperuvian Musicians, Cultural Reclamation, and Artistic Interpretation. PhD diss., The University of Texas at Austin.

Levano, Cesar. 1965. "El prohibido panalivio del negro peruano." *Caretas* (March 19–31): 30–33.

Lévi-Strauss, Claude. [1955] 1977. *Tristes tropiques*. Trans. John and Doreen Weightman. Paris: Plon. Repr. New York: Pocket Books.

Lewis, Marvin A. 1983. *Afro-Hispanic Poetry 1940–1980: From Slavery to "Negritud" in South American Verse*. Columbia: University of Missouri Press.

Lhamon, W. T., Jr. 1998. *Raising Cain: Blackface Performance From Jim Crow to Hip Hop*. Cambridge, MA: Harvard University Press.

Linares, Santiago Coco. 2000. Interview with the author. Lima: March 18.

Lipsitz, George. 1994. *Dangerous Crossroads: Popular Music, Postmodernism and the Poetics of Place*. London and New York: Verso.

——. 1995. Review of *The Black Atlantic: Modernity and Double Consciousness*, by Paul Gilroy. *Social Identities* 1, no. 1:193–200.

Lloréns Amico, José Antonio. 1983. *Música popular en Lima: criollos y andinos*. Lima: Instituto de Estudios Peruanos e Instituto Indigenista Interamericano.

Lockhart, James. [1968] 1994. *Spanish Peru, 1532–1560: A Social History*. 2nd ed. Madison: The University of Wisconsin Press.

López Albújar, Enrique. [1928] 1991. *Matalaché*. 15th ed. Lima: PEISA.

Lott, Eric. 1993. *Love and Theft: Blackface Minstrelsy and the American Working Class*. New York and Oxford: Oxford University Press.

Lott, Lee T. 1995. Review of *The Black Atlantic: Modernity and Double Consciousness*, by Paul Gilroy. *Social Identities* 1, no. 1:200–220.

Lowenthal, David. 1985. *The Past is a Foreign Country*. Cambridge and New York: Cambridge University Press.

Luciano, José, and Humberto Rodriguez Pastor. 1995. "Peru." Trans. Meagan Smith. In *No Longer Invisible: Afro-Latin Americans Today*, ed. Minority Rights Group, 271–286. London: Minority Rights Publications.

MacCannell, Dean. [1976] 1989. *The Tourist: A New Theory of the Leisure Class*. 2nd rev. ed. New York: Schocken Books.

——. 1992. *Empty Meeting Grounds: The Tourist Papers*. London and New York: Routledge.

Mac-Lean y Estenós, Roberto. 1947. *Negros en el Perú*. Lima: n.p.

——. 1948. *Negros en el nuevo mundo*. Lima: Editorial P.T.C.M.

Malcomson, Scott L. 1998. "The Varieties of Cosmopolitan Experience." In *Cosmopolitics: Thinking and Feeling beyond the Nation*, ed. Pheng Cheah and Bruce Robbins, 233–245. Minneapolis: University of Minnesota Press.

Marcus, George. 1995. "Ethnography in/of the World System: The Emergence of Multi-Sited Ethnography." *Annual Review of Anthropology* 24:95–117.

Mariátegui, José Carlos. 1971. *Seven Interpretive Essays on Peruvian Reality*. Trans. Marjory Urquidi. Austin: University of Texas Press.

Mariñez, Pablo A. 1992. "Adiós al poeta afroperuano Nicomedes Santa Cruz." *América Negra* 4:261–265.

——. 1993. "Entrevista con Nicomedes Santa Cruz, poeta afroamericano." *Cuadernos Americanos* 4, no. 40: 110–124.

——. 2000. *Nicomedes Santa Cruz: Decimista, poeta, y folklorista afroperuano*. Mexico: Instituto de Cultura de San Luis Potosí.

Martínez, Gregorio. 1995. "Black Peru." Trans. Fortuna Calvo-Roth. In *Africa's Legacy: Photographs in Brazil and Peru* (Lorry Salcedo-Mitrani). New York: Caribbean Cultural Center.

Martínez, Gregorio, and Fietta Jarque. 1995. *Afro-Peruvian Classics: The Soul of Black Peru* (CD Liner Notes). New York: Luaka Bop/Warner Bros.

Martínez, Mabela. 2000. Interview with the author. Lima: January 24.

Mason, John. 1992. *Orin Òrìsà: Songs For Selected Heads*. New York: Yorùbá Theological Archministry.

Matory, J. Lorand. 1999. "The English Professors of Brazil: On the Diasporic Roots of the Yorùbá Nation." *Comparative Studies in Society and History* 41, no. 1: 72–103.

Medrano Cotito, Juan. 2000. Interview with the author. Lima: February 29.

Méndez G., Cecilia. 1996. "Incas Sí, Indios No: Notes on Peruvian Creole Nationalism and its Contemporary Crisis." *Journal of Latin American Studies* 28, no. 1: 197–225.

Mendoza, Raúl. 2005. "Negros siguen siendo ignorados." *La República*, August 1.

Mendoza Hernández, Teresa. 2000. Interviews with the author. Lima: March 14 and October 24.

Mendoza, Zoila S. 1998. "Defining Folklore: Mestizo and Indigenous Identities on the Move." *Bulletin of Latin American Research* 17, no. 2: 165–183.

——. 2000. *Shaping Society Through Dance: Mestizo Ritual Performance in the Peruvian Andes*. Chicago: The University of Chicago Press.

Millones, Luis. 1985. "Turgurio, the Culture of Peruvian Marginal Population: A Study of a Lima Slum." In *Peruvian Contexts of Change*, ed. William W. Stein, 56–123. New Brunswick, NJ: Transaction Books.

———. 2000. Interview with the author. Lima: March 21.

Minority Rights Group, ed. 1995. *No Longer Invisible: Afro-Latin Americans Today*. London: Minority Rights Publications.

Mintz, Sidney W., and Richard Price. [1976] 1992. *The Birth of African American Culture: An Anthropological Perspective*. Repr. with a new preface. Boston: Beacon Press.

Misztal, Barbara. 2003. *Theories of Social Remembering*. Maidenhead, England and Philadelphia: Open University Press.

Monguió, Luis, and Alicia de Colombí-Monguió. 1993. "José Durand (1925–1990)." In *Homenaje a José Durand*, ed. Luis Cortest, 11–15. Madrid: Editorial Verbum.

Moore, Robin. 1997. *Nationalizing Blackness: Afrocubanismo and Artistic Revolution in Havana, 1920–1940*. Pittsburgh, PA: University of Pittsburgh Press.

Moreno Fraginals, Manuel, ed. 1977. *África en América Latina*. Mexico: UNESCO.

Morillo, Juan. 1999. Interview with the author. Los Angeles: August 27.

Morrison, Toni. 1987. *Beloved*. New York: Alfred A. Knopf.

Mujica, Manongo. 1998. Interview with the author. Lima: August.

Muñoz Cabrejo, Fanni. 2000. "The New Order: Diversions and Modernization in Turn-of-the-Century Lima." In *Latin American Popular Culture: An Introduction*, ed. William H. Beezley and Linda A. Curcio-Nagy, 155–168. Wilmington, DE: Scholarly Resources, Inc.

N.a. 1956a. "Ballet negro 'Pancho Fierro' será repuesto el 30 de julio." *La Prensa*, July 25, 8.

N.a. 1956b. "Cantará en el Municipal vals suyo Chabuca Granda." *La Crónica*, June 4, 12.

N.a. 1956c. "Con las exitosas presentaciones de las Cías., 'Pancho Fierro' y 'Estampas de mi Tierra' vislúmbrase el triunfo del folklore." *La Crónica*, June 8, 23.

N.a. 1956d. "Hoy reopenen 'Pancho Fierro.'" *El Comercio*, July 31, 7.

N.a. 1956e. "Mañana debuta el 'Ballet Negro.'" *La Prensa*, June 6, 6.

N.a. 1956f. "'Pancho Fierro' se despide estrenando el 'Baile Negro.'" *La Prensa*, August 15, 6.

N.a. 1957a. "Diez mil tributaron en Acho homenaje a Chabuca Granda." *La Prensa*, January 18, 6.

N.a. 1957b. "Habrían presentado en Piura un apócrifo 'Pancho Fierro.'" *La Prensa*, January 12, 6.

N.a. 1957c. "'Ritmo Negro del Peru' realizará dos presentaciones antes de viajar a Santiago de Chile y Buenos Aires." *La Crónica*, May 1, 23.

N.a. 1960a. "Exótica brujería negra y estampas del callejón irán al teatro con 'Kumanana.'" *La Crónica*, March 4, 5.

N.a. 1960b. "La compañia de arte negro debutará hoy en La Cabaña." *La Prensa*, March 13.

N.a. 1960c. "Nicomedes Santa Cruz y su conjunto negroide triunfaron ampliamente en debut en La Cabaña." *La Crónica*, March 14, 17.

N.a. 1961a. "Chabuca Granda y 'Limeñisima.'" *Cultura Peruana* XXI (157–158 /July–August).

N.a. 1961b. "En el censo no preguntarán la raza; No hay problema racial en el Perú." *La Prensa*, May 13, 5.

N.a. 1967. "El Niño del bongó." *Suceso* (revista del Correo), October 22, 13.

N.a. 1982. "Victoria Santa Cruz: Adios al Perú." Program from a theatrical performance. Lima: Teatro Municipal.

N.a. 1988. "Lo negroide." In *Documental del Perú: Enciclopedia nacional básica*. Vol. XI (Departamento de Ica), Ed. by Información, Opinión Pública, Publicidad y Encuestas-Editores (Lima). Barcelona, Spain: Ediciones Oceano, S.A.

N.a. 1998a. "El alma negra de David Byrne." *El Sol* (photocopy with unmarked date and page number).

N.a. 1998b. "David Byrne nuevamente en Lima: 'Mi curiosidad musical es un tipo de rebelión'" (photocopy from unidentified newspaper), March 25, C4.

N.a. 1998c. "David Byrne ofrece esta noche concierto." *Gestión*, March 25.

N.a. 1998d. "Gringo alma negra" (photocopy from unidentified newspaper source), 72.

N.a. 1998e. "The Legend of Luaka" (interview with David Byrne and Yale Evelev). Luaka Bop Web site [accessed 2001]: http://www.luakabop.com/label/cmp/main.html.

N.a. 1998f. "Para David Byrne el rock latinoamericano es más interesante." *Expreso*, March 25, 29.

Nájar, Rosario. 1999. "Aproximación cuantitativa a la problemática de los medios de comunicación en el Perú." In *Cultura y globalización*, ed. Carlos Iván Degregori and Gonzalo Portocarrero, 359–384. Lima: Pontificia Universidad Católica del Perú, Universidad del Pacifico, Instituto de Estudios Peruanos.

Los negros hablan sobre los negros. 1988. Lima: TV Cultura and Movimiento Francisco Congo. Videocassette.

"Nicomedes Santa Cruz Gamarra." n.d. Web site [accessed April 20, 2003]: http://es.geocities.com/nicomedessantacruz/.

Nora, Pierre, ed. 1984–1986. *Les Lieux de mémoire*. Paris, France: Gallimard.

———. 1994. "Between Memory and History: *Les Lieux de Mémoire*." In *History & Memory in African-American Culture*, ed. Geneviève Fabre and Robert O'Meally, 284–300. New York: Oxford University Press.

Nuñez, Estuardo. n.d. "La literatura peruana de la negritud." *Hispanoamérica* n.d.: 21–28.

O'Connor, Anne Marie. 1988. "TV Film on Slavery Called Racist Itself." *Miami Herald* International Edition, Sunday, October 9.

Ojeda, Martha. 1997. La proyección de la cultura afroperuana en las obras de Nicomedes Santa Cruz. PhD diss., University of Kentucky.

———. 2003. *Nicomedes Santa Cruz: Ecos de Africa en Perú*. Rochester, NY: Tamesis.

Ortíz, Fernando. [1952] 1996. *Los instrumentos de la música afrocubana*, vol. 1. Repr. La Habana: Publicaciones de la Dirección de Cultura del Ministerio de Educación.

Ossorio, José. 1967. "Encuentro de la canción protesta: Crónica." *Casa de las Américas* 8, no. 45: 139–145.

Pacini Hernandez, Deborah. 1993. "A View from the South: Spanish Caribbean Perspectives on World Beat." *The World of Music* 35, no. 2: 48–69.

———. 1998. "Dancing with the Enemy: Cuban Popular Music, Race, Authenticity, and the World-Music Landscape." *Latin American Perspectives* 25, no. 3: 110–125.

Padilla, Victor "Raul." 1999. Interview with the author. Reston, VA: September 19.

Palma, Angelica. 1935. *Pancho Fierro: acuarelista limeño*. Lima: Sanmarti y Cia.

Palma, Ricardo. [1872–1910] 1957. *Tradiciones peruanas completas*. Madrid: Aguilar.

Parodi, Leonardo "Gigio." 2000. Interview with the author. Lima: January 26.

Pereira, Ricardo. 2000. Interview with the author. Lima: March 2.

Pérez Fernández, Rolando Antonio. 1988. *La binarización de los ritmos ternarios africanos en América Latina*. Havana, Cuba: Casa de las Américas.

Perú Negro. 1974. *Gran premio del festival hispanoamericano de la danza y la canción*. El Virrey. LP. VIR 920.

———. 1979. Unpublished recording of concert broadcast on Venezuelan television, from the personal collection of Lalo Izquierdo. Videocassette.

———. 1993. *Perú Negro Master*. Unpublished recording of Perú Negro's 24th anniversary performance at Lima's Municipal Theater, from the personal collection of Lalo Izquierdo. Videocassette.

———. 2000. *Sangre de un don: Herencia afro peruana*. Times Square Records. Compact disc. TSQD 9013.

———. 2003. *Jolgorio*. Times Square Records. Compact disc. TSQ-CD-9035.

Pi-Sunyer, Oriol. 1981. "Tourism and Anthropology." *Annals of Tourism Research* 8, no. 2: 271–284.

Pinto, David. 2000. Interview with the author. Lima: March 28.

Poniatowska, Elena. 1974. "Habla el peruano Nicomedes Santa Cruz." *Siempre Presencia de México* 1103:39–41, 70.

Poole, Deborah. 1997. *Vision, Race, and Modernity: A Visual Economy of the Andean Image World*. Princeton, NJ: Princeton University Press.

Pratt, Mary Louise. 1992. *Imperial Eyes: Travel Writing and Transculturation*. London and New York: Routledge.

Price, Richard. 1983. *First-Time: The Historical Vision of an Afro-American People*. Baltimore: Johns Hopkins University Press.

———. 1985. "An Absence of Ruins? Seeking Caribbean Historical Consciousness." *Caribbean Review* 14, no. 3: 24–29, 45.

Radano, Ronald. 2003. *Lying up a Nation: Race and Black Music*. Chicago: The University of Chicago Press.

Ratliff, Ben. 2000. "Romance Leavened with Highbrow Folklore (Review)." *New York Times*, August 3, E5.

Remo, Roberto. 1977. "Afroamérica: Las raíces de la unidad." *Cuadernos del Tercer Mundo* 12, no. 2: 96–104.

Revollar, Pilar. 1967. "Victoria Santa Cruz y la danza prohibida." *Ella* 43 (October 28): 6–7.

Ricardo. n. d. [199?]. *Susana Baca Bulletin Board Entry*. Luaka Bop Web site [accessed 2001]: http://www.luakabop.com/susana_baca/bin/bb.cgi.

Ritter, Jonathan Larry. 1998. La Marimba Esmereldeña: Music and Ethnicity on Ecuador's Northern Coast. MA thesis, University of California, Los Angeles.

Robbins, Bruce. 1998. "Introduction Part I: Actually Existing Cosmopolitanism." In *Cosmopolitics: Thinking and Feeling beyond the Nation*, ed. Pheng Cheah and Bruce Robbins, 1–19. Minneapolis: University of Minnesota Press.

Rocca, Luis. 1985. *La otra historia: Memoria colectiva y canto del pueblo de Zaña*. Lima: Instituto de Apoyo Agrario.

Romero, Fernando. 1939a. "Como era la zamacueca zamba." *Turismo* 140:n.p.

———. 1939b. "Instrumentos musicales en la costa zamba." *Turismo* 137 (March):n.p.

———. 1939c. "La zamba, abuela de la marinera." *Turismo* 141:n.p.

———. 1939d. "Ritmo negro en la costa zamba." *Turismo* 135 (January):n.p.

———. 1940. "De la 'samba' de Africa a la 'marinera' del Perú." *Estudios Afrocubanos* IV, nos. 1–4: 82–120.

———. 1946a. "La evolución de 'la marinera'" (Part 1). *IPNA* 6 (May–August): 29–33.

———. 1946b. "La evolución de 'la marinera'" (Part 2). *IPNA* 7 (September–December): 11–21.

———. 1947. "La evolución de 'la marinera'" (Part 3). *IPNA* 8 (January–April): 12–20.

———. 1980. *El papel do los descendientes de africanos en el desarrollo económico-social del Perú*. La Molina, Peru: Universidad Nacional Agraria.

———. 1987. *El negro en el Perú y su transculturación lingüística*. Peru: Editorial Milla Batres.

———. 1988. *Quimba, fa, malambo, ñeque: Afronegrismos en el Perú*. Lima: Instituto de Estudios Peruanos.

———. 1994. *Safari africano y compraventa de esclavos para el Perú: 1412–1818*. Lima: Instituto de Estudios Peruanos.

Romero, Raúl. 1986. "La investigación musical en América del Sur." *Letras* 90:71–92.

———. 1994. "Black Music and Identity in Peru: Reconstruction and Revival of Afro-Peruvian Musical Traditions." In *Music and Black Ethnicity: The Caribbean and South America*, ed. Gerard H. Béhague, 307–330. Miami: North-South Center Press, University of Miami.

———. 2001. *Debating the Past: Music, Memory and Identity in the Andes*. New York and Oxford: Oxford University Press.

Rosaldo, Renato. 1993. *Culture & Truth: The Remaking of Social Analysis*. 2nd ed. Boston: Beacon Press.

Rout, Leslie B., Jr. 1976. *The African Experience in Spanish America, 1502 to the Present Day*. Cambridge: Cambridge University Press.

Rowe, William, and Vivian Schelling. 1991. *Memory and Modernity: Popular Culture in Latin America*. London: Verso.

Safran, William. 1991. "Diasporas in Modern Societies: Myths of Homeland and Return." *Diaspora* 1:83–99.

Salazar Bondy, Sebastián. [1949] 1964. *Lima la horrible*. México: Ediciones Era S.A.

Sandoval, Lucho. 2000. Interview with the author. Lima: March 1.

Santa Cruz (Gamarra), Nicomedes. n.d. [1959?]. *Decimas*. Chilean ed. Santiago de Chile: Ediciones Ercilla.

———. 1962. *Antología de Nicomedes Santa Cruz*. Lima: Teatro Nacional del Ministerio de Educación Pública.

———. 1964a. *Cumanana: Décimas de pie forzado y poemas*. Lima: Librería-Editorial Juan Mejía Baca.

———. 1964b. "Estampas de Pancho Fierro." *Expreso* (Estampa supplement), February 2, 7.

———. 1964c. "Gente Morena." *Expreso* (Estampa supplement), February 16, 7.

———. 1964d. "Ritmos Negros del Perú." *Expreso* (Estampa supplement), February 9, 7.

———. 1966. *Canto a mi Peru*. Lima: Stadium.

———. 1969a. "Glosas criollas: Esos negros musicales inventores de la picardía limeña." *Documental del Perú*, Vol. 15, ed. Información, Opinión Pública, Publicidad y Encuestas-Editores (Lima), 117–122. Barcelona, Spain: Ediciones Oceano, S.A.

———. 1969b. "Navidad negra." *El Comercio* (Dominical supplement), December 21, 12–13.

———. 1969c. "Su majestad 'el cajón.'" *El Comercio*, December 14, 33.

———. 1970a. *Cumanana: Antología afroperuana* (booklet to accompany LP). 3rd ed. El Virrey Industrias Musicales S.A. P6350 001/002.

———. 1970b. "La quijada." *El Comercio* (Dominical supplement), March 1, 25.

———. 1971a. *Décimas y poemas: Antología*. Lima: Campdónico Ediciones S.A.

———. 1971b. *Nicomedes Santa Cruz presenta: Los reyes del festejo* (LP back cover text). El Virrey. LP DVS 769.

———. 1971c. *Ritmos negros del Perú*. Buenos Aires, Argentina: Editorial Losada S.A.

———. 1972. *América Negra*. FTA Industria Peruana. LP. FLPS 123.

——. 1973. "De Senegal y Malambo." *Caretas* 479 (June 21–July 5): 22–24.

——. 1975. *Socabón: Introducción al folklore musical y danzario de la costa peruana: Instrumentos musicales, danzas, y canciones* (booklet to accompany LP)., Lima: El Virrey Industrias Musicales S.A. VIR-948/949-STEREO.

——. 1978. "Aportes de las civilizaciones africanas al folklore del Perú." In *Négritude et Amérique Latine, Colloque de Dakar: 7–12 janvier 1974*, ed. René L. F. Durand, 369–380. Dakar-Abidjan, Senegal: Les Nouvelles Éditions Africaines.

——. 1982. *La décima en el Perú*. Lima: Instituto de Estudios Peruanos.

Santa Cruz (Gamarra), Nicomedes, y su Conjunto Cumanana (Kumanana). 1959. *¡Inga!* El Virrey Industrias Musicales S.A.. LP. DV 412.

——. [1964] 1970. *Cumanana*. 3rd ed. Philips/El Virrey Industrias Musicales S.A. LP. P6350 001/002.

——. 1975. *Socabón*. 2nd ed. El Virrey. LP. VIR-0000948.9/0000949.9.

——. [1964] 1994. *Cuamana*. IEMPSA. Compact Disc. CD-VIR-00001438.

——. [1968] 2000. *Canto negro*. FTA/MegaEntertainment. Compact Disc. CI-1027.

Santa Cruz, Octavio. n.d. "Familia Santa Cruz." Web site [accessed 2002]: http://espanol.geocities.com/familiasantacruz/.

Santa Cruz, Rafael. 1988. "Un 'Matalaché' blanco." *La República*, September 8. Digital copy provided by Rafael Santa Cruz.

——. 2000a. "La familia Santa Cruz." In *Lo africano en la cultura criolla*, 177–186. Lima: Fondo Editorial del Congreso del Perú.

——. 2000b. Interview with the author. Lima: March 24.

Santa Cruz, Victoria. 1978a. "El conjunto nacional de folklore." *Folklore: Reencuentro del hombre con sus raíces* 1:14–17.

——. 1978b. "Importancia del folklore." *Folklore: Reencuentro del hombre con sus raíces* 1:5–7.

——. 1978c. "Negritud en América Latina." *Folkore: Reencuentro del hombre con sus raíces* 1:18–19.

——. 1979a. "Descubrimiento y desarrollo del sentido rítmico." *Folklore: Reencuentro del hombre con sus raíces* 2:4–7.

——. 1979b. "Editorial." *Folklore: Reencuentro del hombre con sus raíces* 2:3.

——. 1988. "La danza." In *Signo e imagen: La marinera*, ed. Willy F. Pinto Gamboa, 84–85. Lima: Banco de Crédito del Perú.

——. 1991. Interview with Raúl Romero (cassette recording, from the private collection of Raúl Romero). Lima: August 10.

——. 1995. *Ritmos y aires afroperuanos*. Discos Hispanicos del Perú S.A. Compact Disc and liner notes. RH.10.0044.

——. 2000. Conversations with the author. Lima: February 21, February 28, March 29.

——. 2005. *Ritmo, el eterno organizador*. Lima: PETROPERU.

Santa Cruz, Victoria, y Gente Morena. 2000. *Con Victoria Santa Cruz y Gente Morena*. 2nd ed. IEMPSA. Compact Disc. CD IEM-0414-2.

Santa Cruz, Victoria, and Nicomedes Santa Cruz. 1961. "Malató." Program from a theatrical performance. Lima: Teatro Principal Manuel A. Segura.

Schechter, John M. 1994. "Los Hermanos Congo y Milton Tadeo Ten Years Later: Evolution of an African-Ecuadorian Tradition of the Valle del Chota, Highland Ecuador." In *Music and Black Ethnicity: The Caribbean and South America*, ed. Gerard H. Béhague, 285–306. Miami: North South Center Press, University of Miami.

Scheuss de Studer, Elena F. 1958. *La trata de negros en Rio de la Plata durante el siglo XVIII*. Buenos Aires: Libros de Hispanoamérica.

Schudson, Michael. 1997. "Lives, Laws, and Language: Commemorative versus Non-Commemorative Forms of Effective Public Memory." *The Communication Review* 2, no. 1: 3–17.

Scott, David. 1991. "That Event, This Memory: Notes on the Anthropology of African Diasporas in the New World." *Diaspora* 1, no. 3: 261–284.

Sims, Calvin. 1996. "Peru's Blacks Increasingly Discontent With Decorative Role." *The New York Times*, August 17, 2.

Smith, Valerie L. [1989a] 1995. "Introduction." In *Hosts and Guests: The Anthropology of Tourism*, 1–17. 2nd ed., 4th paperback printing. Philadelphia: University of Pennsylvania Press.

———, ed. [1989b] 1995. *Hosts and Guests: The Anthropology of Tourism*. 2nd ed., 4th paperback printing. Philadelphia: University of Pennsylvania Press.

Son de los Diablos. 1988. Lima: TV Cultura and Movimiento Francisco Congo. Videocassette.

Soto de la Colina, Carlos "Caitro." 1995. "Yo recuerdo." In *De cajón Caitro Soto: El duende en la música afroperuana*, ed. Bernardo Roca Rey Miró Quesada et al., 41–60. Lima: Servicios Especiales de Edición S.A. del Grupo Empresa Editora El Comercio.

———. 2000. Interview with the author. Lima: October 24.

Soto Herrera, Ezequiel. 2000. Interview with the author. Lima: February 17.

Spiro, Michael, and Mark Lamson. 1996. *Bata Ketu: A Musical Interplay of Cuba and Brazil, featuring vocalists Bobi Cespedes & Jorge Alabe*. Bembé Records. Compact disc. CD 2011-2.

Spivak, Gayatri Chakravorty. 1988. "Subaltern Studies: Deconstructing Historiography." In *In Other Worlds: Essays in Cultural Politics*, 197–221. 2nd ed. New York and London: Routledge.

Stagnaro, Ramon. 1999. Interview with the author. Los Angeles: October 7.

Starn, Orin, Carlos Iván Degregori, and Robin Kirk, eds. 1995. *The Peru Reader: History, Culture, Politics*. Durham: Duke University Press.

Stokes, Susan Carol. 1987. "Etnicidad y clase social: Los afro-peruanos de Lima, 1900–1930." In *Lima obrera 1900–1930*, ed. Steve Stein, 171–252. Lima: Ediciones El Virrey.

Suárez Radillo, Carlos Miguel. 1976. "El negro y su encuentro de sí mismo a través del teatro en el Perú." In *Lo social en el teatro hispanoamericano contemporáneo*, 275–296. Caracas: Equinoccio, Editorial de la Universidad Simón Bolívar.

Taruskin, Richard. 1995. *Text & Act: Essays on Music and Performance*. New York and Oxford: Oxford University Press.

Taylor, Timothy D. 1997. *Global Pop: World Music, World Markets*. New York and London: Routledge.

Templeman, Robert. 1998. "We Are People of the Yungas, We Are the Saya Race." In *Blackness in Latin America and the Caribbean: Social Dynamics and Cultural Transformations*, vol. I, ed. Norman E. Whitten, Jr. and Arlene Torres, 426–444. Bloomington: Indiana University Press.

Thompson, Robert Farris. 1983. *Flash of the Spirit: African & Afro-American Art & Philosophy*. New York: Vintage Books.

Tölölyan, Khachig. 1996. "Rethinking *Diaspora(s)*: Stateless Power in the Transnational Moment." *Diaspora* 5, no. 1:3–35.

Tompkins, William David. 1981. The Musical Traditions of the Blacks of Coastal Peru. PhD diss., University of California, Los Angeles.

———. 1998. "Afro-Peruvian Traditions." In *The Garland Encyclopedia of World Music, Volume 2: South America, Mexico, Central America, and the Caribbean*, ed. Dale A. Olsen and Daniel E. Sheehy, 491–502. New York and London: Garland Publishing, Inc.

Turino, Thomas. 1993. *Moving Away From Silence: Music of the Peruvian Altiplano and the Experience of Urban Migration*. Chicago: The University of Chicago Press.

———. 1996. "From Essentialism to the Essential: Pragmatics and Meaning of Puneño Sikuri Performance in Lima." In *Cosmología y música en los Andes*, ed. Max Peter Baumann, 469–482. Frankfurt and Madrid: Vervuert and Iberoamericana.

———. 2000. *Nationalists, Cosmopolitans, and Popular Music in Zimbabwe*. Chicago: The University of Chicago Press.

———. 2003. "Are we global yet? Globalist discourse, cultural formations and the study of Zimbabwean popular music." *British Journal of Ethnomusicology* 12(ii):51–79.

Urry, John. 2002. *The Tourist Gaze*. 2nd ed. London: SAGE.

Various Artists. 1995a. *Afro-Peruvian Classics: The Soul of Black Peru*. Luaka Bop/Warner Bros. Compact disc. CD 9 45878-2.

Various Artists. 1995b. The JVC/Smithsonian Folkways Video Anthology of Music and Dance of the Americas. JVC, Victor Company of Japan. Videocassettes.

Various Artists. 1998a. *Lo mejor del ritmo negro peruano*. IEMPSA. Compact disc. CD-VIR 00001355.

Various Artists. 1998b. *Música Negra: Grandes exitos*. Disvensa/Sono Radio. Compact disc. CD-DIS 000026044.

Various Artists. 1998c. *Peter Was a Fisherman: The 1939 Trinidad Field Recordings of Melville and Frances Herskovits, Vol. 1*. Rounder. Compact disc. CD 1114.

Various Artists. 1998d. *The Yoruba/Dahomean Collection: Orishas Across the Ocean*. Rykodisc/The Library of Congress Endangered Music Project. Compact disc. RCD 10405.

Vásquez, Abelardo. 2000. Interview with the author. Lima: March 3.

Vásquez Rodríguez, Rosa Elena (Chalena). 1982. *La práctica musical de la población negra en Perú: La danza de negritos de El Carmen*. Havana, Cuba: Casa de las Américas.

———. 2000a. Interview with the author. Lima: March 1.

———. 2000b. "El son de los diablos." Presentation at the Museo de la Cultura Peruana, Ciclo de Conferencias "Lima en sus artes y tradiciones." Lima.

Vásquez Rodríguez, Rosa Elena (Chalena), and Mónica Rojas. n.d. Musical transcriptions of cajón rhythms. Unpublished electronic files from the collection of Chalena Vásquez, cited by permission. Printed copies.

Vásquez, Juan Carlos ("Juanchi"). 2000. Interview with the author. Lima: February 4.

Vásquez, Vicente. 1978. Interview with Rosa Elena (Chalena) Vásquez and Max Brandt. Lima: July 17. Centro de Etnomusicología Andina, Pontificia Universidad Católica del Perú, cassette recording, Rosa Elena Vásquez Collection, C/88/6/286.

Vega, Carlos. 1936. "Eliminación del factor africano en la formación del cancionero criollo." *Cursos y Conferencias* 10, no. 7:765–779.

———. 1953. *La zamacueca (cueca, zamba, chilena, marinera)*. Buenos Aires: Editorial Julio Korn.

Verna, Paul. 1995. "Luaka Bop Revives Peru's Black 'Soul.'" *Billboard* 107, no. 23:1.

Villanueva, Oscar. 2000. Interview with the author. Lima: February 12.

Wade, Peter. 1993. *Blackness and Race Mixture: The Dynamics of Racial Identity in Colombia*. Baltimore and London: The Johns Hopkins University Press.

———. 1997. *Race and Ethnicity in Latin America*. London and Chicago: Pluto Press.

——. 1998. "The Cultural Politics of Blackness in Colombia." In *Blackness in Latin America and the Caribbean: Social Dynamics and Cultural Transformations*, vol. I, ed. Norman E. Whitten, Jr. and Arlene Torres, 311–334. Bloomington: Indiana University Press.

——. 2000. *Music, Race, and Nation: Música Tropical in Colombia*. Chicago: The University of Chicago Press.

Waterman, Christopher. 1990. "'Our Tradition is a Very Modern Tradition': Popular Music and the Construction of Pan-Yoruban Identity." *Ethnomusicology* 34, no. 3:367–379.

Waxer, Lise A. 2002. *The City of Musical Memory: Salsa, Record Grooves, and Popular Culture in Cali, Colombia*. Middletown, CT: Wesleyan University Press.

White, Hayden. 1973. *Metahistory: The Historical Imagination In Nineteenth-Century Europe*. Baltimore: Johns Hopkins University Press.

Whitten, Norman E., Jr., and Arlene Torres, eds. 1998. *Blackness in Latin America and the Caribbean: Social Dynamics and Cultural Transformations*, vol. I. Bloomington: Indiana University Press.

Williams, Brackette F. 1995. Review of *The Black Atlantic: Modernity and Double Consciousness*, by Paul Gilroy. *Social Identities* 1, no. 1: 175–192.

Williams, Patrick, and Laura Chrisman, eds. 1994. *Colonial Discourse and Postcolonial Theory: A Reader*. New York: Columbia University Press.

Williams, Raymond. 1977. *Marxism and Literature*. Oxford: Oxford University Press.

Wolf, Eric R. 1982. *Europe and the People Without History*. Berkeley: University of California Press.

Yates, Frances A. 1966. *The Art of Memory*. Chicago: The University of Chicago Press.

Index

Illustrations are indicated by page numbers in boldface.

eroticism (in Afro-Peruvian dance), 45–46, 76, 102–103, 106, 107, 159, 163, 208–210, 271n11

Espíritu vivo (recorded album), 248

"La esquina del Carmen" (song), 206

ethnography, 5, 11; as strategy of artistic recreation, 1, 32–42, 46, 51, 55, 81, 150–151

festejo: 92–99, 117, 123; and alcatraz, 136; as archetype, 13, 159–162; choreography, 172–173, 184, 209–210; contests, 161, 165, 249–250, 252; Juan Criado, 145; in *Malató*, 57; Perú Negro 137, 159–162; and Senegalese music, 118; and zamacueca, 75. *See also* cajón: in festejo; guitar: in festejo; quijada: in festejo

Festival of the Virgin of El Carmen, 14, 192–202, **193**

Fetiche, 251

Fierro, Pancho (artist), 27, 34, **35**, 36, 40, 41, 74–75, **75**, 76

Figueroa, Chino, 255

"La flor de la canela" (song), 17

folklore, 13, 27–28, 55, 76–78, 93, 117, 121, 123, 126–132; academies 28, 127; European origins of term, 128; folkloricization (Hagedorn), 130–131; in Latin America, 128–129; neo-folklore (Casaverde), 131, 170; neo-folkloricization, 131, 155. *See also* Conjunto Nacional de Folklore, National School of Folklore

Freundt, Julie, 272n4

Fujimori, Alberto, 121–122

Gallardo, Olga, **126**

Gamboa, Gino, 253–254

García Canclini, Néstor. *See* hybridity

gender roles, women, 66, 76

Gente Morena de Pancho Fierro, 44, 117

Ghibelini, Ricardo, 254

Gilroy, Paul. *See* Black Atlantic; double consciousness

Góngora, Linder, **144**, 275n2

González, Lucho, 255

González, Mariano, 88

González, Miki, 14, 202–211, 226, 235, 272n4. See also *Akundún* (recorded album); "Akundún" (song)

Graham, Martha, 67

Granda, Chabuca, 43, 139, 143, **144**, 151, 162, 223, 225–226, 235–236. *See also* "La flor de la canela"; Pancho Fierro (theatrical company): Chabuca Granda in

Graña, Rosa, 29

Guajaja. *See* De la Cruz, José "Guajaja"

"Guaranguito" (song), 235

Guillén, Nicolás, 115, 183

guitar, 4, 148, 161; accompaniment for décimas, 87, 90, 91–92, **92**; in alcatraz, 136; in "Canto a Elegua," 155–156; in festejo, 93, 94, 95, 160, 161; in landó, 110, 112, **112**, 152; in "María Landó," 237–238, **238**; in música criolla, 21; in el son de los diablos, 32, 34–35, 38, 74

habanera, 135, 136

Hacienda San José, 185–187, **186**

Hagedorn, Katherine. *See* folklore: folkloricization

Harlem Renaissance, 85

harp, 34, 74

hatajo de negritos, **193**, 194–196, 246–247; dance, 195–196; music, 195, 198, 199–200; Vásquez transcriptions, 199–200, **201**. *See also* Lurita, José; "Zancudito" (song)

Los Hermanos Santa Cruz, 260

Los Hijos del Sol, 14, 254–255

history, 52, 81, 109–110

Hora Cero, 144, 225–226

huanchigualo 188–190, 206

huayno, 198–200, **201**

Hubert, Jacques, 229

hybridity (García Canclini), 181, 218

IEMPSA, 226

immigrants, Peruvian in U.S., 14, 219–220, 249–258

independence, Peruvian, 3, 87, 100

indigenismo, 28, 54, 86, 129, 273n3

indigenous Peruvians, relations with Black Peruvians, 2

ingá, 39, 163

Instituto Nacional de Cultura, 76

Instituto Negrocontinuo. *See* Baca, Susana: Instituto Negrocontinuo

Izquierdo, Isidoro, **141**, 275n2

Izquierdo, Orlando "Lalo," 128, 132, 276n2; on afro, 134; biography, 140–142; on "Canto a Elegua," 159; on Dance of the Machetes, 135; on Perú Negro choreographic reconstruction process, 150–151; on Perú Negro history, 166, 169; on Ronaldo Campos' cajón patterns, 160; on "Samba Malató," 152, 153

jarana, 20–21, 25, 26, 66, 86, 87, 139, 150

"Johanesburgo" (poem), 101

Joya, Pedro "Chumbeque," 34, 39, 40, 42

Hijos del Sol, 255; landó pattern for cajón, 113
Soto, Orlando, 275n2
Spanish colonialism, 2, 87
staged authenticity (MacCannell), 14, 179, 192, 211–213
Stagnaro, Oscar, 255
Stagnaro, Ramon, 253, 255
Street, Craig, 246–248
Susana Baca (recorded album), 235

"Talara, no digas yes" (poem), 100
"El tamalero" (song), 137
Teatro del Milenio, 14, 262–265
Teatro y Danzas Negras del Perú. *See* Santa Cruz, Victoria: Teatro y Danzas Negras del Perú
Terry, Alberto, 29, 32, 43
Tiahuanaco 2000, 225
La tierra se hizo nuestra. See Perú Negro: *La tierra se hizo nuestra*
timeline, 113, **113**, 156, **157**, 161
Toledo, Alejandro, 122
tondero, 137, 163
Toro, Efrain, 255
"Toro mata" (song), 43, 151, 228, 235
tourism: and anthropology, 177, 180–181, 277n2; postmodern and poststructural perspectives, 180; post-tourism (Urry and Feifer), 180; typologies, 185. *See also* Chincha: tourism
traditions, invented (Hobsbawm and Ranger), 10–11
Túpac Amaru rebellion, 2, 87

Urbina, Tana, 228
U.S.–Peruvian relations, 100, 127

Valcarcel, Luis, 28
vals, 21, 26
Vásquez, Abelardo, 29, 36, 44, 62–63, **63**, 204, 233
Vásquez, Carlos, 88–89
Vásquez, Chalena, 176, 227, 228. *See also* hatajo de negritos: Vásquez transcriptions
Vásquez, Juan Carlos "Juanchi," 45, 126, 209, 261–262
Vásquez, Olga, 30, 31
Vásquez, Pepe, 251
Vásquez, Pipo, 63

Vásquez, Porfirio, 27–28, 87, 88–89, 94, 108, 117, 139, 161
Vásquez, Vicente, 35, 36, 41, 42, 91–92, 109, 111, 152. *See also* agua'e nieve; landó: musical re-creation; "Samba malató" (song)
Vega, Carlos, 105
Velasco Alvarado, Juan. *See* revolutionary government, Peruvian military
Verano Negro, 190–192, **191**
Vestida de vida (recorded album), 229
vihuela, 74, 150
Vilchez, Félix, 228
villancicos, 145, 197
Villanueva, Oscar, **22**, 166, **167**, 262–263, **263**
violin. *See* hatajo de negritos
El Virrey, 101, 223, 279n5

War of the Pacific, 54, 87, 274n16
Watts, Ernie, 255
Wayruro, 254
whitening, 69, 71, 94, 96–97, 107, 252, 270n3. *See also* "No me cumbén" (song)
world music, 14, 215–220, 221–222, 224, 230, 241–243, 245–248, 257–248

"Xanaharí." *See* "Zanahary" (song)

Yoruba, 106, 134, 144, 156, 158, 264, 270n7, 274n20
yunza, 14, 162, 188–192, **189**, 275n22
Yuyachkani, Grupo Cultural, 40, 41

zamacueca, 54, **75**, 271n1; reconstruction, 13, 74–76; as origin of marinera, 101–105, 102, 274n16; Perú Negro, 127, 137; related dances, 163. *See also* cajón: in zamacueca
zamba (dance), 105
zamba-landó, 274–275n22
"Zanahary" (song). *See* "Karambe" (song)
Zanahary (theatrical play), 55–57, 59–63, 65, 276n3. *See also* "Karambe" (song)
"Zanahary" (theatrical scene), 56, 62–63, **63**
"Zancudito" (song), 197, 246–247
zaña (genre), 90
zapateo, 36–37, 75, 91, 94, 137, 161, 198
Zellon, Richie, 260
Zevallos, Jaime, 263

MUSIC/CULTURE

A series from Wesleyan University Press

Edited by Harris M. Berger

Originating editors: George Lipsitz, Susan McClary, and Robert Walser

Listening to Salsa:
Gender, Latin Popular Music, and
Puerto Rican Cultures
by Frances Aparicio

Jazz Consciousness:
Music, Race, and Humanity
by Paul Austerlitz

Metal, Rock, and Jazz:
Perception and the Phenomenology
Musical Experience
by Harris M. Berger

Identity and Everyday Life:
Essays in the Study of Folklore, Music,
and Popular Culture
by Harris M. Berger and Giovanna P.
Del Negro

Bright Balkan Morning:
Romani Lives and the Power of Music in
Greek Macedonia
by Dick Blau and Charles and
Angeliki Keil

Different Childhoods:
Music and the Cultures of Youth
edited by Susan Boynton and Roe-
Min Kok

Music and Cinema:
edited by James Buhler, Caryl Flinn,
and David Neumeyer

My Music:
by Susan D. Crafts, Daniel Cavicchi,
Charles Keil, and the Music in Daily
Life Project

Born in the USA:
Bruce Springsteen and the American
Tradition
by Jim Cullen

Presence and Pleasure:
The Funk Grooves of James Brown and
Parliament
by Anne Danielsen

Echo and Reverb:
Fabricating Space in Popular Music
1900-1960
by Peter Doyle

Recollecting from the Past:
Musical Practice and Spirit Possession on
the East Coast of Madagascar
by Ron Emoff

Locating East Asia in Western Art Music
edited by Yayoi Uno Everett and
Frederick Lau

Black Rhythms of Peru:
Reviving African Musical Heritage in
the Black Pacific
by Heidi Carolyn Feldman

"You Better Work!":
Underground Dance Music in New York
City
by Kai Fikentscher

The Other Side of Nowhere:
Jazz, Improvisation, and Communities in
Dialogue
edited by Daniel Fischlin and
Ajay Heble

About the Author

Heidi Carolyn Feldman is a lecturer in the Department of Communications at the University of California, San Diego.